THE ONE
ALL-AGE BIBLE

FoR CAREN
CHRISTMAS 2017

THE ONE
ALL-AGE BIBLE

GOSPELS

MICHAEL FORSTER

**kevin
mayhew**

First published in 2003 by
KEVIN MAYHEW LTD
Buxhall, Stowmarket, Suffolk IP14 3BW
E-mail: info@kevinmayhewltd.com

9 8 7 6 5 4 3 2 1 0

ISBN 1 84003 974 4
Catalogue No. 1500543

Cover design by Angela Selfe
Edited by Katherine Laidler
Typeset by Richard Weaver

Printed and bound in Great Britain

To Jean
my wife, my friend and my constant 'good news'
in the year of our thirtieth wedding anniversary

Acknowledgements

I'm indebted to a number of people whose help has been invaluable to me in writing this paraphrase:

Katherine Laidler, my editor, whose usual blend of criticism and encouragement has been especially appreciated during this project

Jonathan Bugden, whose knowledge and commitment to the project have been invaluable

Jean, my wife, whose moral support and practical help have been indispensable

Beryl Johnson for her help with the proof-reading.

And to my informal 'reading team' who, from the perspectives of their various ages and faith backgrounds, have critically read the drafts, suggesting improvements and encouraging the author:

Margaret Bodsworth

Laura Doody

Don Dow

Rachael Edwards

Simon Foster

Claire Roberts

Kim Roberts

I am grateful for the generosity of all these and others whose skills and perceptive observations have contributed to this book. After all that, however, like all results of human enterprise it will certainly have short-comings. For all of those, the responsibility remains with me.

MICHAEL FORSTER

Contents

Foreword

This book invites you on a journey of discovery. You can make that journey in at least two ways – the 'walk' and the 'treasure hunt' – either way is OK.

The 'walk'

This will be a hike – energetic and demanding at times, but not taking you below ground – not going far beneath the surface of the text. Still, it's not a bad way to get into it: just read the main text, skipping the boxes and footnotes. That way, the narrative reads continuously, and you can get a good overview of the story of Jesus as he invites you to share his much greater journey through life.

The 'treasure hunt'

This gets you into just some of the layers of subtext concealed within the stories. The boxes offer introductions to help make the subtler points of the text clearer, and the footnotes perform a similar function. Hopefully, they won't interrupt the flow too much, and the better understanding should be worth it. A Glossary at the end of the book gives the deeper meanings of key words and phrases that are used in particular ways and have deeper significance than the base meaning of the words.

If you want to get an idea of where you're going before you set out on the journey, there's a 'route planner' showing the general outline at the beginning of each gospel.

The best of both

Of course, you can chop and change between those approaches, or do a bit of both at different times. The important thing is that you enjoy reading, and encounter the Person at the heart of the stories as vividly as you may.

Health warning

Please bear a couple of things in mind as you read this book.

Firstly, in writing this book, I've drawn heavily on the expertise of others who, for example, know the languages of the Bible and have studied some of the ancient documents.

Secondly, this isn't a new translation but a paraphrase (written in pretty colloquial style in places). So, don't confuse this book with Holy Scripture – it's not. It's my attempt to make that same Scripture accessible and understandable on a relatively superficial level (even using the 'treasure hunt' approach won't get you *that* far beneath the surface, because to help you do so would have meant writing an encyclopaedia).

It's also true that there are many passages where the best brains in the business struggle, and certainly don't agree – so often the best I can do is to give you *one* possible understanding. I shan't be offended if you want to check out my text against a standard translation – quite the contrary in fact: I'd be very pleased, since that's what I've put the chapter and verse numbers in for. And if you *really* want to go digging – for even richer treasure – then there are commentaries, Bible study notes, videos, and no shortage of computer software programmes on the market that can take the backache out of the excavations.

My hope – and my prayer – is that reading this text may help you to encounter Christ in a meaningful way. If it does that, I'll be well pleased – and you'd better be ready, because he'll change your life!

MICHAEL FORSTER

General introduction to the Gospels

Suppose you became famous, and four of your best friends each decided to write your life story. Would they all say the same things? Most probably, they'd each want to show the qualities that they personally liked best – or thought most important – about you. So they'd pick out those aspects of your life that helped them to do that, and tell the stories in a way that highlighted what they most loved about you.

The gospel writers all tell the story of Jesus, but they do it differently from their own particular point of view, and give us a much better picture of him and his friends than we'd get from just one.

In the Bible there are four books that bear the title 'gospels': Matthew, Mark, Luke and John. The fourth stands out as distinctive from the other three.

The first three gospels are known as the 'Synoptic' gospels because they're seen as giving a kind of 'synopsis' of Jesus' life and ministry. In places, the general wording is identical in the three, but the glory is in the detail – sometimes changing, adding or removing as little as a single word is enough to bring out that particular writer's style or emphasis.

One important thing they have in common is that they portray Jesus' ministry as a journey. His physical journey reflects his spiritual one on which he invites all who are willing to follow him. Jerusalem is the high point of the journey: the closer he gets to Jerusalem, the nearer Jesus is to the climax of his ministry, his 'enthronement' on the cross at Golgotha and his vindication in the resurrection. The inspired gospel writers constantly challenge us to follow him on his journey as he offers himself for the salvation of the world.

John would agree with all that, but he shapes his presentation of the gospel differently. We still get a strong sense of progression, but John wants us to see Jesus' ministry very much in the Passover context. Again, this is unmistakably there in the Synoptics, but it is John who particularly highlights it for us. He alone actually records the title 'Lamb of God' as used for Jesus – right at the start of Jesus' ministry, in fact. The Passover lamb had been sacrificed every year since Moses led the people out of Israel – as a reminder that their liberation had not been cheap but immensely costly. So, as well as being the new and greater 'Moses', who will lead his people to freedom in the full sense of the word, Jesus is actually the sacrificial Lamb who will pay the cost of that freedom with his own blood. This is one of John's big themes – not entirely unique to him, but certainly unique in the way he highlights it.

Another of John's 'big themes' – again, not absent from the Synoptics but brought to dizzy heights in John – is the status of Jesus as Son of God; not simply declared such at his baptism, or shown as such in the manner of his conception and birth, but actually co-equal with God in eternity. The glory of this gospel is in the subtext: layers and layers and layers of it! Remember that digging I talked about in the Foreword? Well, this gospel could keep you at it for a lifetime, even with a JCB – and we all know you can't dig for buried treasure with a JCB; you need to use tiny trowels to make sure you don't miss anything.

Look, can I help it if this is one of the most exciting subjects imaginable? *Of course* I go on about it! Why don't you just leave me to chunter away to myself and get on with your own digging?

Matthew

The Gospel according to Matthew

A complete summary of how Matthew's particular concerns show could take up a book on its own, but let me give a few quick pointers. Not that you won't find the same themes in other gospels, mind you – but they're particularly strong in this one.

Matthew firmly grounds Jesus in the Jewish tradition. He's particularly concerned to show Jesus as the fulfilment of Jewish hopes, so not only does he make frequent direct quotations of prophecies but he includes countless other subtle references to the Hebrew Bible as well. And while all the gospels point us back to the Hebrew scriptures, and show Jesus as fulfilling them, Matthew has his eleven 'formula quotations' as they're called, in which he very specifically refers to prophecies, beginning with words like, 'This fulfilled what God had said through the prophet . . .'

Similarly, the theme of Jesus as a second (but infinitely greater) Moses runs through the New Testament but Matthew – with his particularly Jewish flavour – gives it special emphasis by telling us the story of the killing of the innocents in 2:16-18.

Matthew was also very interested in Jesus' attitude to the law, as an aspect of another special concern – the nature of the Christian Church and its relationship with the established religion of Judaism. This in turn means he has to show Jesus confronting the traditional religious people and authorities. This, and the claim that Jesus is the Messiah, means that we're going to see a lot of conflict. However, the key thing to remember is that Matthew is showing Jesus not throwing over the old traditions but actually strengthening them. In the famous 'antitheses', for example (Matthew 5:21-44), characterised by the words 'but *I'm* telling you . . .', Jesus is actually *increasing* the demands of the law. Even where he seems to be setting it aside (for example, in terms of Sabbath observation), he's really pointing to the true meaning and intention of it.

Now, as I suggested earlier, the fact that Matthew gives these themes special emphasis doesn't mean that I'm saying he has a monopoly on them. You'll find similar ideas in the other Gospels, but Matthew takes his equivalent of a yellow highlighter to them.

Matthew Route Planner

You might find this helpful to give you a quick overview of the journey ahead.

Prologue

Jesus' family tree

1 [1-17] There's a long list of names here, tracing Jesus' human ancestry and clearly linking him to important figures (notably David) in God's history with his people. If you're into this sort of stuff it's actually very useful – you can pick up some insights into Matthew's underlying ideas, and it's particularly interesting to compare it with Luke 3. So if genealogies are your thing, why not settle down with a standard Bible and a good commentary[1] and enjoy it? Otherwise, come with me and we'll get straight into the story.

The birth narrative

> Right from the very conception of Jesus, God's Spirit is at work challenging the smallness of mortal minds: breaking the strictures of conventional society, confronting our concern with outward appearances with his inward truth, and making us look again at the things we count most important.

[18-21] Now, this is how the birth of Jesus, the Messiah, came about. Mary, his mother, was engaged to be married to a man called Joseph, but before the big day arrived, she was found to be pregnant – not by Joseph, though; this was a miracle brought about by the Holy Spirit, no less. Now, Joseph was a good sort and really didn't want to make it any harder for Mary than it needed to be – so he decided he'd break off the engagement quietly, with as little publicity as possible. But no sooner had he made his mind up to do it than God sent an angel to him in a dream. 'Joseph, son of David,' said the angel, 'listen to me. Don't go doing anything hasty, now – it's OK to marry Mary; there's no disgrace or anything. The child she's carrying is a work of God's Holy Spirit. She's going to have a son, and you're to give him the name Jesus – because he's going to save God's people from their sin.'

---

1. For those who haven't come across these before, Christian bookshops sell a range of commentaries on the Bible: some one-volume works covering the whole Bible (also useful to prop open heavy swing doors) and much more manageable ones concentrating on individual books. The latter are obviously more detailed, but the former are cheaper in the long run and easy to use for cross-referencing.

[22-23] So in this way God fulfilled the promise he'd made through the prophet: 'Look, a virgin[1] will conceive and give birth to a son, and they'll give him the name Immanuel' – meaning 'God with us'.

[24-25] Of course, that changed everything – so when Joseph woke up he did exactly as the angel from God had said: the engagement stood, and he and Mary got married. But the marriage wasn't consummated – not until after her son had been born, and Joseph gave him the name 'Jesus'.

The universe proclaims Christ's birth

> A bright, vivid star, possibly caused by the lining up of two stars along the same sight line, proclaims Christ's birth and kingship to the farthest corner of the known world. God is using the whole universe to draw people to the ultimate revelation of his glory – Jesus. With all that lined up against him, poor Herod stood no chance!

2 [1-6] King Herod was on the throne, Jesus had been born in Bethlehem in Judea, and wise men from the East were in Jerusalem. 'Where's the baby?' they asked. 'Where's the child who's been born to be King of the Jews?[2] We know he's around somewhere, because we saw his star rising, and we've come all this way to worship him. So, where is he?' Of course, it wasn't long before word got back to Herod, and he wasn't happy at all. And if Herod was worried, *everybody* was worried – everybody in Jerusalem, at any rate. So Herod got the scribes and chief priests together, and asked them, 'Where's this Messiah supposed to be born, then?'

'In Bethlehem of Judea,' they told him. 'That's what the prophet said: "You, Bethlehem in Judah, you're not to be sniffed at where the rulers of Judah are concerned – because it's from you that the great ruler will come, who's going to guide my people, Israel, like a shepherd."'

[7-8] Herod called the wise men to him in secret, and got them to tell him exactly when the star had first appeared. 'Right,' he told them, 'now, you go and look for this child – and I mean *look* – and then come back and tell me where he is, so that I can go and worship him too. Because I'd really like to.'

---

1. Isaiah's (Hebrew) word meant 'young woman' and could also mean 'virgin'. Matthew is less ambiguous by his choice of a (Greek) word specifically meaning 'virgin'.
2. No wonder Herod panicked – 'King of the Jews' was *his* official title!

[9-11] So, off they went, with the star still leading them, until it stopped right over the place where the child was. Wonderful! Of course, they wasted no time in going inside, where they found the child, with his mother Mary, and knelt down to worship him. And they hadn't come empty-handed – they'd brought gifts: gold, frankincense and myrrh.

[12] They didn't tell Herod about it, though: they were warned in a dream to keep him in the dark, and went back to their own country by a different route.

No God on my patch

When God makes himself known in the world, it's usually the powerful who try to push him out, and the innocent who suffer – and all too often it's a case of 'women and children first'.

There's a fascinating parallel here with Moses, who was also saved from a baby-murdering ruler, called 'out of Egypt' and prepared for the task of freeing his people from slavery. Jesus is the new, and greater, Moses, freeing his people from slavery to sin and death. For Jewish readers, this would have been a shorthand way of showing what Jesus' mission was. This device forms a significant theme in all the Gospels, but Matthew is unique in using this parallel to Moses in the birth narrative. The 'Exodus' imagery reaches its climax, in fact, in John, whose emphasis upon Jesus as the 'Lamb of God' also points us to the Passover and the Exodus as a way of understanding who Jesus is.

[13-15] Just after the wise men left, Joseph had a dream: one of God's angels appeared to him and said, 'Time to get up and go, Joseph – now! Take the baby and his mother, and go like the wind for Egypt – and stay there until I tell you to leave. King Herod's just about to start searching for the baby to put an end to him.' So Joseph was up in a flash, took the baby and mother, and got them all out of there to Egypt, to hide until Herod died. Now, this fulfilled what God had said through the prophet: 'I called my son out of Egypt.'[1]

[16-18] Of course, it didn't take Herod long to realise that he'd been outwitted by the wise men – and he was hopping mad! He sent soldiers to Bethlehem with what must have been the worst orders they'd ever been given: to kill every male child in the city who was under two years old –

---

1. Hosea 11:1.

he worked that out from what the wise men had told him about the time the star first appeared to them. Now, there's a prophecy about this, too – from Jeremiah: 'Listen to the raised voice in Ramah – horrible wailing and screaming – Rachel, weeping for her children. And she simply couldn't be comforted, because her children are no more.'[1]

[19-23] Herod died, and the angel wasted no time in going to see Joseph again, in a dream, where he was staying in Egypt. 'OK, Joseph, get moving – and don't forget the family. You can go back to Israel now, because the ones who were trying to destroy the child are dead themselves.' Joseph didn't need telling twice, and he, Jesus and Mary were soon back in Israel. When they got there, though, Joseph found out that Herod's son, Archelaus, had succeeded his father to the throne – so settling down in his territory wasn't particularly inviting. Another dream, another warning, and Joseph retreated to the area around Galilee where he made a home for his family in a town called Nazareth. And – yes, you've guessed it – there's a prophecy about that, too: 'He will be called a Nazorean.'[2]

---

1. Jeremiah 31:15.
2. The interesting thing is, although Matthew says this prophecy exists, no one's been able to find it! There are references that could be related, but the vital word is different. Personally, I'd leave it to the scholars to debate this, and just get on with enjoying the story.

Jesus in Galilee

John prepares the way

Right at the start of his ministry, Jesus is identified as the one who will bring new life to the world. John is telling people they need to change. Well, no disrespect to John, but telling people to change isn't that hard, and most of us are a bit too good at it! Actually offering them new life, well, that's something else. And Jesus, empowered by the Spirit of God, is just the one to do it.

3 [1-6] At that time, John the Baptiser came into the desert of Judea and started preaching. 'You've got to change your ways,' he said, 'because God's going to remind you all that he's king[1] around here.'[2] This is what Isaiah was foretelling when he said, 'A voice is calling in the desert, "Prepare the way for God. Build a straight road for him."'[3]

John made a strange sight, dressed in camel skins held together with a leather strap. He had a funny idea of convenience food too: all he seemed to live on was a diet of locusts, and honey that he took straight from the comb. Rather him than me is what I say. It didn't seem to put people off, though – they came from all over the district to hear him preach, to confess their sins and to be baptised by him in the River Jordan.

[7-12] John always had a colourful turn of phrase, but he really got into his stride on one particular day. It was the Pharisees and the Sadducees – and they were walking straight towards the place where he was doing baptisms. 'You revolting poisonous snakes!' he shouted. 'So, who warned you to run away from God's judgement? I suppose you think that saying the right words is going to save you, do you? Well, if you're really saved it'll show in your lives. Oh, and don't give me any of that "We're Abraham's descendants, so we're OK" rubbish, either. Let me tell you, God can make descendants of Abraham out of these rocks – it doesn't mean a thing! You'd better take notice: God's coming like a forester with his axe to take out any dead wood and burn it – and

---

1. In the standard texts, this is Matthew's first use of the classic term 'kingdom of heaven' (see Glossary).
2. The gospels often talk about the 'kingdom of God', which sounds a bit like a place. What it really meant was the 'king*ship* of God' – God's reign as Sovereign in creation, which as Ezekiel found is about bringing new life (Ezekiel 37:1-14).
3. Isaiah 40:3.

believe me, wood doesn't come much deader than you. All I'm doing is baptising people with water, for repentance, but there's someone *seriously* important coming along behind me – I'm not even good enough to help him undo his shoes. Now, he's really going to start something – his baptism will be with the Holy Spirit, and with fire. It's harvest-time in heaven, folks, and he's coming equipped – harvesting the wheat and burning the chaff in the fire. Need I say more?'

Jesus is baptised

¹³⁻¹⁷ Then Jesus arrived in Jordan, from Galilee, looking for John to baptise him. 'What?' John protested. 'It's me that needs your kind of baptism, not you mine.'

'Just do it, John,' Jesus answered. 'Right now, it's an important part of fulfilling God's purpose.'

So, John did it. And at the moment that Jesus came out of the water, he had a vision: God's Spirit, like a dove, resting on him. Then there was a voice from heaven. 'This is my Son,' it said, 'my special Son – like no other – and he's fulfilling all my expectations!'

Jesus resists temptation

Even when we're tempted to rebel, God is with us in that experience. The particular temptations Jesus suffered are very familiar to us:

- Abuse of power: Jesus knew his power was for others, not for him.
- 'Tabloidism' – sensationalising to draw attention: Jesus knew he had to appeal to people on a much deeper level than that.
- Beating the world at its own game: Jesus knew he had to offer a radical alternative.

The Church has succumbed to all these temptations in the past – still does, and doubtless will again – but God understands because he's been there!

4 ¹⁻⁴ Then the Holy Spirit led Jesus away into the desert to face the temptations of the devil. For forty days, and nights as well, he went without food, so it is probably an understatement to say that by the end of it all he was famished! That, of course, gave the perfect opportunity for the devil to tempt him.

'Look, you're supposed to be the Son of God, aren't you? So, tell these stones to turn into bread. Go on – you can do it – you know you can. Live a little, why don't you?'

Jesus answered, 'Scripture says that we don't only need bread to live on – we need all the wisdom God speaks to us, as well.'[1]

⁵⁻⁷ Something more spectacular was clearly needed, so the devil whisked Jesus off to the top of the Temple – right up on the pinnacle of the building, and that's mighty high. 'You could jump off,' he murmured persuasively. 'Well, if you're really the Son of God, that is. So, are you? Go on – throw yourself off – because I know my Bible, too, and it says, "He'll give orders to his angels about you, and they'll hold you in their arms – you won't even strike your foot against a stone."'[2]

'Another thing the Bible says,' Jesus answered. '"Don't put God to the test."'[3]

⁸⁻¹¹ Well, things weren't exactly going as planned, so the devil decided that serious measures were needed – like a good, high mountain. 'Look at it: you can see all the empires of the world from here,' the devil breathed. 'All the wealth, all the power – and it's all there for you. Just do things my way – let me be the big thing in your life. Not a lot to ask for all that, is it? Go on, what d'you say – we could be good together.'

This was really a step too far! 'Go away, Satan – and I mean *away*. The Bible's very clear. "You're to have just one God," it says, "one God to serve and to worship: God, Yahweh, the Great I AM."[4] Got it? So that leaves you well out of the picture, doesn't it? Now just push off!'

Well, what could he do? He pushed off. And immediately, angels from God came to be with Jesus.

Jesus begins his ministry

¹²⁻¹⁷ Jesus got wind of the fact that John had been arrested[5] – time for a quick retreat[6] and a change of focus. He moved from Nazareth to the Galilee region and set up his home base in Capernaum, near the sea, in

---

1. Deuteronomy 8:3.
2. Psalm 91:11-12.
3. Deuteronomy 6:16.
4. Deuteronomy 6:13.
5. You'll find more detail about this in 14:3.
6. Jesus does this a number of times – not out of cowardice but common sense. There are some things that are worth dying for and others that aren't – and he was saving himself for when it really mattered.

the area of Zebulun and Naphtali. So that was another prophecy fulfilled: '. . . Zebulun and Naphtali . . . Galilee of the nations, on the road from Jordan to the sea . . . the people not so much walking as blundering around in the dark – well, they've seen a terrific light! They seemed to be living in a land of total darkness, and the light has shined on them.'[1]

From that time, Jesus began[2] preaching his message of repentance. 'Turn away from everything that separates you from God,' he said, 'because the kingdom of heaven has come right to your door, and you'd better believe it!'

Jesus calls the first disciples

[18-22] He walked on the beach by the Sea of Galilee and that's where he found Simon (who's also called Peter) and his brother Andrew, throwing a net into the sea – because that's what fishermen do – and made them an offer they couldn't refuse. 'Why don't you come and follow me?' he said. 'I can teach you to fish for people.' Sounded intriguing. Simon and Andrew didn't hang around – they left the nets behind and took off after Jesus. Immediately. Just like that. He wasn't done yet, either. He'd hardly gone any further when he found two more brothers, James and John. They were in the boat with their father, Zebedee, mending their nets – but not for long. Jesus called them, and they immediately left the lot – boat, business, not to mention poor old Dad in the boat with the nets to mend – and followed Jesus.

[23-25] Jesus took them all round Galilee; he taught in synagogues, preached the good news of the kingdom of heaven, and healed people of every kind of sickness and disease – whatever it was they were suffering from, Jesus could handle it. So, of course, it wasn't long before everyone was talking about him, not just in Northern Israel but all the regions round about. And people brought their sick friends and relatives to him – people oppressed by demons, or suffering from paralysis or epilepsy, all kinds of stuff – and he cured them. It was amazing: everywhere he went he had crowds following him: all sorts of people from all over the place: Galilee, the Decapolis,[3] from Jerusalem, the whole of Judea, the other side of the Jordan – the entire region seemed to be moving and changing because of him!

---

1. Isaiah 9:1-2.
2. Keep your eyes peeled for these words – or very similar ones – repeated elsewhere, indicating a new stage in Jesus' work.
3. Literally 'Ten Towns' – a group of mainly Gentile cities.

Jesus' first big speech: mainly on discipleship

The sermon on the Mount

Jesus' ministry involved constant teaching. In other Gospels (notably Luke) this teaching is more spread out, but Matthew wants to show the coherence of it by putting it together and presenting it as one 'sermon'. This is part of the Gospel-writer's role: not merely to give the facts but to arrange the material so as to help us grasp its meaning – including the distinctive meaning it has for him.

5 [1-10] Seeing the crowds, Jesus moved into the hills and his disciples gathered round for him to teach them.[1] Here's what he said:

The Beatitudes

Congratulations[2] to all who are poor in spirit – humble if you prefer –
    because the kingdom of heaven is truly theirs!
Congratulations to all who are suffering,
    because they're going to be comforted!
Congratulations to gentle people who don't think they've always got something to prove,
    because they're going to inherit the earth!
Congratulations to all those who are hungry and thirsty for a real relationship with God,
    because, let me tell you, they're going to be satisfied!
Congratulations to all who are kind,
    because they'll *receive* kindness too!
Congratulations to people who love God with their whole heart,
    because they'll see him – *really* see him!
Congratulations to all who try to *make* peace – not just keep it –
    God will call them his very own children!
Congratulations to all those who are persecuted because their faithfulness to God really shows,
    because the kingdom of heaven truly belongs to them.

---

1. 7:28-29 indicates that the 'crowds' were still listening, but they were probably not quite so close by as the more committed 'disciples'.
2. The original word has no direct translation in English. Most people use 'Blessed' and if you want to substitute that I won't mind. Some translations say 'Happy' but that's really not good enough as most people think of happiness as a 'feel good' thing. We could use 'How fortunate'. The point is that Jesus is saying these people are in a good position to be close to God and in tune with his ways.

[11-12] Congratulations to *you* when people ridicule you, and persecute you, and tell slanderous stories about you, all because of your loyalty to me. Be glad about it – proud of it – because it's an indication of your real faith, and it'll all be made up to you in the end with interest – after all, they did the same thing to the prophets who went before you, so it's really no surprise, is it!

Salt and light

[13] *Of course* you're different – you're salt for the earth! And if salt loses its distinctive flavour, what use is it? It's only fit to be thrown out and trampled underfoot!

[14-16] You're the light of the world – as conspicuous as a city set on a hill. Now, you don't go to the trouble of lighting a lamp only to hide it under a measuring jug, do you? – you put it on a lampstand so the whole house can have the benefit. Well, then, let *your* light shine out among people – not for your own glory, but so that they'll see the way you live and give the glory to God, your Father in heaven.

The old traditions

[17-20] Look, don't go thinking I've come to chuck out the old ideas, because I haven't. I've come not to abolish but to *complete* them – get you all to see what they really mean. And I'm telling you this: as long as there's a heaven and an earth, all of them are still going to matter – not a letter, not a single stroke of a pen, not a splash from a careless scribe's inkpot will even begin to fade from the law until everything has been completely fulfilled and we don't need it any more. So anyone who breaks even the most insignificant of these laws – and goes round teaching others to behave the same way – well, they won't exactly rank very highly in the kingdom of heaven, that's all I can say. Of course, those who *do* keep them – and teach other people to, as well – they'll be among the greats, no mistake about that. Because I'm telling you that you'll need a kind of commitment that the scribes and Pharisees can't begin to understand, or you won't even get into the kingdom of heaven.

Jesus gets to the true heart of the law

Jesus now goes on to give some examples of how true faithfulness means going beyond mere legalism. The question for him is not, 'What does the law literally say?' but 'What is its true purpose and intention?' The examples take the form of six 'antitheses' which begin with words such as 'You've heard what used to be said' and go on to 'But *I'm* telling you . . '.

21-26 You've heard what used to be said to people, way back: 'Don't commit murder' – and anyone who does will be liable to the judgement of the courts? Yes, well, that's fine as far as it goes, but *I'm* telling you that even giving in to the anger underlying it will make you liable to the judgement of God himself. You go round insulting one another and you'll be held to account – and throwing around insults like 'Idiot!' will put you in danger of hell. So next time you're getting ready for worship, and you remember that someone's got a grievance against you, go to them first – get right with them, and then you can think about worshipping God. Setting relationships straight isn't something you can just keep putting off. Is someone suing you for something? Settle out of court before it all runs away with you and you find yourself locked up for it – because there'll be no half-measures then, and you'll end up paying the full penalty.

27-30 You've heard what used to be said: 'Don't commit adultery.' But *I'm* telling you that just looking lustfully at someone means you've already as good as done it. Dangerous things, eyes – if seeing is going to lead you in that direction, why, you'd be better off being blind! And however useful your hand might be, if it's going to get you into trouble you might be better off without that, too – better maimed than damned is what I say.[1]

31-32 Something else that was always said: 'If anyone wants to divorce his wife,[2] he's got to do it in writing.' But *I'm* telling you that anyone who divorces his wife – for anything other than unfaithfulness, which annuls the marriage anyway – is conniving at adultery. And if someone does it, don't go thinking you can move in with the wife afterwards, because you'll effectively be committing adultery, too.

---

1. He had a real way with words, did Jesus! A nice bit of rhetoric here, but just don't go taking him too literally!
2. Women couldn't divorce men, in that culture, but men could divorce women very easily, leaving them vulnerable.

[33-37] And again, you've heard what used to be said, way back, that sacred oaths have to be honoured. But *I'm* telling you, you shouldn't need to make them in the first place because your word should be trustworthy. So don't swear by heaven, because that's God's throne, not your personal property. And don't swear by the earth, either, because that's his, too – his footstool, if you like – or by Jerusalem, the Holy City, or even by your own head because that's God's as well – try wishing your hair a different colour if you don't believe me! The point is that your word alone should be enough. Let 'Yes' mean 'Yes', and 'No' mean 'No' – if you have to add any more it means you're no better than the devious society you live in.

[38-42] You've heard what used to be said: 'An eye for an eye and a tooth for a tooth?'[1] Well, again, that's fine as far as it goes, but *I'm* telling you, you can't even go that far. Don't be always insisting on your individual rights, defending your own property, as though those things were what mattered. If someone gives you a smack[2] on your right cheek, well, offer your left one, too. Someone wants to sue you for your shirt? Be generous! Give your jacket as well – it's worth more! And next time some jumped-up tin soldier forces you to carry his pack for a mile, well, show him what civilisation really is, and carry it for two! Beggars? Don't be selfish – give to them. And if someone asks to borrow something, don't come out with pious excuses – share a bit!

[43-47] You've heard what they used to say: 'Love your friends' – which seems to imply that you should hate your enemies. But *I'm* telling you: love your enemies; pray for people who have a go at you. This is so that you can truly be children of your Father in heaven who doesn't have any favourites at all. Doesn't he send sunshine to bad people as well as good, rain to both faithful and unfaithful? I mean, what's so special about loving people who love you – anyone can do that. Even the tax gatherers are canny enough to stick together![3] And if you only speak to people who're the same as you, what makes you different from anyone else? Even outsiders do that.

[48] In other words, your example of true goodness should be God, your heavenly Father – model yourselves on him!

---

1. In the Law of Moses, this was a limit not a licence – the *absolute maximum* allowed, intended to stop the excesses that had led to blood feuds.
2. More than just a slap, a *contemptuous* gesture.
3. Jews gathering taxes for the Roman occupiers were despised by their fellow Israelites.

What about religious rituals?

There's a fine but important line between witnessing for Christ and showing off! Jesus doesn't say rituals are unimportant, but that they're *too* important to be abused. He concentrates on three kinds of observance that are important in most if not all religions: giving, prayer and fasting. There's a lot about 'rewards' here, which should be thought of as pleasant consequences rather than handouts: the 'rewards' of true religion are much better than we can get from other people – so let's not miss them by chasing after empty praise!

6 [1-4] Now, don't fall into the trap of making a big show of your religiosity, just to look good to other people. Anything you get from them won't be worth the rewards that serving God could have given you. I mean, it's good to give, but don't go sounding off and drawing attention to it like the 'holier than thou' brigade – I'm telling you straight, they've had all the reward they're going to get. When you give, do it quietly – so even your other hand doesn't know about it – and your reward will be of the kind only God can give.

[5-8] Same when you pray – don't be like all that pretentious lot who make a big show of it – they'll pray anywhere, synagogues, street corners, just as long as it's nice and public. I'm telling you straight, they've had all the reward they're going to get. When you want to pray, go to your own place, shut the door, and pray discreetly. And the God who sees what you do discreetly won't let it go unrecognised. And don't go in for all that pious prattle, either – you know, words so long that by the time you've finished you've forgotten where you started! Funny how people think the more words they say, the better the prayer will be. Don't be like them. What's the point? Your Father knows what you need before you even begin to ask. There's a lot more to prayer than giving God shopping lists, you know!

Now we come to the Lord's Prayer. It's interesting that Jesus doesn't say, 'Use these exact words', but 'Pray like this'. It's open to question whether he ever intended us simply to sit and recite the words, or whether he really wanted to offer us a pattern that could inform *all* our praying.

[9-10] So, pray along these lines:

Our Father, enthroned in heaven,

may you be truly honoured, your reign established, your purpose fully achieved, on earth just as in heaven.[1]

[11-13] Give us day by day the food we need, and forgive us our wrongdoing as we forgive people who wrong us. And don't let our faithfulness be tested unreasonably, but help us to stay out of trouble.

[14-15] You see, it's a two-way thing, forgiveness. And if you're forgiving towards others, then you'll be more open to the forgiveness God wants to give you – but if you can't *offer* forgiveness, then you're not really in any position to receive it, are you?

[16-18] Oh, yes – fasting. When you do it, don't go round looking miserable – you know, the way some two-faced folk do, who make themselves ugly to make sure everyone knows. I'm telling you straight, they've had all the reward they're due. But when you're fasting, spruce yourself up so that no one else will know you're doing it – except your Father who's in on it – and your reward will be of the kind only God can give.

What about worldly possessions?

[19-21] Look, it's pointless becoming obsessed with worldly treasures that get moth-eaten, rusty or stolen. Focus on the heavenly treasures that moths, rust and thieves can't get at. It's simple enough, really: whatever you count as 'treasure' will decide where your true loyalties are.

[22-23] It's all about how you see things. Think of the eye as a lamp for the body. If it's healthy, you'll be all light, so you'll see things properly and know the way to go; but a bad eye's going to keep you completely in the dark – think about it: if even the light's dark then how dark will the darkness be?

[24-25] I mean, can you imagine a slave trying to serve two owners at once? The slave would either end up hating one and loving the

---

1. As the ending suggests, this section of the prayer isn't only looking forward to God's final victory at the end of time (although, of course, it does that); it's a desire that God and his ways should be honoured in the here and now – and a strongly implicit commitment to try to make that a reality in our own lives.

other, or be loyal to one and loathe the other. It's God or wealth, and you can't be a slave to both! That's why I'm telling you: don't get obsessed with things like food and drink, or clothes. I mean, isn't there more to life than that stuff?

26-30 Take a look at the birds. When did you last see a sparrow digging its garden? But your heavenly Father provides for them, doesn't he, and aren't you worth more to him than they are?

And is getting yourself into a stew about things going to give you a single hour's extra life?

And what's all this hang-up about clothes? Take a look at the wild flowers – when did you see one of them working for its living, or going to dressmaking classes? And yet, I'm telling you that even Solomon in his best ceremonial outfit never looked as good as one of those. But, look, if God dresses up the weeds that are going to finish up as fuel for burning, how much more care do you think he's going to take of you? Talk about little faith!

31-33 So don't go getting all hung up about what you're going to eat, or about having 'nothing to wear' – those are the kinds of things that people without faith keep harping on about. Your heavenly Father knows that you need these things. Instead, why not set your sights first and foremost on his kingdom and his justice, and trust him to provide all that other stuff as well?

34 So let worrying about tomorrow wait – it'll bring enough problems with it when it comes, without starting early. Today's troubles are quite enough to be going on with.

What about one another?

7 1-5 Don't get judgemental with others, and they'll have no reason to act that way towards you, will they? Because judgementalism breeds judgementalism, and you get back what you give.

I mean, how is it you can see a speck of sawdust in your neighbour's[1] eye, but you can't see a whacking great roof rafter in your own? How have you got the nerve to say, 'Let me take that speck out of your eye,' when the rafter's still sitting there in yours? Hypocrite! Try dealing with the rafter in your eye first – you might then be able to see more clearly to help your neighbour with that little speck of dust!

---

1. Here the word used refers to another member of the faith community – but the word 'Christian' hadn't been thought of yet!

[6] You've got to be realistic – there's no point in giving holy things[1] to dogs, or expensive jewellery to pigs, now, is there? All they'll do is trample it underfoot and then set on you!

What about our relationship with God?

This section emphasises God's goodness by contrasting it with the much lesser goodness of human beings. One biblical scholar has called it 'beggar's wisdom' – beggars know that if they ask persistently enough they'll get something, even from grudging mortals, so how much more will our generous God respond if we pray persistently! It's really meant to show God's goodness, and how God values our prayers – not necessarily that if we ask often enough God will give us that Ferrari! Neither should it be taken to mean that people who are poor or sick just haven't prayed enough.

[7-11] Ask for something, and you'll be given it; go searching – really searching – and you'll find; keep on knocking, and the door will be opened. Because everyone who keeps asking gets something; everyone who really searches finds, and for all who keep pounding on that door, it *will* be opened. I mean, look at your own families. So, your child wants some bread: are you going to say, 'Have a stone, instead – it's the same shape'? Or maybe one of your children says, 'Hey, I'd really like some fish!' So, are you going to say, 'Try a nice, wriggly snake instead – they've both got scales'? I think not, somehow. So if you, poor sinful mortals that you are, know how to be decent parents, how much more does your Father in heaven know how to give good things to you?

So what does it all amount to?

[12] In every situation, treat other people the way you'd like them to treat you. That's really what the whole of scripture – God's revealed will and purpose – is about.

And finally: don't be led astray

To rephrase an old song, 'It ain't what you *say*, it's the way that you *do* it'. In the end, faith in Christ is about lifestyle, not just

---

1. Early Christians interpreted this as meaning the bread and wine of communion, but it probably refers to good teaching.

about easy professions of faith or recitations of dogma – no special codes and passwords here. The ultimate question is about whether the way we're living is in keeping with God's will for us, revealed in Jesus. So the sermon ends with strong advice to stick to the path he has beaten for us.

[13-14] Don't go blindly following the crowd – look for the little gate that's easy to miss. Oh, yes, there's a nice big, obvious gate and a lovely wide road that'll lead you straight to destruction, and there'll always be plenty of people choosing that way. The gate that leads to life, well, that's something else. It's narrow – you've got to look for it. And the road beyond it – well, I can't tell you a lie – it can be hard going. Not a lot of people find it.

[15-20] And watch out for the spin-doctors who come to you looking like little lambs but underneath it all are about as cuddly as fierce and hungry wolves. Oh, you'll know them – you'll know them by their results. After all, you don't get grapes from thorn bushes, now do you – or figs from thistles? Put it another way: good trees, good fruit; bad trees, bad fruit. And you know what happens to trees that give bad fruit, don't you? – cut off at the roots and into the fire, that's what. So you'll know these characters by the 'fruit' they produce.

[21-23] You know, it's not everyone who comes to me bowing and scraping and saying 'Lord, Lord' who'll get into the kingdom of heaven – oh, no! It'll be those whose lives fulfil the purpose of my Father in heaven. Oh, of course, they'll come – when the great day arrives, they'll be there, saying, 'Lord, Lord, didn't we say all those wise things in your name? Didn't we cast out demons from people and do all kinds of spectacular miracles in your name?' Well, I'm not going to be taken in by all that. 'Hey, have we met?' I'll say to them. 'Out of my sight, you rotten lot!'

[24-27] You hear what I'm saying and live by it, and you'll be like a really sensible guy who built a house on solid rock. Rain? You've never seen anything like it – and wind, too – but that house stood firm because its foundations were solid. Of course, if you don't then you'll be like the other chap who built his house on the sand. Seemed easier, see – none of that sweaty labour digging foundations – until the storm came. Well, the rain came down in sheets, the wind blew, and when that house fell, wow, did it fall!

[28-29] When Jesus finished saying this, the crowds were totally amazed because he taught with real authority – not like the kind of sermons they were used to getting from the scribes!

It ain't what you say, it's the way that you do it

Being a good teacher was important, but for Jesus' work to be effective his authority had to be shown in his actions as well as in his words. So, as well as *telling* people how to have good lives, he *acted* to change people's lives for the better.

Including the excluded

A man with leprosy

8 [1-4] Jesus left the mountain, with the crowd still following him, and a man came up to him who had leprosy.[1] The man knelt down in front of Jesus and said, 'Lord, if you really want to, you can make me well again – not to mention socially acceptable.'

Jesus reached out and touched him – not something recommended in polite society.[2] 'Oh, I do want to,' he said. 'So be healed.' Immediately, the man's skin healed up. 'Now, don't you go telling everybody about this,' Jesus warned him. 'Just go and see the priest and get all the legal stuff sorted out – thank offerings, that sort of thing – then you can go home again.'

A 'heathen'

[5-13] Jesus was just going into Capernaum when a Roman Centurion[3] came to him for help. 'Lord,' he said, 'I've got this servant, and he's ill at home and he's really desperate.'

'I'm on my way,' said Jesus. 'I'll see him right.'

'You can't do that, can you, Lord? I mean, you're not allowed – I'm not fit for it according to your law. Look, just say the word – that's all it will take, and my servant will be well again. Oh, I know all about

---

1. Not sure if it was true leprosy – all kinds of unpleasant skin diseases were called leprosy in those days, including the real thing, of course. Whatever it was, no one wanted him around!

2. Not only that: Jesus risked being 'quarantined' himself for doing it. How's that for solidarity!

3. And not just any old heathen either – an officer in the forces of occupation.

authority – I'm under it, and I've got soldiers under me. When I tell someone, "Go", he goes. And if I tell him, "Come here", he comes. And I've only got to say the word and my slave will do exactly what I command. Oh, yes, I know authority.'

Jesus was amazed! 'I don't mind telling you,' he said to the people round him, 'I've never seen faith like this in anyone in Israel. I'm telling you, people are going to come from everywhere – from the farthest east and west – to share with Abraham, Isaac and Jacob in the great feast of the kingdom of heaven, and those who think it already belongs to them – the ones who *should* inherit it – will find themselves shut out in the dark. Oh, there'll be some wailing and tooth-gnashing going on then, you can be assured of that!' Then he turned to the centurion. 'Go home,' he said. 'It's done – just as you had faith it would be.' And the centurion's servant was healed at that very moment.

A woman

[14-15] Next stop was Peter's house – and Peter's mother-in-law was down with a fever. Well, that was soon dealt with. When Jesus touched her hand, the fever went. Then she got up from her bed and served him.

Everyone included . . .

[16-17] By the time evening came, all kinds of people were there, some possessed by evil spirits, others just plain sick. The evil spirits were despatched without a word, and the sick were healed. So he fulfilled a prophecy of Isaiah: 'He took our oppression away from us, and healed our diseases.'[1]

. . . if they truly want to be

> The next section illustrates an important distinction. While Jesus was there for everybody, unconditionally, when it came to people actually becoming *disciples*, he was careful to make sure they knew what it involved. So there's a different tone when he's speaking to people in general ('the crowds') from when he's talking to disciples or would-be disciples.

---

1. Isaiah 53:4. Sometimes, prophets speaking about the future used a form of past tense to illustrate the power of God's word. In effect, they were saying, 'God has decided it, so it's as good as done.'

¹⁸⁻¹⁹ Jesus decided to get away from the crowds for a bit, and began to take his friends off to the other side of the lake. One of the scribes came up to him. 'Hey, Teacher,' he said, 'wherever it is that you're off to, I think I'll tag along.'

²⁰ 'Oh, you will, will you?' Jesus answered. 'Well, it's not quite as easy as that – foxes have holes to sleep in, birds have their nests, but for the Son of Man there's nowhere half that comfortable to get his head down.'

²¹ One of his disciples came up to him. 'Lord,' he said, 'I'll be very happy to come with you, just as soon as I've buried my father.'[1]

²²⁻²³ 'You just stay with me,' Jesus answered. 'Let the people who are spiritually dead themselves worry about things like that!' And he got into the boat, followed by his disciples.

Jesus calms the storm

> Having shown us Jesus' authority as a teacher and as a changer of individual lives, Matthew now moves to the climax of this section: Jesus' authority over the whole created order.

²⁴⁻²⁵ Next thing anybody remembers, the wind had got up and the whole sea seemed to be shaking like an earthquake. The boat was being swamped and where was Jesus? Fast asleep! Not for long, though – 'Lord, save us!' the disciples started shouting at him. 'We're all going to die!'

²⁶ Jesus wasn't impressed. 'What are you afraid of? Talk about little faith!' Then a word from Jesus – a stern one – and the wind and sea stopped raging and everything was quiet.

²⁷ They were all completely amazed. 'Now, just who is this guy?' they were asking. 'Even the wind and the sea do as he tells them!'

The healing of the Gadarene demoniacs

²⁸⁻³¹ Then it was on to the other side – to the Gadarene region – where they were met by two people possessed by demons, who came out from

---

1. Most probably his father wasn't dead. The disciple was postponing following Jesus for as long as his father remained alive – which could have been years! This would explain Jesus' response.

among the tombs. Ferocious characters, they were – which was why sensible people avoided the area. Suddenly they were yelling furiously at Jesus, 'What business do you have with us, Son of God? Have you come to start punishing us ahead of time, is that it?' As it happened, there was a herd of pigs feeding some way away, so the demons obviously decided that some home was better than none and said, 'Look, if we've got to leave these bodies, can we go into the pigs instead?'

³²⁻³⁴ 'Go!' Jesus answered, so they did – and in next to no time those peacefully feeding pigs were charging madly down the steep bank into the sea, where they drowned. The swineherds didn't hang around to ask questions – just took off into the town and told the whole story. So, of course, the entire town got up and came out to Jesus, pleading with him to get out of their area.

Jesus has the authority to forgive[1]

9¹⁻² Then it was back to the boat, across the sea and home to Capernaum for Jesus and his friends. Some people were carrying a paralysed man on a stretcher. Jesus was pretty impressed by their faith and said to the paralysed man, 'Don't be downhearted, son – your sins are forgiven.'[2]

³⁻⁸ The scribes nearby responded predictably, of course. 'Blasphemy!' they whinged. 'This guy's blaspheming!'

Jesus knew exactly what was in their minds, and said, 'Why do you always have to pick holes like that? All right, I suppose anyone could say, "Your sins are forgiven", but to say, "Get up and walk", well, that's another matter, isn't it![3] So, if you want to see some real authority, that's OK by me.' He turned to the man on the stretcher and said, 'Stand up, get hold of that stretcher, and go home.' And he did. And when the crowds saw it, they were completely awestruck and started praising God for giving that kind of authority to a human being.

---

1. This story is more usually entitled something like 'Jesus heals a paralysed man', but if we take the passage in context we know that the story is really about authority, in keeping with the others in this section. In this case, the real issue is not the healing but the forgiving.
2. This doesn't mean Jesus thought the man's illness was a punishment – Jesus never went in for all that 'blame the victim' stuff – but it was what people in those days believed, so the man would certainly be *feeling* in need of forgiveness.
3. Because any ordinary person would risk looking a bit silly when it didn't happen!

Eating with the undesirables

[9-11] Then Jesus came across a guy called Matthew, a tax collector, sitting at the custom desk taxing the traders. 'Follow me,' he said, and the man just got up and followed him. Next thing everybody knew, Jesus was sitting down to dinner with him, and every tax collector and general undesirable in the area seemed to be joining them. 'Hey, what's the idea?' the Pharisees demanded of Jesus' disciples. 'Why does your teacher fellow share food with characters like this?'

[12-13] Jesus heard them – well, he'd have found it difficult not to, the commotion they were causing – and said, 'The people who are fit and healthy hardly need a doctor, do they? Doctors go to people who need them, and so do I. Why don't you just go away and take a look at your Bibles? You could start with, "It's kindness that I want from you, not rituals and sacrifices".[1] I didn't come to invite the righteous to my banquet – I came to invite the ones you call sinners to share it!'

Empty rituals

[14] Next, it was John's disciples who came to him. 'Look,' they said, 'the Pharisees are always fasting, and so are we – so why's it not good enough for your disciples, too?'[2]

[15-17] 'Oh, right,' Jesus answered, 'I suppose you'd ask wedding guests to go into mourning while the bridegroom's with them, would you? When the bridegroom's been taken away, there'll be plenty of time for that! New days, new ways: no one with any sense patches an old coat with new, unshrunk cloth – you just end up with a worse tear than ever. And you don't put new wine into old wineskins, either – not if you know your wine. It's just inviting disaster. The new wine will burst out of the skins and they'll both be lost. New wineskins for new wine.'

New life and healing

[18-19] As Jesus was saying this, one of the local religious leaders came up and knelt in front of him. 'Please help,' he said. 'It's my daughter – she's

---

1. Hosea 6:6. This isn't belittling the sacrifice tradition, but rather saying that what God wants is a proper relationship with and between his people: all the true spiritual qualities that the various sacrifices were intended to represent.
2. Fasting was only required at specific times, but some groups saw it as a kind of religious badge of honour and took it to extremes.

just died. You can save her, though – it's what you do, isn't it? Just come and lay hands on her and I know she'll be OK.' Jesus didn't hang around – he went with him, and his disciples followed.

[20-22] Just as they were getting going, a woman who'd suffered from a haemorrhage for twelve years came up behind him and touched just the fringe of his coat. 'That's all it'll take,' she told herself. 'If I can just touch the edge, I'll get better.'

Jesus turned round to face her. 'Don't be downhearted, daughter,' he said. 'Your faith has healed you!' And immediately she was made well.[1]

[23-26] When Jesus got to the synagogue leader's house, the place was full of people, including professional mourners making a racket. 'You may as well go,' he said, 'because this is one death that's not going to last.' They all had a good laugh at him over that, but he insisted they leave. Jesus went in to where the girl was, took her by the hand, and she stood up. Not surprisingly, it was the talk of the district.

Two men who can't see . . .

[27-31] As Jesus moved on, two blind men followed, calling out after him, 'Son of David, help us! Son of David, help us!' When he got to the house he was aiming for, they followed him right inside.

Jesus said, 'Do you truly believe I have the power to do this for you?'

'Oh, yes, Lord,' they answered.

Jesus touched their eyes: 'As your faith says, so let it be done.'

While their eyes were beginning to focus, Jesus warned them, 'Just make sure you don't go telling anyone else about this.' Not that that made any difference, of course – they just went and spread the story all over the district.

. . . and one who can't speak

[32-33] After those two had gone, someone else came along who was possessed by a demon that made him mute. The demon was soon despatched and the power of speech restored, and everybody was amazed yet again. 'We've never seen anything like this in Israel,'[2] they said.

---

1. This illness would have made the woman 'unclean'. For a full healing, she needed a proper encounter with Christ.
2. A damning indictment on the religious establishment! If the power of God could be seen anywhere, it should have been in Israel.

[34] The Pharisees had an answer, of course – well, they would, wouldn't they! 'Of course he can cast out demons,' they scoffed, 'because he's in league with the most powerful demon of them all!'

Jesus delegates his authority

> Having firmly established the authority of Jesus, Matthew now shows how he doesn't jealously cling to it but delegates – shares his power with his disciples. It's a cliché, of course, but still true and worthy of reflection, that the world today might be a much better place if we learnt to share, rather than grasp power.

[35-38] Then Jesus took off all over the place – all the cities and villages – teaching in synagogues, preaching the good news of the kingdom of heaven, healing people of every kind of sickness and disease. He looked upon the people with real compassion – seeing them as sheep without a shepherd.[1] 'There's a great harvest, here,' he said to his disciples, 'but far too few labourers to bring it all in. So get praying to the Chief Harvester to send in more workers.'

Time to commission the 'harvesters'

Jesus calls the Twelve to be Apostles

10[1-4] Jesus called a meeting of his twelve closest disciples and gave them his authority to cast out evil spirits wherever they'd gained a hold over people, as well as healing people of every kind of sickness and disease. Want to know who they were? I'll tell you. First came Simon – who was known also as Peter – and his brother Andrew, and then Zebedee's two sons, James and John. He also commissioned Philip and Bartholomew, Thomas, Matthew (the tax collector, would you believe?), another James – the son of Alphaeus – and Thaddaeus. Finally, another Simon – this time Simon the patriot – and Judas Iscariot, the guy who was eventually going to betray him.

---

1. This is another huge indictment of the spiritual leadership of Israel – reading Ezekiel 34 with this reference in mind is enlightening.

Jesus' second big speech: mainly on mission

[5-8] Those were the twelve Jesus sent out as missionaries, and he made clear what he expected of them. These are the instructions he gave them:

Get your priorities sorted

Now, you've got to stay focused. Don't get distracted by trying to convert Gentiles, and keep away from the Samaritan towns.[1] Concentrate on what I call the 'lost sheep' among the Israelites themselves. As you go, tell everyone the good news – that the kingdom of heaven has come near. And don't stop at just saying it – show it: heal sick people, bring the dead back to life, heal those with anti-social diseases, get rid of demons who're oppressing people. And you're not there to line your pockets, like some people we know of – you've been given a free gift, so share it equally freely.

[9-15] Don't get weighed down with provisions: no fund-raising or getting kitted out with spare gear. Just go in what you stand up in – after all, God knows that his harvesters deserve to be provided for! In every place you come to, find some appropriate people to stay with – people who are open to your message. Give the traditional blessing of peace as you enter the house. If they accept it, they'll get the benefit; if they don't, then that's their problem – you can't force it on them, can you![2] If people reject your message, then don't let's have any pretence about it. Shake the dust off your shoes as you leave, showing that you've not been welcome, because I'm telling you that Sodom and Gomorrah will do better than that town on judgement day!

Don't expect to have it easy

[16-20] Look, I'm sending you out to live like sheep among wolves.[3] So you've got to be as canny as snakes and, at the same time, as un-threatening as doves. And make no mistake, these people can be

---

1. This wasn't Jesus being prejudiced – he was always open to including outsiders, as we've seen already, but the specific mission to the Gentiles (non-Jews) would come later. For now, the disciples' attention had to be concentrated on a smaller, more immediate task.
2. In the Jewish tradition, blessings aren't just imposed on people; they need to be accepted. It's a bit like giving someone a cheque – if they can't be bothered to cash it, then they're not going to get the benefit and you'll still have the money!
3. No alternative, then, but to rely upon the Shepherd.

dangerous: they'll put you on trial on trumped-up charges; they'll have you publicly flogged – and that's just the religious people! You'll be tried by the highest human authorities, just because you're committed to me – but that'll be your opportunity to testify and get my story out to the wider world! So when you find yourself being handed over, don't start fretting about what words you're going to use – all that will be given to you at the time, because you aren't there to speak for yourselves. Just let God's Spirit speak through you.

21-23 Oh, it's going to get nasty – you'll find families split apart, all turning on one another – and people will hate you with a passion, just because of me. But those who can hang on, keep the faith right to the end – they'll be saved. Don't waste your time on lost causes – if you get a hammering in one town, head for the next, because I'm telling you straight, you won't have converted everybody in this district by the time the Son of Man comes, however fast you move or however much you put up with.

24-27 Look, why should disciples get on any better than their teachers? Why should a slave expect more than the master? They do well if they can just be like them. So if people are calling the main man the devil incarnate, you can imagine what sort of names they're going to dream up for his family! So don't let them get to you. Don't worry, it'll all come out in the end – whatever nasty little secrets they try to hide now will all be made known. On the other hand, I don't have a secret life, so whatever I say quietly[1] to you can be shouted in public, and any personal conversations we may have can be broadcast from the rooftops. No problem!

28-31 It's not the civil authorities you need to reckon with, just because they can take away your earthly life; the one you should be really in awe of is the one who has life-or-death power over your entire being. And he's the one you can trust. Look, sparrows are two a penny, aren't they? But not one of them dies without your Father knowing and feeling it. As for you, he even counts every hair of your head! So don't go worrying yourselves, because you're worth a sight more than any number of sparrows.

---

1. In standard translations, you'll find 'quietly' expressed here as 'in the dark', but Jesus is contrasting himself with those who use darkness as cover. When he seeks privacy with his disciples, it's not because he's got something to hide; they can repeat his words confidently in public – 'the light'.

32-33 Put it this way: if you're prepared to speak for me, just to ordinary people, I'll do the same for you to my Father in heaven, no less! But if you disown me to others, well, don't expect to have it both ways as far as my Father in heaven's concerned. OK?

34-39 Don't go thinking that my coming here is going to make everything hunky-dory, just like that – real peace isn't that easy! My coming means trouble – big trouble. It'll tear families apart – son from father, daughter from mother, oh yes, and daughter-in-law from mother-in-law. It won't be people outside that'll be the problem – people's enemies will be right there in their own households. Folk are going to find themselves having to choose – if you want to put your worldly ties and relationships before your loyalty to me, well, that's your choice and you'll have made it. People won't be able to follow me and avoid the cross – however hard they try. Life's a funny thing – the more you grasp at it, the more it eludes you, but those who put their lives and lifestyles on the line for me will find what real living is about!

40-42 When people welcome you, and accept you, they're welcoming and accepting me – and in that case they've welcomed the one who sent me. You see, it's not just leaders who get the benefits – anyone who welcomes them as being from God will get the same. Anyone who gives even so much as a cold drink to one of these because they're my disciples – well, they won't go unrewarded.

Jesus, John and great expectations

11 ¹ After Jesus finished this teaching session for the Twelve, he headed out to the towns to get on with his own public preaching.

2-6 Meanwhile, John the Baptiser was in prison, hearing reports of what the Messiah was doing – and it didn't quite seem to fit. So he sent some of his own disciples to check Jesus out. 'Hey, Jesus, what's the story? I mean, are you really the one we've been waiting for, or should we be looking for someone more like what we expected?'

Jesus answered, 'Why don't you just go back to John and tell him what you've seen and heard: blind people seeing, deaf hearing, dead people raised back to life, and the good news being targeted on the most needy. And congratulations, I say, to everyone who isn't put off just because I don't fit with their preconceived ideas!'

[7-15] So they went away to report back, and Jesus started speaking to the crowds about John:

Remember how you all went chasing out into the desert to hear him? Well, what were you expecting? Someone weak, like a reed shaken in the wind? Not likely! Or was it someone in beautiful clothes? Look, if you'd wanted that sort of thing you'd have gone to a palace or somewhere. So, what *were* you looking for? A prophet, maybe? Oh, yes – but you got a lot more than that, didn't you! This is the one that scripture foretold: 'Look, I'm sending my messenger ahead of you – the one who's going to prepare the way before you.'[1] I'm telling you straight, in the old order of things, there's no mother's son greater than John – but of those who are already in the kingdom of heaven, even the lowest is greater than he is! Ever since John the Baptiser first started preaching, the kingdom of heaven's been provoking violent reactions – not to mention those who've wanted to use it to sanctify their own violence! Everything in the prophets, and in the law, pointed forward to this – and if people's minds are open they'll recognise in John the 'Elijah' figure who was prophesied. If you've got ears, use them!

[16-19] You know what this generation's like? It's like silly children, sitting in a market place playing funerals, jeering at one another: 'We played the flute but you wouldn't dance – we cried but you wouldn't join in.' You really want it both ways, don't you! I mean; along comes John, abstaining from food and strong drink, and you say, 'He's possessed by a demon, you know,' but when you see the Son of Man *enjoying* his food and his drink, you say, 'Ooh, look – he's greedy, he's drunk and he's got terrible friends, all those tax collectors and sinners!' Well, the things I've done are all the vindication I need.

[20-24] Following this, he almost inevitably rounded on the cities where his great miracles had been performed, because after everything they'd seen, they'd showed no indication at all of turning away from their Godless ways. 'A curse upon you Chorazin and Bethsaida!' he said. 'My, are you in trouble! Even Tyre and Sidon would have turned from their rotten ways and made sackcloth and ashes[2] fashionable if they'd seen

---

1. Malachi 3:1 and Exodus 23:20.
2. Wearing sackcloth and ashes was a traditional expression of being sorry for sin.

the works of power I did for you – but on the day of judgement, they'll come out better than you will![1] And what about you, Capernaum? Reckon you've got a first-class ticket to heaven, do you? Think again – hell's more suitable for you. I mean, even Sodom might still be standing if the people there had seen the signs you've seen – but come the judgement, Sodom will be comfortable compared with you!'

25-27 So, Jesus gave thanks to God: 'Father, I really thank you. I mean, you're God of all things, and you've chosen to make blindingly obvious to simple, uneducated people these matters that the so-called wise and learned just can't get a handle on! Oh, yes, Father – that's truly your goodness in action!'

He continued, 'My Father's given me authority in all things, you know. I mean, we're so close you wouldn't believe it. No one's as close to the Son as the Father, and no one understands the Father the way the Son does – unless of course the Son chooses to make him known.

28-30 'Hey, is your religion a burden to you – all those laws and petty regulations? Then come to me – I can set you free from all that! Oh, I'll make demands of you, but good ones – and compared with all that 'i'-dotting and 't'-crossing, it'll be positively therapeutic! So, come and learn from me and you'll find true peace for your souls![2]

Never on a Sabbath day!

> Jesus made it very clear that the Sabbath day was to be a blessing, not a burden.

Picking the corn

12 1-8 It was about that time that Jesus was walking through the cornfields one Sabbath day, with some very hungry disciples who were picking some of the heads off the corn as they went, and eating them. Harmless enough, you'd think, but not if you're a Pharisee with

---

1. Tyre and Sidon, destroyed by God for impenitence (see, for example, Isaiah 23), became a byword for pagan insolence towards God – but the towns Jesus had visited had even less excuse!
2. Jesus isn't offering anarchy, here – he made clear in chapter 5 that he's not about disregarding the law. The point is that he's getting us back to its true purpose – to provide a framework within which we can relate to God properly. So his true law sets us free instead of being a burden to us!

an axe to grind. 'Hey, Jesus,' they called, 'what do you think you're doing, letting your disciples break the law on the Sabbath?'[1]

'Oh, get real, please!' Jesus answered. 'Try reading your Bibles – don't you remember what King David did when he and his companions were hungry? I mean, he only went into the holy of holies and stole the bread intended for worship, which the law says only the priests can eat – that's all! And surely you must know the law that says that priests in the Temple break the Sabbath but aren't counted guilty? Well, I'm telling you, you're looking at something a sight greater than the Temple. But then again, if you had any idea of what the Bible really means when it says, "It's kindness that I want from you, not rituals and sacrifices",[2] then you wouldn't go around making wild accusations against innocent people – because they're with me, and the Son of Man has authority over the Sabbath.'

Healing: the man with the withered hand

[9-14] Moving on, Jesus went to the local synagogue, where there was a man in the congregation whose hand was paralysed – which gave the Pharisees the chance they needed. 'OK,' they said to Jesus, 'tell us whether it's legal to heal people on the Sabbath.' Not that they were the least bit interested in either the man or the answer, of course – it was just another chance to catch Jesus out.

'Look,' Jesus answered, 'if one of you has a sheep that falls into a pit, are you going to tell me you wouldn't go and rescue it, Sabbath or no Sabbath? You can bend the law soon enough when it's your valuable property that's at stake, oh yes! Well, we're talking about a human being – worth infinitely more than an animal – so to answer the *real* question: of course it's legal to do good on the Sabbath.' Then he turned to the man and said, 'Stretch out your hand,' and it became as sound as a bell – well, as sound as a good hand, anyway. The Pharisees, though, were unimpressed – they sloped off into an unholy huddle to plot his downfall.

---

1. Now, you might think they meant stealing, but it was even pettier than that. Working on the Sabbath was illegal, and, as far as they were concerned, if you're going to pick an ear of wheat you might as well take a combine harvester to the whole field!
2. Hosea 6:6. See my note on 9:13.

Jesus: God's Chosen One

15-17 Time for another strategic retreat, but not without the crowds following him. He healed all the people who needed it, but with strict instructions to them not to go shouting it around the place. This fulfilled what the prophet Isaiah had said about the kind of man he would be:

18-21 Look: I'm presenting to you my special servant, the one who has my full support,
the one I've chosen before all others, the very delight of my being!
In fact, I've even put my own Spirit within him,
he's going to bring about justice all through the world.
Not that he's going to make a big song and dance, mind you,
none of this public shouting and yelling for him:
he won't even break off a damaged reed,
or snuff out a candle that's nearly burnt out.
But for all that, he'll be determined in creating justice.
He'll fulfil the hopes of the whole world.[1]

Servant of God or of Satan?

22-24 Then some people brought to Jesus a man possessed by a demon that made him both blind and mute, and Jesus cured him – another example of giving the voiceless a voice and the blind their sight. 'Amazing!' said the people in the crowds. 'Hey, this couldn't by any chance be the long-promised "Son of David", could it?'

Now, the Pharisees couldn't let that kind of idea take hold, so they cut in with their own explanation. 'Look,' they said, 'the only reason this guy can cast out demons is that he's in league with the devil himself!'

25-29 Jesus knew exactly how their minds were working. 'Use a bit of sense!' he said to them. 'Everyone knows that any kingdom that's divided against itself ends up being destroyed. That's true at every level – a divided city, or even a feuding family – none of them can survive. So if you're saying that Satan is casting out Satan, then clearly the underworld's in a state of civil war and can't stand. Put it another way: if it's from the devil that I get my power of exorcisms, where do your own exorcists get theirs? I think you've just defeated your own arguments, which rather makes my point! On the other hand, if my powers of exorcism come from the Spirit of God, then it means that the kingdom

---

1. Isaiah 42:1-4.

of God[1] has come and camped on your doorstep – with all that implies. Or again, can you imagine someone going to burgle a strong man's house without tying up the strong man first?[2] Only then is it safe to start looting the place!

What we say and do shows what we are

[30-37] 'Look, you're either with me or against me – there's no neutrality here. You decide whether you're going to be with me, bringing things together, or out there creating division. I'm telling you, people can be forgiven for any kind of sin, any kind of blasphemy, but when you start committing blasphemy against the Holy Spirit, then you put yourself out of reach of forgiveness. You can say what you like about the Son of Man, and still be open to forgiveness, but when you start trying to make out that good's bad and vice versa, then there's no getting through to you, is there? Not now, and not in eternity, either.[3] Look, you either say the tree's good and its fruit's good too, or you say the tree's evil and then you have to say its fruit's evil – because the one inevitably leads to the other. You revolting, poisonous snakes! How d'you expect to say anything good when you're evil at heart? Because the mouth can only speak from what the heart has stored up. Good people can produce good things because they've got this inner store of goodness – but evil people produce evil, from what they've hoarded up inside themselves. I'm telling you, the day's coming when you'll be judged for every thoughtless word that's passed your lips. You'll stand or fall in the end, by the things you say.'

The demand for proof

[38-42] 'OK, then,' the Scribes and Pharisees demanded, 'give us some proof – a supernatural sign; that might convince us.'

'Only a generation that's completely lost any trace of real faith would ask for something like that,' Jesus answered. 'You're not getting any sign except the sign of Jonah. Remember Jonah: three days and

---

1. 'Kingdom of heaven' would be more usual for Matthew. This is probably a literary device, echoing 'Spirit of God' with 'kingdom of God'. The meaning is the same.
2. 'Binding Satan' was a traditional Jewish image. Jesus is clearly saying the only reason he can do the things he's doing is that he's effectively rendered Satan helpless.
3. It's important to read this in context. The Pharisees are convincing themselves that what's good is bad and vice versa – shutting themselves off from the 'Spirit of Truth' who, Jesus said elsewhere, leads us into all truth. So it's not that God's withholding forgiveness from them, but that they've got themselves into a position where they can't accept it *because they can't recognise their need of it!*

three nights in the belly of a sea creature? Well, the Son of Man will be three days and three nights in the bowels of the earth.[1] Just wait and see: the people of Nineveh are going to rise up at the judgement and condemn all of this generation,[2] because when Jonah preached they repented – whereas you've got something a sight greater than Jonah standing right in front of you and you're rejecting it! Likewise, the Queen of Sheba will stand in judgement on this generation,[3] because she travelled from the other side of the world to learn from the wisdom of Solomon, and you've got something infinitely greater than Solomon right on your doorstep and can't recognise it!

Evil spirits and vacant possession

[43-45] 'You know what happens when an evil spirit leaves a person? It goes walkabout looking for another home. And if it doesn't find one, what does it do? It thinks, "I know, I'll go back where I was before – nice place, that." And just suppose that when it gets there it finds it all nice and clean with vacant possession. "Hey, this is a bit of all right," it thinks. "I'll get a few friends round." So it goes and finds seven other spirits even more evil than it is itself, and they all move in with it. What a rave that's going to be! And the person ends up worse off than before the original exorcism happened. That's how it's going to be for all of this generation!'[4]

The true family of Jesus

[46-50] 'Hey, Jesus!' someone said. 'Your mother and your brothers are standing outside – it seems they want a word.'[5]

'My family?' Jesus answered. 'OK, you tell me – who are truly my family?' He looked around, and pointed to his disciples. 'There!' he said. 'There's my true family! Because a proper relationship with me isn't about blood ties and family trees – it's about commitment to the work of my Father in heaven – that's what makes you my family!'

---

1. I found this puzzling for years, but didn't think it was proper to ask – so now I'll save you the hassle. Simple arithmetic tells us that Jesus didn't spend that time in the tomb – Friday afternoon until Sunday morning isn't three days and three nights. So, was Jesus' arithmetic that bad? No. This saying was a Jewish figure of speech for 'a short time'. It's the parallel that's important here, not the calculation.
2. The people of Nineveh, of course, were foreigners – the Pharisees weren't going to like this!
3. Another foreigner – Jesus really is driving the point home!
4. So just getting rid of evil isn't enough – there needs to be a positive presence of good to fill the spiritual vacuum.
5. One of various indications that even Jesus' own family weren't totally sure of him.

Jesus' third big speech: mainly on the kingdom of heaven

A ministry in parables

We have seen a few short passages that are very much like parables, but so far Matthew hasn't used the word itself. Now, he draws together some parables of Jesus along with explanations both of the individual parables and of the general principle.

13 1-3a The same day that all this happened Jesus went out and sat on the beach, but the crowds followed him, of course, and it all got a bit too cosy for comfort – so he found a boat to use as a floating platform while the crowd stood on the shore. Then, with a bit of space around him, he started teaching using parables:

The parable of the sower

3b-9 Listen: there was this sower who went out sowing seed – as sowers do – and some of his seed landed on the pathway, so the birds thought it was dinner time and snaffled it all. Then some of it fell among rocks – not a lot of soil there, so the wheat died as fast as it grew. No roots, you see – no way of getting water when the sun got up – you know how it is. Anyway, some other seeds fell in the briar patch and the wheat that grew there just got choked to death by all the weeds. So far, not so good – but some of the seed fell on good soil, and, wow, did it grow! I mean, some of it produced anything between thirty and a hundred times its own weight. OK? End of story. If you've got ears, fine – use them.

Why parables?

10-17 'Jesus,' his disciples said, 'why do you do this? I mean, why do you have to talk in riddles all the time?'

Jesus answered:

Well, whether they're riddles depends on your state of mind. Your minds have been opened to things about the kingdom of heaven, so you understand them – other people's haven't, so they don't. You know what it's like: people who've already got a headstart will always end up doing better, but if they don't have a clue to begin with they probably won't get the point however you dress it up. It's a riddle to them because, as the saying goes, 'You see but don't really perceive it; you hear but you don't understand.[1] They exactly fulfil Isaiah's prophecy, don't they! Remember what he said: 'You hear but you don't understand, you see but don't really take anything in. Because these people's minds are closed, their ears are bunged up, they've got their eyes shut to make sure they don't see – or hear – anything they don't want to. I mean, they don't want to do anything radical like repenting and being healed, now do they!'

But congratulations to you because your eyes can see, and your ears can hear. I'm telling you straight: there've been prophets and people of real faith who've longed to see the things you're seeing now – really strained to hear what you're hearing – but weren't able to.

Interpreting the parable of the sower

[18-23] OK, then – take the parable of the sower. People hear the message about the kingdom, but don't get to grips with it, so it gets taken away again before it has a chance to grow – that's the seed on the path. Then we had seed sown on rocky ground, didn't we? Well, that's the people who hear and get all enthusiastic, but it doesn't last. It's shallow faith, and at the first hint of trouble they're off back to their old ways. Now what? Oh, yes – the seed in the briar patch. Well, some people truly do have good intentions, you know, but then they are swamped by all the cares and pleasures of the world, and before long it's as though they never heard. But the good soil – well, that's something else. People hear the word, they really take it on board, and you start to see the results – it's that good fruit thing again. OK, now?

The parable of wheat and weeds

[24-30] Then he put another parable in front of them.

Think of the kingdom of heaven as like someone who sowed a field full of really good seed, but then, while respectable people were in their beds, this enemy came along and scattered weed seeds and then slunk away without being seen. Well, everything seemed fine until the crop grew, and then the weeds came sprouting up as well. 'Hey, boss, what's going on?' the slaves asked. 'I mean, that seed you

---

1. An allusion to Isaiah 6:9-10, used in a way to suggest that it was a commonly used saying.

gave us to sow – it was OK, wasn't it? So, how come we've got all this other rubbish among the wheat?'

'This is spite,' the farmer answered. 'Sabotage!'[1]

'So, shall we rip them up?'

'No,' the farmer said. 'You'll only go pulling up wheat along with it.[2] Just let them all grow together until harvest – we'll separate them then, and you can burn the rubbish and put the wheat in the barn.'

The parable of the mustard seed

[31-32] Then Jesus presented them with another parable.

The kingdom of heaven, well, it's like a mustard seed that someone might sow in a field. Now, you know it's the smallest of seeds, but when it grows it's quite a different story – the biggest of all the shrubs, virtually a tree, in fact. So much so that the birds come and shelter in its shade.

[33] And another parable:

The kingdom of heaven is like yeast. Suppose a woman mixes a little bit of yeast with a lot of flour – what happens? *All* the flour is affected by that little bit of yeast.

[34-35] This was Jesus' way of teaching – talking in riddles as far as the crowds were concerned.[3] In this way he fulfilled what had been prophesied: 'I'll open my mouth to speak parables; I'll reveal secrets hidden from the dawn of time.'[4]

Interpreting the parable of the wheat and weeds

[36-43] Then Jesus went into the house with his disciples, leaving the crowds behind. One of the disciples said, 'OK, then – so what did all that stuff about weeds in the field mean?'

Jesus explained:

The one who sows the good seed in the field – that's the Son of Man; the field is the whole world, and the good seed represents the people

---

1. The weeds were probably darnel – indistinguishable from wheat until it was fully ripe, but deadly if eaten.
2. The darnel roots would be entangled with the wheat, and impossible to separate.
3. Remember that in Matthew 'the crowds' represent the people outside Jesus' group of followers. So what was a 'parable' to an insider would have seemed like a riddle to an outsider. Check back to verses 10-17 to see this spelled out more.
4. Psalm 78:2.

who've responded to God's calling. The bad seed is the ones who haven't. The saboteur is the devil, the harvest is the end of the age, and the reapers are God's angels. So, at the end of all things, there'll be the harvest. Some people are going to be like the weeds – and there'll be a fair bit of weeping and tooth-gnashing going on among them – and others will be like the good wheat, and they'll shine like the sun itself in their Father's kingdom. Got ears, have you? Then use them!

Three parables: images of the kingdom in treasure, pearls and fish

⁴⁴ The kingdom of heaven's like treasure buried in a field. Someone finds it – so what does he do? He buries it again, that's what – and goes off in great delight to sell every last thing he's got and buy the field – just to get that treasure.

⁴⁵⁻⁴⁶ Another example: the kingdom of heaven is like a trader who deals in fine pearls, and one day he comes across a real cracker – worth a mint! So what does he do? Only goes out and sells up every last thing he owns, to buy it, that's all!

⁴⁷⁻⁵² Then again, the kingdom of heaven could be thought of as a big fishing net, thrown into the sea and catching every imaginable kind of fish. When it was full they hauled it in, sorted through the fish and put the good ones into baskets but threw out the inedible ones. That's how it'll be at the end of all things – angels sorting the bad from the good and slinging them into the furnace – wailing, gnashing of teeth, all that stuff.

Jesus ended by saying, 'Are you getting all of this?'

'Oh, yes,' they said, 'we're getting it.'

Treasures old and new

'Right,' said Jesus. 'So what's special about the scribes trained for the kingdom of heaven¹ is that they're like a householder whose treasures include not just old things but new things as well.'

---

1. Jesus seems to be having a dig at the traditional scribes, trained for the old order, who only knew the old stuff! The 'scribes' trained for the new order (in other words, his followers) would also know about the new revelation of God, in him.

The ministry continues

> In this latter part of the Galilean ministry, the question 'Who is Jesus?' simply will not go away. It's implicit or explicit in everything that happens: from the fear aroused in Herod to the obedience of the wind and waves; from the Pharisees' and Sadducees' demand for proof to the foretelling of his own death and resurrection.

Jesus is rejected at home

⁵³⁻⁵⁸ Well, that was that – time to move on. So Jesus went to the synagogue in his home town and started teaching there. 'Where did this guy get all this stuff from?' the people asked. 'All the eloquence, the miracles? He's a carpenter's son, isn't he – mother called Mary, brothers James and Joseph, Simon and Judas? His sisters live round here, too – just a local boy. What right's he got to be special?'

'Well, there you go,' Jesus said. 'Prophets never get any street cred in their home towns or their own families.' That's why he didn't perform so many miracles there – there simply wasn't the faith.

Sex, politics and religion

14¹⁻² About this time, Jesus' reputation had reached the ears of the local ruler, Herod,[1] who immediately got his loincloth in a twist. 'It's John the Baptiser!' he ranted. 'I know it is – John the Baptiser, come back to haunt me – where else would anybody get powers like that?'

³⁻¹¹ Perhaps I'd better start at the beginning. It all began when Herod arrested John and slung him in prison – and that was all on account of Herodias, his brother Philip's widow. You see, John had pointed out – in pretty strong terms even for a hairy prophet – that it was against the law for Herod to marry her. Herod would have executed John, but the crowds liked the guy so he had to be careful.

Then Herod's birthday came around, and things got complicated. Herodias's daughter danced at his party, and the old boy got a bit carried away – finished up promising to do whatever she asked. What she asked for, with a little prompting from her mother, was John the Baptiser's

---

1. Herod Antipas – not to be confused with Herod the Great whom we met earlier. This is his son.

head, on a platter. Now, Herod wasn't happy, but what could he do – break his word in public? So he gave the order: John was beheaded in his cell, and his head put on a platter and presented to the girl, who promptly passed it on to her mother.

¹²⁻¹⁴ John's disciples then came and collected his body to give it a decent burial, before going to tell Jesus the whole gruesome story.

Jesus listened and decided to make another strategic retreat. He hopped into a boat and went to a quiet place where he could get a bit of solitude. Fat chance of that, though – the crowds heard about it and followed him on foot by the land route. So, when Jesus came ashore, there they were, but compassion prevailed and he healed the sick among them.

The feeding of the five thousand

¹⁵⁻²¹ Come the evening, the disciples said to Jesus, 'Look, this is a pretty isolated place, and it's getting late – the crowds must be starving. Send them away and let them go and get some food to eat.'

'Now, why would they want to go away?' Jesus responded. '*You* give them something to eat.'

'Oh, sure – with five loaves and a couple of fish!'

'Oh, give them to me,' Jesus said. He told the crowds to sit down on the grass, and then took the food, said a prayer of thanksgiving, broke the loaves into pieces and handed them to his disciples who went and served the crowds. The amazing thing is that everyone had as much as they needed. More than that – when they cleared up at the end they collected twelve baskets full of scraps! The number of people fed amounted to about five thousand men – and that's not counting women and children!

Subduing the waters of chaos

It's funny stuff, water: it can give life, but it can destroy it, too. Jews knew all about the delicate balance of creation: when God created the earth, he brought the waters of chaos under control – but he didn't completely tame them. So water represented the danger of overwhelming chaos. Noah had needed a boat to survive it – but to be able to walk on it unaided would be the mark of someone *really* special!

²²⁻²⁵ Jesus didn't hang around. He ordered his disciples to get into the boat and set out for the other side of the lake, while he stayed behind, got the crowd to disperse, and then took to the hills¹ – he needed some space to pray. Evening began to fall – and there he was, all alone up a mountain, while the boat with his disciples in it was out in the middle of the lake being given a fair old battering by the waves because the wind was in the wrong direction. Then, at some unearthly hour of the morning – somewhere between three and six o'clock – Jesus went out to catch up with them, walking on the surface of the lake.

²⁶ Not surprisingly, this caused a bit of a stir: the disciples were terrified. 'It's a ghost!' they started screaming.

²⁷ 'Come on, get a grip,' Jesus called out. 'It's me – don't panic.'

²⁸ 'Lord, is that really you?' Peter shouted. 'If it is, just say the word and I'll be able to come to you.'

²⁹ Jesus just said one word: 'Come!' and Peter was out of the boat, walking on top of the water towards Jesus.

³⁰ Then he noticed just how strong the wind was and panic set in. He barely had time to yell out, 'Save me, Lord!' as he started to go under.

³¹ Straightaway, Jesus reached out, grasped hold of him and lifted him up. 'So little faith!' he said. 'Why didn't you simply trust me?'

³²⁻³³ And then something truly amazing happened – as soon as Jesus got Peter back into the boat and climbed in himself, the wind dropped – just like that. All ways round, it was pretty impressive stuff, and the disciples were completely awestruck. 'You're the one!' they said. 'No, seriously – you are – *the* One. You're the Son of God.'

Healings at Gennesaret

³⁴⁻³⁶ So they finished the crossing and got to Gennesaret. In no time at all, Jesus had been recognised and the word spread rapidly through the whole region. Everyone brought their sick friends and relatives to him – they even pleaded to be allowed to touch just the edge of his coat, and all who did that were cured.

---

1. According to John's account of the feeding of the five thousand, the crowd had got entirely the wrong end of the stick and wanted to make him an earthly king whether he wanted it or not. The disciples were probably in danger of being caught up in the hysteria – so it made sense to get them out of harm's way while he stalled the crowd and then took off into the hills to spend some quality time with God.

Opposition from the religious authorities

15 [1-9] Then a delegation from the Jerusalem Pharisees and scribes turned up.[1] 'Jesus,' they said, 'we've been hearing that your disciples don't observe the sacred traditions – they don't wash before meals.'

'Well, if we're talking about breaking the traditions,' Jesus answered, 'perhaps I can ask you about *your* observance, or lack of it. After all, God does say, "Honour your father and mother", but you tell people they can escape their obligations to their parents by saying, "Sorry, old things, but I can't provide for you in your old age because I've promised the money to God"! So you maintain your own tradition by emptying the word of God of its power – I mean, come on! What a bunch of hypocrites! You know, Isaiah was right about you, wasn't he? What was it he said? Oh, yes: "These people pay me lip service, but their real values are a million miles from me! They bring me all this meaningless worship, and proclaim human ideas as if they were holy writ!"'[2]

[10-20] Jesus called the crowd nearer to him, and said, 'Now, listen and get this straight: it's not what goes into your mouth that makes you "unclean" – it's what comes out of it!'

Then his disciples came up to him, and said, 'You do realise, do you, that you really got the Pharisees rattled over the way you spoke just now?'

'Look,' Jesus retorted, 'anyone can claim to be a plant God planted, but just saying it won't save them being uprooted if it's not true! Oh, just let them get on with it – blind guides trying to lead blind people! You know what happens then, don't you – they both end up in the ditch!'

'There you go again,' Peter exclaimed, 'talking in riddles! Just what *are* you on about?'

'Haven't you got it yet?' Jesus replied. 'Don't you see? What goes *into* the mouth just passes through the system and finishes up being flushed away down the sewer. But what comes *out* of the mouth begins at the very heart of your being – and you know the sort of stuff that's sluicing around in there, don't you: all kinds of evil intentions like murder, adultery, promiscuity, stealing, lying . . . It's *that* kind of thing that makes a person ritually unclean, not eating without washing!'

---

1. Jerusalem! So Jesus was rattling cages at a very high level!
2. Isaiah 29:13.

Who's the gospel for?

[21-28] Things were definitely hotting up, and it seemed like a good time for another strategic retreat – this time to the area around Tyre and Sidon, completely outside Israelite territory. It wasn't going to be that simple, though – a Canaanite woman recognised him and started pestering the life of him. 'Will you do me a kindness – yes, you, Jesus – Son of David[1] – a devil's got my daughter and we need you to exorcise it.'

Jesus didn't answer but kept walking – so she carried on shouting until his disciples said, 'For goodness' sake, Jesus, will you just tell her to clear off – she's getting to be a pain in the neck.'

'I was sent to Israel,' Jesus answered. 'There are quite enough lost sheep wandering around there for now, without looking any further.' The woman became really desperate, and finished up kneeling in front of Jesus. 'Lord, please help me!' she wailed.

Jesus looked at her. 'It's really not on, you know,' he said, 'to take food meant for children and throw it to the dogs.'

The woman wasn't having any of that. 'Oh, I know,' she said, 'and I also know that those same dogs get to eat the scraps that drop from the table – come on, I'm really not asking for very much, now am I?'

'Wow, that's some faith!' Jesus answered. 'OK, you've got what you asked for.' And immediately the woman's daughter was healed.

Healing many people

[29-31] After Jesus had moved on from there, he went along the shore of the sea of Galilee[2] and sat down a little way up the mountainside. Crowds came to him again, with all the sick friends and neighbours they could drag or carry, and put them down at his feet to be cured. It was a stunning sight – mute people were speaking, lame walking, the blind suddenly able to see – and everybody praised the God of the Israelites[3] when they saw it.

---

1. An astonishingly perceptive title for a non-Jew to have used for Jesus – just one indication that she really did have exceptional faith.
2. The Decapolis area, on the Gentile side of the lake (see Mark 7:31).
3. Mark spelt it out – Matthew, a more subtle writer, gives us this clue that they were in Gentile territory.

The feeding of the four thousand

> Another miraculous feeding coming up. So, why bother to record both, if they're so similar? – after all, quite a lot of Jesus' miracles are barely mentioned, but this one's retold in detail. The difference here may be that it's Gentiles who are being fed – having been the beneficiaries of the last two miracles. The point's being rammed home that when people considered 'outsiders' are open to what Jesus offers, they will receive!

[32-39] Jesus called his disciples together. 'You know, I can really feel the crowd's hunger,'[1] he said. 'I mean, they've been traipsing around after me for three days now, and they haven't got anything to eat. I can't send them home in this state, can I? – some of them probably won't even make it.'

'Well, that's all very fine, Jesus,' his disciples answered, 'but where in this desert of a place are we going to get enough food to feed a crowd like this?'

'We can begin with whatever you've got,' Jesus retorted. 'Let's be seeing it, then.'

'All we've got,' they said, 'is seven loaves, and a handful of little fish.'

That was more than enough for Jesus – next thing anyone knew, he had the crowd sitting down on the ground. Then he took the loaves and fishes, gave thanks to God, broke them and gave them to his disciples who passed them on to the crowds. Everyone who joined in the meal was completely satisfied, and when they gathered up the leftovers there were seven baskets full. Altogether, about four thousand men had been fed – and that doesn't include the women and children! Jesus got the crowds to go away, hopped into a boat and took off for Magadan on the other side of the lake.[2]

---

1. The word 'compassion', used here in some standard translations, is often weakened to 'pity' – which is a pity! Literally, 'compassion' means 'co-suffering' – it means actually feeling the suffering of another, rather than just feeling sorry for them. Important, of course, because Jesus didn't come just to feel sorry for us, but to share our suffering!
2. Some of the early manuscripts say 'Magdala'. It could be an alternative name for the same place, no one knows for certain.

The demand for proof

16
[1-4] This time it was an unholy alliance of Pharisees and Sadducees[1] that came to try and trip Jesus up by asking for a sign from heaven.[2] 'You're priceless!' Jesus told them. 'You can look at the sky in the evening and say, "Hey, it's red – nice day tomorrow," or in the morning you can say, "Look, a red sky – better get ready for a storm!" So you can interpret the sky, but you can't even get close to understanding the signs of the times. All you're doing by going on asking for signs is showing yourselves up as the pathetic, faithless generation you really are – and the only sign you're going to get is the sign of Jonah!'[3] And with that, he walked off.

The disciples still don't get it!

[5-12] When the disciples arrived, guess what – after all that had happened, they'd forgotten to bring any food! 'You've got bigger issues to worry about, anyway,' Jesus told them, 'like the Pharisees and Sadducees, for example – the "yeast" they use that pervades and corrupts all their teachings – that's what you need to be concerned about.'

The disciples missed the point completely. 'He's just miffed because we forgot to get the bread,' they moaned to one another.

'Oh, what is it with you!' Jesus exclaimed. 'How can anyone have so little insight – why are you still going on about bread? Haven't you caught on yet? I suppose you've forgotten the five loaves we used to feed five thousand, and the seven we used to feed four thousand – and all the baskets of scraps we collected up? Can't you see anything that isn't slapping you in the face? How could you possibly fail to see that I wasn't just going on about bread? I say again, beware of the yeast of the Pharisees and Sadducees!'

At last, they got it – they understood that it was the teachings of the Pharisees and Sadducees, with their insidious, all-pervasive nature, that Jesus was talking about.

---

1. The enemies of Jesus must have been getting desperate! The Sadducees were the hereditary, aristocratic priests, and normally they and the Pharisees could scarcely bring themselves to give each other the time of day.

2. Haven't we been here before? Some folk just don't seem able to learn!

3. Jesus obviously wasn't going to waste time repeating himself to people who weren't listening – but flick back to 12:40-41 if you want to refresh your memory about what this means.

So, who is Jesus?

13-20 Next port of call was the district of Caesarea Philippi, where Jesus said to his disciples, 'What is it that people are saying, about who the Son of Man is?'

'All sorts of things,' they told him. 'Some say you're John the Baptiser come back; others say you're Elijah. Some are even saying you're Jeremiah or one of the other prophets.'

'OK,' Jesus said. 'Now, who do *you* say that I am?'

Simon Peter was right there with the answer. 'You're the Messiah,' he said. 'Son of the living God, no less.'

'Congratulations, Simon, son of John!' Jesus exclaimed. 'You didn't get this from any human source, did you? – this is something my Father in heaven has specifically made clear to you. And I'm telling you, you're truly "Peter" – the very rock on which I'm going to build my faith-community[1] – and even the power of death itself will be completely ineffective against it. I'm going to make you the gatekeeper of the kingdom of heaven – what you say goes. If you forbid something, then it's forbidden, and if you allow something, it's allowed – no arguments.' Then he gave his disciples a solemn warning not to go telling everybody that he was the Messiah.[2]

Jesus prepares his disciples

We're well into the last days of Jesus' Galilean ministry, and he needs to prepare his disciples. If we were responsible for assessing their progress, we'd probably conclude they were nowhere near ready for the ordeal ahead, and suggest to Jesus that he reschedule! Fortunately, Jesus has more faith – both in God and in people.

Jesus foretells his death and resurrection

21-28 From that time, Jesus began trying to prepare his disciples for what had to happen in the future: going to Jerusalem, being tortured and abused by the chief priests, elders and scribes, being killed, and finally

---

1. In Greek, 'Petros' meant 'Peter' while 'Petra', the feminine form, was used for 'rock'. Jesus is making one of his subtle twists of language.
2. The time wasn't yet ripe. People still thought the Messiah would be a warlord – so bandying words like that around in such a climate would have been distinctly counter-productive!

being raised to life on the third day. Peter took Jesus to one side and started having a real go at him. 'No! God won't allow it. God *can't* allow it! It's not going to happen to you – end of story!'

Jesus rounded on him. 'Get out of my way, Satan!' he said. 'You're a stumbling block, that's what you are – you're seeing everything from a human point of view when it should be from God's!'[1] Then Jesus reminded them all, 'If anyone's really determined to be a follower of mine, they've got to be prepared not to call their life their own – ready to take up the cross and follow in my footsteps. Those who are obsessed with safeguarding what they have in this life will lose it. On the other hand, those who are prepared to lose what they have now for my sake will discover real life through letting go. What good does it do to gain the whole world if in doing so you lose your true self? What are you going to have that's worth enough to buy it back? Because the Son of Man's going to be coming with a full escort of angels and in all the glory of his Father, and he'll recompense everyone for the choices they've made. I'm telling you straight, there are people standing here, right now, who won't taste death before they see the kingdom of the Son of Man being inaugurated.'[2]

Transfiguration: a glimpse of Christ glorified

Remember those echoes of Moses in the Nativity story (see the introduction to 2:13-16)? Here's another such device. Thinking of Jesus as the new and greater Moses is an inspired 'shorthand' by which Matthew could spark people's imagination and help them understand just who Jesus was. The high mountain and the presence of special companions recalls Exodus 24, while the shining face calls to mind Exodus 34. Then, when Moses and Elijah appear in the vision, Jesus' fulfilment of the scriptures is graphically emphasised.

---

1. Notice the neat reversal of the previous congratulations. Now, the rock that was going to be a firm foundation is turned into one that people will fall over, and the inspiration is now human, not divine, rather than vice versa. To call Peter 'Satan' might not have been quite as harsh as it sounds, as the word could be used as a synonym for anything that was in opposition to God.
2. The kingdom was in an important sense inaugurated with the death and resurrection of Jesus. This verse doesn't *necessarily* refer to the second coming. Also, see 'coming of the Son of Man' in the Glossary of Key Words and Phrases.

17 ¹⁻⁹ Six days later, Jesus called together Peter, James and John, and went up a high mountain with them – no one else, just them – and was transfigured right there in front of them. His face shone like the sun, his robes were brilliant white, and then Moses and Elijah appeared, talking with Jesus. 'Hey, Lord, this is terrific,' Peter called out. 'I mean, this is *so* the place to be! Why don't I build three shelters – one for you, one for Moses and one for Elijah?'

Before he finished speaking, he was interrupted from a great height. There was this cloud – silver lining and all – came right over all of them, and a voice said, 'This is my special Son – he's living up to all my expectations – so listen to him!'

Well, that did it – the disciples hit the deck and stayed there, shaking gently with fear. Jesus came over and put his hand on them. 'Come on,' he said, 'on your feet – there's nothing to be afraid of.' And there wasn't. When they looked up they couldn't see anything out of the ordinary at all – just Jesus. So they started off down the mountain. 'Now, watch you don't go spreading this around,' Jesus warned them. 'Not until the Son of Man has been raised from the dead.'

¹⁰⁻¹³ 'OK,' the disciples answered, 'but the scribes have always taught us that Elijah's going to return publicly first.'

'Yes, I know,' Jesus said, '"Elijah is certainly coming, and he's going to put everything right". Fine. Well, I'm telling you, Elijah's already been, but of course he wasn't what they expected – prophets never are – so they couldn't or wouldn't recognise him, but did with him as they saw fit. And they're about to make the same mistake again with the Son of Man.' Then the disciples realised that he was talking to them about John the Baptiser.

Faithless disciples

> The parallel with Moses continues. Moses came down from the mountain to find that his people's faith had failed them, and Jesus comes down from the mountain to find something very similar. The account of the healing of the epileptic boy may well have been placed here to emphasise the parallel.

¹⁴⁻²¹ When they got back to where the crowds were, a man came rushing over and knelt in front of Jesus. 'Lord,' he said, 'will you do a kindness for my son? He's got epilepsy, and the fits put him in terrible danger – falling into the fire, or into water, that sort of thing – so I brought him to your disciples, but a fat lot of good they were!'

'Oh, great!' Jesus rounded on his disciples. 'You're no better than the rest of this faithless generation, are you! I sometimes wonder how much more of this I'm expected to put up with! Bring the lad over to me.' One stern word from Jesus, and the demon instantly left the boy.

'So, why couldn't we do that?' the disciples asked Jesus, when they got him in private.

'It's not just about saying the right word,' Jesus answered. 'That kind of authority only comes from faith. Because I'm telling you straight, if you only had faith as tiny as a mustard seed, you could say to this very mountain, "Move from here and go over there," and it would happen – nothing would be impossible for you.'[1]

Jesus foretells his death and resurrection a second time

[22-23] As they were regrouping in Galilee,[2] Jesus tried again to get his disciples to understand. 'The Son of Man,' he said, 'is going to be given up to the worldly authorities – then he's going to be killed, before finally being raised to life on the third day.' As you'd expect, his disciples weren't happy about that, which is probably why they didn't pursue the conversation.

[24-27] When they got to Peter's house in Capernaum, the Temple tax officials had a go at Peter. 'Your teacher doesn't pay the Temple tax,' they said. 'Why?'[3]

'Oh, he does, he does!' Peter objected.

When Jesus got inside, he raised the subject himself with Peter. 'It's not compulsory to pay it,' he said, 'but I've got more important battles to fight than this one – and anyway, we aren't here to cause offence just for the sake of it. So, go fishing, and you'll find the money to pay this year's tax in the fish's mouth.'

---

1. A couple of points here. Firstly, Jesus' emphasis was on the power of God working through even the tiniest faith – not on the power of human faith. Secondly, since a world where this was happening all the time would be unthinkable, Jesus was clearly using a picture to say that God would do impossible things if only there were an atom of faith for him to work with.
2. Probably in preparation for Jesus' fateful journey to Jerusalem.
3. It wasn't compulsory, but for a Jew not to pay it was like going to church and not putting anything in the collection – in other words, it was embarrassing.

Jesus' fourth big speech: mainly on community relationships

Real greatness

[1-2] Jesus' disciples came to him with a question. 'Who's the greatest in the kingdom of heaven?' they asked.

Jesus looked round for a child, and asked one to stand in the middle of them before he answered:

[3-11] I'm telling you straight, you've got to change your whole outlook on things – forget the rat-race and learn to live without all that status-obsession, the way children have to – before you even get a foot in the door of the kingdom of heaven! Anyone who can rediscover the humility of this child[1] – find importance in what the world calls insignificant – that person will be counted truly great in the kingdom of heaven. Then anyone who welcomes someone like that in my name also welcomes me.

Temptations

But don't go thinking you can take advantage of humble people[2] and get away with it. What's coming to those who do that will make them think that drowning would have been nice by comparison! The world's always going to have stumbling blocks[3] in it, but a curse upon those people who deliberately put them in place! And if it's your own hand or foot that trips you up, maybe you'd better cut it off and ditch it – better maimed than damned, remember. And if it's your eye that makes you stumble, then you're better off losing it – better half blind but saved than fully sighted and lost![4] So, remember, just be careful not to treat selfless, unassuming people with contempt – because I'm telling you, they're never out of God's sight!

The parable of the lost sheep

[12-14] Think about it: suppose a shepherd has a hundred sheep and one of them's wandered off. What's he going to do – won't he leave the

---

1. Jesus was streetwise enough to know that children aren't that humble. He was really talking about letting go of obsessions with status (children in that culture simply had to live without it) and finding significance in apparently insignificant roles.
2. Often called 'little ones' or 'the least'. Jesus has subtly merged the child image with people who choose service over self-aggrandisement.
3. A familiar image used by Jesus. This is what he accused Peter of being in chapter 16!
4. As with 5:29-30: a nice bit of rhetoric, but just don't go taking it too literally!

ninety-nine and go searching for that one? And if he finds it, I'm telling you he's *really* got something to celebrate – more so than over the ninety-nine who never strayed in the first place. Well, so it is for your Father in heaven – he doesn't want even one of these apparently unimportant people to be lost.

Dealing with failure in the faith community

[15-20] If you think another disciple's going off the rails, try and keep it between the two of you. Have a quiet word when you're alone, and if that works, then leave it at that. Of course, some may not listen, so you might need to take a couple of other people along so that you've got two or three witnesses to what's said. If the individual still won't listen to you, it's a matter for the community to decide. And if they won't listen to the decision of the whole church, then they've put themselves beyond it, haven't they? I'm telling you straight, this authority is vested in the community – remember what I said to you: if you forbid something, then it's forbidden, and if you allow something it's allowed – no arguments. And I'm also telling you straight that when you agree to pray for something my Father in heaven will grant it – because wherever two or three people get together truly in my name, I'm there at the heart of it all.[1]

Forgiveness that's hard to live up to

> God's forgiveness is unlimited, Jesus tells us, but he then goes on to tell a parable that *appears* to limit it – can't God forgive us unless we're as good as he is to begin with? Forgiveness isn't just a one-way process – it's really about reconciliation, about putting right a relationship. And how can we possibly have a good relation-ship with God if we're being rotten to each other?

[21-27] Peter came to Jesus and said, 'Tell me, if someone repeatedly offends me, how many times do I have to forgive them? I mean, should I go as far as seven times?'[2] Jesus answered like this:

Oh, I wouldn't stop at seven times – I'd say seventy-seven times.[3]

---

1. This doesn't mean that we've got a magic formula – see the introduction to 7:7-11.
2. The rabbis' conference had suggested three times as the limit – so Peter was really going well beyond the expectations already.
3. Could Jesus have been referring back to Genesis 4:24, and contrasting the unlimited vindictiveness of a human being with the unlimited forgiveness of God?

That's why I use examples like this, to illustrate the kind of kingship God exercises[1] – what the 'reign' of God really means. A king once decided to sort out his accounts with his slaves – and found that one of them owed him a billion pounds.[2] As you'd expect, the slave couldn't pay it. So the king ordered that he should be sold – along with his wife and children, of course, and all that he owned, too – so that some payment could be made. Naturally, the slave was terrified, and decided to do the sensible thing – he threw his dignity to the winds and grovelled. 'Please don't do that!' he blubbered. 'If you're patient with me, I'll pay you everything – honestly, I will.' So, the king took pity on him and decided to let him go – and cancelled the debt completely. So the slave walked away owing nothing, because of the king's generosity.

[28-30] Now, it was a pity that as the slave left he should happen to bump into another slave – who owed him a couple of pounds. The first slave grabbed the other by the throat and said, 'I want my money – and I want it now! Pay up!'

The second slave did exactly the same as the first had done – he grovelled, too. 'I'll pay you everything,' he cried. 'Just be patient with me.' But the first slave was completely unmoved, and had his colleague thrown into prison, to stay there until the debt was paid.

[31-34] As you'd expect, when all the other slaves heard about it, they weren't happy – in fact, they were hopping mad – and they went to the king and told him the whole story. So the king sent for the slave again. 'You despicable slave!' he said. 'I showed kindness to you, because you begged me and won my sympathy. Didn't it ever occur to you that you should show similar kindness towards your own colleagues – just as I'd done for you?' The king was far too angry for any pleading to do any good – the slave had really blown it on that front – and he handed him over to be put in prison until he paid it all off.[3]

[35] So how do you think you can expect to receive forgiveness from God if you aren't able to forgive each other? And I mean *really* forgive!

---

1. The standard texts use 'kingdom of heaven' here.
2. In the Bible, the figure given is ten thousand – the largest number that a single Greek numeral could express – in order to illustrate the unlimited nature of forgiveness. So this is probably the best equivalent here, in terms of the *spirit* of the parable.
3. Remember the amount? Could you pay off a debt like that?

Jesus in Judea

The journey to Jerusalem

Jesus begins the journey that will bring his mission to a climax, with his confrontation with the religious authorities in Jerusalem, leading to the final conflict and victory of his earthly ministry. As the journey proceeds, Matthew never lets us forget the massive authority of Jesus that was such a threat to the establishment. All the way along the route, it is demonstrated in powerful words and actions.

19 [1-2] When Jesus had finished these sayings, he left Galilee, heading south across the Jordan, with great crowds of people following him and being cured by him.

Marriage and commitment

[3-12] Some Pharisees decided to have another go at catching him out. 'Hey, Jesus, is there any reason at all why a man can legally divorce his wife?'[1]

'Don't you read your Bibles?' Jesus asked. 'Doesn't it say that when God made people he "made them male and female",[2] and that "because of this, to this very day, when children grow up into men and women, they move away from their parents and set up new homes together, and become one flesh"?[3] So they aren't just two separate people any more – they're one flesh! In other words what God has joined together isn't open to being separated by human decisions.'

'In that case,' they argued, 'why did Moses say we can give the woman a divorce certificate and tell her to sling her hook?'

'That,' said Jesus, 'was simple pragmatism, because he knew you weren't capable of meeting the ideal. But that's not the same as saying it's what God intended, now is it? And I'm telling you that if someone divorces his wife, except for unfaithfulness, and marries someone else, then he's committing adultery.'

'Well,' his disciples chimed in, 'if we're going to get saddled with a woman for life, then perhaps we shouldn't marry at all!'

---

1. Remember what 'divorce' meant then – in effect, a man's right to consign his wife to the scrap-heap when he was tired of her.
2. Genesis 1:27.
3. Genesis 2:24.

'It's certainly true that not everyone can live up to these standards,' Jesus answered. 'You have to be born to it, really. Some people do seem to be destined for celibacy, while others have it imposed upon them, and then there are those who accept celibacy as a God-given gift[1] – but whether we're talking about celibacy or marriage, it's still a serious commitment, so you don't get off that lightly!'

Jesus blesses the children

13-15 Then some people started bringing children to Jesus, so that he could pray and lay hands on them. The disciples told them to get lost, but Jesus wasn't having that. 'Get out of the way and let the little children come to me,' he said, 'because it's to people like these that the kingdom of heaven truly belongs.' Then he blessed them, and continued on his journey.

The rich man's ambition

16-22 Then someone said, 'Teacher, can you advise me – I'd like to do something really good – spectacularly good, in fact – something that'll guarantee I get eternal life.'

'Good?' Jesus echoed. 'You think a human being can attain goodness? Look, it's God's laws, not human achievements, that count – so keep the commandments.'

'Like, which ones?' the man asked.

'You know,' Jesus answered. 'You shall not murder, commit adultery, steal, or lie about people; you *shall* honour your parents, love your neighbour the way you love yourself . . .'

'Yes I know those,' the young man persisted, 'and I've done all that since I was just so high – but it doesn't seem enough. What's missing?'

'Ah,' said Jesus. 'You evidently want to fulfil the *spirit* of the law, completely. Excellent! Go, then, and sell all your stuff, and give the money to the poor. Then you'll have real treasure in heaven – the kind that lasts for eternity. Then come and follow me.'

Well, talk about a let-down! That wasn't what the guy had wanted to hear at all – because he was remarkably rich – and he went away very unhappy.

---

1. Or 'for the sake of the kingdom of heaven'.

Depend upon God

23-30 Jesus turned to his disciples. 'I'm telling you straight,' he said, 'if there's one thing the rich can't afford it's a ticket to the kingdom of heaven. You'd see a camel go through the eye of a needle before you saw a rich person earn their way in.'

The disciples were aghast. 'Well, in that case, what hope is there for anyone at all?' they asked.

Jesus gave them one of his knowing looks. 'Ah, now there's the heart of it,' he said. 'It's more than any human being can ever achieve – but depend on the power of God, and anything's possible!'

'Fine,' Peter answered. 'Well, we've given up everything to be your disciples – so what's going to be in it for us, then?'

Jesus said to them, 'I'm telling you straight, in the new world order, when the Son of Man's enthroned, so will you be – on twelve thrones, ruling over the twelve tribes of Israel. And all those who've given up their homes or families for my sake will be recompensed a hundred times over[1] – and they'll inherit eternal life as well. But an awful lot who are ahead of the game now will come in last, and vice versa.'

God's generosity: the workers in the vineyard

> Jesus clearly wants to show that God's love can't – and needn't – be earned, because he immediately follows this conversation with a parable where those who have done the least work receive exactly the same as those who think themselves the most deserving. I wonder whether, two thousand years on, we dare to say that we've really understood this parable!

20 1-16 Jesus went on:

You see, the kingdom of heaven, well, it's like a landowner who needed some workers in his vineyard – so he went out early to the market place to hire them. They were happy enough to agree a standard day's wages, and he told them to go and get started. Come the middle of the morning, he went out and hired some more. 'I'll pay you a fair wage,' he said, and that was good enough for them. He did the same at midday and again half-way through the afternoon. Then, at about five, he went and found some more workers standing around.

---

1. Think about it: if everyone's sharing everything, and 'holding all things in common ownership' (Acts 2:44), then everyone 'owns' countless houses, etc.! It's really saying that everyone will be abundantly provided for because of the community principles.

'What's this,' he said, 'no work to do?'

'We're not wanted,' one of them explained.

'You are now,' the landowner said. 'Go and get started.'[1]

Then, come the evening, he called his manager. 'Pay the men off,' he said, 'starting with the ones who arrived last.'

When the workers who'd started at five got a day's wage, the ones who'd been there longer thought, 'This is a bit of all right – he's obviously going to give us some extra.' Were they in for a disappointment! All they got was the standard day's wage they'd agreed – so they were soon sounding off about the landowner being unfair. 'Look,' they said, 'those guys only worked an hour, and you've paid them the same as we got who slogged right through the hottest part of the day.'

'But what's the problem?' the landowner answered. 'I agreed a day's pay, and I've given you a day's pay. Look, if I were you I'd take what's yours and go – if I choose to give the last workers the same that's my decision; I take it it's OK for me to do what I like with my own money? Or is it just that you're so mean-spirited that you resent my generosity?'[2]

So, those who've been shoved to the back of the queue will be first, and the ones who think they've clawed their way to the front will be last.

Jesus foretells his death and resurrection a third time

[17-19] Continuing on the way towards Jerusalem, Jesus took the Twelve to one side and spelled out to them what was going to happen. 'Look, we're going to Jerusalem – so it's showdown time. The Son of Man will be handed over, first to the chief priests and scribes – they'll condemn him to death – and then to the Gentile authorities who'll humiliate him first, and then have him flogged and crucified, and on the third day he'll be raised to life.'[3]

---

1. Get the picture? With only an hour left, they couldn't possibly earn their pay, any more than a rich person could pay their way into heaven. It's all about God the gracious giver, not about what we're worth!

2. Now that's hit the nail on the head! It's about generosity, not earnings!

3. This is the third time Jesus has described his death – with progressively more detail. Each time, the context suggests that he's doing more than just preparing them for the experience. He's saying that his victory will be startlingly different from their expectations – reached through suffering servanthood and humiliation, not through military glory.

More jockeying for position – they still haven't learnt!

[20-23] Then James' and John's mother came to Jesus and knelt in front of him to ask him a favour. 'It's about my sons,' she said. 'Can you, sort of, well, promise – make it clear to everyone – that they'll be the top guys alongside you in your kingdom?'

Jesus said, 'You really don't have any idea what you're asking, do you?' He turned to James and John. 'I mean, have you got the stomach to drink from the cup that I'm soon going to have to drink from?'[1]

'What? That – oh, sure!' James and John answered.

'Well,' Jesus told them, 'drink my cup you certainly will, but to have the top places in my kingdom – that's not mine to give. That's not something you can aspire to or earn – it's a gift from my Father.'

[24-28] When the word got round, the other ten were hopping mad with James and John, but Jesus called them to him and spelt it out yet again. 'Look,' he said, 'you know how it is in the rest of the world: kings on thrones giving orders to everyone else, bullies having all the clout – a proper rat-race – well, you'd better get it into your heads that it's not going to be like that among you. One of you wants to be thought of as great? Fine, then be a good servant to all the rest. And if you want to be put first in the kingdom, then you'll need to be like a slave, just like the Son of Man who didn't come to be waited on but to serve others, and to pay the cost of human freedom with his own life!'

> Having said this, Jesus deliberately moves towards Jerusalem – towards the fulfilment of these words – and the principle is powerfully demonstrated by an act of service towards two people whose form of greeting shows recognition of Jesus' status as Messiah.

Sight for the blind

[29-34] Moving on out of Jericho, with a crowd following him, Jesus came to where two blind men were sitting, begging by the side of the road. 'Lord!' they shouted. 'Son of David – will you do a kindness for us?' The people in the crowd tried to shut them up, but they weren't having any of it and just kept shouting more loudly, 'Do us a kindness, Lord, Son of David!'

---

1. The 'cup of suffering' would be a familiar metaphor to any Jew, and Jesus is trying yet again to get it into the disciples' heads that his route to glory is through suffering. He'll still be trying to do that when he enacts this idea at the Last Supper – and they still won't make sense of it!

Jesus stopped and came over to them. 'So, what is it you want me to do for you?'[1]

'Lord, we just want to be able to see!' Jesus could feel their distress – *really* feel it. He touched their eyes; they got their sight back and followed him.

Jesus in Jerusalem

> All this time, Jesus has been trying to change people's ideas about kingship, authority, and in particular about the nature of the promised Messiah. He's been trying to point them back to the 'suffering servant' of Isaiah's prophecy. Now he fulfils the Zechariah prophecy, entering Jerusalem in humility. Could this be a last – almost desperate – attempt to get people (including his own disciples) to see that he's not going to be what they want him to be?

21 [1-11] They were approaching Bethphage at the Mount of Olives within sight of Jerusalem. 'Right,' Jesus said to two of his disciples, 'I'd like you to go into the village, and immediately you get there you'll find a donkey tied up with her colt beside her. Untie them and bring them to me, here. Oh, and if anyone challenges you, just say, "The Lord needs them," and he'll let you take them without any hesitation.'

Jesus enters the city

All this was needed for the prophecy to be fulfilled: 'Look, your king's coming to you – but gently – riding a donkey, and with the colt, the donkey's foal'.[2]

The disciples went off on their errand, found the donkey and colt, and threw their own coats over the animals' backs, and Jesus sat on the colt to ride into town.[3] The crowd[4] got in on the act too – talk about putting out the red carpet! Some of them used their own coats, while

---

1. This is the humble servant talking – not the expert of people's expectations. You or I would probably have just assumed that blind people wanted to see, but Jesus knew better than to make assumptions.
2. Zechariah 9:9.
3. So why did he need two animals? The colt would have been uncontrollable if separated from its mother, so it had to be a question of 'Mother comes too'.
4. Most probably pilgrims going to Jerusalem for the Passover and likely to be in a pretty hyped-up state.

others tore branches off the trees to put on the road, and by the time they got to Jerusalem they were a real sight: crowds in front of Jesus, crowds behind him, all shouting, 'Saviour![1] Son of David!' and joining in the traditional festal chant, 'Congratulations to the one who's coming in God's name! Praise God in the highest!' By the time Jesus himself reached Jerusalem the entire city was in complete uproar – positively seismic, it was! Everybody was asking 'Who on earth *is* this guy?' and the crowds were yelling out, 'It's Jesus, the holy man from Nazareth – you know, in Galilee!'

A confrontation in the Temple

[12-17] And this was just the beginning: Jesus went to the Temple and laid into the traders. He turned over the money-changers' tables, pulled the chairs out from under the dove-sellers.[2] 'You know what scripture says,' he roared at them. '"My house is to be a place for prayer" – you've turned it into a thieves' kitchen!'[3] Then the blind and lame[4] approached him, and Jesus cured them.

Of course, the chief priests and scribes didn't like it one bit when they saw what he was doing and heard the children joining in the general acclamation. 'Do you hear what these brats are saying about you?' they demanded of Jesus.

'Yes,' Jesus replied. 'Interesting, that – you have read the Bible, of course, where it says, "and yet you bring praise from the very mouths of tiny children!"'[5] Jesus left them to ponder that, and went away to Bethany for the night.

A curse on the fruitless fig tree

Now we have an acted parable that sums up the previous events. Religion that's lost its values, a Temple without true faith, is like a fig tree with no fruit. And ultimately its fate is sealed: destruction.

1. The word 'Hosanna' literally means 'Save us', but it had come to be used as a shout of praise more than as a prayer in itself. Here the crowd are praising Jesus as Saviour.
2. The Temple offering had to be made in special coinage – without the hated Roman emperor's head on it – and people also needed pure doves for the ritual. So, of course, the chancers had moved in and turned it into a nice little earner!
3. Isaiah 56:7; Jeremiah 7:11.
4. They were usually excluded from the Temple and its life – an important barrier was broken here.
5. Psalm 8:2 (Septuagint).

> Jesus isn't being petty and vindictive – he's summing up the meaning of what he did in the Temple.

[18-19] Next morning, a hungry Jesus was back in Jerusalem again, where he saw a fig tree at the side of the road – but the only thing he found on it when he inspected it was leaves. 'Right, that's it,' he said, 'you're dead!' And the tree withered, immediately.

[20-22] 'Hey, will you look at that!' the disciples said. 'Now, is that power, or is that power!'

'I'm telling you straight,' Jesus answered. 'Have faith – real faith – and you'll do a lot more than's just been done to the fig tree. Why, you could tell this mountain to decamp into the sea and it'd do it! If you ask for something – the kind of thing you can ask for in faith – you'll get it.'[1]

Who does he think he is!

> The antagonism between Jesus and the religious authorities is now coming to the boil. They confront him and he tells three dreadfully pointed parables designed to show their faith up for the sham it is.

[23-31a] Next stop was the Temple and, while he was teaching, the chief priests and elders came to have a go at him. 'What authority do you think you have for the things you're doing?' they asked. 'And just who do you think gave it to you?'

'I'll answer your question,' Jesus countered, 'if you can answer mine.[2] The baptism that John introduced – did he do that on heavenly authority or was it just a human invention?'

That did it – suddenly they were arguing amongst themselves. 'Look we can't say it was from heaven,' they muttered, 'or he'll ask why we rejected it. And we can't say it was just a human invention, because the crowd will tear us apart – they all think John was a prophet!' So they had to say, 'Well, actually, Jesus, we're not really sure.'

'In that case,' Jesus retorted, 'you won't mind if I don't tell you where *my* authority comes from – will you!'

---

1. It may be worth taking another look at the footnote to 17:20 . . .
2. This was a standard technique in theological debate in those days – a good way of getting to the heart of the matter.

The parable of the two sons

or

It ain't what you say, it's the way that you do it!

Jesus continued:

> Look, tell me what you think about this. A man has two sons, OK? And one day he collars the first one and says, 'Go and do a bit of work in the vineyard, will you?'
>
> 'Work! Me? Not likely!' the guy says – but then he changes his mind and goes anyway.
>
> So the father goes to the other son and says the same thing.
>
> 'Sure, Dad,' the son answers – but then he changes his mind and doesn't bother.
>
> OK, so you tell me – who actually did what his father wanted?

'The first one, obviously,' they answered.

[31b-32] 'I'm telling you straight,' Jesus said to them, 'swindlers and prostitutes are entering the kingdom of God[1] in front of you – because John came, pointing you toward the way of faith, and you didn't believe him, but the swindlers and prostitutes did. And even after you saw that, you just couldn't get down off your high horses and admit it, could you!'

The parable of the vineyard

> The religious authorities would be familiar with images of Israel as God's vineyard. Jesus highlights the fact that all God's prophets have been abused and murdered, and his Son doesn't expect to be treated any better. In other words, he's got them rumbled!

Jesus went on:

> [33-41] OK, listen to another parable, then. There's a landowner, and he plants a vineyard – fences it round, digs a winepress, builds a watchtower. Then he lets it out to tenants and goes abroad. Harvest time comes, and he sends servants to bring him the profits. What do the tenants do? They beat up the first one, kill the next and throw stones

---

1. Matthew chooses 'God' instead of his more usual 'heaven' here, possibly to make it more personal for the purpose of this passage. The focus is the priests' and elders' rejection of a proper relationship with God.

at the third. So, the landowner sends some more – and they are all treated in the same way.

Finally he sends his son. 'They'll respect my son,' he says. So do they? Not a bit of it.

'It's the son,' they say, 'the one who's down to inherit it all. If we get rid of him, perhaps we can take over!' So they grab hold of him, drag him outside the vineyard and kill him.

Now, what's the owner going to do to those tenants, when he finally comes himself to the vineyard?

'Oh, that's easy,' they answered. 'He'll kill them – preferably slowly and horribly – and then he'll re-let the vineyard to some decent people who'll give him what he's due.'

[42-44] Jesus said, 'Don't tell me you haven't read the Bible passage that says, "The stone that the expert builders rejected has turned out to be the cornerstone – only God could have done this, and it's really amazed us!"[1] So, I'm telling you that the kingdom of God's[2] going to be removed from your charge, and given to a new set of people who'll help it to be fruitful. People falling over this stone will injure themselves, and it'll be curtains for anyone it should fall on.'[3]

[45-46] The chief priests and the Pharisees finally got the point and realised that Jesus was talking about them! They'd have arrested him on the spot, but they knew better than to take on the crowds who thought Jesus was a prophet.

The parable of the wedding banquet

Here's another story showing that the response of faith is really about commitment, not just saying the right things.

22 [1-10] Jesus told them another parable.

This is how things are in the kingdom of heaven. Think of a king who gives a big wedding reception for his son. He sends his messengers

---

1. Psalm 118:22-23.
2. Again Matthew uses the unusual (for him) 'kingdom of God'. See the note on 21:31b above.
3. A similar twist to chapter 16 where the rock that provided stability could also be a dangerous stumbling block.

out to all the people who've been invited,[1] but they don't want to know. So he sends some more messengers. 'Tell those invited guests,' he says, 'that since they originally promised to come I've gone to a lot of trouble: the food's cooked – I've slaughtered my best cattle to provide it – and everything's ready – so it's time they got themselves over here.' Well, after they've had a good laugh, some of the guests go back to their own farms and businesses while others grab the messengers and beat them to death. The king – well, he just goes ballistic – sends out his army to kill the guests and destroy their property. 'Right,' he says to his servants, 'the wedding's still on, but the invited guests didn't exactly live up to the privilege – so get out there and bring in anybody you can find – OK?' So the servants go out again and everybody comes – good, bad, clean, smelly, they're all there and the place is full of guests!

> Luke has a version of this parable, with different details, but the paragraph that follows only occurs in Matthew. It seems odd for the king, who obviously represents God, to be so ungracious, but in this text Jesus is pointing out that while God invites us just as we are, he also calls us to *change*!

[11-14] Then the king comes in and what does he see? One of the guests isn't exactly properly dressed for a wedding. 'Just what are you trying to pull?' he asks him. 'You know it's an insult to the host to go to a wedding without changing first?' Then he calls the doormen. 'Sling this guy out!' he orders. 'Out into the outer darkness – where all the wailing and tooth-gnashing happens.'

That's the trouble, you see – a whole lot of people are *called* by God, but very few make it all the way.

More catch questions

Should we pay taxes?

[15-22] Then the Pharisees got down to some serious plotting in an effort to trap Jesus. They got together with some of Herod Antipas's cronies, and cooked up a dilemma. 'Excuse us, teacher,' they oiled, 'but we know you're a man of integrity and all that stuff – not afraid of anyone,

---

1. For a formal banquet, two invitations would have been usual – one to let everyone know it was happening and give them a chance to respond, and then another to tell them the meal's actually ready.

always ready to speak the truth. So we were wondering whether you think it's right for us to pay taxes to the Roman Emperor or not.'[1]

'You really are the most tiresome bunch of hypocrites,' Jesus said. 'I know what your game is, trying to catch me out. Look, show me a coin, somebody.' They showed him a coin, and he asked, 'Now, tell me, whose head is this on the coin – and whose inscription?'

'Caesar's,' they answered.

'Exactly!' Jesus responded. 'So give to Caesar whatever he's got a right to, and to God what belongs to God. That plain enough for you, is it?'

That told them – caught them completely off guard – and they left him.

Marriage in heaven

[23-33] Next to try their luck – on the very same day, would you believe! – were the Sadducees, who didn't believe in life after death. They had a question for Jesus. 'Teacher,' they said, 'you know that according to the law of Moses if a man dies childless, then his brother has to marry his widow so that she can have children? Well, we've got an interesting case for you. There were these seven brothers, see, and the first one got married but then died without having become a father. So the next brother married his widow, but they didn't have any children either. Well, would you believe it – all seven of them in turn married her and died childless – and then she died herself. So, we were wondering – in the afterlife,[2] whose wife will she be? I mean, she's legally married to all seven, isn't she?'[3]

'Now you're really showing your ignorance!' Jesus said. 'Resurrection life is a totally different order from this one – marriage and remarriage don't enter into it! And as for resurrection itself, haven't you read the title God gives himself, "I am the God of Abraham, Isaac and Jacob" – which, since he's the God of the living, not of the dead, would be pretty difficult without a resurrection, wouldn't it?' The crowd nearby were completely astounded at the sheer power of his argument.

The greatest commandment

[34-40] When word got to the Pharisees that Jesus had effectively silenced the Sadducees, they ganged up and went to have another go themselves.

---

1. They must really have thought they'd got him now. If he said, 'Yes', he'd lose his street cred among devout Jews, and if he said, 'No', then Herod's lot would be straight on to the Romans, accusing him of sedition.

2. In which, you may remember, the people asking the question didn't believe!

3. This was supposed to show that belief in resurrection was unrealistic – as if God would be defeated by a simple problem like that!

'Teacher,' their appointed spokesman began, 'which of all the command-ments is the greatest one?'

'Love God with all your heart, soul and mind,' Jesus told him. 'That's the greatest, and the primary law. And the second's very like it – love your neighbour as yourself. Everything in scripture ultimately depends upon those two commandments.'

Who is the Messiah?

[41-46] Jesus took the opportunity, while they were all together, to ask the Pharisees a question. 'What do you believe about the Messiah?' he asked. 'Whose descendant is he?'

'He's the son of David,' they answered.

'OK,' Jesus continued, 'so how is it that David – under the inspiration of the Spirit – calls him "Lord", when he says, "God said to my Lord, 'Take your place on my right, while I make your enemies a rest for your feet'"?[1] I mean, if David calls him Lord, how can he be David's son?'[2] That put an end to all their game-playing – not one of them could answer him, and from that time no one dared ask any more questions.

The confrontation intensifies

> Jesus now launches a direct and startlingly vehement attack upon the attitudes of the Pharisees. The basic message is that status-seeking is not to play any part in Christian discipleship.

23

[1-12] Jesus then addressed the crowd and his disciples at the same time:

I'm not denying the function of the scribes and Pharisees. They've inherited Moses' seat of authority. So, if you want to obey everything they tell you, right down to the very last detail, that's fine. Just don't *do* the things they do, that's all – because they don't practise what they preach. They load up other people with all kinds of baggage, but do they lift a finger to help? Not likely! They parade their good works for the world to see, and do all they can to make their piety obvious. Oh, and don't they just love the best seats at official functions, and to be bowed and scraped to in public and called 'Rabbi'! Of course, you won't be called 'Rabbi', because you're never going to be above learning, are you? – and there's only one teacher in our outfit.

---

1. Psalm 110:1.
2. Jesus isn't denying that he's a descendant of David. He's saying he's not *only* that.

And don't go thinking of any human being as your spiritual father – because you've only one of those and that's the one in heaven. Same goes for status symbols like being called 'teacher', because only the Messiah has the right to be called that. Just remember what I said – greatness, in the new order, is going to be about servanthood. So all those who go around full of their own importance will be brought down and the ones who accept humble positions will be raised.

Seven curses

> Matthew has spent the whole gospel building up our sense of Jesus' authority, shown in his teachings, healings and exorcisms. That same authority is now exercised in pronouncing divine judgement – a curse – on sterile, meaningless religiosity.

[13-15] But a curse upon you, scribes and Pharisees, hypocrites that you are! You've no intention of entering the kingdom of heaven, but you stand there at the very entrance to it, stopping others from going in.

A curse upon you, scribes and Pharisees, hypocrites that you are! You'll travel right across the world to make a single convert, but since you're on the road to ruin yourselves, where do you think that convert is going to end up!

[16-24] A curse upon you, blind guides, with your petty word-games! You say, 'If you're forced into taking an oath, swear on the sanctuary, because that's not really serious, rather than on the gold within it which would be binding.' What a load of blind simpletons you are! So let me ask you: which is greater – the sacred gold, or the sanctuary that makes it sacred? There again, you say, 'Just swear by the altar and you can wriggle out of it, but don't swear by the gift that's on the altar or you'll be committed.' You just refuse to see it, don't you – which is greater, the gift or the altar that sanctifies it? So if someone swears by the altar, that includes everything that's on it, and the sanctuary includes everything in it – including the One whose house it is! And if you swear by heaven, then you swear by God's very throne – and the One who sits on it!

A curse upon you, scribes and Pharisees, hypocrites that you are! Oh, you're so careful about tithing,[1] aren't you? – when it's minute

---

1. The legal requirement to give one-tenth of everything to God (in token recognition that the other nine-tenths are rightfully his, also).

quantities of herbs that are at stake – but the really big legal obligations like justice and kindness and faith you conveniently forget about! Those are the things you should be really focused upon – without neglecting the others, of course.

You blind guides! It's as if you carefully strain a gnat out of a drink, but swallow whole the camel that's floating in it and don't even notice![1]

25-28 A curse upon you, scribes and Pharisees, hypocrites that you are – obsessed with outward appearances! It's like washing the outside of a cup or a dish, when it's the inside that's filthy with greed and ill-gotten gains. You blind Pharisee! Why not clean the inside first – then the outside will be clean as well.

A curse upon you, scribes and Pharisees, hypocrites that you are. You're like whitewashed graves – beautiful on the outside, and full of decaying corpses within. That's you, outwardly oh so good and inwardly full of filth!

29-39 A curse upon you, scribes and Pharisees, hypocrites that you are! You build monuments to the prophets and decorate the tombs of great people from the past. And then you say, 'Of course, if we'd been around then, *we* wouldn't have joined in torturing and killing them – oh, no, not us'! And so your own testimony shows that you're no better than the ones who murdered the prophets. Well, now you're getting the full measure of what they deserved!

You revolting poisonous snakes! How can you escape being punished for this? And now I'm sending you my own prophets, my own wise teachers, and you're going to do the same to them, aren't you? – crucify them, flog them in your so-called 'holy' places, hound them from town to town – and you'll bring on yourselves the retribution still pending for every martyrdom from Abel to Zechariah![2] I'm telling you straight, this generation will suffer all these things!

Oh, Jerusalem! Jerusalem! The city that kills the prophets, and stones God's messengers to death! If you only knew how much I've longed to gather your people together just like a mother hen gathering her brood under her wings for protection – but you wouldn't have

---

1. This joke would have been even funnier in Jesus' own language (Aramaic) in which the words for 'gnat' and 'camel' were very similar.
2. According to the scriptures of Jesus' time, these were the first and last martyrs – so the persecution of Jesus' disciples is the culmination of the persecution of all God's messengers.

any of it!¹ Well, you've got the Temple you always wanted, and it's empty – devoid of any spirituality. I'm telling you that you won't be seeing me again, unless and until you're prepared to take me seriously.

Jesus' fifth big speech: mainly on future judgement

Jesus came with a mission of reconciliation for all who would accept the offer. However, the failure of established religion to respond will mean that he has precipitated a crisis which he says will take two forms. In the short term, the Temple, symbol of religious power, will be destroyed and the people scattered – this actually happened in AD 70. Since discipleship has to engage the world, Jesus' followers will all be affected by this event – it will foreshadow a much greater judgement to come at the end of the age, but the main focus of this speech, delivered in highly symbolic language, is the more immediate local upheavals referred to above. As far as the final judgement is concerned, when this will happen is not even for Jesus to know – so don't get taken in by people who claim to know what even Jesus himself didn't claim to!

It's not at all improbable that this speech would have been heard in three different ways: by the religious establishment as predicting the downfall of their Temple and traditions; by the Romans as typical Jewish apocalyptic about the end of the world and by those more open to Jesus' message as both of the above – although previous indications suggest that even the disciples wouldn't have really got the point until much later.

So this is subversive literature – real cloak and dagger stuff! Now, read on . . .

The destruction of the Temple

24 [1-2] As Jesus left the Temple, his disciples were raving on about what a wonderful building it was. 'You think so?' Jesus replied. 'I'm telling you straight, there won't be a single stone left standing on top of another – the whole thing's going to be flattened.'

---

1. A vitally important verse, this. The vehemence of Jesus' words is the product of an anger born of love for the nation and its religion – not hatred of it! None of this long diatribe has given Jesus any kind of pleasure at all.

The apocalypse

[3-14] When he was sitting on the Mount of Olives, his disciples came up to him, privately. 'Look, are you going to tell us when this disaster's going to happen?' they asked him. 'And what sort of clues should we be looking for about the end of everything and your coming back again?'

Jesus answered:

> Oh, don't get hung up on that! Don't be fooled – all kinds of frauds and posers will come along in my name, saying, 'Hey, guys, I'm the Messiah!'– and they'll fool a lot of people. Oh, and the same goes for wars and dire rumours – I mean, you're always going to have those things going on, but that doesn't mean the end's just round the corner. Yes, of course nations will make war on one another, there'll be all the usual famines and earthquakes and things – but that's just the start of it: the beginnings of the labour-pains of a new age coming to birth!

Persecutions

> Then you'll be betrayed, arrested, tortured – they'll put you to death – the whole world's going to hate you, because of your connection with me. Then a lot of people will stumble and fall away; disciples will give one another away, hatred will grow, some will run off after bogus spiritual leaders. And in all the general lawlessness, a lot of people's love will cool off rapidly. But anyone who keeps the faith through it all will be saved. The good news of the kingdom is to be proclaimed as a testimony to every nation, and only when that's been fully accomplished – then and only then – will the end truly come.

The desolating sacrilege

[15-28] When you see the ultimate desolating sacrilege standing in the place it's got no right to be, as Daniel said[1] (work it out for your-selves),[2] that is *not* the time to hang around! Time to take to the hills, pronto: if you're up on the housetop, don't stop to get anything

---

1. Daniel 9:27; 11:31; 12:11.
2. This editorial insertion would be understood by Jews who knew their Bible, but completely meaningless to Romans. Since Daniel promises devastating judgement against the 'desolator', this clever encryption was a wise precaution by the gospel writers.

from inside; if you're in the field, don't go home to get your coat. It'll be particularly ghastly for pregnant women and nursing mothers – and you'd better pray that it doesn't happen in the winter[1] or on the Sabbath.[2] At that time there'll be misery such as hasn't been seen since the creation of the world, and won't be again – in fact, if events were to run their full course no one could be saved, not even the faithful people, but that won't be allowed to happen. And don't believe it when people say, 'Look, here's the Messiah', or 'There he is', because these will be great times for impostors – false messiahs and prophets. Oh, they'll do all the impressive tricks, claiming that they're 'signs', intent on deceiving people – even some who are faithful. Remember, I've given you advance warning. So when they say, 'He's out in the desert!' don't go running off after them; and if they say, 'He's in a secret place, I'll show you', don't be fooled by that. You know how lightning lights up the entire sky – you can hardly be in any doubt about it, can you? Well, that's how it'll be at the coming of the Son of Man. You know what they say, 'You can always find a corpse by looking for vultures gathering'? Well, it'll be that obvious!

The coming of the Son of Man

[29-35] As soon as that stage is over, the sun will go dark, the moon will stop giving light, stars will fall from heaven, and the entire order of things will be shaken up. Then will appear the greatest sign of all: the sign of the Son of Man, and every family in the land will quake with fear when that happens![3] They'll recognise 'the Son of Man coming on the clouds of heaven',[4] with power and terrific glory. Then he'll send his messengers with a great clarion call, and gather faithful people from all points of the compass.[5]

Take the fig tree as an example: when the branches soften and the leaves start to sprout, you know that summer's coming. Well, in the

---

1. . . . when roads would be quagmires.
2. . . . when supplies for the journey would be unobtainable.
3. Almost certainly, Jesus is referring – in highly symbolic language – to the effect of his own vindication after the people have rejected him.
4. Daniel 7:13-14. In that passage, the 'Son of Man' doesn't come to earth, but comes to *God* to receive glory and power. So while, of course, this *may* be about the second coming, there again it may very well not.
5. Again, often interpreted to mean the end of the world, but more likely to mean the worldwide mission to gather people into the Church: the risen Christ commissions and sends out his messengers to make and gather disciples in all parts of the world (28:19).

same way, when you see these things happening, you'll know that the 'desolating sacrilege' I told you about[1] is right at the very gates. I'm telling you straight, this generation won't have disappeared until all these things have happened.[2] Trust me on this – I'm giving you my word on it, and that's more solid and reliable even than the universe itself!

Keep watching!

[36-44] Mind you, if you're looking for a date for the final big event, I can't help you. No one knows that, not the angels in heaven, not the Son, only the Father – because the coming of the Son of Man will be like the story of Noah. Remember that? There they all were, eating and drinking, marrying and planning their futures together, right up until the last moment when Noah went into the ark – and they knew nothing about it until the flood hit them and it was too late. Well, that's how the coming of the Son of Man will be: two workers in the field – one prepared, and saved, the other completely caught out by it; two women grinding corn together, one ready to be saved, and the other taken utterly by surprise. So keep alert, because you just don't know when it's going to be. Get this, though: if someone knew their house was going to be burgled, they'd stay awake and defend it, wouldn't they? So you'd better do likewise, because the Son of Man will come at a time when you least expect him.

Faithful and unfaithful servants

[45-51] Put it another way: suppose a servant's given responsibility for caring for the family while his boss is away: if he wants to be in the good books when the boss returns, he's going to care for that family very well, now isn't he? There'll probably be some serious promotion in it for him. A bad servant would be quite another matter – he might take advantage: drink the boss's best wine, ill-treat the rest of the household, throw wild parties for people who don't appreciate a

---

1. See verse 15.
2. There's the key to the issue. If Jesus had been accurately predicting the literal end of the world in the previous verses, you wouldn't be here to read this. However, if he was predicting the worldly events of AD 66-70, then we don't have a problem with this verse. The point is that he's using the imminent historical apocalypse as an image *foreshadowing* the big one.

nice place. Boy, is he in for a shock when the boss arrives home unexpectedly! A fate definitely worse than death, you can safely assume – more of that wailing and gnashing of teeth stuff!

The parable of the ten bridesmaids

25 [1-13] There again you could think of the kingdom of heaven like this. Ten bridesmaids, each carrying a lantern, went to meet a bridegroom. Now, five of them had the common sense to take some spare oil with them, but the other five didn't think of it. Then the bridegroom didn't turn up exactly when they expected, and they all dozed off while they were waiting, to be awoken right in the middle of the night when the cry went up, 'The bridegroom! Look lively, everybody!' That's when the bridesmaids found out that their lanterns were going out. So the ones who'd come unprepared had to try to beg oil from the sensible ones, but they weren't having any of that! 'If we give you our oil,' they said, 'we shan't have enough for ourselves and we'll all end up in the dark – what good would that do anybody? You'd better go shopping.'

So the bridesmaids went off looking for oil, and while they were gone the bridegroom arrived and everyone who was ready went in with him to the feast, shutting the door behind them. Then along came the other bridesmaids, calling out, 'Lord, Lord, open the door for us! Open the door!'

He answered, 'I'm telling you straight, I don't know you!'

Keep on the alert, then, because you don't know either the date or the time!

A parable of trust and responsibility

> It's probably the greatest honour God can give to humanity: responsibility. You only give that to someone who matters. You've either got to trust them an awful lot, or love them like crazy to take the risk.
>
> Being special to God doesn't mean being birds in a gilded cage. It means the privilege of being right in there with him when he's about his creative work.

[14-30] Imagine a man who was going on a journey – so he called his staff to a meeting, and gave each of them part of his property to look

after: five talents¹ to one of them, two to the next, and one to the third, giving each servant as much responsibility as he thought he could handle. Then he went away and left them to it.

So the one with the five talents went and did a bit of business and finished up with five talents clear profit, and the one with two doubled his money as well. The third one, though – well, he wasn't so adventurous, and he just decided to keep the money he had safe, and not actually use it. So he dug a hole and hid the money underground.

Then the dreaded day arrived – and so did the boss. And he wanted to know what they'd done with the money he'd entrusted to them. So the one who had five talents said, 'You gave me five talents, boss, and look – I've made five more.'

'Great!' exclaimed his boss. 'Well done! You're a good servant, and you've done a good job with the little bit I gave you, so now I'm going to give you a lot more responsibility – but first, hey, let's celebrate!'

Then the servant with two talents came up. 'Remember you gave me two talents? Well, I went and doubled it, so here's your money and the profits with it.'

'Terrific!' the boss said. 'You're a good servant, too. I gave you a little and you did well, so let's see how you handle it if I give you more. Come and join the celebration!'

Then the servant who'd only been given one talent came forward. 'Well, it's like this, you see. I, um, well . . . look, you're a good business-man, right – tough and ruthless? I mean, you make profits out of nothing! I knew I couldn't measure up to your standards, so I panicked. I hid your money away in the ground. Here it is – you've still got what belongs to you.'

'You pathetic, idle, worthless individual!' his master said, angrily. 'Oh, so you knew I was tough, did you? You knew I was ruthless? Then why didn't you at least put the money in a bank where it would get interest? Well, I'll have that talent back, thank you very much, and I'll give it to the guy who ended up with the ten talents. At least he'll make some good use of it! That's the way it is: those who have get more, and those who don't have lose even the little they have already. As for this worthless waste of space, sling him

---

1. A talent was a coin, like a present-day pound or dollar – and this parable of Jesus is where we get the modern use of the word to mean a gift or skill that God has given us to develop and use.

outside into the darkness and let him do his weeping and moaning there!'

Preparing for the last judgement

So, what does 'being ready' mean? In a parable that starts off sounding as though it's about the final 'end times', Jesus shows that 'waiting' isn't just about sitting around! Those who will be ready to meet Christ *then* will be those who have recognised him *here and now*. Those who will enter his kingdom *then* will be the ones who have already become part of it *now*! So this parable is not just about Jesus' second coming but also about recognising his continual presence in the world, and responding to the challenge that this presents.

[31-46] When the Son of Man comes, gloriously arrayed, with all the angels with him, then he'll be seated on the throne of glory itself. All the nations will be gathered together in front of him, and he'll divide them up the way a shepherd separates the flock – sheep on the right, goats on the left. Then the king will say to the ones on the right, 'Hey, congratulations – come on in! Time to take the share in my kingdom that's been prepared for you from the beginning of all things – after all, when I was hungry, didn't you give me some food, and when I was thirsty, wasn't it you that gave me a drink? When I was a stranger, you made me welcome; when I was naked, then you clothed me. I was sick, and you nursed me, and when I was in prison, who came to see me? You did!'

Then the faithful people will say, 'Lord, what are you going on about? When did we ever see you hungry or thirsty and help you? When were you a stranger and we took you in – or naked and we clothed you? And as for visiting you when you were sick or in prison – well, that's completely news to us. When was it?'

The king will answer, 'I'm telling you straight, if you did it to the least of these who are my brothers and sisters, well then, you did it for me.'

Then he'll turn to the ones on the left. 'A curse on you!' he'll say. 'Go away from me into the place of eternal destruction! Just where were you when I needed you? There I was, starving hungry, and you couldn't give a crust! I was thirsty, but could you spare me a drink? Not likely! I was a stranger, but you refused to welcome me, naked and you couldn't spare me a single item of clothing, sick or in prison and – oh, you kept well away then, didn't you!'

And they'll answer in the same way: 'What? When was this? When did we see you hungry or thirsty, or a stranger, or naked, or sick or in prison if it comes to that? When did we see all that and not help you?'

'I'm telling you straight,' the king will answer, 'if you didn't do it for the most insignificant of my brothers and sisters, then you didn't do it for me.' And these will go into eternal destruction, but the faithful will go to everlasting life.

The Passion Narrative

The pace quickens now, as Matthew moves us determinedly towards the climax of his story – the death and resurrection of Jesus. Matthew balances the story very carefully. On the one hand, he doesn't want Jesus to be seen as the helpless victim – this is the path he's chosen, in obedience to his Father and in fulfilment of the scriptures. On the other hand, that doesn't get the culprits off the hook – they can hardly claim to be acting out of commitment to God's purpose! And who are the culprits? Certainly the religious authorities, but also Judas, the traitor, and the 'crowd' who have been there in the background throughout the gospel, never quite really committing themselves either way until this point.

A crucial point is the link between Passover and the death of Christ. The Passover was the celebration of God's great act of liberation when, through Moses, he led his people out of slavery. The gospel says that he's about to do it again now, in Jesus – but this time the slavery is our addiction to all that keeps us from being fully committed to God – fully 'in the kingdom of heaven'.

The plotting thickens

26 [1-2] When Jesus finished all this teaching, he said to his disciples, 'You know it's going to be Passover in two days? Well, that's the time when the Son of Man will finally be betrayed and crucified.'

[3-5] Then the chief priests and elders met at the house of Caiaphas, the High Priest, where the plot was hatched to arrest Jesus discreetly and kill him – but how? 'We can't do it in public,' they said, 'not with all these crowds here celebrating the festival – they'll go ballistic!'

Jesus is anointed

[6-13] As if to prove their point, a woman came up to Jesus while he was having a meal at Bethany, in the house of Simon the Leper,[1] and poured a whole alabaster jar of really expensive perfume all over his head. The disciples didn't appreciate it at all. 'What a terrible waste!' they said. 'This perfume could have been sold for a small fortune and the money could have been given to charity.'

Jesus knew exactly what was going on. 'What's your problem?' he demanded. 'Why are you getting at her when she's performed such a beautiful service for me? Look, you'll always have poor people around that you can be kind to, but you won't always have me. You realise what she's done? She's prepared me for burial in advance. This is an unforgettable act! I'm telling you straight, she'll go down in history – wherever my story is told, she'll be remembered!'

Betrayal!

[14-16] Judas, one of the Twelve, made his decision. He went to the chief priests, and said, 'What's it worth to you to know when it's safe to grab Jesus?' They agreed thirty pieces of silver, and from that time on Judas was on the lookout for a chance to betray him.

The Last Supper

[17-25] On the first day of the Festival period the disciples said, 'Jesus, where do you want us to set the Passover meal up for you?'

Jesus told them to go and meet a man who'd evidently got it all in hand. 'Say to him,' Jesus said, '"The Teacher says, 'The crunch moment[2] is very close, and I'll be celebrating Passover at your house with my friends.'"'

The disciples did exactly as Jesus said, and got the Passover meal ready, and that evening they sat down together – Jesus and the Twelve. While they were eating, Jesus said, 'I'm telling you straight, one of you's a traitor – he's going to give me away.'

They were horrified. 'You surely don't mean me, Lord?' each of them was asking.

---

1. Strange name, since had he truly been a leper he'd have been banished to a leper colony. Matthew doesn't give us any explanation, leaving us to assume, perhaps, that Simon was a leper whom Jesus had healed.
2. Matthew used a particular Greek word: *Kairos*. It doesn't just mean 'the time', but a very special time – 'the time of fulfilment', or 'the time of God's purpose': 'the time of God-given opportunity'.

'It's someone who's been dipping into this common dish with me,' Jesus emphasised. 'He's going to betray me. Well, the Son of Man is fulfilling the scriptures, but a curse on the one who betrays him – that man's going to wish he'd never been born!'

Judas (the one, you may remember, who'd already agreed the betrayal) said quietly, 'You *surely* don't mean *me*, Rabbi?'

'You've got it!' Jesus murmured back.

The Lord's Supper

The Church has debated the next passage for centuries. What we can say is that it's a graphic acted parable of what's about to happen: Jesus' body torn and broken, his blood poured out, and in some infinitely mysterious way that sacrificial self-giving is going to strengthen and sustain his people like food. We, as it were, 'feed on the life and death of Christ'.

²⁶⁻³⁰ Later in the meal, Jesus took a loaf of bread, gave thanks to God, broke it and gave it to his disciples. 'Take this and eat it,' he said. 'This is my body.' Then he took a cup, gave thanks and gave it to them. 'Drink from this – all of you – because this is my blood, opening up a new covenant – a whole new relationship with God. It's poured out for many people, for the forgiveness of sins. I'm telling you, I shan't be drinking this "fruit of the vine"[1] again until I share it with you when we celebrate the new life in my Father's kingdom!'

A hymn ended the meal, and Jesus led his disciples out for the last time towards the Mount of Olives.

Jesus foretells the disciples' failure

³¹⁻³² 'You're all going to stumble[2] and fall away tonight, because of what happens to me,' Jesus told them. 'Remember what scripture says: "The

---

1. Jesus is quoting the traditional Jewish blessing that he has just used – it's not specifically recorded but its omission from a Passover celebration would have been unthinkable, so the gospel writers can safely leave their readers to assume that it would have been used.
2. Remember earlier in the story when Jesus spoke of rocks becoming stumbling blocks? The same pun again. This time, the most dependable rock of all – Jesus (or more correctly, what happens to him) is going to cause them to stumble! Their faith still isn't ready to cope with a suffering Messiah!

shepherd will be struck down and the sheep will be scattered."[1] But after I've been raised, I'll be in Galilee ahead of you.'

[33-35] Peter said, 'I don't care if everybody else deserts you – *I* never will!'

'I'm telling you straight,' Jesus answered, 'this very night, before the cock-crow, you'll deny that you even know me, not just once but three times!'

'Look, Jesus,' Peter insisted, 'just get this straight – even if I have to die with you I'm never going to deny you!' And so said all the rest.

Jesus' agonising prayer

[36-46] Then Jesus went with them all to a plot of land called Gethsemane[2] and said, 'You sit here, while I go and pray over there.' Then he took Peter, James and John (the two sons of Zebedee) with him, and began to get into a terrible state. 'I don't mind admitting, I'm terrified – scared to death!' he told them. 'Please don't leave me – stay awake with me!' Then he went a few paces further, threw himself flat on the ground, face down, and prayed. 'My Father,' he pleaded, 'if there's any other way, please take this bitter cup[3] away from me! But in the end the only thing that matters is your will, not mine.' Then he came back to his disciples and found them asleep. 'Peter,' he said, 'couldn't you keep awake for my sake just for one hour? Wake up – and pray for yourself that you don't get tested more than you can take. Yes, I know your spirit's willing – it's the weakness of the flesh that worries me!'

Jesus went away to pray a second time. 'My Father,' he said, 'if the only way to deal with this cup is to drink it, then let your will be done!' Returning to the disciples, what should he find? They were asleep again – not surprising, since they were tired out! So he left them again, to go away and pray a third time in the same words as before. Then he came back to the disciples. 'Still asleep?' he said. 'Still resting? Well, the moment's here, and the Son of Man's betrayed into the clutches of people who hate him! Come on, wake up – we've got to get going[4] – look, the traitor's here.'

---

1. Zechariah 13:7.
2. Literally, Gethsemane means 'oil-press' – appropriate on the Mount of Olives.
3. The 'cup of suffering' was a familiar Jewish image. Jesus used it when challenging James and John in 20:20-23.
4. Going, that is, not in retreat but into action. This is the moment for which he's saved himself with those earlier strategic withdrawals.

The arrest

[47-56] Even as he spoke, Judas, one of his own chosen Twelve, arrived, and he'd come mob-handed – a crowd of people armed to the teeth with swords and clubs, sent by the chief priests and elders. Now, Judas had it all arranged. 'You'll know the one you're to arrest,' he said, 'because I'm going to kiss him – he's my friend, see!' With that, he went up to Jesus. 'Greetings, Rabbi!' he said, and kissed him.

'Such friendship!' Jesus said. 'You'd better just get on with it – it's quite a job you came here to do.' Then they came forward and arrested Jesus. For a few moments it was chaotic. One of the disciples lashed out with a sword. He landed a glancing blow and the High Priest's slave lost an ear. 'Now, stop that and put the sword away!' Jesus ordered him. 'People who live by violence end up dying that way too – it's not my way! If it was, don't you think I could ask my Father for a battalion of angels, and he'd send them? But, then, how would the scriptures that foretold all this be fulfilled?'

Jesus turned to the crowds. 'Just look at you!' he said. 'You come after me, armed to the teeth as if I were some sort of dangerous desperado – but I've been teaching openly in the Temple every day, so why didn't you just take me then? Still, I suppose at least you're fulfilling another prophecy![1] Then the disciples all turned tail and ran for their lives.

The 'trial' before Caiaphas[2]

[57-68] The people who had arrested Jesus led him away to the house of Caiaphas, where he was waiting with the scribes and elders. Peter followed at a safe distance and hung around in the courtyard with the guards so he could hear the trial. The chief priests – and in fact the entire council – were determined to make something stick, so that they could have Jesus executed, and they hunted around for false witnesses to testify against him. It wasn't finding witnesses that was the problem, though – there were plenty of them, all willing to lie in their teeth for a consideration – it was finding two who'd say the same thing! Eventually, they produced two people with the same story: 'This guy said, "I can destroy this Temple and rebuild it in three days flat!"'

The High Priest rose to his feet. 'Well, what do you have to say about that testimony?' Jesus said nothing, so the High Priest got heavy. 'I'm

---

1. Isaiah 53:12, probably – 'He was counted as one of the common criminals!'
2. It hardly deserved to be dignified with that title. Apart from the perjury involved, the very time at which it was held was illegal. Trials had to be held in the full light of day.

commanding you, on oath, in the name of the living God himself, to answer my question: are you expecting us to believe that *you* are the Messiah, the Son of God?'[1]

'That's what *you* say,' Jesus answered. 'But let me tell you, you're about to find out what that really means. You're going to find out what's meant by "the Son of Man seated at the right hand of God and coming on the clouds of heaven".'[2]

'That's it!' The High Priest ripped his robe. 'Blasphemy! What more witnesses do we need? He's convicted himself!' He turned to the assembly. 'So, what's your verdict?'

'Death!' they all roared. Then they really laid into Jesus: spat in his face, hit him – some even slapped him in a contemptuous gesture, and said, 'OK, Mr Messiah – prophesy. If you're so all-fired special, tell us who hit you!'

Peter denies Jesus

69-75 Meanwhile, Peter, sitting outside in the courtyard, was being intimidated by a solitary slip of a servant girl! 'Hey,' she said, 'you're one of the friends of that Galilean guy, aren't you?'

Peter quailed. 'Who, me? I haven't a clue what you're on about!'

He decided to take refuge out in the porch, only to be spotted by another girl. 'This fellow was with Jesus, from Nazareth,' she asserted.

Well, she really had him rattled! 'I swear to God I don't know the guy!' he spluttered.

There was no hiding place, though – some of the other spectators went for him next. 'You must be one of them,' they said. 'It's your accent that gives you away!'

Peter started cursing at them, and finally said, 'I swear to you, I don't know the man! OK?'

At that moment the cock crowed, and Peter remembered what Jesus had told him: 'Before the cock-crow, you'll deny three times that you know me.' He went out and dissolved into terrible tears of remorse.

---

1. The very idea would appear ludicrous, with Jesus standing in front of him, bound and humiliated!
2. Caiaphas would indeed witness the enthronement and vindication of Jesus – but not in the way he understood Daniel's imagery.

The trial before Pilate

> Having secured a conviction for blasphemy, the Temple authorities could, under the law of Moses, stone Jesus to death – but under Roman occupation that didn't count. So now they had to get the Roman authorities to do their dirty work. Just one problem – the Romans weren't the least bit interested in the law of Moses.

27 [1-2] Morning light saw another frantic conference of the chief priests and elders to find the grounds on which they could induce the Romans to execute Jesus. Having hatched their plot, they tied Jesus up and took him to Pontius Pilate, the Governor.

Judas on a guilt trip

[3-10] Meanwhile, Judas – the traitor – saw that Jesus was going to be executed, and had some serious regrets about what he'd done. So he scurried back to the chief priests and elders, and tried to return their money. 'I've sinned,' he wailed, 'I've sinned because I've betrayed innocent blood!'

'Oh, don't come to us with your problems!' they scoffed. 'Go and deal with it yourself.' Judas threw down the thirty pieces of silver in the Temple, and then went out and hanged himself.

'Now, whatever are we going to do with these?' the chief priests said. 'It's illegal to put blood money into the Temple funds.' So they decided to use the money to buy the potter's field and use it as a cemetery for foreigners – and it's been called the Field of Blood ever since. In doing this, they fulfilled Jeremiah's prophecy: 'They took the thirty silver pieces – the lordly sum they'd valued me at – and paid them for the potter's field, as God had commanded.'[1]

Back to the trial

[11-18] Jesus stood before the Roman Governor, who asked, 'Are you the King of the Jews?'

'Those are your words,' Jesus answered, but when the chief priests and elders started hurling accusations again he didn't dignify them with an answer. So Pilate said, 'Don't you hear all these accusations

---

1. This actually sounds more like Zechariah 11:13 – well, sort of – with a hint of Jeremiah added for flavouring!

they're bringing? Still Jesus didn't answer – not to a single one of the charges – leaving the governor thoroughly frustrated.[1]

As it happened, the governor had a custom of releasing one prisoner, chosen by the crowd, at the Festival time – and he had in custody a particularly notorious revolutionary called Jesus Barabbas. So he asked the crowd, 'Whom do you want me to release to you: Jesus Barabbas, or Jesus called the Messiah?[2] He knew perfectly well that it was only because of their own petty jealousy that the authorities had brought Jesus to him.

[19-26] Even Pilate's wife was pleading on Jesus' behalf! She sent a message to Pilate as he sat in judgement. 'Just keep your distance from this,' she advised, 'and be careful how you treat this guy. I've had a really terrible time because of dreams about him!' But the chief priests and elders were stirring up the crowds to ask for Barabbas to be released, and have Jesus killed.

'Well?' the Governor demanded, 'What's it to be, then? Which one of these do you want?'

'Barabbas!' the crowd screamed.

'So what am I supposed to do with the Jesus who's called the Messiah?' Pilate asked.

'Have him crucified!' they yelled.

'Now, why should I want to do a thing like that?' Pilate asked. 'What harm's he done?'

They just shrieked all the more loudly, 'Crucify him!'

Well, Pilate knew when he was beaten, and he could see that there was a riot brewing, so he called for water and publicly washed his hands. 'This man's blood is not going to be on *my* hands!' he declared.

'Fine!' came the reply. 'It's our responsibility – ours and our children's!' So Pilate released Barabbas, and handed Jesus over to be flogged before being crucified.[3]

---

1. In Roman civilisation, judges thought it a little unseemly to convict and sentence a defendant without adequate defence – so Jesus' silence didn't help Pilate to feel any better!

2. Can these names *really* be a coincidence? Jesus Barabbas would have been a lot closer to the popular idea of Messiah – a political revolutionary. The crowd chose him in preference to the real Messiah, the true 'Son of the Father' – the real meaning of 'bar Abbas'!

3. It looks as though, once the crowd had accepted the guilt, Pilate decided to pile it on by passing a gratuitously brutal sentence – flogging, itself a ferocious and often fatal punishment, followed by crucifixion. There was simply no legal reason to inflict both.

The mocking

[27-32] It wasn't that simple, though. Before the flogging came ritual humiliation at the hands of the governor's troops. The whole squad gathered round as they stripped Jesus' clothes off him and dressed him in one of their scarlet capes instead. Then they plaited some thorns into a crown and thrust it on his head. Next, they put a long reed in his right hand for a sceptre, and then started mocking him – kneeling before him and chanting, 'Hail, King of the Jews!' Then they spat on him and hit him over the head with the reed. When they'd had all the fun they wanted with him, they put his own clothes back on him and led him away for crucifixion. On their way out they came across a man called Simon, from Cyrene, and forced him to carry Jesus' cross.

The crucifixion

[33-44] When they got to the place called 'Golgotha' (which means 'the place of the skull') Jesus was offered a mixture of wine and gall to drink, but he wouldn't accept it. When they'd crucified him, they divided up his clothes among themselves by gambling for them, and then sat down to keep watch. They fixed a placard over his head, reading, 'This is Jesus – the King of the Jews!' and crucified two rebels with him, one either side. People who passed by ridiculed him, shaking their heads and saying, 'OK, then – you who reckoned you could destroy the Temple and rebuild it in three days – you can start by saving yourself! If you're the Son of God, then just step down from the cross – surely you can do a little thing like that!'

All the Temple officials joined in too – priests, scribes, elders,[1] all mocking him. 'He saved others,' they jeered, 'but he can't save himself, can he! Oh, come on – he's the King of Israel – so let him just come down from the cross and we'll all believe in him, won't we! I mean, he always trusted in God – supposed to have this incredible faith – so let God rescue him, then! If he wants to, that is – after all, didn't the guy claim to be the Son of God?' Even the rebels, crucified on either side, joined in and taunted him in the same way.

The death of Christ breaks all barriers

Matthew obviously wants to make clear that the decisive moment in redemption is the *death* of Jesus. It is at that point that the

---

1. What an unholy alliance! It must have taken an awful lot of hatred to unite all of those against him!

> power of the grave is broken, and the veil that has marked a barrier between the people and God – and also a priestly class-distinction, since only they could pass it – is torn completely open. Powerful stuff, indeed!

[45-46] There was a horrible darkness everywhere. It lasted from midday, when Jesus was crucified, until three o'clock in the afternoon. And at about three, Jesus gave a great and terrible cry: 'My God,' he screamed, 'my God – why have you deserted me?'[1]

[47-49] Some of the people said, 'Hey, listen to that! He's calling Elijah.'[2] One kind person ran over to where the soldiers were sitting, soaked a sponge in their wine and held it up on a stick for Jesus to drink. But others just scoffed, 'What are you doing that for? If Elijah's coming to save him, leave it to him!'

[50] Then Jesus gave another great cry, and gave up his life.

[51-53] At that precise moment the curtain that hid the holy of holies in the Temple was ripped in two from top to bottom. The earth shook so violently that even the rocks themselves were broken up. As that happened, graves broke open as well, and the bodies of faithful people who had died rose back to life again (after Jesus' resurrection, they were to be seen by many people in Jerusalem).

[54-56] The centurion guarding Jesus, along with the other guards, watched all this with amazement and terror, and said, 'Surely it must be true that this was the Son of God!' They weren't the only ones there – there were a lot of women as well, standing quite a long way away. They were the ones who'd been with Jesus, providing for him, all the way from Galilee, and they included Mary Magdalene and the other Mary – the mother of James and Joseph – and the mother of the two sons of Zebedee.

---

1. Psalm 22:1. It has been suggested that Jesus used this cry deliberately to point us to the psalm, and that he was not actually feeling such despair himself. However, we have to ask what it means for Jesus truly to share our experience of death. For me, this haunting cry makes the whole gospel infinitely more real. God, in Jesus, did not merely 'dress up' as a human being – he truly became human and went through all that this implies.
2. It seems they might have misheard him – mistaking 'Eli', the Hebrew word for addressing God, for 'Elias'.

The burial

[57-61] In the evening, a rich man came along. His name was Joseph, and he came from Arimathea and was a disciple of Jesus. He went to see Pilate to ask to be allowed to take Jesus' body – a request to which Pilate acceded. So Joseph took Jesus' body, wrapped it lovingly in a clean piece of linen, and placed it in his own tomb, hewn out of the rock and completely unused.[1] He rolled a huge stone across the mouth of the tomb, and left. Mary Magdalene and the other Mary were there, still on watch, sitting across from the tomb.

[62-66] Next day, the chief priests and the Pharisees went to see Pilate, and said, 'Your Excellency, we're really worried about what that poser said when he was alive – that after three days he'd rise again.[2] Look, we'd like you to put a bit of security on the tomb – just for the three days. Otherwise, we know what those disciples of his are capable of – they'll steal the body and then go round telling everyone that he's been raised from the dead.[3] Then the final fraud[4] will be even worse than the first – and that was bad enough!'[5]

'Oh, OK, OK, whatever!' Pilate sighed. 'Take a squad of my troops and go and deploy them if it'll make you any happier!' So they took the soldiers to the tomb and sealed the stone to secure it.

The Resurrection

Although Christians can justly claim that the resurrection vindicated Jesus, we must beware of confusing its message. It's quite clear that God wasn't just trying to prove something and score some points over the opposition – if that had been his intention, even in part; he'd surely have made certain of it by at least having some witnesses to the big event itself. As it is, he appears to have left the whole question open to debate by having not a single eyewitness account of the moment of actual resurrection in the whole of scripture.

---

1. Rich people's tombs could have space for several bodies. This one was *completely* unused.
2. Well, they got that wrong too. He said he would *be raised* – a small but vital detail since he was giving God the credit for it, not claiming it for himself.
3. That's better!
4. A phoney resurrection.
5. The claim to be Messiah.

This, of course, is totally in keeping with Jesus' ministry. He was calling people to *faith*, which meant people had to respond freely. To provide irrefutable proof – of a forensic quality that would make rejection impossible – would defeat that object. Matthew's overwhelming (although not exclusive) emphasis is on the effect of the resurrection on the faith community itself.

28[1-10] As the Sabbath ended and the first day of the week dawned, Mary Magdalene and the other Mary went to visit Jesus' tomb. Suddenly, the earth shook as an angel came from heaven, rolled the stone away from the tomb and sat on it. And this was no ordinary angel: his entire being shone like lightning, his robe was brilliant white[1] – and he certainly put the fear of God into the guards who quaked with terror and went into a dead faint! The angel reassured the women. 'Don't be frightened,' he said. 'I know what you're here for – you're looking for Jesus, who was crucified. But have I got news for you! He's not here – he's been raised to life, just the way he always said. Come on, see for yourselves – look at the empty space where you witnessed him being laid to rest. Then, when you've seen, go and take the good news to his disciples. Tell them, "He's been raised from the dead, and is going ahead of you to Galilee – there you'll see him!" You have the word of an angel on that!'

The women rushed out of the tomb, bubbling over with a heady mixture of joy and fear, and headed off to tell the disciples. Before they'd gone far, though, whom should they meet but Jesus himself! 'Hello!'[2] he said, in a low-key sort of way. There was nothing low-key in the women's reaction, though – they fell down and took hold of his feet, in a gesture of adoration. 'Don't be frightened,' Jesus said. 'Go and tell my disciples to go to Galilee – that's where they'll see me.'

[11-15] While the women were on their way, some of the soldiers who'd been on guard went into Jerusalem and told the whole story to the chief priests, who then got together with the elders and concocted a plan of action. First, they gave the soldiers a hefty bribe, and then told them what their story was to be. 'Say you were asleep,' they said. 'Yes,

1. Daniel 10:6, perhaps.
2. Sounds a bit feeble compared with the traditional translations, but the original word translates as a very ordinary daily greeting – which would be more natural if you were about to give someone the shock of their lives and didn't want to make it even worse by using emotionally charged language!

that's it: you were asleep and the disciples came and stole the body. Oh, don't worry about the governor getting to hear it – we can easily square things with him and make sure you don't get into trouble.' The soldiers grabbed the money and did as they were told – and that's the story still being put around now.[1]

16-20 The eleven disciples went to the mountains of Galilee, as per Jesus' instructions, and when they saw him they worshipped him – although one or two needed a bit longer for it to sink in – not surprisingly, given the circumstances! Jesus came closer, and said, 'All authority in heaven and earth has now been given to me. So go – go and make disciples everywhere, and baptise people in the name of the Father, the Son and the Holy Spirit. Teach people to be faithful to every command I've given you. And remember: I'm always with you[2] – right to the very end of time!'

1. 'Now', of course, refers to Matthew's time of writing, not the present day. Matthew uses the term 'the Jews' here, but in fact this idea is put forward by many people today who do not believe the story of the empty tomb. Matthew had his own reasons for pointing to 'the Jews' in particular, but we should be careful how we interpret that.
2. Remember the name Jesus was given at birth? – 'Immanuel', meaning 'God with us'. So this was not just a thirty-year blip in history – Jesus reveals 'God with us' as a reality in all times, places and circumstances!

Mark

The Gospel according to Mark

It's likely that Mark wrote the first of our four accounts of the gospel. Nothing's certain in these areas, but that's the most widely accepted theory. His gospel is the shortest, and the most fast-paced. He had just one urgent task to perform (the more urgent if the theory that his was the first written account is correct): to present Jesus as the Son of God and the Messiah.

It's possible that Mark was a worried man. The Christian faith had spread like wildfire through the known world, but the written records relating directly to Jesus' life consisted generally of collections of sayings and stories, probably originally compiled from eye-witness accounts for teaching and preaching purposes. Mark was passionately convinced that being a Christian was not about following the teachings of Jesus, but following Jesus himself. And at that time there were no authoritative writings that could enable people to do that in quite the way that Mark wanted to make possible. For that, people needed to encounter the word of God in the life, ministry, death and resurrection of Jesus taken as a coherent whole.

Perhaps with that in mind, Mark's narrative is short but very vivid. There's an awful lot he doesn't tell us that other writers do – but the material he chooses is presented in much more detail.

Even so, Mark wasn't writing a biography. In a biography, the personal development of the central character, as a whole person, underlies the story. Mark isn't interested in, for example, whether Jesus liked sport, or whether he had a sweet tooth! So it's obvious that this is a very special form of book that Mark decided to write. His concern is with who Jesus is and what his life means for those who choose to follow him – or otherwise.

Mark Route Planner

You might find this helpful to give you a quick overview of the journey ahead.

111

Jesus in Galilee

Introduction

> Mark sets out his stall. This book is not about ethics, rules or philosophical debate. It's about a *person*: Jesus Christ, the Son of God. And there are two things about that person that Mark wants us to keep in mind. On a human level, Jesus was the fulfilment of the hopes and dreams of the past – the inspired prophecies. He was much more than that, though: in him, God was getting involved in human affairs in an unprecedented and decisive way.

John prepares the way

1 [1-3] The beginning of the gospel of Jesus Christ, the Son of God, as the Prophet Isaiah foretold: 'Look, I'm sending my messenger ahead of you – the one who's going to prepare the way before you. A voice, calling out in the desert, "Prepare the way for God. Build a straight road for God to travel."'[1]

[4-8] So John the Baptiser appeared as was said – 'in the desert' – preaching a baptism by which people could show that they turned away from sin and accepted God's forgiveness. People came from all over the district of Judea, and even from Jerusalem itself.

John made a strange sight, dressed in camel skins held together with a leather strap. He had a funny idea of convenience food, too: all he seemed to live on was a diet of locusts, and honey that he took straight from the honeycomb. Rather him than me is what I say. 'There's someone *seriously* important coming along behind me,' he proclaimed. 'I'm not even good enough to help him undo his shoes. Now, he's really going to start something. All I'm doing is baptising people with water, for repentance – his baptism will be with the Holy Spirit.'

[9-11] At that time, Jesus arrived in Jordan, from Nazareth in Galilee, and John baptised him. As Jesus came out of the water, he had a vision: God's Spirit, like a dove, hovering over him. Then there was a voice from heaven. 'You are my Son,' it said, 'my special Son – like no other – and you're fulfilling all my expectations!'

---

1. The quotation is actually a mixture of Malachi 3:1, Exodus 23:20 and Isaiah 40:3.

Jesus resists temptation

[12-13] Then the Spirit immediately drove[1] him out into the desert where he stayed for forty days, being tempted by Satan, with only wild animals and angels for company.[2]

God's glory and human blindness

In the first main section of his book, Mark will show how God's glory was revealed in Jesus by the authority he demonstrated in teaching, healing, forgiveness, exorcism, in his freedom in respect of the law, and even his command over natural forces. He will also show how that revelation fell largely on blind eyes. The point, however, is not human failings but divine grace. Mark concludes this section of the gospel with a healing miracle (8:22-26) in which blind eyes are opened, showing us that ultimately God's glory is not ours to understand and to grasp, but his to reveal.

Jesus calls the first disciples

[14-15] After John was arrested, Jesus came into Galilee proclaiming the gospel. 'The time's come, folks!' he said. 'The kingdom of God has come right to your door, and you'd better believe it. So turn away from everything that separates you from God.'

[16-20] As Jesus walked on the beach by the Sea of Galilee, he saw Simon and his brother Andrew throwing a net into the sea – because that's what fishermen do – and made them an offer they couldn't refuse. 'Why don't you come and follow me?' he said. 'I can teach you to fish for people.' Sounded intriguing. Simon and Andrew didn't hang around – they left the nets behind and took off following Jesus. Immediately. Just like that. And he wasn't done yet, either. He'd hardly gone any further when he found James and John. They were in the boat mending their nets – but not for long. Jesus called them, and on hearing him they immediately left the lot – boat, business, not to mention their father Zebedee – and followed Jesus.

---

1. Whereas Matthew and Luke would both say, 'led', Mark chose 'drove', portraying Jesus as being in the tradition of some Old Testament prophets whose experience of the Spirit of God was overwhelming.
2. When Matthew and Luke came to write their gospels, they filled in the details of this (Matthew 4:1-11, Luke 4:1-13), but Mark's in a hurry to get us into the main ministry of Jesus.

²¹⁻²² They headed for Capernaum and, when the Sabbath day arrived, Jesus went to teach in the synagogue. They were totally amazed, because he taught with real authority – not like the kind of sermons they were used to getting from the scribes!

Exorcising a demon

> The 'Messianic secret'. This comes up in this next passage and is worth noting. On various occasions, Jesus told either demons or people to keep quiet. It seemed he didn't want his Messianic status known. Scholars put forward various explanations for this; here's one that fits in with the overall thrust of Mark's approach. Simply to be known as the Messiah would be unhelpful to Jesus – and to everybody else – until his ministry reached a point where the nature of that Messiahship became clear in his journey to the cross, his great 'enthronement' at Golgotha, and his ultimate glorification. Only then would it be appropriate for the proclamation to be made, for only in that light could it be fully understood.

²³⁻²⁸ Immediately, in the synagogue, he encountered a man with an evil spirit. 'What do you want with us, Jesus of Nazareth?' the spirit screamed at him. 'Have you come to destroy us? Oh, we know who you are, all right – God's holy messenger!'[1]

'Shut up and come out of him!' Jesus commanded the spirit, which threw the guy into a convulsion, gave one final defiant scream, and left. Everyone was completely amazed. 'Hey, what's this?' they asked one another. 'Some radical new teaching, or something? He gives orders to evil spirits and they obey him – man, that's some authority! And in next to no time he was famous throughout the whole surrounding region of Galilee.

---

1. Now this might just be my interpretation, but you can decide for yourselves. Remember that much is made in the gospels of Jesus being rejected in the synagogues and by the religious establishment generally – and telling his disciples to expect the same. Many radical preachers have received similar treatment, especially when they tried to practise what Jesus preached. William Booth, for example, might never have started the Salvation Army if the mainstream Church hadn't objected to his socially challenging ministry. The message of the gospel can be, and often has been, discomforting, even for the Church, such that we close our ears, preferring not to hear it.

Healing Simon's mother-in-law

[29-31] Immediately, Jesus moved on from the synagogue to the house where Simon and Andrew lived – James and John were with him, too. Now, Simon's mother-in-law was down with a fever, as Jesus was swiftly told. Jesus didn't hang around – he went to where she was, took her hand and lifted her up. The fever subsided and then she waited on them.[1]

Jesus' influence and reputation spread

[32-39] By the time evening came, as the sun went down, all kinds of people were there, some possessed by evil spirits, others just plain sick, and the entire local population had gathered to watch. The evil spirits were despatched, and the sick were healed – and the evil spirits weren't allowed to get a word in because they knew who Jesus was.[2]

Then in the morning, well before daybreak, Jesus went out to find a quiet place to pray, No chance of that, though – not with Simon and his guests chasing after him. 'Everyone's wondering where you've got to!' they told him.

'OK,' Jesus sighed, 'let's move on. We can go and make a start in the next towns. I've got to preach there, as well – after all, that's why I'm here.' And he went all over Galilee, preaching in their synagogues and performing exorcisms.

Healing a man with leprosy

> According to the laws of the time, people suffering from leprosy were strictly quarantined. The illness was regarded as incurable – the person was in effect dead already, so being cured would be tantamount to being raised to new life!

[40-45] A man suffering from leprosy came up to Jesus and knelt down. 'If you really want to, you can make me well again – not to mention socially acceptable.'

---

1. The indication is that a woman was here admitted to discipleship – that her 'service' was valued, and the healing enabled her to do it.
2. Two points here. Firstly, we are back to the 'Messianic secret' mentioned in the introduction earlier. Secondly, if the demons think that just knowing and acknowledging Jesus to be divine is going to be enough to save them, they've got another think coming! Just believing or saying the right things – even 'Jesus is Lord' – isn't enough!

Jesus was horrified at the man's suffering.[1] 'I do want to,' he said. 'So be healed.' Then he reached out and touched him – not something recommended in polite society.[2] Immediately, the man's skin healed up. Jesus gave him strict instructions. 'Now, don't you go telling everybody about this,' he said. 'Just go and see the priest and get all the legal stuff done – thank offerings, that sort of thing – then you can go home again.' But, of course, the guy just went out and told everyone, and the news spread, so that before long Jesus couldn't go into a town for fear of being mobbed, preferring instead to stay in the rural places – but even there, people came from everywhere to surround him.

Jesus and the law

> It's worth noting at the start of this passage that Jesus never encouraged a cavalier attitude to the law. What he did was emphasise its true purpose and fight against the use of it to maintain oppressive and unjust social structures. The following cluster of stories illustrates this from different perspectives.

Jesus has the authority to forgive[3]

2[1-12] When Jesus got back to Capernaum some days later, the word spread like wildfire and the house was so crowded no one else could get in. They couldn't even get near the door, in fact – absolutely packed, it was, with Jesus preaching to everybody who could hear.

So when four men arrived, carrying a paralysed friend on a stretcher, they had no chance of getting to see Jesus – not by any socially acceptable means anyway. So they just took the outside staircase up onto the flat roof, and calmly started removing it – the roof, that is, not the staircase – until they'd made a big enough hole to let the stretcher down with the man on it. Jesus was well impressed by their faith and said to the paralysed man, 'Son, your sins are forgiven.'[4]

---

1. The word often translated as 'had pity' really means 'was angry'. Such suffering is completely contrary to God's will: hence Jesus' response, 'I will'.
2. Not only that: Jesus risked being 'quarantined' himself, for doing it. How's that for solidarity!
3. This story is more usually titled something like 'Jesus heals a paralysed man', but if we take the passage in context we know that the story is really about authority, in keeping with the others in this section. In this case, the real issue is not the healing but the forgiving.
4. This doesn't mean Jesus thought the man's illness was a punishment, but it was what people in those days believed, so the man would certainly be *feeling* in need of forgiveness.

The scribes nearby responded absolutely predictably, of course. 'Blasphemy!' they thought. 'Why does this guy talk like this? Blasphemy – that's what it is! Who other than God has the right to forgive sins?'

Jesus immediately knew exactly what was in their minds, and said, 'Why do you always have to pick holes like that? All right, I suppose anyone could say, "Your sins are forgiven", but to say, "Get up, pick up your stretcher and walk", well, that's another matter isn't it it![1] So, if you want to see some real authority, that's OK by me.' He turned to the man on the stretcher and said, 'I'm telling you to stand up, get hold of that stretcher, and go home.' And immediately, he did. And when the crowds saw it, they were completely awestruck and started praising God. 'Well!' they said. 'We've never seen anything like it in our lives!'

Eating with the undesirables

[13-17] Jesus went out again near the sea, and, of course, the crowd followed as always, so he taught them. Moving on, he came across a guy called Levi, the son of Alphaeus, a tax collector, sitting at the custom desk taxing the traders. 'Follow me,' he said, and the man just got up and followed him. Next thing everybody knew, Jesus was sitting down to dinner with him and just about every tax collector and general undesirable in the area seemed to be joining Jesus and his disciples – because he had quite a following. 'Hey, what's the idea?' the Pharisees demanded of the disciples. 'Why does your teacher share food with characters like this?'

Jesus heard them – he could hardly fail to, the commotion they were causing – and said, 'Well, the people who are fit and healthy don't need a doctor, do they? Doctors go to those who need them, and so do I. I didn't come to invite the righteous to my banquet – I came to invite those you call sinners to share it!'

Empty rituals

[18-22] Now, as it happened, John's disciples were fasting – and so were the Pharisees[2] – so, of course, people started making comparisons. 'Look,' they said, 'John's disciples and the Pharisees are always fasting, so why's it not good enough for your disciples, too?'

---

1. Because any ordinary person would look a bit silly when it didn't happen!
2. Fasting was only required at specific times, but some groups saw it as a kind of religious badge of honour and took it to extremes.

'Oh, right,' Jesus answered, 'I suppose you'd ask wedding guests to fast while the bridegroom's with them, would you? Really good manners that'd be, wouldn't it! When the bridegroom's been taken away, there'll be plenty of time for that! New days, new ways: no one with any sense patches an old coat with new, unshrunk cloth – you just end up with a worse tear than ever. And you don't put new wine into old wineskins, either – not if you know your wine. It's just inviting disaster. The new wine will burst out of the skins and they'll both be lost. New wineskins for new wine.'

The Sabbath

The Sabbath day was a vital feature of Jewish life. No work was to be done on it at all. The underlying principle was of community: having a day off is just not quite the same if the rest of the world's mad bustle is still going on around us. Furthermore, in households with several people working, a *common* rest day meant that regular time *together* could be assured. On this purely human level, then, the Sabbath was a good idea, and Jesus wasn't trying to destroy it. The problem lay in defining work. Was walking to visit a relative 'work'?[1] Lawyers had been busy trying to pin everything down clearly, and the result was that God's gift of rest became a burden – another cause for anxiety!

Picking the corn

23-28 Then there was the time when Jesus was walking through the cornfields one Sabbath day with his disciples, who were picking some of the heads off the corn as they went, and eating them. Harmless enough, you'd think, but not if you're a Pharisee with an axe to grind. 'Hey, Jesus,' they called, 'what do you think you're doing, letting your disciples break the law on the Sabbath?'[2]

'Oh, get real, please!' Jesus answered. 'Try reading your Bibles – don't you remember what King David did when he and his companions were desperate and hungry? I mean, he only went into the holy of holies,

---

1. Hence the reference in Acts 1:12 to 'a Sabbath day's journey'. Yes, they'd even defined that!
2. Now, you might think they meant stealing, but it was even pettier than that. Working on the Sabbath was illegal, and, as far as they were concerned, if you're going to pick an ear of wheat you might as well take a combine harvester to the whole field.

when Abiathar was High Priest, and stole the bread intended for worship, which the law says only the Priests can eat – and gave some to his companions, too – that's all! The Sabbath was made for people's benefit, not people for the Sabbath! So the Son of Man has authority even over the Sabbath.'[1]

Healing: the man with the withered hand

3 [1-6] Jesus went to the synagogue, where there was a man in the congregation whose hand was paralysed – so, of course, they were all watching to see whether Jesus would heal on the Sabbath and give them a chance for another go at him. Jesus said to the man, 'Come here.' Then he turned and asked, 'OK, you tell me what the law says we should do on the Sabbath: good or harm – save life or kill?'

Not a word!

Jesus glared at them in a mixture of anger and pity for their stubborn minds, and then turned to the man and said, 'Stretch out your hand,' and it became as sound as a bell – well, as sound as a good hand, anyway. The Pharisees, though, were unimpressed – they just sloped off into an unholy huddle with Herod's cronies[2] to plot his downfall.

A ministry of parables and miracles

> Both parables and miracles had a purpose in Jesus' ministry: to reveal both his own authority and the kingdom of God. Yet, the striking theme running through all of these is the blindness not only of Jesus' enemies but of his friends and even his closest family who simply did not get the message.

[7-12] Time for a strategic retreat,[3] with his disciples, to the sea – but not without a crowd following him. They came from all over the place: from Judea, including Jerusalem itself, from Idumea, from the Gentile side of the Jordan, from the region of Tyre and Sidon – a great crowd of people who'd heard what he was doing and thought they'd try and get

---

1. Matthew 12:1-8 includes a fuller argument by Jesus.
2. The Pharisees hated the Herodians who gave support to the Roman occupiers of what should have been God's own country – so this can only mean the two parties hated Jesus even more than they despised each other.
3. The gospels record a number of these retreats, and it's important to understand that Jesus wasn't running away because he was afraid of trouble. Rather, he was saving himself for the purpose for which he was born. When the time came, he would go to his suffering faithfully, but this wasn't the time.

a piece of the action. Jesus was ready for them – he'd already told his disciples to have a boat ready, so he could avoid being trampled in the rush – because his fame as a healer was spreading and every sufferer under the sun seemed to be crowding in to touch him. And when any evil spirits encountered him, they prostrated themselves in front of him, saying, 'You're the Son of God! You're the Son of God!'[1] He gave them strict instructions not to go shouting it around the place.[2]

Jesus calls the Twelve to be Apostles

> The apostles were called first and foremost to be close to Jesus, and only secondarily to be sent out in mission. So, the Church exists first and foremost to *be* the people of God — but, in order that it should not be an exclusive club, it is also sent out into the world. Christ first gathers, and then he sends – neither image is complete without the other.

[13-19a] Jesus went up a mountain, and gave twelve of the disciples the title of 'apostles'.[3] They were to keep close to him and really get to know him, so as to be able to go out and preach – he also gave them his authority to send evil spirits packing. Want to know who the twelve were? I'll tell you. First came Simon (whom Jesus surnamed Peter), Zebedee's two sons James and John (he called them 'Boanerges', which means 'Sons of Thunder'!). Then came Andrew, Philip, Bartholomew and Matthew. Then there were Thomas, another James – the son of Alphaeus – Thaddaeus, and another Simon – this time Simon the Patriot[4] – and finally Judas Iscariot, the guy who was eventually going to betray him.

The ultimate blasphemy

[19b-22] Then Jesus went home, and guess what – the crowd gathered again! It got so that he couldn't even enjoy a meal in peace. His family got wind of it and went out to get him and take him back with them

---

1. The use of Jesus' title could be seen as a futile attempt to exert control over him. It could also be an attempt at blackmail, threatening to expose his true identity before the appropriate time.
2. On the 'Messianic secret', see the introduction to 1:23-28.
3. Basically, it meant someone who was commissioned or sent on a mission.
4. Some translations read 'Cananaean' or 'Canaanite', but the word really refers to a political movement, not to the place of a similar name. Luke calls him a 'Zealot' which identifies him as a member of a fanatical group of freedom fighters.

because people were saying, 'The guy's lost it, you know – completely barking!'[1] The scribes who'd come from Jerusalem to investigate were even less polite. 'He's possessed!' they said. 'The only reason he can cast out demons is that he himself is in league with the devil!'

[23-30] Jesus called them to him, and started talking in parables[2] again:

Use a bit of sense! How can Satan send Satan packing? Everyone knows that any kingdom that's divided against itself ends up being destroyed. That's true at every level – a divided city, or even a feuding family – none of them can survive. So if you're saying that Satan is rebelling against himself, then clearly the underworld's in a state of civil war and can't stand. Put it another way: can you just imagine someone going to burgle a strong man's house without tying up the strong man first?[3] Only then is it safe to start looting the place!

I'm telling you straight, people can be forgiven for any kind of sin, any kind of blasphemy, but when you start committing blasphemy against the Holy Spirit, then you put yourself out of reach of forgiveness. When you start trying to make out that good's bad and vice versa, then there's no getting through to you, is there? – so you're stuck in your sins for ever.[4]

He said that because they'd called his Spirit unclean!

Who are the true household of Jesus?

This story re-echoes a prominent theme in the gospels: being part of the household of Jesus is not about being born to it, but about a deliberate decision and commitment to be 'about the Father's business'.

[31-35] Then Jesus' family turned up and stood outside, sending messages and calling for him. 'Hey, Jesus!' someone in the crowd said. 'Your mother and your brothers are standing outside – it seems they want a word.'

---

1. One of various indications that even Jesus' own family weren't totally sure of him.
2. We think of parables as stories with messages, which they often are, but the word translated as 'parable' can also mean 'riddles' which only those whose minds have been opened can understand.
3. 'Binding Satan' was a traditional Jewish image. Jesus is clearly saying that the only reason he can do the things he does is that he's effectively rendered Satan helpless.
4. It's important to read this in context. The Scribes are convincing themselves that what's good is bad and vice versa – shutting themselves off from the 'Spirit of Truth' who, Jesus said elsewhere, leads us into all truth. So it's not that God's withholding forgiveness from them, but that they've got themselves into a position where they can't accept it *because they can't recognise their need of it!*

'My family?' Jesus answered. 'OK, you tell me – who are truly my family?' He looked around and said, 'Here's my true family! Because a proper relationship with me isn't about blood ties and family trees – it's about commitment to the work of God – that's what makes you my family!'

It has been said that Shakespeare's plays are clichéd, so many lines from them having passed into colloquial English that we're probably familiar with them even if we haven't read Shakespeare first-hand. The same might be said for Jesus' parables – for example, many people who have never read the Bible nonetheless know about the 'Good Samaritan', and they have probably used the term to describe a person showing particular kindness to others. The purpose of parables was to make the truth accessible, but to those with closed minds they appeared more like riddles. The Greek word used in the Gospels could mean either parable or riddle, and Jesus' explanation plays on this, as we shall see.

4 [1-9] Once again, Jesus started to teach by the sea, but huge crowds meant that it all got a bit too cosy for comfort – so he found a boat to use as a floating platform while the crowd stood beside the sea. Then, with a bit of space around him, he started teaching using parables.

The parable of the sower

Listen: there was this sower who went out sowing seed – as sowers do – and some of his seed landed on the pathway, so the birds thought it was dinner time and snaffled it all. Then some of it fell among rocks – not a lot of soil there, so the wheat died as fast as it grew. No roots, you see – no way of getting water when the sun got up – you know how it is. Anyway, some other seeds fell in the briar patch and the wheat that grew there just got choked to death by all the weeds – so that was pretty fruitless. So far, not so good – but some of the seed fell on good soil, and, wow, did it grow! I mean, it just went on and on, producing more and more – anything between thirty and a hundred times its own weight. OK? End of story. If you've got ears, fine – use them.

The nature and purpose of parables

[10-12] Some of the people standing around near the Twelve came and asked why on earth he had to talk in riddles all the time.

Jesus answered:

Well, whether they're riddles depends on your state of mind. Your minds have been opened to things about the kingdom of God, so you understand them. Those on the outside haven't, so they don't. It's riddles to them, because, as the saying goes, they see but they don't really perceive, they hear but don't understand. Otherwise, they'd turn from their bad ways and be forgiven, wouldn't they![1]

[13-20] Do you *really* not understand this parable? In that case, how are you going to understand any of them? OK, then. What the sower's sowing is the word of God. The path? Well, that's where the word's sown but it gets snatched away again before it has a chance to grow. Then we had seed sown on rocky ground, didn't we? Well, that's the people who hear and get all enthusiastic, but it doesn't last. It's shallow faith, and at the first hint of trouble they're off back to their old ways. Now what? Oh, yes – the seed in the briar patch. Well, some people really do have good intentions, you know, but then they're swamped by all the cares and pleasures of the world, and before long it's as though they never heard. But the good soil – well, that's something else. People hear the word, they really take it on board, and you start to see the results – it's that good fruit thing again. OK, now?

[21-25] Look, you don't go to the trouble of lighting a lamp and then hide it under a measuring jug, or shove it under the bed, do you? – you put it on a lampstand. Well, nothing's hidden now that won't be revealed, and whatever people keep secret now will be brought to light. Got ears, have you? Then use them! And don't just hear – really listen, because what you give out to others you'll get back, and with interest![2] That's the way it is: those who have get more, and those who don't have, lose even the little they have already.

[26-29] Think of the kingdom of God like this: a man scatters seed on the ground, OK? Then he goes off to sleep at night, gets up in the morning, and so it goes on – and all the time the seed's sprouting and growing without him – he doesn't know how it happens. The earth just gets on with producing the harvest – first a stalk, then it sprouts a seed

---

1. An allusion to Isaiah 6:9-10, used in a way to suggest that it was a commonly used saying. It corresponds better to the Aramaic translation (the everyday language of Jesus and his hearers) than it does to the Hebrew or Greek versions.
2. See Matthew 7:2.

head, and finally the seeds themselves appear in the seed head. Next job for the farmer comes when it's ready for harvesting, and then he gets stuck in with the cutter.

30-32 What else can I use to illustrate the kingdom of God? Well, it's like a mustard seed that someone might sow in a field. Now, you know it's the smallest of seeds, but when it's sown in the ground and grows it's quite a different story – the biggest of all the shrubs, stretching out its branches so that the birds come and shelter in its shade.

33-34 This was Jesus' way of teaching – talking in riddles as far as the others were concerned,[1] but he explained everything to his disciples in private.

Stilling the storm

> Water is a powerful symbol in the Bible. In creation, God brought the waters of chaos under control, but there was always the fear of their breaking out again. When psalmists, for example, wanted to express despair they would often sing of being overwhelmed by water. So what more appropriate way for the full authority of Jesus to be demonstrated than in calming the raging waters of the sea?

35-41 That evening, Jesus said, 'Let's go across the lake to the other side.' So they left the crowd and pushed off in the boat with Jesus, and with other boats around them. Next thing anybody remembers, the wind had got up and the whole sea seemed to be shaking like an earthquake. The boat was being swamped, and where was Jesus? Fast asleep on a pillow in the back of the boat! Not for long, though – the disciples saw to that! 'Teacher! Wake up! Don't you care if we die?'

Jesus had a stern word with the elements. 'Shut it!' he called. 'Just calm down, OK?' The wind and sea stopped raging and everything was quiet. Jesus wasn't impressed with the disciples, though. 'What are you afraid of? Talk about little faith!'

They were all completely awestruck. 'Now, just who is this guy?' they were asking. 'Even the wind and the sea do as he tells them!'

---

1. Remember that 'the crowds' represent the people outside Jesus' group of followers. So what was a 'parable' to an insider would have seemed like a riddle to an outsider. Check back to verses 10-17 to see this spelled out more.

Exorcising demons

5 [1-9] Then it was on to the other side – to the Gerasene region – where they were confronted by a man who lived among the graves and was in the clutches of an evil spirit.[1] He was a ferocious character – completely unmanageable, by any means known at the time. They'd tried everything, even heavy chains and shackles, but he just ripped them apart. It was more than any mortal man could do to control the guy – he just roamed around, night and day, either among the graves or in the mountain areas, howling and harming himself.

He saw Jesus from way in the distance, and charged over and bowed low. Then, suddenly, he was yelling furiously at Jesus, 'What business do you have with me, Jesus – Son of the Most High God? In the name of God, don't you start punishing me ahead of time!'

Well, it was understandable, since Jesus had just given the demon its marching orders. 'OK, evil spirit – time to move house. Come out of him.'

Then Jesus asked, 'What's your name?'

'My name?' came the reply. 'My name is Legion, because there's a lot of us in here.'

[10-20] Then the demons started crawling – begging not to be sent out of the area.[2] As it happened, there was a large herd of pigs, grazing unsuspectingly on the hillside. 'Send us into the pigs,' they begged. 'Quite a desirable residence for a demon, is a pig.'[3]

So Jesus agreed to that, and the demons left the man and moved into the pigs – about two thousand of them – and in next to no time, those peacefully feeding pigs were charging madly down the steep bank into the sea, where they drowned. The pigmen didn't hang around to ask questions – just took off into the town and the countryside round about and told the whole story. So, of course, the entire town got up and came out to see for themselves and found the man who'd been terrorising them sitting quietly there, completely sane and fully dressed. They were awestruck – no, they were terrified.[4]

---

1. Living among the tombs would make him ritually unclean anyway, so it was a vicious circle.

2. The theory probably was that they'd have a lot less hassle in a Gentile district than in a Jewish one, now that Jesus was around.

3. Pigs, of course, like demons, demoniacs and graveyards, were ritually 'unclean' under Jewish law, so it does seem appropriate – although I'm not at all sure the pigs would agree.

4. Understandably, really – they were afraid of Legion, but at least he stayed among the tombs. Jesus was obviously more powerful – and he was going to break out of the tomb.

Well, the people who'd seen what happened told their story, and that did it. Suddenly, everybody was pleading with Jesus to get out of their area.

As Jesus was getting back into the boat, the guy who'd been possessed came scurrying over, begging to be allowed to go with him, but Jesus had another idea.

'No, don't do that,' he said. 'Go home, instead – back to your family and your friends, and let them see what a kindness God's done for you.' Which the man did – and how! He proclaimed it all over the Decapolis region, leaving people completely amazed.

New life and healing

> This is an interesting juxtaposition of stories. Jairus's daughter was facing literal death, and Jesus is shown to be the Lord of life as he calls her back. But is it really coincidence that the woman with the haemorrhage is put right in the middle of that story? The 'unclean' nature of her illness means that she is excluded from life, condemned to live on the fringe, barely 'touching the edge' of the life of the community. So, naturally, she feels unworthy to do any more than 'touch the edge' of Jesus' clothing. His response is to call her to centre stage, invite her to look him full in the face and, as a result of that encounter, to come back from her living death to life in all its fullness.

21-24 Back across the sea again, the usual crowd gathered round Jesus. Then one of the local religious leaders, a man called Jairus, came up and prostrated himself in front of him. 'Please help,' he said. 'It's my daughter – she's right on the edge of death. You can save her, though – it's what you do, isn't it? Just come and lay hands on her and I know she'll be OK.' Jesus didn't hang around – he went with him, and the crowd followed, crushing against him as he walked.

25-34 Among them was a woman who'd suffered from a haemorrhage for twelve years. She'd had a rough time, going from one healer to another – all at a price, as you'd expect. Now she'd spent all her money and was getting worse, not better. Well, she'd heard about Jesus. She crept up behind him and touched his coat. 'That's all it'll take,' she told herself. 'If I can just touch the edge, I'll get better.' Immediately, the haemorrhage stopped and her whole body felt different – she knew she was healed.

Immediately, Jesus knew that power had gone from him. He turned round and asked, 'Who touched my coat?'

The disciples, of course, thought it was a hoot! 'Oh, get real, Jesus!' they said. 'You can see how the crowd's jostling around you – and you ask, "Who touched me?"'

Jesus just carried on looking round. The woman knew something awesome had happened to her, and she struggled forward, shaking with fear and apprehension.[1] She fell on the ground at Jesus' feet and poured out the whole story.

'Daughter,' said Jesus, 'your faith has made you better! Go in complete peace and be healed of your illness.'[2]

[35-43] Even as he spoke, some of the people from the synagogue leader's house arrived. 'No point in bothering the teacher any more,' they told Jairus. 'We're sorry, but she's dead.'

Jesus overheard. 'Don't worry,' he said to Jairus. 'Just trust me.'

This wasn't a time for public demonstrations, so Jesus told everybody else to stay behind but let Peter, James and John – James's brother – follow him. They went to the synagogue leader's house, and – what a scene! People were weeping and wailing enough to wake the dead – except that they hadn't. Jesus went in. 'What's all the fuss about?' he demanded. 'This is one death that's not going to last.'

They all had a good laugh at him over that, but Jesus shooed them out of the room and then took the girl's parents and the people with him in to where the girl was. He took her by the hand,[3] and said, '*Talitha cum*' – in other words, 'Little girl, get up.' Immediately, she was on her feet and walking around – she was about twelve years old at the time. Everybody, of course, was totally awestruck by it all, but Jesus warned them in no uncertain terms to keep quiet about it, and then told them to give the girl something to eat.

Jesus is rejected at home

6[1-6a] Well, that was that – time to move on. So Jesus went, with his disciples following him, to the synagogue in his home town and

---

1. Probably because she knew that her touch would technically have made Jesus ritually unclean – she probably expected him to be not particularly happy!
2. This illness would have made the woman 'unclean'. For a full healing, she needed a proper encounter with Christ.
3. Touching a corpse – yet another challenge to the purity laws, since he would then be ritually unclean.

started teaching there. 'Where did this guy get all this stuff from?' a lot of the people asked. 'All the eloquence! The miracles he performs! He's a carpenter, isn't he? – son of Mary, brothers James and Joses, Judas and Simon? His sisters live round here, too – he's just a local boy.'

'Well, there you go,' Jesus said. 'Prophets never get any street cred in their home towns or their own families.' That's why he couldn't perform any miracles there, other than laying hands on a few sick people to cure them. He was astounded at their lack of faith.

The mission widens

6b-13 Then Jesus took off all over the place – teaching in every city and village he came to. He called a meeting of his twelve closest disciples and started sending them out in pairs, granting his authority over evil spirits. He warned them not to get weighed down with provisions, other than a hiker's staff – no fund-raising or getting kitted out with spare gear. He said, 'When someone gives you shelter, stay with them until you finish in that town.[1] If people reject your message, then don't let's have any pretence about it. Shake the dust off your shoes as you leave, as a testimony that you've not been welcome.'

So that's what they did – preached, called people to repentance, kicked out the demons and healed loads of sick people, anointing them with oil.

Sex, politics and religion

Now we're introduced to Herod Antipas – not to be confused with Herod the Great whom we met earlier. This is his son – and not one to be particularly proud of.

14-16 The local ruler, Herod, got wind of all this because Jesus' reputation was going before him. Some people said, 'It's John the Baptiser, raised from the dead – where else would anybody get powers like that?'

'No,' others argued, 'it's Elijah.'[2]

'Well, a prophet, anyway,' some others said, 'like the old-timers, you know.'

When Herod got a sniff of it, he lost the plot completely. 'It's John the Baptiser!' he ranted. 'I know it is – John that I beheaded, come back to haunt me.'

---

1. Wasting time on hunting around for a nicer place to stay wasn't part of the brief.
2. The return of the prophet Elijah was widely expected by Jews as heralding the Messiah.

[17-23] Perhaps we'd better start at the beginning. It all began when Herod arrested John and slung him in prison – and that was all on account of Herodias, his brother Philip's widow, whom Herod had married. You see, John had pointed out – in pretty strong terms even by hairy prophets' standards – that it was against the law for Herod to marry his own brother's wife. Herodias held a king-sized grudge against John and wanted him dead, but Herod was terrified of the guy, because he knew he was right, so gave him his protection. Don't get me wrong – John's preaching drove him round the bend, but he still used to listen.

Herodias got her chance when Herod's birthday came around, and he threw a party for everyone who was anyone. Herodias's daughter danced at his party, and the old boy got a bit carried away. 'Anything you want!' he drooled. 'Just ask, and it's yours – anything up to half my kingdom.'

[24-29] So she went out and asked for advice – from her mother, of all people! 'What shall I ask for?'

Mother didn't need a second thought. 'The head of John the Baptiser,' she told her daughter.

Daughter didn't hang around – she immediately ran in to Herod and said, 'John the Baptiser's head, please – preferably detached – on a platter.'

Now, Herod wasn't happy, but what could he do – break his word in public and lose face into the bargain? So he immediately gave the order to a guard: John was beheaded in his cell, and his head put on a platter and presented to the girl, who promptly passed it on to her mother.

When John's disciples heard of it, they came and collected his body to give it a decent burial.

The missionaries return

[30-34] The apostles came back to Jesus, brimming over with news about the things they'd done and the sermons they'd preached. 'Let's find somewhere private,' Jesus said. 'We could all do with a bit of rest while we talk.' He wasn't wrong there – so many people were coming and going around them they hadn't even had a chance to eat!

So it was decided to make another strategic retreat. They hopped into a boat and went to a quiet place to be on their own. Fat chance of that, though – they were instantly recognised by countless people who followed them on foot by the land route. So, when Jesus came ashore, there they were, but compassion prevailed – he saw them as sheep without a shepherd[1] – and he gave the time to teach them.

The feeding of the five thousand

[35-44] When it got late, the disciples said to Jesus, 'Look, this is a pretty isolated place, and it's getting late – they must be starving. Send them away and let them go and get some food to eat.'[2]

'You give them something to eat,' Jesus responded.

'Oh, sure – we'll just go and spend about six months' wages[3] on bread for them to eat, shall we!'

'Well, let's see,' Jesus sighed. 'How much bread have you got between you? Well, go and look!'

They checked, and said, 'We've got five loaves and a couple of fish.'

'Oh, give them to me,' Jesus said. He told them to sit down in groups of hundreds and fifties on the grass, and then took the food, said a prayer of thanksgiving, broke the loaves into pieces and handed them to his disciples who went and served the people, and then distributed the fish as well. The amazing thing is that everyone had as much as they needed. More than that – when they cleared up at the end they collected twelve baskets full of scraps! The number of men that were fed amounted to about five thousand.[4]

Subduing the waters of chaos

Here come the waters of chaos again (see on 4:35-41). You may remember that when God released the waters of chaos in Genesis 7, Noah needed a boat to survive – but to be able to walk on the waters unaided would be the mark of someone *really* special!

[45-52] Jesus didn't hang around after that. He immediately ordered his disciples to get into the boat and set out for the other side of the lake, while he stayed behind, got the crowd to disperse, and then took to the

---

1. This is a huge indictment of the spiritual leadership ('shepherds') of Israel – reading Ezekiel 34 with this reference in mind is enlightening.
2. Exodus 16 and Numbers 11 both recount how Moses fed the masses in the desert – and here's Jesus, the new but greater Moses, in a remote place doing the same.
3. The original says '200 denarii', and one denarius was about a day's pay!
4. It's interesting that all three of the synoptic gospels (Matthew, Mark and Luke) refer to 'men' specifically; Matthew makes it clear that the word isn't just a sexist way of saying 'people' by adding 'not counting women and children'.

hills[1] – he needed some space to pray. Evening began to fall – and the boat with his disciples in it was out in the middle of the lake while he was all alone on land. He could see that the boat was struggling to make headway because the wind was in the wrong direction. Then, at some unearthly hour of the morning – somewhere between three and six o'clock – Jesus went out to catch up with them, walking on the surface of the lake. Actually, he was going to go straight past them,[2] but the disciples were terrified. 'It's a ghost!' they started screaming.

'Come on, get a grip,' Jesus called out. 'It's me – don't panic.'

And then something really amazing happened – as soon as Jesus got into the boat with them, the wind dropped – just like that. All ways round, it was pretty impressive stuff, and the disciples were completely awestruck. You see, they'd completely missed the point of the miracle of the loaves – it was beyond the grasp of their understanding.[3]

Healings at Gennesaret

53-56 So, they finished the crossing and got to Gennesaret and tied up at the shore. They'd no sooner got out of the boat than Jesus was recognised and the word spread rapidly through the whole region. Everyone brought their sick friends and relatives to him wherever he went. In the villages, the towns, or even out in the countryside, they found him – they even pleaded to be allowed to touch just the edge of his coat, and all who did that were cured.

Opposition from religious authorities

7 [1-8] Then some Pharisees turned up with a delegation from the Jerusalem scribes.[4] As always they had their eyes peeled for anyone breathing out of turn, and it didn't take them long to notice Jesus' disciples eating in a ritually unclean way – not washing their hands. Now,

---

1. According to John's account of the feeding of the five thousand, the crowd had got entirely the wrong end of the stick and wanted to make Jesus an earthly king whether he wanted it or not. The disciples were probably in danger of being caught up in the hysteria – so it made sense to get them out of harm's way while he stalled the crowd and then took off into the hills to spend some quality time with God.
2. Mark gives no indication as to why Jesus meant to walk past and not help. It's been suggested that it was a test of their faith, and that they failed the test by yelling out to him.
3. The feeding of the five thousand and the calming of the storm have parallel themes: they're supposed to arouse faith in God in times of crisis.
4. Jerusalem! So Jesus was rattling cages at a very high level!

for Jews, and especially Pharisees, this was more than just hygiene – it was a sacred tradition. And if they'd been in the market place, they'd have to do a purification ritual before they touched any food. They had lots of other similar traditions too – like the ritual washing of crockery. Anyway, the Pharisees and scribes buttonholed Jesus.

'Jesus,' they said, 'we've been hearing that your disciples don't observe the sacred traditions – they don't wash before meals.'

'You know,' Jesus answered, 'Isaiah was right about you hypocrites, wasn't he? What was it he said? Oh, yes: "These people pay me lip service, but their real values are a million miles from me! They bring me all this meaningless worship, and proclaim human ideas as if they were holy writ!"[1] You set aside God's own commandments in favour of human tradition.'

9-17 'Oh, yes,' Jesus went on, 'you've got some very smart ways round God's laws, haven't you! After all, Moses did say, "Honour your father and mother", but you tell people they can escape their obligations to their parents by saying, "Sorry, old things, but I can't provide for you in your old age because I've promised the money to God"! So you maintain your own tradition by emptying the word of God of its power – oh, come on!'

Jesus called the crowd nearer to him, and said, 'Now, listen and get this straight: there's nothing outside you that makes you "unclean" if it's taken in – it's what comes out that does that!'

When Jesus went inside the house, leaving the crowd behind, the disciples asked him what he meant – it all sounded like riddles to them!

18-23 'Haven't you got it yet?' Jesus replied. 'Don't you see? What goes in from the outside can't make someone "unclean" because it only affects the stomach, not the heart – it just passes through the system and finishes up being flushed away down the sewer.' (In saying this, he effectively abolished all the food taboos!) Then he went on, 'But what comes *out* is what makes you spiritually unclean – because you know the kind of things that are sluicing around in there, don't you? – all kinds of evil intentions like murder, adultery, promiscuity, stealing, lying . . . It's *that* kind of stuff, coming from within, that makes a person ritually unclean!'

---

1. Isaiah 29:13.

Who's the gospel for?

²⁴⁻³⁰ Things were definitely hotting up, and it seemed like a good time for another strategic retreat – this time to the area around Tyre and Sidon, completely outside Israelite territory. He found a pleasant spot and tried to shut out the world for a time, but it wasn't going to be that simple.

Immediately, a woman whose daughter was possessed by an evil spirit heard about him, and she came and bowed down in front of him. Now, she was actually Greek – Syro-Phoenician to be precise – and she begged Jesus to exorcise her daughter.

'You'll have to join the queue,' Jesus answered. 'I've got to feed the family first[1] – it's really not on, you know, to take food meant for children and throw it to the dogs.'

The woman wasn't having any of that. 'Oh, I know,' she said, 'and I also know that those same dogs get to eat the scraps that the children drop from the table – come on, I'm really not asking for very much, am I?'

'OK, you've made your point well,' Jesus answered. 'You daughter's OK now – the demon's gone.' The woman went home and found her daughter calmly resting in bed, and no hint of the demonic presence.

Jesus gives both sight and speech

³¹⁻³⁷ Jesus moved on from the area of Tyre, going via Sidon to the Decapolis district on the Gentile shore of the sea of Galilee. There, the people brought a man who was not only deaf but could hardly speak[2] – and they pleaded with Jesus to lay hands on him. Well, Jesus wasn't having a consultation turned into a sideshow, so he took the guy aside to a private place. First he put his fingers in the man's ears, and then he licked his finger and touched the man's tongue.[3] Jesus looked up to heaven and sighed deeply. 'Ephphatha!' he said, meaning, 'Be opened!' Immediately, everything was fully functioning – the guy could hear, and he spoke as plainly as anyone else. Jesus gave strict instructions to everyone not to broadcast what he'd done, but the more he told them not to, of course, the more they went and did it. They were absolutely astonished. 'There's nothing he can't do,' they said. 'He can make the deaf hear and the mute speak!'

---

1. Note the 'first'. Jesus always knew his mission was to the Gentiles as well as to Israel, but he clearly believed it was a good strategy to focus on the smaller, local task first.
2. This is a closer translation of the Greek word usually rendered 'dumb'.
3. Not just a healing touch but an act of communication, so the man was able to participate in the act rather than just having it done *to* him.

The feeding of the four thousand

> Another miraculous feeding coming up. So, why bother to record both, if they're so similar? After all, quite a lot of Jesus' miracles are barely mentioned, but this one's retold in detail. The difference here may be that it's Gentiles who are being fed – having been the beneficiaries of the last two miracles. The point's being rammed home that when people considered 'outsiders' are open to what Jesus offers, they will receive!

8 [1-10] At about that time, when as usual a crowd had gathered round, Jesus called his disciples together. 'You know, I can really feel these people's hunger,'[1] he said. 'I mean, they've been traipsing around after me for three days now, and they haven't anything to eat. If I send them home in this state, some of them probably won't even make it – they've come a long way.'

'Well, that's all very fine, Jesus,' his disciples answered, 'but where in this desert of a place are we going to get enough food to feed them?'

'We can begin with whatever you've got,' Jesus retorted. 'Let's be seeing it, then.'

'All we've got,' they said, 'is seven loaves.'

That was more than enough for Jesus – next thing anyone knew he had the crowd sitting down on the ground. Then he took the loaves, gave thanks to God, broke them and gave them to his disciples who distributed them to the people, who in turn passed them on to the crowds. They had a few fish as well, so Jesus said a blessing and told the disciples to hand those out, too. Everyone who joined in the meal was completely satisfied, and when they gathered up the leftovers there were seven baskets full. Altogether, about four thousand people had been fed! Jesus got the crowds to go away, and immediately hopped into a boat with his disciples and took off for the region of Dalmanutha.[2]

---

1. The word 'compassion', used here in some standard translations, is often weakened to 'pity' – which is a pity! Literally, 'compassion' means 'co-suffering' – it means actually feeling the suffering of another, rather than just feeling sorry for them. Important, of course, because Jesus didn't come just to feel sorry for us, but to share our suffering!
2. It seems no one knows where this is, but Matthew (15:39) says they went to Magadan, which might be another name for Magdala.

The demand for proof

[11-13] The Pharisees came to Jesus, trying to trip him up by asking for a sign from heaven. 'Oh, dear me!' groaned Jesus. 'Why does this generation go on and on, asking for signs? I'm telling you straight, you're not getting one!' And with that he went back to the boat and left again for the other side.

The disciples still don't get it!

[14-21] Now, guess what – after all that had happened, the disciples had forgotten to bring any food, and only had one loaf in the boat with them! 'You've got bigger issues to worry about, anyway,' Jesus told them, 'like the Pharisees and Herod's cronies, for example – the "yeast" they use that pervades and corrupts all their teachings[1] – that's what you need to be concerned about.'

The disciples missed the point completely. 'He's just miffed because we forgot the bread,' they moaned to one another.

'Oh, what is it with you!' Jesus exclaimed. 'Why are you still going on about bread? Haven't you caught on yet? Are you completely devoid of understanding? Is it that you have eyes but can't see, and ears but can't hear?[2] I suppose you've forgotten the five loaves I broke to feed five thousand – how many baskets of leftovers did you collect afterwards?'

'Twelve,' they admitted.

'And the seven we used to feed four thousand – how many baskets of scraps did we collect up?'

'Seven.'

'And you *still* don't understand?'[3]

The blind can see, though!

> The first major section of the gospel ends with the miracle of vision: after all the displays of blindness the key to it all is revealed. When all's said and done, it doesn't depend on our ability to see, but on God's power to open our eyes. Thank God for that!

---

1. Slavish adherence to, respectively, the laws of Moses and of Rome.
2. Now the disciples face the same criticism as Jesus levelled at outsiders in 4:12.
3. As Paul would emphasise in his letters, it's all about grace, not works. Salvation is free to all whose minds are open enough to accept it – not to be earned by slavishly following rules and regulations, as the Pharisees thought.

[22-26] The next place they came to was Bethsaida, where some people brought a blind man to meet Jesus. They begged him to touch the guy, so Jesus took him by the hand and led him away from them, out of the village.[1] First, Jesus put saliva on the man's eyes, then he did the laying on of hands. 'Can you see anything?' he asked.

'You know, I do believe I can!' the man answered. 'People – yes, definitely people – thought they were trees at first, but they're walking about.'

After Jesus had put his hands on the man's eyes again, the guy really made an effort to focus. Then his sight was fully restored and everything was crystal clear to him. Jesus sent him home. 'Don't even bother to go back to the village,' he said.

---

1. Once again, there's all the difference in the world between healing a suffering human being and pulling off a publicity stunt. Jesus knew the difference, whereas sometimes we can confuse the two.

The great journey to glory

Jesus has been calling people to follow him, and has certainly shown the authority behind that call, and now the journey really begins. They are to follow him not simply on an itinerant ministry, but on the journey that will lead to his glorification. The trouble is, though, that he's still dealing with people whose eyes are blinded – blinded now by the traditional expectations of the Messiah. They're ready to follow him to glory, but not yet to accept that the glory will come through suffering! The second main section of the gospel begins with the vital question, and ends with another miracle of opening blind eyes (10:46-52).

So, who is Jesus?

Do the disciples yet understand what all this is about? It's good news and bad news: Peter has certainly recognised who Jesus is – but he's still understanding that identity in terms of human expectation, not divine purpose.

[27-30] Jesus led his disciples on to the villages of Caesarea Philippi. On the way, he said to them, 'What is it that people are saying, about who I am?'

'All sorts of things,' they told him. 'Some say you're John the Baptiser come back, others say you're Elijah. Some are even saying you're one of the other prophets.'

'OK,' Jesus said. 'Now, who do *you* say that I am?'

Simon Peter was right there with the answer. 'You're the Messiah,' he said. Jesus gave his disciples a warning not to go telling everybody about him.[1]

Jesus prepares his disciples

We're well into the last days of Jesus' Galilean ministry, and he needs to prepare his disciples. If we were responsible for assessing their progress, we'd probably conclude they were nowhere near ready for the ordeal ahead, and suggest to Jesus that he reschedule! Fortunately, Jesus has more faith – both in God and in people.

---

1. Again, the time wasn't yet ripe. People still thought the Messiah would be a warlord – so bandying words like that around in such a climate would have been distinctly counter-productive!

Jesus foretells his death and resurrection

[31-33] Now, Jesus began trying to prepare his disciples for what had to happen in the future: suffering, rejection, being tortured and abused by the chief priests, elders and scribes, being killed, and finally rising to life after three days.

Jesus really laid this on the line, but Peter took him to one side and started having a go at him.

Jesus rounded on Peter, one eye also on the disciples. 'Get out of my way, Satan!' he said. 'You're seeing everything from a human point of view when it should be from God's!'

[34-38] Then Jesus called the crowd to join them, and said, 'If anyone's really determined to be a follower of mine, they've got to be prepared not to call their life their own – ready to take up the cross and follow in my footsteps. Those who are obsessed with safeguarding what they have in this life will lose it. On the other hand, those who are prepared to lose what they have now for my sake and that of the gospel will discover real life through letting go. What good does it do to gain the whole world if in doing so you lose your true self? With what do you propose to buy it back again? Put it this way: if anyone in this faithless generation finds me or my words an embarrassment in these faithless times, well, don't expect to have it both ways when the Son of Man comes in the glory of his Father, with all the angels with him – that's all.

9 [1] 'I'm telling you straight, there are people standing here, right now, who won't taste death before they realise that the kingdom of God has come with power.'[1]

Transfiguration: a glimpse of Christ glorified

[2-10] Six days later Jesus called together Peter, James and John, and went up a high mountain with them – no one else, just them – and was transfigured right there in front of them. His robes were brilliant white – whiter than any kind of bleach on earth could have got them. Then Moses and Elijah appeared, talking with Jesus. 'Hey, Rabbi, this is terrific,' Peter called out. 'I mean, this is *so* the place to be! Why don't I build three shelters – one for you, one for Moses and one for Elijah?' The

---

1. The kingdom was in an important sense inaugurated with the death and resurrection of Jesus. This verse doesn't necessarily refer to the second coming. Also, see 'Coming of the Son of Man' in the Glossary of Key Words and Phrases.

poor guy was babbling desperately because he didn't know what to say, probably because they were all scared witless.

Suddenly there was this cloud coming right over all of them, and a voice said, 'This is my special Son – listen to him!'

And that was it! Suddenly they couldn't see anything out of the ordinary at all – just Jesus. So they started off down the mountain and Jesus warned them not to go spreading it around – not until the Son of Man had been raised from the dead. So they kept quiet about it – but that didn't stop them wondering what this rising from the dead business meant.

[11-13] Then they asked, 'The scribes have always taught us that Elijah's going to return publicly first – why?'

'Yes, I know,' Jesus said. '"Elijah is certainly coming, and he's going to put everything right", unquote. Fine, and isn't it also written about the Son of Man, how he's to suffer abuse and contempt? Well, I'm telling you, Elijah's been, and they did with him as they saw fit, just as it was prophesied about him.'

Faithless disciples

[14-19] When they got back to where the disciples were, there was a great crowd gathered around, watching them have a terrific argument with some scribes[1] who were there. Immediately they saw Jesus, the crowd got even more hyped up and came running over to him. 'What are you all getting so worked up about?' Jesus asked.

'Well, it's like this, Teacher,' one of the crowd explained. 'I came here to bring my son to you – he's got this bad spirit, see – stops him from talking – and whenever it grabs him it throws him down on the ground and makes him gnash his teeth, foam at the mouth, and go as stiff as a board. It's ghastly! So, anyway, I asked your disciples to do an exorcism, but a fat lot of good they were!'

'Oh, great!' Jesus rounded on his disciples. 'You're no better than the rest of this faithless generation, are you! I sometimes wonder how much more of this I'm expected to put up with! Bring the lad over to me.'

[20-24] So they brought the boy over. The evil spirit took one look at Jesus and went on the offensive in a big way – threw the boy to the ground in

---

1. See 1:22. Having contrasted Jesus' authority with the ineffectual **scribes**, Mark now specifically includes the **scribes** in this story as a foil for the disciples' lack of faith. The two groups aren't as different as Jesus might have hoped! The vital difference, though, lay not in the disciples' own abilities but in the fact that they had Jesus to turn to.

a terrific fit. 'So, how long's this been happening to him?' Jesus asked the father.

'Ever since he was a lad,' the father replied. 'It's awful – sometimes it throws him into the fire, or into water. Well, that could be fatal, couldn't it? Look, if you can do anything, for pity's sake help us!'

'If *I* can?' Jesus echoed. 'If *you* can, more like. For someone with real faith, anything's possible.'

Immediately, the father shouted back, 'Well, of course I've got faith – but it's nothing compared with yours! I *need* your help!'

²⁵⁻²⁷ Jesus could see the crowd getting bigger and closer by the second, so he spoke sternly to the spirit. 'OK, you deaf and mute spirit, I'm giving you an order. Come out of him – and stay out.'

The demon came out, but not before he gave the boy one last fit. 'That's done it!' the bystanders said. 'The kid's dead.' But Jesus just took the lad's hand and lifted him to his feet, and the boy rose.

²⁸⁻²⁹ When Jesus had gone into the house, the disciples asked him privately, 'So, why couldn't *we* do that?'

'That kind,' Jesus replied, 'only respect real authority – the kind that comes from prayer.'

Jesus foretells his death and resurrection a second time

³⁰⁻³² From there they moved on through Galilee – but Jesus wanted to keep a low profile so he could concentrate on getting his disciples to understand. 'The Son of Man,' he said, 'is going to be given up to the worldly authorities – then he's going to be killed. But, three days afterwards, he'll rise again.' His disciples just couldn't get it, though – and they didn't have the nerve to ask what he meant!

Real greatness

³³⁻³⁷ When they reached Capernaum, and Jesus got them somewhere private, he asked, 'Just what was it you were haggling about on the way here?'

Well, they weren't going to tell him that – because they'd been bickering amongst themselves about which of them was going to be the greatest! Jesus sat down and gathered the Twelve around him. 'Look,' he said, 'if anyone really wants to be first in my book, they've got to be willing to be last – bottom of the pile – slave to everybody.' He looked round for a child, and asked one to stand in the middle of them. He put his arms around the child and said, 'Anyone who welcomes someone like this in my name also welcomes me, and anyone who welcomes me welcomes the one who sent me.'

[38-41] 'Hey, Teacher,' John said to him, 'we found this guy doing exorcisms in your name, but don't worry, we soon put a stop to that – he wasn't following us,[1] you see.'

Jesus wasn't impressed:

So what! What do you think you're doing, stopping someone who's doing good – after all, anyone who does great things in my name is going to find it pretty difficult to speak against me, don't you think? Look, it's quite simple: anyone who isn't actually opposing us is effectively on our side.[2] Anyone who gives you even so much as a cold drink because you bear the name of Christ[3] – well, they won't go unrewarded.

[42-50] Don't go thinking you can take advantage of humble people[4] and get away with it. What's coming to anyone who does that will make them think that drowning would have been nice by comparison! And if your own hand tempts you into sin, maybe you'd better cut it off and ditch it – better maimed than damned, wouldn't you say? And if it's your foot, the same applies: lose it – better alive and lame than standing on both feet in eternal fire! Or there again, if your eye leads you astray, get shot of it. Being in the kingdom of God with one eye's a sight better than being in hell with two – you know, where the worm never dies, and the fire never goes out.

You see, everyone's going to be salted with fire.[5] Now, we all know salt's good, but it's not a lot of use if it's not salty any more – what are you going to use to make salt salty again? So keep yourselves well salted and live together in peace.

---

1. Interesting: 'following us', not 'following you'. It's a distinction the Church must always keep in mind.

2 It's interesting to compare this with Matthew 12:30 and Luke 11:23 where Jesus apparently says exactly the opposite. It just goes to show: we have to read things in context, because Jesus always spoke into particular situations.

3. It's likely that this phrase relates directly back to the 'in your name' of verse 38.

4. Often called 'little ones' or 'the least'. Jesus has subtly merged the child image with people who choose service over self-aggrandisement.

5. Jesus is combining two images: the fire (in this case suffering) that refines and purifies, and salt which has a preserving as well as flavouring and purifying function. We're called to maintain our distinctiveness, in order to be a good influence in the world, and the suffering that this entails will itself be part of the process.

Jesus in Judea

10 [1-2] Then Jesus moved on, heading into Judea across the Jordan, with great crowds of people around him and, as usual, being taught by him.

Marriage and commitment

[3-12] Some Pharisees decided to have another go at catching him out. 'Hey, Jesus, is it legal for a guy to divorce his wife?'[1]

'What did Moses command you to do?' Jesus asked.[2]

'Oh,' the Pharisees replied, 'he said we can give the woman a divorce certificate and tell her to sling her hook.'

'That,' said Jesus, 'was simple pragmatism, because he knew you weren't capable of meeting the ideal. But that's not the same as saying it's what God intended, now is it? Doesn't Scripture say that when God made people he "made them male and female",[3] and that "because of this, to this very day, when children grow up into men and women, they move away from their parents and set up new homes together, and become one flesh"?[4] So they aren't just two separate people any more – they're one flesh! In other words that what God has joined together isn't open to being separated by human decisions.'

Later, in private, the disciples pressed him on the point, and he said, 'If someone divorces his wife, and marries someone else, then he's committing adultery – and the same applies to a woman who divorces her husband.'[5]

Jesus blesses the children

[13-16] Then some people started bringing children to Jesus, so that he could lay hands on them. The disciples told them to get lost, and when

---

1. Remember what 'divorce' meant then – in effect, a man's right to consign his wife to the scrap-heap when he was tired of her.
2. Interesting: the Pharisees are concerned about their rights, whereas Jesus emphasises God's *commandment*. He's coming from a totally different starting point. Incidentally, the Bible's full of subtle little twists like this, and it's worth developing an eye for them because they're hugely revealing.
3. Genesis 1:27. Jesus grounds the marriage relationship in nothing less than God's purpose for creation. We are made for relationships of trust and mutuality.
4. Genesis 2:24.
5. This seems a strange thing to say given that a woman in Jewish society was not allowed to divorce her husband. Possibly these words are a later addition, interpreting Jesus' words for a Greek audience, where women had such a right.

Jesus saw that, he really got annoyed. 'Get out of the way and let the little children come to me,' he said, 'because it's to people like these that the kingdom of God truly belongs. I'm telling you straight, you've got to change your whole outlook on things – forget the rat-race and learn to live without all that status-obsession, the way children have to – before you even get a foot in the door!' Then he took the children in his arms and blessed them with the laying on of hands.

The rich man's ambition

> This man wanted to know what he could *do* to secure eternal life. The idea that it can be earned or bought isn't exactly uncommon today either! We find it so hard to accept a gift, don't we? – so hard, in fact, that we sometimes end up missing out on the best things in life.

[17-22] Just as Jesus was getting going on his journey, someone ran up to him, knelt down and said, 'Good Teacher, can you advise me – I'd like to do something that'll guarantee I get eternal life.'

'Save the flattery for God,' Jesus answered. 'He's the only one you should be calling good – and he's what this is all about, isn't he! Look, it's God's laws, not human achievements, that count – and you know his commandments: don't murder, don't commit adultery, don't steal, don't lie about people, don't swindle; *do* honour your parents . . .'

'Teacher,' the man persisted, 'I've done all that since I was just so high – but it doesn't seem enough.'

Jesus really warmed to the guy. 'There's one thing missing,' he said. 'Go and sell all your stuff, and give the money to the poor. Then you'll have real treasure in heaven – the kind that lasts for eternity. Then come and follow me.'

Well, talk about a let-down! The poor man's face was a picture of gloom! That wasn't what he'd wanted to hear at all – because he was remarkably rich – and he went away very unhappy.

[23-31] Jesus looked round at his disciples. 'It's tough,' he said. 'If there's one thing the rich can't afford it's a ticket to the kingdom of God.'

The disciples were completely shocked at what he said. 'My dear friends,' Jesus said kindly, 'it's really, really hard to get into the kingdom of God. You'd see a camel go through the eye of a needle before you saw a rich person earn their way in.'

The disciples were aghast. 'Well, in that case, what hope is there for anyone at all?' they asked.

Jesus gave them one of his knowing looks. 'Ah, now there's the heart of it,' he said. 'It's more than any human being can ever achieve – but depend on the power of God and anything's possible!'

'Fine,' Peter began to answer. 'Well, we've given up everything to follow you.'

Jesus said to them, 'I'm telling you straight, all those who've given up their homes or families for my sake, and for the sake of the gospel, will be recompensed a hundred times over.[1] Now, in this life, I'm talking about: houses and brothers, sisters, mothers, children, land – but there'll be a cost because there'll be persecutions, too – and afterwards, eternal life as well. But an awful lot who are ahead of the game now will come in last, and vice versa.'

Jesus foretells his death and resurrection a third time

[32-34] Continuing on the way towards Jerusalem, Jesus was striding on ahead like a man with a mission – which the disciples found pretty alarming, and the others who were following weren't any too happy either. So he took the Twelve to one side again and spelled out to them what was going to happen. 'Look, we're going to Jerusalem – so it's showdown time. The Son of Man will be handed over, first to the chief priests and scribes – they'll condemn him to death – and then to the Gentile authorities who'll humiliate him first, and then have him flogged and crucified, and on the third day he'll rise to life.'[2]

More jockeying for position – they still haven't learnt!

[35-40] Then James and John, Zebedee's sons, came to Jesus. 'Teacher,' they said, 'we'd like you to do something for us.'

'Oh, yes?' Jesus answered.

'Can you, sort of, well, promise that we'll be the top guys alongside you in your kingdom?'

Jesus said, 'You really don't have any idea what you're asking, do you? I mean, have you got the stomach to drink from the cup that

---

1. If everyone's sharing everything, and 'holding all things in common ownership' (Acts 2:44), then everyone 'owns' countless houses, etc! It's really saying that everyone will be abundantly provided for because of the community principles.

2. This is the third time Jesus has described his death – each time with progressively more detail. The context suggests that he's doing more than just prepare them for the experience. His victory will be startlingly different from their expectations – reached through suffering servanthood and humiliation, not through military glory.

I'm soon going to have to drink from?[1] Can you go through my baptism?'[2]

'What? That – oh, sure!' James and John answered.

'Well,' Jesus told them, 'drink my cup you certainly will – and go through my baptism too – but to have the top places in my kingdom, well, that's not mine to give. That's not something you can aspire to or earn – it's a gift of God.'

[41-45] When the word got round, the other ten were hopping mad with James and John, but Jesus called them to him and spelt it out yet again. 'Look,' he said, 'you know how it is in the old order of things: kings on thrones giving orders to everyone else, bullies having all the clout – a proper rat-race – well, you'd better get it into your heads that it's not going to be like that among you. One of you wants to be thought of as great? Fine, then be a good servant to all the rest. And if you want to be put first, then you'll need to be like a slave, just like the Son of Man who didn't come to be waited on but to serve others, and to pay the cost of human freedom with his own life!'

> Having said this, Jesus deliberately moves towards Jerusalem – towards the fulfilment of these words. Yet, even after the long journey (spiritual as well as geographical) the disciples still can't see that Jesus' triumph in Jerusalem is going to be a very different matter from the worldly takeover they've always expected. We might well ask: 'If they couldn't grasp it after all that, what hope is there for us?' The conclusion of this second main section reminds us of the answer: God can open our blind eyes. The difference here, though, is that the blind man, once sighted, becomes a follower of Jesus. God, then, can work the miracle that opens eyes and creates disciples.

Sight for the blind

[46-52] Jesus moved on through Jericho. As he was leaving, with his disciples and a crowd following him, Jesus came to where Bar-Timaeus son of

---

1. The 'cup of suffering' would be a familiar metaphor to any Jew, and Jesus is trying yet again to get it into the disciples' heads that his route to glory is through suffering. He'll still be trying to do that when he enacts this idea at the Last Supper – and they still won't make sense of it!

2. He's not talking about a religious ceremony here – baptism is the way to new life, and for Jesus that meant going through suffering and death.

Timaeus, a blind beggar, was sitting by the side of the road. 'Jesus!' he shouted. 'Son of David – will you do a kindness for me?' A lot of people tried to shut him up, but he wasn't having any of it and just kept shouting more loudly.

Jesus stopped and said, 'Get that guy over here.'

So they went to the blind man. 'Hey, this is really your day,' they said. 'He's asking to see you.' The man didn't waste any time – just threw his cloak on the floor, jumped to his feet and scuttled over to where Jesus was waiting.

'So,' Jesus asked, 'what is it you want me to do for you?'[1]

'Teacher, I just want to be able to see!'

'Off you go, then,' Jesus said. 'Your faith's healed you.'

Immediately, the man got his sight back and followed Jesus on the road.[2]

Jesus in Jerusalem

> Here begins the ultimate journey, on which Jesus calls us to follow him. But it is the hardest journey of all, as it calls us finally to relinquish all our ideas of status, power, victory, etc., and recognise the greatest victory in defeat, the highest success in failure, the way to the best possible life through a willingness to die. This will be the ultimate revelation. When it is complete, some 'blind eyes' will have been unexpectedly opened while others will have remained resolutely shut.

11 [1-10] They were approaching Bethphage and Bethany at the Mount of Olives within sight of Jerusalem. 'Right,' Jesus said to two of his disciples, 'I'd like you to go into the village, and immediately you get there you'll find a colt tied up – one that's never been ridden. Untie it and bring it to me here. Oh, and if anyone says, "What are you two up to?" just say, "The Lord needs it and he'll return it immediately."'

The disciples went off on their errand and found the colt tied up outside a door, right on the street. As they untied it, the people around

---

1. This is the humble servant talking – not the expert of people's expectations. You or I would probably have just assumed that a blind person wanted to see, but Jesus knew better than to make assumptions.
2. The road to Jerusalem – but also the road through suffering to new life. Some translations say, 'in the Way'. Mark has given us a little parable of discipleship, wrapped up in a miracle.

said, 'Hey! What do you think you're up to, untying that colt?' But as soon as the disciples told them what Jesus had said, they stopped arguing about it and let them go.

Jesus enters the city

So they brought the colt to Jesus, and threw their own coats over its back and Jesus sat on the colt to ride into town. Everybody got in on the act – talk about putting out the red carpet! Some of them used their own coats, while others cut foliage from the fields to put on the road. They were a real sight: crowds in front of Jesus, crowds following behind him, all shouting, 'Saviour![1] Son of David!' and joining in the traditional celebratory chant, 'Congratulations to the one who's coming in God's name!' Then they added, 'Blessed is the coming kingdom of David, our father! Praise God in the highest!'

> The next part of this story is remarkable. Traditionally, this story is often called the 'Triumphal entry', but in fact the entry, in Mark, is far from triumphal. The crowds milling outside the city don't seem very keen to follow Jesus into it. It's all getting a little too hot for them! It's OK to hail Jesus as Messiah out in the country, but to do so in the city itself would be another matter: only those really committed would follow Jesus there – and the crowd aren't.

[11] Jesus himself got to Jerusalem and went to the Temple, but when he'd had a look round it was getting late and he went back to Bethany with the Twelve.[2]

---

1. The word 'Hosanna' literally means 'Save us', but it had come to be used as a shout of praise more than as a prayer in itself. Here the crowd are praising Jesus *as* Saviour.

2. There's a huge sense of anti-climax here. After all that big build-up, Jesus simply goes in, looks round and goes away! I think Mark *wants* us to feel disappointed. Misunderstood throughout his ministry, Jesus has made a last-ditch attempt to show the crowd that he's not the kind of Messiah they expect – by making his entry into Jerusalem not on an all-conquering warhorse but on a gentle colt. The crowd have stayed true to form in two ways. Firstly, the ecstatic behaviour shows that they've completely failed to grasp the point and still think of Jesus as a political liberator; and secondly, for all the fuss they made while he was safely outside the city, where are they now? The message is clear: the crowd will not truly follow in the way of Jesus. For all the apparent popularity, he will make his final journey alone.

A curse on the fruitless tree

Next, we come to an acted parable. Religion that's lost its values, a Temple without true faith, is like a fig tree with no fruit. And ultimately its fate is sealed: destruction.

Jesus isn't being petty and vindictive – he's summing up the meaning of what he is subsequently to do in the Temple.

[12-14] Next morning, a hungry Jesus was back in Jerusalem again, where he saw a fig tree in the distance. When he went over to it, though, all it had on it was leaves – not surprising, really, since figs were out of season. 'Right, that's it,' he said, 'you're dead!' And his disciples overheard.

A curse on fruitless religion

[15-19] Then they came to Jerusalem, where he went into the Temple and laid into the traders. He turned over the money-changers' tables, pulled the chairs out from under the dove-sellers, and stopped people from taking short cuts through the court.[1] 'You know what scripture says,' he roared at them. '"My house is to be a place for prayer for people of all cultures"[2] – you've turned it into a thieves' kitchen!'

That did it as far as the chief priests and the scribes were concerned: Jesus had definitely got to go. The fact was that he terrified the life out of them because the masses were in awe of his teaching. That evening, Jesus and his disciples left the city.

[20-25] Passing that way next morning, they saw what was left of the fig tree – withered away to its very roots. 'Hey, Rabbi, will you look at that!' Peter exclaimed. 'One curse from you, and it's dead.'[3]

'Faith in God's what you need,' Jesus retorted. 'I'm telling you straight, you could say to this mountain, "Get up and decamp into the sea," and if you had real faith it'd be done for you. That's why I'm telling you, if you ask for something – the kind of thing you can ask for

---

1. The Temple offering had to be made in special coinage – without the hated Roman emperor's head on it – and people also needed pure doves for the ritual. So, of course, the chancers had moved in and turned it into a nice little earner!
2. This indicates the real point of all this. The Temple should have been a place where people of any tradition could worship God, but the legalism of the religious authorities had kept people of other cultures out. Symbolically, Jesus is destroying the old, closed Temple which is a barrier, and replacing it with an open one which is what it was always intended to be. Or, to put it differently, he's replacing the lifeless, fruitless Temple with a living, fruitful one.
3. Lifeless tree or lifeless religiosity, it makes no difference – both have got to go.

in faith – believe you've got it, and you'll get it.[1] Oh, yes, and when you're praying, think of it as an opportunity to forgive anyone you've got a grievance against – then, the way'll be open for your Father in heaven to forgive you.'

Who's the authority here?

We now witness a series of confrontations in which the real issue is authority. The religious leaders, in various ways, are trying to assert theirs – if need be by simply undermining Jesus' credibility. The final story in the set points us back to the devastating truth that it is not the outward show or status that is important. The poor widow, who for sheer love gives the little that is her all to God, receives the highest commendation.

Just who does he think he is?

[27-33] Next stop was Jerusalem, and while he was in the Temple the chief priests the scribes and the elders came to have a go at him. 'What authority do you think you have for the things you're doing?' they asked. 'And just who do you think gave it to you?'

'I'll answer your question,' Jesus countered, 'if you can answer mine.[2] The baptism that John introduced – did he do that on heavenly authority or was it just a human invention? Go on, then – answer me!'

That did it – suddenly they were arguing amongst themselves. 'Look, we can't say it was from heaven,' they muttered, 'or he'll ask why we rejected it. And we can't say it was just a human invention, can we!' The fact was they were scared – the people generally believed that John was a prophet, and wouldn't take kindly to the religious experts saying otherwise. So they had to say, 'Well, actually, Jesus, we're not really sure.'

'In that case,' Jesus retorted, 'you won't mind if I don't tell you where my authority comes from – will you!'

---

1. A couple of important points here. Firstly, Jesus' emphasis was on the power of God working through even the tiniest faith – not upon the power of human faith. Secondly, since a world where this was happening all the time would be unthinkable, Jesus was clearly using a picture to say that God would do impossible things if only there were an atom of faith for him to work with.
2. This was a standard technique in theological debate in those days – a good way of getting to the heart of the matter.

The parable of the vineyard

> The religious authorities would be familiar with images of Israel as God's vineyard. Jesus highlights the fact that God's prophets have traditionally been abused and murdered, and his Son doesn't expect to be treated any better.

12
[1-12] Then Jesus started speaking in parables. He said:

There's a landowner, and he plants a vineyard – fences it round, digs a winepress, builds a watchtower. Then he lets it out to tenants and goes abroad. When the time comes, he sends a servant to bring him some of the profits from his vineyard. What do the tenants do? They beat the servant and send him back empty handed. So the landowner sends another – and that one gets his head split open and his dignity shredded. He sends yet another, and this time they go right over the top and kill the guy. And so it goes on – servant after servant either killed or beaten. Eventually there's only one more person he can send – a really dear son. 'They're bound to respect my own son,' he thinks. So do they? Not a bit of it.

'It's the son,' they say, 'the one who's down to inherit it all. If we get rid of him, perhaps we can take over!' So they grab hold of him, kill him and sling his body outside the vineyard. Now, what's the owner going to do? He'll come down on those tenants like a ton of grapes, destroy them completely and re-let the vineyard to others.

Don't tell me you haven't read the Bible passage that says, 'The stone that the expert builders rejected has turned out to be the cornerstone – only God could have done this, and it's really amazed us!'[1]

They'd have arrested him on the spot, but they knew better than to take on the crowds. The penny had finally dropped that the parable was against them! So they went away.

More catch questions

> The stakes are rising now: the conflict between Jesus with his Good News of grace and the legalistic old guard with their bad news of rules and regulations.

1. Psalm 118:22-23.

Should we pay taxes?

13-17 Then the Pharisees became all the more determined to trap Jesus. They got together with some of Herod Antipas's cronies, and cooked up a dilemma. 'Excuse us, Teacher,' they oiled, 'but we know you're a man of integrity and all that stuff – not afraid of anyone, always ready to speak the truth. So we were wondering whether you think it's right for Jews to pay taxes to the Roman Emperor or not. Should we pay, or refuse?'[1]

'I know what your game is,' Jesus said, 'trying to catch me out. Look, show me a coin, somebody.' They showed him a coin, and he asked, 'Now, tell me, whose head is this on the coin – and whose inscription?'

'Caesar's,' they answered.

'Exactly!' Jesus responded. 'So give to Caesar whatever he's got a right to, and to God what belongs to God. That plain enough for you, is it?'

That told them – left them completely dumbstruck.

Marriage in heaven

18-23 Next to try their luck were the Sadducees, who didn't believe in life after death. They had a question for Jesus. 'Teacher,' they said, 'you know that according to the law of Moses, if a man dies leaving his widow childless, then his brother has to marry his widow so that she can have children? Well, we've got an interesting case for you. There were these seven brothers, see, and the first one got married but then died without having become a father. So the next brother married his widow, but they didn't have any children either. Well, would you believe it – all seven of them in turn married her and died childless – and then she died herself. So, we were wondering – in the afterlife,[2] whose wife will she be? I mean, she's legally married to all seven, isn't she?'[3]

24-27 'Now you're really showing your ignorance!' Jesus said. 'Resurrection life is a totally different order from this one – marriage and remarriage don't enter into it! And as for resurrection itself, haven't you read

---

1. They must really have thought they'd got him, now. If he said, 'Yes', he'd lose his street cred among devout Jews, and if he said, 'No', then Herod's lot would be straight on to the Romans, accusing him of sedition.
2. In which, you may remember, the people asking the question didn't believe!
3. This was supposed to show that belief in resurrection was unrealistic – as if God would be defeated by a simple problem like that!

in the book of Moses – you know, the bit about the burning bush – the title God gives himself, "I am the God of Abraham, Isaac and Jacob" – which, since he's the God of the living, not of the dead, would be pretty difficult without a resurrection, wouldn't it? Sorry, lads – wrong again!'

The greatest commandment

[28-34] Now, one of the scribes overheard the argument and was impressed, so he decided to ask a question. 'Which of all the commandments,' he asked, 'is the greatest one?'

Jesus answered, 'Well, the first priority is: "Listen, Israel: our God is the only God, and you're to love God with all your heart, soul, mind and strength." And here's the second: "Love your neighbour as yourself." There simply aren't any greater commandments than these.'

'No doubt about it, Teacher,' the scribe said, 'you're well on the mark there. One God, no other, and loving him with all your heart, your intellect, your strength, and loving your neighbour as yourself – well, that's worth more than any number of ritual offerings and sacrifices, don't you think?'[1]

Jesus was impressed. 'When it comes to the kingdom of God,' he said, 'you're not far off.' No one dared challenge him again, after that.

Who is the Messiah?

[35-37] When Jesus was teaching in the Temple, he said, 'It's a funny thing, the way the scribes call the Messiah "Son of David". I mean, David himself – under the inspiration of the Spirit – says, "God said to my Lord, 'Take your place on my right, while I make your enemies a rest for your feet.'"[2] I mean, if David calls him Lord, how can he be David's son?'[3] The crowd loved it!

[38-40] Jesus went on, 'Now, be careful not to be taken in by the scribes, parading their fancy outfits and revelling in the public glory. Oh, and don't they just love the best seats in the synagogues and the top table at official functions! At the same time as they're depriving widows of their

---

1. This isn't belittling the sacrifice tradition, but rather saying that what God wants is a proper relationship with and between his people: all the true spiritual qualities that the various sacrifices were intended to represent.
2. Psalm 110:1.
3. Jesus isn't denying that he's a descendant of David. He's saying he's not *only* that, but actually much, much more.

homes,[1] they'll make long pretentious prayers in public. Oh, yes, they'll find they get the worse judgement!'

The widow's generosity

[41-44] Jesus went and sat near the big offertory box, and watched the crowds making their offerings. The rich put in sizeable amounts, but then a really poor widow came up and dropped in two copper coins – worth less than a penny between them. Jesus called his disciples over. 'I'm telling you straight,' he said, 'this really hard-up widow's given more than all those others put together. They only gave what they wouldn't miss, didn't they? – but she, for all her poverty and need, has given everything she had to live on.'[2]

The destruction of the Temple

Anyone who wants to think of God as little more than a hot-water bottle – there to provide comfort and reassurance – would probably be better off not reading this bit. As has already been seen, proclaiming God's free, unconditional love issues a challenge to the powerful vested interests in the world – especially the religious ones. So, while God wants nothing for us but love, peace and true happiness, the very offer of those things will provoke violent reactions from those with positions to defend. And they'll defend them even to their own destruction.

13 [1-4] As Jesus left the Temple, one of his disciples said, 'Hey, Teacher, will you get a load of this! Great stones! Incredible buildings!'

'You think so?' Jesus replied. 'Well, take a good look at these great buildings, because there won't be a single stone left standing on top of another – the whole thing's going to be flattened.'

When he was sitting on the Mount of Olives, opposite the Temple, Peter, James, John and Andrew came for a private chat. 'Look, are you going to tell us when this disaster's going to happen?' they asked him.

---

1. Remember, a widow would have no legal rights and no rights to property. So the religious establishment's strict legalism was directly contrary to the compassionate demands of Jesus.
2. Now, you need *real* faith to do that!

'What sort of clues should we be looking for?'

> This next passage needs to be handled carefully. It's tempting to try to use it to predict the end of the world, but if we read closely we find Jesus is warning us against precisely that. You might like to flip back to the introduction to Matthew 24, to see how Jesus is drawing a parallel between the short-term, temporal showdown that can already be foreseen, and the longer-term, cosmic one that is not for us to predict.

The apocalypse

[5-8] Jesus answered:

Oh, don't get hung up on that! Don't be fooled – all kinds of frauds and posers will come along in my name, saying, 'Hey, guys, I'm the one!' – and they'll fool a lot of people. Oh, and the same goes for wars and dire rumours – I mean, you're always going to have those things going on, but that doesn't mean the end's just round the corner. Yes, of course nations will make war on one another, there'll be all the usual earthquakes and famines, and things – but that's just the start of it: the beginnings of the labour-pains of a new age coming to birth!

Persecutions

[9-13] But you take care, now — because, make no mistake, these people can be dangerous: they'll put you on trial on trumped-up charges; they'll have you publicly flogged – and that's just the religious people, but don't worry, the politicians will get stuck in, too. You'll be tried by the highest human authorities, just because you're committed to me – but that'll be your opportunity to testify – get my story to the wider world! So when you find yourself being handed over and put on trial, don't start fretting in advance about what words you're going to use – just say what's given to you at the time, because you aren't there to speak for yourselves. Simply let God's Spirit speak through you.

Oh, it's going to get nasty – you'll find families split apart, all turning on one another – and people will hate you with a passion, just because of me. But anyone who keeps the faith through it all will be saved.

The desolating sacrilege

[14-20] When you see the ultimate desolating sacrilege standing in the place it's got no right to be[1] (work it out for yourselves),[2] that is *not* the time to hang around! Time to take to the hills, pronto: if you're up on the housetop, don't stop to get anything from inside and save your precious possessions; if you're in the field, don't go home to get your coat. It'll be particularly ghastly for pregnant women and nursing mothers – and you'd better pray that it doesn't happen in the winter.[3] At that time there'll be misery such as hasn't been seen since the beginning when God created the world, and won't be again – in fact, if events were to run their full course no one could be saved, not even the faithful people, but that won't be allowed to happen.

[21-23] And don't believe it when people say, 'Look, here's the Messiah', or 'There he is', because these will be great times for impostors – false messiahs and prophets. Oh, they'll do all the impressive tricks, claiming that they're 'signs', intent on deceiving people – even some who are faithful. Remember, I've given you advance warning.

The coming of the Son of Man

[24-27] As soon as that stage is over, the sun will go dark, the moon will stop giving light, stars will fall from heaven, and the entire order of things will be shaken up. Then they'll recognise 'the Son of Man coming in clouds',[4] with terrific power and glory. Then he'll send his messengers, and gather faithful people from all points of the compass and right across the whole universe.

Remember the fig tree

[28-32] Take the fig tree as an example: when the branches soften and the leaves start to sprout, you know that summer's coming. Well, in the same way, when you see these things happening, you'll know that

---

1. Daniel 9:27; 11:31; 12:11.
2. This editorial insertion would be understood by Jews who knew their Bible, but completely meaningless to Romans. Since Daniel promises devastating judgement against the 'desolator', this clever encryption was a wise precaution by the gospel writers.
3. . . . when roads would be quagmires.
4. Daniel 7:13. In that passage, the 'Son of Man' doesn't come to earth, but comes *to God* to receive glory and power. So while, of course, this *may* be about the second coming, there again it may not.

the 'desolating sacrilege' I told you about[1] is right at the very gates. I'm telling you straight, this generation won't have disappeared until all these things have happened.[2] Trust me on this – I'm giving you my word on it, and that's more solid and reliable even than the universe itself!

Mind you, if you're looking for a date for the final big event, I can't help you. No one knows that, not the angels in heaven, not the Son, only the Father.

Keep watching

[33-37] Stay alert! Watch! You just don't know when the time's going to be. Think of a man going on a journey. Before he leaves home, he calls his staff to a meeting, and gives each of them responsibility for some of the work, and tells the doorkeeper to keep watch. So watch – because you just don't know when he's going to come back. Could be evening, or midnight, maybe cock-crow or early in the morning. And you don't want him coming and catching you all napping, now do you? So I'll say to you what I say to everybody: watch!

The Passion Narrative

The plotting thickens

14[1-2] Just two days before the Passover – the feast of unleavened bread – the chief priests and scribes were in an unholy huddle, plotting to arrest Jesus discreetly and kill him – but how? 'We can't do it in public,' they said, 'not with all these crowds here celebrating the festival – they'll go ballistic!'

Jesus is anointed

[3-9] As if to prove their point, a woman came up to Jesus while he was having a meal at Bethany, sitting at table in the house of Simon the

---

1. See verse 14.
2. There's the key to the issue. If Jesus had been accurately predicting the literal end of the world in the previous verses, then you wouldn't be here to read this. However, if he was predicting the worldly events of that same century, then we don't have a problem with this verse. The point is that he's using the imminent historical apocalypse as an image *foreshadowing* the big one – not predicting it exactly.

Leper,[1] and poured a whole alabaster jar of really expensive perfume – pure nard, it was – must have cost a bundle! – all over his head. The other guests didn't appreciate it at all. 'What a terrible waste!' they said. 'This perfume could have been sold for a small fortune and the money could have been given to charity.' So they all had a go at her about it.

Jesus knew exactly what was going on. 'Leave her alone!' he said. 'Why are you getting at her when she's performed such a beautiful service for me? Look, you'll always have poor people around – and if you really cared that much you could be giving to them right now! – but you won't always have me. You realise what she's done? She's prepared me for burial in advance. This is an unforgettable act! I'm telling you straight, she'll go down in history – wherever my story is told, she'll be remembered!'

Betrayal!

[10-11] Judas Iscariot, one of the Twelve, made his decision. He went to the chief priests, and offered to let them know when it would be safe to grab Jesus. They thought all their birthdays had come at once, and promised to make it worth his while – money-wise. So Judas was on the lookout for a chance to betray him.

The Last Supper

[12-16] On the first day of the Festival period when the Passover lamb was due to be sacrificed, the disciples said, 'Jesus, where do you want us to set the Passover meal up for you?'

Jesus told two of them, 'Go into the town, and look for a man carrying a water jar.[2] Follow him. And when he goes indoors, say to the house-holder, "The Teacher says, 'Where's the guest room you've provided so that I can celebrate Passover with my friends?'" He'll show you a large upstairs room, all furnished and ready – set the table there.' The disciples set out and it all happened the way Jesus had said. So the Passover meal was prepared.

---

1. Strange name, since had he truly been a leper he'd have been banished to a leper colony. Mark doesn't give us any explanation, leaving us to assume, perhaps, that Simon was a leper whom Jesus had healed.
2. There wouldn't be many of those – carrying water was seen as women's work and beneath a man's dignity! What a sign of the kingdom! If we want to serve Jesus, then we need to be prepared to 'follow', in more senses than one, the Man who carries water!

[17-21] That evening they sat down together – Jesus and the Twelve. While they were eating, Jesus said, 'I'm telling you straight, one of you's a traitor; he's going to give me away – one who's actually sharing food with me!'[1]

They were horrified. 'You surely don't mean me?' each of them was asking.

'It's one of the Twelve,' Jesus said. 'Someone who's been dipping into this common dish with me,'[2] Jesus emphasised. 'Well, the Son of Man is fulfilling the scriptures, but a curse on the one who betrays him – that man's going to wish he'd never been born!'

The Lord's Supper

The Church has debated the next passage for centuries. What we can say is that it's a graphic acted parable of what's about to happen: Jesus' body torn and broken, his blood poured out, and in some infinitely mysterious way that sacrificial self-giving is going to strengthen and sustain his people like food. We as it were, 'feed on the life and death of Christ'.

[22-25] Later in the meal, Jesus took a loaf of bread, gave thanks to God, broke it and gave it to them. 'Take this,' he said. 'This is my body.' Then he took a cup, gave thanks and gave it to them, and they all drank. 'This is my blood,' he said, 'opening up a new covenant – a whole new relationship with God. It's poured out for many people. I'm telling you straight, I shan't be drinking the "fruit of the vine"[3] again until I drink it in the new life in the kingdom of God!'

[26-31] A hymn ended the meal, and Jesus led his disciples out for the last time towards the Mount of Olives.

---

1. For Jews, to share table fellowship included an obligation to be at peace – at the very least while the food remained in the body. Judas was therefore contemplating an even more unspeakable act than we would immediately appreciate.

2. That didn't help much – it could have been any of them! But bearing in mind the note above about table fellowship, and noting also that only close friends would eat from a common dish, brings home the full extent of Judas' treachery.

3. Jesus is quoting the traditional Jewish blessing that he has just used – it's not specifically recorded but its omission from a Passover celebration would have been unthinkable, so the gospel writers can safely leave their readers to assume that it would have been used.

Jesus foretells his disciples' failure

'You're all going to fall away tonight,' Jesus told them. 'Remember what scripture says: "The shepherd will be struck down and the sheep will be scattered."[1] But after I've been raised, I'll be in Galilee ahead of you.'

Peter said, 'I don't care if everybody else deserts you – *I* never will!'

'I'm telling you straight,' Jesus answered, 'this very night, before the second cock-crow, you'll deny that you even know me, not just once but three times!'

At that, Peter got seriously heated. 'Look, Jesus,' he insisted, 'just get this straight – even if I have to die with you I'm never going to deny you!' And so said all the rest.

Jesus' agonising prayer

[32-42] Then they went to a plot of land called Gethsemane[2] and Jesus said, 'You sit here, while I pray.' Then he took Peter, James and John with him, and began to get into a terrible state. 'I don't mind admitting, I'm terrified – scared to death!' he told them. 'Please don't go away – stay awake and watch!' Then he went a few paces further, threw himself flat on the ground, face down, and prayed that, if it were possible, he might be spared this dreadful time. 'Abba,[3] Father,' he pleaded, 'anything's possible for you. Please take this bitter cup[4] away from me! But in the end the only thing that matters is your will, not mine.' Then he came back to his disciples and found them asleep. 'Simon,' he said, 'are you sleeping? Couldn't you keep awake for just for one hour? Wake up – and pray for yourself that you don't get tested more than you can take. Yes, I know your spirit's willing – it's the weakness of the flesh that worries me!'

Jesus went away to pray a second time – using the same words as before. Returning to the disciples, what should he find? They were asleep again – not surprisingly, since they were completely exhausted – and they didn't know what to say to him. Then he came back for the third time. 'Still asleep?' he said. 'Still resting? Well, that's enough. The moment's here, and the Son of Man's betrayed into the clutches of people

---

1. Zechariah 13:7.
2. Literally, Gethsemane means 'oil-press' – appropriate on the Mount of Olives.
3. 'Abba' was the familiar, affectionate form of 'Father', similar to our 'Daddy'.
4. The 'cup of suffering' was a familiar Jewish image. Jesus used it when challenging James and John in 10:38.

who hate him! Come on, wake up – we've got to get going[1] – look, the traitor's here.'

The arrest

[43-52] Immediately, even as he spoke, Judas, one of his own chosen Twelve, arrived, and he'd come mob-handed – a crowd of people armed to the teeth with swords and clubs, sent by the chief priests, scribes and elders. Now, Judas had it all arranged. 'You'll know the one you're to arrest,' he said, 'because I'm going to kiss him – he's my friend, see! Grab him, take him away and guard him well.' With that, he went up to Jesus. 'Rabbi!' he said, and kissed him.

Then they came forward and arrested Jesus. For a few moments, it was chaotic. One of the bystanders lashed out with a sword. He landed a glancing blow and the High Priest's slave lost an ear. Jesus turned to them. 'Just look at you!' he said. 'You come after me, armed to the teeth as if I were some sort of dangerous desperado – but I've been teaching openly in the Temple every day, so why didn't you just take me then? Still, I suppose at least you're fulfilling another prophecy![2] Then the disciples all turned tail and ran for their lives. There was a young man who'd followed him there – wearing nothing except for a linen cloth. The mob made a grab for him, but he wriggled out of the cloth and ran for his life – absolutely naked.

The 'trial' before Caiaphas[3]

[53-59] They led Jesus away to the High Priest, where he was waiting with all the chief priests, scribes and elders. Now, Peter had followed at a safe distance and was sitting in the courtyard with the guards, warming himself by the fire. The chief priests – and in fact the entire council – were determined to make something stick, so that they could have Jesus executed, and they hunted around for false witnesses to testify against him. It wasn't finding witnesses that was the problem, though – there were plenty of them, all willing to lie through their teeth for a fee – it was finding two who'd say the same thing! Eventually, they produced some who'd stand up and perjure themselves consistently with

---

1. Going, that is, not in retreat but into action. This is the moment for which he's saved himself.
2. Isaiah 53:12, probably – 'He was counted as one of the common criminals!'
3. It hardly deserved to be dignified with that title. Apart from the perjury involved, the very time at which it was held was illegal. Trials had to be held in the full light of day.

false testimony: 'We heard him say, "I'll destroy this Temple, which was made with human hands, and build another, not made with hands, in three days flat!"' Mind you, even then they didn't fully agree about it.

[60-65] The High Priest rose to his feet in the middle of the assembly. 'Well, what do you have to say about that testimony?' Jesus said nothing, so the High Priest asked him directly, 'Are you seriously claiming that *you* are the Messiah, the Son of the Blessed One?'[1]

'I am,' Jesus answered, 'and you're about to find out what's meant by "the Son of Man seated at the right hand of God and coming on the clouds of heaven"'.[2]

'That's it!' The High Priest ripped his robe.[3] 'What more witnesses do we need? He's convicted himself!' He turned to the assembly. 'So, now what's your verdict?'

The death sentence was unanimous. Then they really laid into Jesus: spat in his face, covered his face and slapped him, saying, 'Prophesy!'[4] And the guards joined in the abuse.

Peter denies Jesus

[66-72] Meanwhile, Peter, sitting outside in the courtyard, was being mercilessly hounded by a solitary slip of a servant girl! She saw Peter warming himself, and said, 'Hey, you're one of the friends of that Jesus guy from Nazareth, aren't you?'

Peter quailed. 'Who, me? I haven't a clue what you're on about!'

The cock crowed.

He decided to take refuge out in the porch, but this girl wasn't that easily put off. 'This fellow's one of them,' she asserted. He denied it a second time.

There was no hiding place – some of the other spectators went for him, next. 'You must be one of them,' they said. 'It's obvious that you're a Galilean!'

---

1. The very idea would appear ludicrous, with Jesus standing in front of him, bound and humiliated!
2. Caiaphas would indeed witness the enthronement and vindication of Jesus – but not in the way *he* understood Daniel's imagery.
3. Actually part of the judicial procedure laid down in the law. No one is an island, and the guilt of one affects all. The tearing of the Priest's robes at the time of judgement is a powerful symbol of the way society is ripped apart by crime.
4. So why cover his face and then demand prophesy? Go to Luke 22:64 for a possible answer.

Well, Peter started cursing at them, and finally said, 'I swear to you, I don't know the man you're going on about! OK?'

Immediately, the cock crowed for the second time, and Peter remembered what Jesus had told him: 'Before the cock crows twice, you'll deny three times that you know me,' and he dissolved into terrible tears of remorse.

The trial before Pilate

15 [1-5] Morning light saw another frantic conference of the chief priests, elders and scribes, to find the grounds on which they could induce the Romans to execute Jesus. Having hatched their plot, they tied Jesus up and took him to Pilate,[1] who asked, 'Are *you* the King of the Jews?'

'Those are your words,' Jesus answered, and then the chief priests and elders started hurling accusations again.

Pilate said, 'Haven't you any answer? Don't you hear all these accusations they're bringing?' Still Jesus didn't answer – leaving the governor thoroughly frustrated.[2]

[6-15] As it happened, the Governor had a custom of releasing one prisoner, chosen by the people, at the Festival time – and he had in custody a good selection of murderous revolutionaries, including a guy called Barabbas. So when the crowd started reminding him of his custom, he asked them, 'Do you want me to release to you the King of the Jews?'[3] He knew perfectly well that it was only because of their own petty jealousy that the chief priests had brought Jesus to him.

But the chief priests stirred up the crowds to ask for Barabbas to be released instead.

'So what am I supposed to do with the man whom *you* call the King of the Jews?' Pilate asked.

---

1. Pontius Pilate, that is – the Roman Governor of Judea and the only person who could legally sentence anyone to death. The fact that they purported to hate everything that Pilate represented didn't stop them from fraternising with the enemy when it suited their purpose.
2. In Roman civilisation, judges thought it a little unseemly to convict and sentence a defendant without adequate defence – so Jesus' silence didn't help Pilate to feel any better!
3. Pilate had no respect at all for the people he was governing, and we can hear the contemptuous sarcasm in his voice as he parades a bound, battered and utterly humiliated prisoner, and refers to him to the people as the 'King of the Jews'! We see in stark relief the contrast between the world's ideas of power and glory, and God's!

'Have him crucified!' they yelled.

'Now, why should I want to do a thing like that?' Pilate asked. 'What harm's he done?'

They just shrieked all the more loudly, 'Crucify him!'

Well, Pilate knew not to push things too far, realising it was worth his while to keep the crowd sweet,[1] so he released Barabbas, and handed Jesus over to be flogged before being crucified.

The mocking

[16-21] It wasn't that simple though! Before the flogging came ritual humiliation at the hands of the governor's troops. The whole squad gathered round as they dressed him in a purple cloak. Then they plaited some thorns into a crown, put it on his head, and started mocking him: 'Hail, King of the Jews!' Finally, they hit him over the head with a cane, spat on him and knelt in mock homage. When they'd had all the fun they wanted with him, they put his own clothes back on him and led him away for crucifixion. They grabbed a passer-by called Simon, from Cyrene (father of Alexander and Rufus), coming into Jerusalem from the country, and forced him to carry Jesus' cross.

The crucifixion

[22-32] They took Jesus to the place called 'Golgotha' (which means 'the place of the skull') and offered him a mixture of wine and myrrh to drink, but he wouldn't accept it. Then they crucified him and divided up his clothes, gambling to decide who should take what. This was about nine in the morning. The placard over his head read, 'The King of the Jews!' They crucified two rebels with him, one either side. People who passed by ridiculed him, shaking their heads and saying, 'OK, then – you who reckoned you could destroy the Temple and rebuild it in three days – you can start by saving yourself – just step down from the cross – surely you can do a little thing like that!' All the chief priests joined in mocking him, too. 'He saved others,' they jeered, 'but he can't save himself, can he! Oh, come on – he's the king of Israel – so let him just come down from the cross – seeing's believing, after all!' Even the rebels, crucified on either side, joined in and taunted him.

---

1. Remember, it was Passover time, and the city was teeming with pilgrims in a religious fervour – and Pilate knew from bitter experience how easily they could get out of hand.

The death of Christ

[33-41] At midday, there was an eerie darkness everywhere. It lasted until three o'clock in the afternoon. And at three, Jesus gave a great and terrible cry. 'My God,' he screamed, 'my God – why have you deserted me?'[1]

Some of the people said, 'Hey, listen to that! He's calling Elijah.'[2] One individual ran over to where the soldiers were sitting, soaked a sponge in their wine and held it up on a stick for Jesus to drink, saying, 'Let's just wait and see whether Elijah will come to save him!'

Then Jesus gave another great cry, and breathed his last.

At that precise moment, the curtain that hid the holy of holies in the Temple was ripped in two from top to bottom. When the centurion who was standing facing him saw how he died, he said, 'Surely it must be true that this is the Son of God!'

They weren't the only ones there – there were women as well, standing quite a long way away. They included Mary Magdalene and the other Mary – the mother of the younger James, and Joses – and Salome. They were the ones who'd followed Jesus when he was in Galilee; and there were quite a lot of other women who'd come up to Jerusalem with him.

The burial

[42-47] Now, this was the day before the Sabbath – the day of Preparation – so Joseph from Arimathea knew he had to move quickly (Joseph was a respected Council member who was also searching for the kingdom of God). So, in the evening, he plucked up his courage and went to see Pilate to ask to be allowed to take Jesus' body. Pilate was astonished that Jesus was already dead, and sent a centurion to check. When the officer came back and confirmed it, Pilate agreed to Joseph's request. So Joseph took Jesus' body, wrapped it lovingly in a clean piece of linen, and placed it in a tomb, hewn out of the rock. He rolled a huge stone across the mouth of the tomb. Mary Magdalene and the other Mary, the mother of Joses, watched where Jesus was buried.

---

1. Psalm 22:1. It has been suggested that Jesus used this cry deliberately to point us to the psalm, and that he was not actually feeling such deep despair himself. However, we have to ask what it means for Jesus truly to share our experience of death. For me, this haunting cry makes the whole gospel infinitely more real. God, in Jesus, did not merely 'dress up' as a human being – he truly became human and went through all that this implies.
2. It seems they might have misheard him – mistaking 'Eli', the Hebrew word for addressing God, for 'Elias'.

The Resurrection

> Considering the subject matter, the next part of the story is written in a remarkably low-key way by Mark. In particular, he reports no joy but only fear on the part of the women. This is the ultimate example of Mark's emphasis on human blindness in the face of God's revelation. Even these most faithful of Jesus' friends cannot comprehend the gospel when it appears (at least to our modern-day eyes) to stare them in the face! The real point, though, is that it's not words but the Word that we have to encounter. The women, like all creation, are blind to God's revelation until a personal encounter with [the risen] Christ opens their eyes!

16 [1-8] As the Sabbath ended, Mary Magdalene, with the other Mary – the mother of James – and Salome, got together some spices so that they could anoint Jesus' body in the traditional way.[1] Then, very early on the Sunday, they went to the tomb just after daybreak. 'The trouble is,' they were saying on the way, 'who's going to shift the stone that's across the tomb entrance?' Then, when they looked, they found that the stone was already rolled back – and it was no lightweight, let me tell you! Very odd – but it got odder still.

They went in – nervously, no doubt – and found some young man in a white robe, sitting as calm as you like to the right of the burial chamber.

'Don't be frightened,' he said. 'You're looking for Jesus, from Nazareth, who was crucified. But have I got news for you! He's risen – he's not here. See for yourselves – look at the empty space where they laid him to rest. Then, when you've seen, go and tell his disciples, and Peter, that he's going to Galilee ahead of you – there you'll see him, just as he told you.'

Well, they didn't hang around – rushed out of the tomb, trembling with fear and amazement, and said nothing to anyone at all, they were so frightened.

> Things get a little bit complicated here. The various ancient manuscripts give us three possible endings (the oldest finishing at this point). In itself, that's really not so surprising given that every single copy was hand-written. The important thing for us is that,

---

1. Presumably, in the hurry to get Jesus buried before the Festival, there hadn't been time for these vital rituals.

whichever ending we follow, Mark has proclaimed the Good News of the life, death and resurrection of Jesus Christ, Son of God.

The shorter ending

This conclusion puts the emphasis on proclamation. Mark's main purpose in writing his book was to assist in the proclamation that was, of course, already happening. So this paragraph shows God glorified in the *proclamation* of his Good News.

9-10 They went and gave a quick run-down of what they'd been told to the disciples who were with Peter. After this, Jesus used them to send out to the whole world, from east to west, the holy and imperishable gift: the proclamation of wholeness and eternal peace!

The longer ending

Some of the old manuscripts have this additional section, which serves a different but important purpose: to emphasise the need for even those closest to Jesus to encounter him as the risen Christ before their eyes were fully opened to the truth.

9-20 Now, after Jesus rose from the dead, early on the Sunday, the first person he appeared to was Mary Magdalene (remember her – the one from whom he'd cast out seven demons?). Anyway, she went and told his grief-stricken friends. And, what do you know – they didn't believe her!

Then he appeared, but differently, to a couple of them who were walking out into the country, and they went back and told the rest, but – yes, you've guessed it – they didn't believe them either!

Then, later on, he showed himself to the eleven while they were having a meal – and had a real go at them for not believing the others, stubborn, sceptical crew that they were. Then he said to them, 'Right, it's procla-mation time. So get out there and proclaim! Tell the whole creation the good news. People will accept it or not – with the salvation that goes with it – that's for them to choose. And you'll know the ones who believe – you'll recognise the signs – because they'll do great things in my name: they'll exorcise demons, speak in tongues – even handle snakes or drink poison without being harmed by it[1] – and they'll heal the sick with the laying on of hands.

The Ascension

When the Lord Jesus had finished talking to them, he was exalted to heaven to sit at the right hand of God. And his disciples? They went out and got on with the proclamation – and the Lord worked through them all the signs he'd promised.

---

1. Now, I really wouldn't try this at home – or anywhere else, come to that – if I were you. There are plenty of creative ways for us to test and prove our faith – ways that benefit other people, rather than simply draw attention to, and invite harm on, ourselves.

Luke

The Gospel according to Luke

'Jesus saves.'

As with the other Gospel writers, Luke had various things he especially wanted to tell us about Jesus. One of these, which he was particularly keen to emphasise, could be expressed in the simple statement above. Other writers also say that Jesus saves, but Luke makes a special point of it, and in choosing which stories to include and how to present them he highlights the saving nature of Jesus' work.

However, he doesn't only mean that Jesus saves from death or from hell: Jesus also saves from all things that make our present life less than it could be – in particular, rejection, social exclusion, prejudice and such-like. Luke saw that Jesus was especially concerned for the powerless people who were mistreated, neglected or simply undervalued. All kinds of people who were looked down on or excluded by others found them-selves saved from their humiliation by Jesus – and negative social attitudes challenged. While by no means neglecting other aspects (or having a monopoly on these insights, for that matter), Luke chooses to highlight these events. It's not that only Luke shows these things but that Luke particularly underlines them. It's thought that he might have been a medical doctor, which could account for his particularly compassionate approach.

This concern for the excluded shows in Luke's emphasis upon Jesus' attitude to Gentiles (people not born Jews and generally considered to be outsiders). It's likely that Luke himself was a Gentile. If so, no doubt he'd had some experience of the early Church's prejudices before he wrote his account of the gospel. And he wrote it, as far as we can tell, for a particular person (Theophilus) who was a Gentile too, and who might have particularly needed to encounter the compassionate, all-welcoming Christ presented by Luke's writing. Not everyone, though, would have warmed to this aspect of Jesus, and Luke pulls no punches in showing us this. Those who had a vested interest in keeping the social barriers in place were seriously threatened by Jesus, and reacted with hostility and eventually violence. So while Jesus, seen through Luke's eyes, is com-passionate, he is no wimp! Those who would oppress the vulnerable find a courageous and fiercely committed opponent in Jesus.

Some other things we know about Luke:

- He was not an eye-witness of Jesus' work – he makes clear in his introduction that he is relying on others for that.

- He was with Paul on his missionary journeys before any of the gospels were written.
- He was also the author of the book of Acts.

Luke Route Planner

You might find this helpful to give you a quick overview of the journey ahead.

Prologue

Dedication

We don't know who Theophilus (verse 3) was. His name simply means 'Friend of God,' which leads some people to think that this is Luke's rather stylish way of addressing his readership in general. Equally, Theophilus could have been a wealthy patron whom Luke needed to impress in order to get his book published, or he could have been a Gentile convert wanting to know more about Christianity. Whoever the intended recipient, the importance of the gospel as a record of the birth, life, death and resurrection of Jesus is unaffected.

1 [1-4] Many people have set pen to papyrus in order to create a proper record of the way God's purposes have been fulfilled among us – and they've been careful to be true to those early accounts from people who actually saw it all at first hand and became ministers of the word. So, I did my research very carefully and now I'm ready to provide a structured account for you, Most Excellent Theophilus, so that you can be quite confident about the things that you've learnt already.

The Birth Narrative

The book begins, as it will end, by highlighting the vital role played by women in this fulfilment of God's purpose. The empowering and honouring of those whom society counts worthless is a fundamental theme of Luke, and women represent one group of such people.

We meet two women who are both, for different reasons, thought of as of little importance. In that culture, a woman's only role of any significance was to bear and raise children. If she couldn't do that – whether because like Elizabeth she was 'barren' (and too old) or like Mary a virgin – then she would be regarded as insignificant. God takes two such women and gives them a central role in his purpose.

Elizabeth who 'couldn't conceive'

[5] It was during the time that Herod was king in Judea: Zechariah was a priest from a long and respected tradition – the order of Abijah – and his wife Elizabeth was a descendant of Aaron, no less.

[6-7] Now, let's be clear about this: neither of them had anything to be ashamed of. They kept all the commandments, obeyed all the rules, and there was no reason for God to be punishing them at all.[1] And yet they had no children – Elizabeth was infertile,[2] and anyway they were both getting on a bit in the age stakes.

[8-12] One day it was Zechariah's turn to do the priestly duties, and he went into the Temple to burn incense. All the worshippers were there, on the other side of the curtain, praying. Then an angel appeared, standing on the right-hand side of the altar, making Zechariah jump. The poor guy was terrified.

[13-20] 'Hey, calm down, Zechariah,' the angel said. 'Your prayer has been heard – and it's going to be answered. Your wife Elizabeth is going to give you a son, and you're to call him John.[3] Not only will he give *you* enormous joy – the day he's born will be a great day for an awful lot of people. God's got a very special purpose for him: because of him, a lot of people are going to get to know God again. He's not to drink wine, or anything alcoholic for that matter, and right from the start he'll be filled with God's Spirit. He'll go before God like a second Elijah, bringing reconciliation and faith – generally getting people ready to meet him.'

Zechariah was struggling to take all this on board. 'How can I believe a thing like that?' he said. 'I mean, I'm no youngster, and my wife's getting on a bit, to put it mildly.'

'I am Gabriel,' the angel told him. 'I stand in the very presence of God himself – and I've been sent to give you this good news. Now if you find it hard to believe an authoritative word like that – a word that's to be fulfilled right in your own time – well, you'd better have a

---

1. That would have been most people's explanation for their childlessness in those days.
2. The fertility of men was rarely, if ever, questioned in ancient society.
3. In that, as in other cultures, naming someone was a mark of authority, even ownership. So for *God* to name a child signified that God had chosen that person for a special purpose. In the case of John, the name was given before birth, giving resonant echoes of passages such as Jeremiah 1:5: 'Before you were formed in the womb, I knew you, and before you were born I had a purpose for you.'

bit of time for silent reflection. So you can be quiet – mute, in fact – we'll stop you speaking until the time all these things happen.'

²¹⁻²⁵ All this time, the congregation were waiting for Zechariah to come out – and they were starting to get worried.[1] When he did emerge, he couldn't talk, of course – which led them to guess that he'd seen a vision while he was in there. He kept making signs to them, but was quite unable to speak out loud. As soon as his duties were completed, he went home.

Not long after this, Elizabeth his wife found she was pregnant and shut herself away for five months. She was filled with a terrific sense not only of joy but of relief. 'This is what God's done for me,' she said. 'He's completely vindicated me – taken away all the disgrace I've suffered at the hands of other people.'

Mary who 'couldn't conceive'

²⁶⁻²⁸ Elizabeth had been pregnant for six months when God sent the angel Gabriel off with another message – this time to a town in the Galilee region, called Nazareth, and specifically to a young virgin there. She was engaged to a man called Joseph – a descendant of David – and the virgin herself was called Mary. The first thing Mary knew, he was right there in front of her, saying, 'Greetings, O great chosen one – hey, is God impressed by you!'

²⁹⁻³³ Now, Mary was a bit mystified, as you might expect, and wondered what it was all about. 'Chill out, Mary!' the angel said. 'God's well pleased with you, and no mistake. You're going to have a son – Jesus, you'll call him – and he'll be seriously great. "Son of the Most High" is what he'll be known as, and God's going to give him the throne of David, his great ancestor. He'll reign over Israel for ever – no, really – no end to it!'

³⁴⁻³⁷ 'Well, that's all very well,' Mary answered, 'but isn't the fact that I'm still a virgin a bit of a problem?'

'Oh, not for God,' the angel answered. 'The Holy Spirit's going to take care of things. You'll be overshadowed by the power from on high – know what I mean? So the child's going to be holy – Son of God, no

---

1. Traditionally, Jews believed that being in the immediate presence of God was dangerous, and it seems likely that the priests were advised not to delay in case the congregation became anxious about their having come to harm – which seems to fit with this.

less. Where God's concerned anything can happen – well, take your cousin Elizabeth, for example. A bit on the old side, wouldn't you say? But she's pregnant too – six months gone now – and there was everybody saying she wasn't up to it! Like I said, where God's concerned, "impossible" just isn't in the vocabulary.'

[38] 'What can I say?' Mary said. 'God's the boss, so – well, whatever you say's OK by me.'

And the angel didn't hang around any longer.

Turning the world upside down

> Many find the idea of a virgin birth difficult to comprehend, but in the time of the birth of Jesus it was also a threatening idea, undermining as it did one of the great pillars of the male-dominated establishment. In every area of human power-play, God was indeed lifting up the lowly and bringing down the powerful!

[39-40] Mary was a woman in a hurry when she went to a town in the Judean hills, to Zechariah's house, and called out, 'Elizabeth!'

[41-45] When Elizabeth heard Mary's voice calling her name, she felt the baby within her jump – and God's Spirit filled her so that she cried out, 'Congratulations to you, of all women – and to the baby, the fruit of your womb! I can't believe this! It's you – the mother of my Lord – and you've come to see me! You know, when I heard your voice, my own baby jumped for joy within me! Well done, Mary – it took real faith for you to accept what you were told God was going to do through you.'

The song of the defiant oppressed

[46-50] Mary answered:

My whole being is praising and thanking God.
　　My spirit is bubbling with joy for God, my saviour.
I mean, he's really turned things round, hasn't he? – before this I was just a nothing –
　　but from now on the whole world's going to sit up and take notice.
God – the almighty God – he's done really great things for me –
　　no doubt about it, he's terrific!
He shows kindness to his faithful people,
　　always has, from one generation to the next.

⁵¹⁻⁵³ Honestly, has he shown his power, or has he shown his power!
All those people with their airs and graces, and their big ideas –
where are they now?
God's really turning things upside down –
down for the powerful, up for the so-called 'ordinary folk'!
This is going to mean food for the hungry –
the rich can fend for themselves!

⁵⁴⁻⁵⁵ 'God's really making a difference for his people – all Israel, I
mean.
He's not forgotten us – he's remembered and shown kindness to us.
Of course, we always knew he would – this is fulfilling his promise
to all our ancestors –
Abraham, and his children, and all who follow after him, for ever
and ever!

⁵⁶ Mary stayed with Elizabeth for about three months before going back
to her own home.

John the Baptiser is born

⁵⁷⁻⁶⁶ Well, things progressed well, and soon the time came: Elizabeth's
child was born. The whole neighbourhood was celebrating because
they knew God had shown kindness[1] to her in a big way. So, as tradition
demanded, when the baby was eight days old they gathered for the
great circumcision ritual.[2] Of course, he'd be called Zechariah, after his
father – well, it was traditional. But Elizabeth wasn't done with surprises
yet. 'John,' she announced. 'We're calling him John.'

'What!' the neighbours were shocked. 'There's nobody of that name
in the family at all,' they objected. Then they began making signs to
Zechariah, to see what he wanted to do. Zechariah got something to
write on and wrote down, 'His name's John.' Well, that settled it – the
father had spoken. Everybody was amazed, of course – and all the

---

1. Here's an example of where 'kindness' is a better translation than 'mercy' (see the
Glossary for more detail). Luke specifically tells us that Elizabeth had nothing about
which to feel guilty – that her infertility was not any kind of punishment. So there was no
specific need for mercy (as we now tend to understand it) in connection with this.
2. Circumcising boy babies was and remains very important in Jewish culture. No doubt
it had practical beginnings but by the time of Jesus it was a vital mark of the child's
Jewishness, and took place as part of the naming ceremony.

more so when Zechariah got his voice back and started praising God as soon as he'd written those words.[1]

Pretty awe-inspiring stuff, it was, for the neighbours – the entire region was talking about it for ages afterwards. And people who knew them simply couldn't stop wondering what it all meant. 'Just what sort of guy's he going to turn into?' they asked – it was obvious that God was at work in all this.

Zechariah prophesies great things

> We now have one of the most magnificent hymns of praise in Christian literature. Zechariah brings together two great historic promises of God – the promise, or covenant, made to Abraham, and also the promise of a great successor to David who would re-establish his wise and just rule. Zechariah sees these promises both being fulfilled in Jesus, the Messiah for whom John, Zechariah's newborn son, is to prepare the way. An honour indeed!

[67-79] Then Zechariah was filled with the Holy Spirit of God, and started to prophesy:

Blessed be God,[2] the God of Israel,
    because he's visited and redeemed[3] his people.
He's raised up a great saviour for us
    in the line of David, his servant.
Well, isn't this what he promised through all those prophets,
    to save us from our enemies, liberate us from the clutches of people who hate us?
So, by doing this he's shown the kindness promised to our ancestors,
    remembered the covenant of old,

---

1. So, having lost the 'power' of speech when he questioned God's way, Zechariah gets the 'power' back when he publicly and irrevocably accepts the loss of prestige.

2. A very traditional Jewish expression of praise. God would often be referred to as 'the Blessed One' by strict Jews who thought the actual name 'God' too awesome to be pronounced by mortal lips.

3. The word 'redeemed' is often reduced to 'saved', but it's much more than that. It's (at least theoretically) possible to rescue someone without any cost to oneself. 'Redeemed', though, actually means 'bought back' and was often used in reference to slaves. God's 'rescuing' of his people was in fact an enormously costly act, as Luke will show us later – and there really is no other word to express the scale of that but 'redeemed'.

the solemn promise he made to our ancestor Abraham
that he said he would give to us: that we'd be liberated from the
fear of our enemies
and set free for a proper relationship with him, to serve him for
all our days![1]
And you – son – well, you've got a really special place in this!
'The prophet of the Most High', everyone'll call you!
   because you're going to be right there in front – going ahead of
   the Lord – preparing his way,
   giving people a taste of what salvation's all about
   by helping them find forgiveness for their sins.
And that's all about God's tender kindness –
   bursting on us like a visit from the sun itself, out of heaven,
   giving light to people who're lost in darkness,
   whose lives are overshadowed by death –
   and guiding our footsteps in ways of peace.

[80] So, the child grew up – became strong in mind and spirit – and went
to live in the desert until the start of his public ministry.

Jesus is born

In this classic story, we can't escape the revelation that God's priorities
are different from ours – it's to shepherds, generally regarded as
socially undesirable, that the Good News is first revealed, with not
a word, apparently, to the religious ruling classes. It's also interesting
to note a contrast with the general expectations, in which God's
glory was to be imposed on the world by force. Here we see God
humbling himself in order to enable relationships, rather than
using coercive power. Surely this is glory of a completely different
kind – and an infinitely higher order!

2 [1-7] At the time that Mary and Elizabeth were preparing for mother-
hood, Augustus, the Roman Emperor, decided that all the people in
the world[2] should be counted. Now, that was a novel idea to the locals
for a start. Everyone had to go back to their family's home town to regis-
ter themselves, and for Joseph – being descended from the great king

---

1. 'All *our* days' – salvation isn't just about going to heaven – it's about truly being God's
people here and now!
2. By 'the world', of course, he meant the Roman Empire.

David himself, no less – that meant travelling to Bethlehem. He made the journey with his wife, Mary, who was expecting a baby – and, of course, that was the time the infant decided to be born! So it was that Mary had her first child; she wrapped him in strips of cloth, and put him to bed in the animals' feeding trough – well, the family guest room was full, so they had to make do.[1]

The shepherds are told the good news

[8-12] Now, in that area, there were some shepherds spending the night in the fields to keep an eye on their flocks, when suddenly an angel appeared – and the whole place was lit up with God's glory. They were terrified, but the angel said, 'Now, there's nothing to be afraid of – quite the opposite, in fact, because have I got great news for you guys! And not just for you – for everyone – celebration time for all people! The Saviour's been born – for you – yes, I mean *you* – in King David's birthplace, so you know what that means – a Saviour, the Messiah, the Lord – need I say more? OK, then, here's how you'll recognise him. You'll find him wrapped in strips of cloth and lying in a cattle feeding trough.'

[13-14] And suddenly the angel wasn't alone. The whole sky was full of them, singing and dancing as though their immortality depended on it. 'Glory to God in the highest heavens,' they thundered. 'And here on earth, peace for all who are open to him!'

[15-20] When the angels had gone, the shepherds looked at each other in amazement. 'We'd better get over there,' they said. 'Like, now! Got to get to Bethlehem and cop an eyeful of whatever it is God's up to. Hey, he's told us – *us!*' So off they went at a cracking pace, and found Mary and Joseph – and, sure enough, there was the baby lying in the feeding trough. Of course, then it all came tumbling out – everything the angels had said about the baby – and everyone who heard it was just amazed by the shepherds' story. Everyone except Mary, who simply listened, took it all in, and thought deeply about what it meant. And the shepherds? Well, they went back to work – bubbling over with praise for God who'd chosen them to hear the good news, and then let them see it with their own eyes.

---

1. People who study these things now know that the word previously translated 'inn' should really be 'guest-room'. Now, why whoever was in it didn't move out for a pregnant young woman is an interesting question.

Jesus is named

²¹ When Jesus was eight days old, it was time for the naming ceremony. So they circumcised him and named him Jesus – the name the angel had said they should call him, even before he was conceived.[1]

²²⁻²⁴ Then the time came when they had to do the purification rituals,[2] and Mary and Joseph went to present Jesus in the Temple – that's what the law of Moses says: 'Every first-born male is to be consecrated to God'.[3] So they followed the law carefully[4] and made the necessary sacrifice: 'either a pair of turtle doves, or two young pigeons'.

Simeon's and Anna's long vigils end

If you have the privilege (and, believe me, it is one) of meeting people who live in places of fear, even despair, and yet manage to stay hopeful, you will find they are an inspiration. They are God's witnesses to hope who, simply by being there in the way they are, enable other hearts and minds to be kept open. A vigil can be a very powerful thing, and now we meet two people whose faithful service of God took just that form.

²⁵⁻²⁸ Now, there was a man living in Jerusalem – Simeon, his name was – who had truly amazing faith. He was patiently waiting for the day when Israel would be a place of peace and truth again. God's Holy Spirit was really with him, and had promised him that he wouldn't die until he'd seen the Messiah with his own eyes. And it was that same Spirit that led him into the Temple this particular day, just as Jesus' parents brought him there to do what the law required. Simeon took the baby into his arms and praised God:

---

1. See the note on 1:13.
2. These requirements are set out in Leviticus 12. Ritual cleanliness was an important part of the culture, and much of it probably originated from the early community's experience of infections associated with blood and unhealed wounds. They didn't have the science to understand the process, but they were able to make the connections – so people who could pose a threat were excluded. However, this was believed also to cut them off from God, so as soon as it was safe to do so a religious ceremony was required to reconcile them both to the community and to God.
3. See Exodus 13, for example. It applied not just to children but to livestock as well – a token recognition that all life is a gift of God and belongs to him.
4. Luke's emphasising that Jesus was from a devout, law-abiding family. It was important that followers of Jesus could be seen as faithful people, not religious rebels.

[29-32] O God, now you're letting your servant go to his rest, in peace,
    just the way you promised,
because these eyes of mine have actually seen your salvation,
    prepared by you in full sight of all the nation:
a light to lighten the whole world,
    and to make known the glory of your presence here in Israel!

[33-35] Now, as you'd expect, the child's parents were completely awestruck by what Simeon said – but the old man wasn't done yet. After he'd given them a blessing, he said, 'This child has a great destiny – to bring about the falling and rising of many, many people in Israel. He'll become a symbol of everything that some people want to oppose – he'll show people in their true colours. And that'll bring pain to you too – like a dagger though the heart.'

[36-38] Also in the Temple was Anna, a prophet – the daughter of Phanuel of the tribe of Asher. She was just amazingly old! She'd lived with her husband for seven years after they were married, and then been a widow right up to the age of eighty-four. She was always in the Temple – never left the place – stayed there, day and night, praying and fasting. And at this precise moment she also came to where they were. Well, she really started praising God – and talking about the child to all the people who were watching, as she was, for the redemption of Jerusalem.

Home to Nazareth

[39-40] After they'd done all the things they had to do under the law, they went back to Galilee – Nazareth, to be precise, their home town. Well, the child grew up. He developed amazing wisdom, and it was quite clear that God was working in him.

Young Jesus in the Temple

[41-52] Jesus' parents went to Jerusalem every year to celebrate the Passover festival – and in the year when Jesus was twelve years old it turned into quite an event. Everything was fine until the festival was over and they set off for home. Well, everyone except Jesus did anyway – he stayed behind in Jerusalem but his parents didn't know that. So they merrily walked away from Jerusalem for a whole day, thinking he was some-where in the group of pilgrims, before they started scouting around their family looking for him. No joy, of course, so off they trudged back to Jerusalem, where they hunted for three days trying to find him. And where do you think he was? In the Temple – calmly sitting among the

teachers there, listening to them and asking questions. And the people around were well impressed with his intellect. His parents were amazed when they found him. 'What do you think you're doing, child!' his mother said. 'We've been hunting all over for you – worried sick, we've been.'

Jesus looked at them calmly. 'Searching for me? Why? Didn't you know that I had to be in my Father's house?' They hadn't a clue what he meant by that. Jesus went back with them to Nazareth, and from then on treated them with respect. His mother couldn't get all this out of her mind, though, and spent a lot of time thinking about it. Meanwhile, Jesus grew up – in wisdom as well as in years – and gained a lot of respect both from God and from the people around him.

Jesus in Galilee

John prepares the way

John the Baptiser is a vital figure, forming the bridge between the old covenant and the new – while very definitely standing within the old himself, as Luke and others make clear elsewhere. The birth narratives have served to set out some of the great themes of the gospel, the better for us to understand the work of Jesus as God's Messiah – which starts in earnest here.

3 [1-4] Let's begin by getting the time clear. This was the fifteenth year of Tiberius Caesar's reign;[1] Pontius Pilate was the governor of Judea and Herod was the tetrarch[2] of Galilee. Herod's brother, Philip, was tetrarch of Ituraea and Trachonitis, and Lysanias had the same position in Abilene.[3] Annas and Caiaphas were High Priests at the time.[4] Anyway, the word of God came to Zechariah's son John, in the desert, and he went into the Jordan area and started preaching a baptism by which people could show that they turned away from sin and accepted God's forgiveness, as the prophet Isaiah foretold:

[5-6] A voice, calling out in the desert, 'Prepare the way for God.
Build a straight road for God to travel.
Raise up all the valleys,
  flatten every hill!
Smooth out the uneven ground,
  and make every rough patch level!
Then God will reveal his glory.
Everyone's[5] going to see it together.[6]

[7-9] John always had a colourful turn of phrase, but he really got into his stride on one particular day when he saw the crowd coming towards

---

1. This would have been about AD 28-29.
2. A relatively minor ruler – although accorded the title 'King', he governed on behalf of the real political power which was the Roman Empire.
3. What *is* helpful to bear in mind is that the Herod mentioned here wasn't the same Herod whom Matthew describes as being around when Jesus was born. This was his son – although he wasn't much better than his father.
4. To be strictly accurate, Annas was the *ex* High Priest – there was only ever one at a time – but he was still respected and carried a fair bit of clout.
5. The standard text says, 'all flesh'.
6. Isaiah 40:3-5.

him to be baptised. 'You revolting poisonous snakes!' he shouted. 'So, who warned you to run away from God's judgement? I suppose you think that saying the right words is going to save you, do you? Well, if you're really saved it'll show in your lives. Oh, and don't give me any of that "We're Abraham's descendants, so we're OK" rubbish either. Let me tell you, God can make descendants of Abraham out of these rocks – it doesn't mean a thing! You'd better take notice: God's standing like a forester with his axe, poised to take out any dead wood and burn it – and, believe me, wood doesn't come much deader than you.'

¹⁰⁻¹⁴ 'So, what are we supposed to do?' the people asked.

John answered, 'Look, if you've got two suits in your wardrobe, you can share with someone who hasn't got any, can't you? And if you've got lots of food – same principle.'

Even some tax collectors[1] came to him for baptism. 'And what about us – what do we have to do?'

'Just be fair,' John answered. 'Collect the taxes you're supposed to, and don't go lining your own pockets by cheating.'

'And us?' It was some soldiers. 'What do we have to do?'

'Don't bully people and rob them,' came the reply, 'don't abuse your position by falsely accusing people – and be satisfied with the wages you're paid.'

¹⁵⁻¹⁸ Now, this was a time of great expectations – and, not unnaturally, people were wondering whether John might be the Messiah. John was very clear about that. 'All I'm doing,' he said, 'is baptising people with water, but there's someone *seriously* important coming along behind me – I'm not even good enough to help him undo his shoes. Now, he's really going to start something – his baptism will be with the Holy Spirit, and with fire. It's harvest-time in heaven, folks, and he's coming equipped – harvesting the wheat and burning the chaff in the fire.' He really hammered the point, trying to get people to hear the good news he was preaching to them.

¹⁹⁻²⁰ Now, John had seriously been getting to King Herod by denouncing him for marrying Herodias, his brother's wife – and a fair stack of other things – so Herod had John slung into prison.

---

1. Tax collectors were despised, not so much because they were dishonest as for working for the occupying power. John doesn't get into the complicated political arguments (not that he was afraid to – they just weren't the point in this case) but calls for justice in their dealings.

Jesus is baptised

²¹⁻²² When everybody who wanted to had been baptised, and he himself had been baptised as well, Jesus started praying. As he did so, heaven opened up above him and God's Holy Spirit came down on him in physical form, like a dove. Then there was a voice from heaven. 'You are my Son,' it said, 'my special Son – like no other – and you're fulfilling all my expectations!'

Jesus' family tree

²³⁻³⁸ Like Matthew, Luke includes a genealogy of Jesus – but he does it differently. As with Matthew, I'm not including it here – you can easily find it in a standard Bible if that's your thing, and – again, as with Matthew – a good commentary will help you through it. One of the important functions this passage fulfils is to address the 'divine/human' issue about Jesus. Jesus, Luke wanted to tell us, was fully human, but also wholly divine. He showed this by tracing his ancestry right back through Adam, whom he also called 'son of God'. So Jesus perfectly fulfils what should have been the destiny of the whole human race.

Jesus resists temptation

To hear some people talk, you'd think God had just *pretended* to be human in Jesus! Of course, that would have been dishonest and patronising; most of all, though, for Jesus' obedience to his Father to be of any significance at all, he had to have the capacity to disobey – he had to be tempted, just the same as we are.

This links with the purpose of the genealogy. Remember, Luke had been with Paul on his missionary journeys, and would have heard Paul speaking of Jesus as the 'second Adam'. This was not in any way belittling Jesus; rather, it was a bit like Matthew's use of Moses – a shorthand way of saying what Jesus was about. The first Adam was tempted and gave in to it. Now the true Son of God, fully human, faces temptation and wins. By linking Jesus with Adam in the previous chapter and then moving on to this story, Luke is giving us a very helpful peg on which to hang our thinking about Jesus.

4 ¹⁻⁴ Jesus was full to bursting with the Holy Spirit after his baptism in the River Jordan, and the Spirit led him into the desert to face the temptations of the devil. Forty days he was there, with nothing to eat –

now that's serious fasting – and by the time it was over he was famished.

The devil seized the opportunity. 'Look, you're supposed to be the Son of God, aren't you? So, tell these stones to turn into bread. Go on – you can do it – you know you can. Live a little, why don't you?'

Jesus answered, 'Scripture says that we don't only need bread to live on.'[1]

5-8 Then the devil filled Jesus' head with images of all the glorious empires in the world. 'Want to rule the world?' he whispered tantalisingly. 'Just do things my way, and you will. I could give you all this, and then more. Power, authority, wealth – you name it. It's mine to give, you know.'

Jesus answered, 'The Bible's very clear. "You're to have just one God," it says, "one God to serve and to worship: God, Yahweh, the Great I AM."[2] Got it? So that leaves you well out of the picture, doesn't it?'

9-13 Something more spectacular was clearly needed, so the devil whisked Jesus off to the top of the Temple – right up on the pinnacle of the building, and that's mighty high. 'You could jump off,' he murmured persuasively. 'Well, if you're really the Son of God, that is. So, are you? Go on – throw yourself off – because I know my Bible too, and it says, "He'll give orders to his angels about you, and they'll hold you in their arms – you won't even strike your foot against a stone."[3]

'Another thing the Bible says,' Jesus answered, 'is, "Don't put God to the test."[4]

Well, the devil had done all he could for the time being, so he left Jesus to it. But he was just biding his time.

14-15 Then Jesus returned – full of the Spirit's power – to Galilee. He was the talk of the neighbourhood – the entire region, in fact – and he taught in the synagogues to the great acclaim of everyone.

Jesus begins his ministry

Jesus' ministry begins as it will continue, and as it will end. False expectations lead to confusion, disappointment and ultimately rejection. All this is foreshadowed in his reception and rejection at Nazareth.

---

1. Deuteronomy 8:3
2. Deuteronomy 6:13
3. Psalm 91:11-12
4. Deuteronomy 6:16

Jesus is rejected at home

[16-17] Then he came to Nazareth – the place where he'd grown up – and went as usual to the synagogue on the Sabbath. Everything seemed fine at first; they asked him to read, and gave him the scroll with the book of the prophet Isaiah. Jesus found the place and began to read:

[18-19] The Spirit of God is upon me,
> because he's anointed me
>> to proclaim good news to the poor,
> He's sent me to announce freedom to captives,
>> sight to blind people,
>>> liberation for the oppressed.
> In short, to proclaim God's year of jubilee.[1]

[20-27] Every eye was fixed on Jesus as he rolled up the scroll, passed it back to the steward, and sat down. 'Today,' he announced, 'right here, in front of you, this scripture has been fulfilled.'[2]

They were well impressed. How eloquently he spoke! It still seemed strange, though, for such words to come from an ordinary man they all knew. 'Isn't this just Joseph's son?' they said to one another.

Then Jesus really got into his stride. 'Oh, I know what you're going to say,' he said. '"Doctor, heal yourself! If you can do miracles in Capernaum, why not here in your own town?" Well, I'm telling you straight, there never was a prophet who was accepted in the place where that prophet had grown up! The truth is there were plenty of widows in Israel during Elijah's time – remember, when there was all that famine and drought? – but where was Elijah sent to do his work? Zarephath, in Sidon – that's where! And do you think there weren't enough people with leprosy in Israel during Elisha's lifetime? None of them were healed though – only Naaman, and he was a Syrian!'

[28-30] By this time the people's hackles weren't just raised, they were positively in orbit! Seething and tooth-grinding were in full swing! Suddenly the whole congregation was on its feet – and they weren't about to give him a standing ovation! Out of the synagogue they went – dragging

---

1. Isaiah 61:1-2; 58:6. According to Jewish law, jubilee was a regular event (every fiftieth year) in which all debts were cancelled, slaves were freed, land returned to its original owners – a new beginning.
2. In Jesus, all is fulfilled. The 'jubilee' had come, not as a once-in-fifty-years event, but as a final reality.

Jesus with them – until they got to the top of the steep hill, ready to throw him off the cliff. But Jesus wasn't that easy to dispose of – he walked straight through the middle of them and left them standing there.

> So, having shown how Jesus' authority was not accepted in his home town, and also demonstrated that this was hardly surprising, Luke now specifically highlights that authority not in words but in actions – actions of healing in which not only this-worldly but also other-worldly ills are no match for Jesus.

[31-32] Jesus headed down to Capernaum, another city of Galilee. And on the Sabbath day he was teaching. They were totally amazed because he taught with real authority.

Exorcising a demon[1]

[33-37] In the synagogue he encountered a man with an evil spirit. 'Leave us alone!' the spirit screamed at him. 'What do you want with us, Jesus of Nazareth? Oh, we know who you are, all right – God's holy messenger!'[2]

'Shut up and come out of him!' Jesus commanded the spirit, which threw the man into a convulsion, gave one final defiant scream, and left. Everyone was completely amazed. 'Hey, what is this?' they asked one another. 'Some radical new teaching or something? He gives orders to evil spirits and they obey him – man, that's some authority! Some power!' And he became famous throughout the whole surrounding region.

Healing Simon's mother-in-law

[38-39] Jesus left the synagogue to go into Simon's house. Now, Simon's mother-in-law was ill with a fever, and they asked Jesus to help her. Jesus didn't hang around – he went and stood over her and dismissed the fever with a word! The fever subsided, and she rose and waited on them.[3]

---

1. You might find it helpful to refer to the introduction to the parallel passage beginning at Mark 1:23.
2. Similarly, you might find the footnote to the same parallel passage interesting.
3. The indication is that a woman was here admitted to discipleship – that her 'service' was valued, and the healing enabled her to do it.

Jesus' influence and reputation spread

[40-44] As the sun went down, all the people who had sick relatives – whatever the illness might be – brought them to him, and he healed them with the laying on of hands. Evil spirits came out of some of them, yelling out, 'You're the Son of God!' but he stopped them and wouldn't let them go on speaking, because they knew that he was the Messiah.[1]

Then in the morning, at daybreak, Jesus went out to find a quiet place. The people were looking for him and they'd have kept him there with them, given half a chance, but he said, 'I've got to preach the good news of the kingdom of God in other places as well, you know – after all, that's why I was sent.' So he continued, preaching in synagogues in Judea.

Jesus calls the first disciples

5[1-11] The shore of Lake Gennesaret was getting a bit too crowded for comfort with the crowd pressing all around Jesus wanting to hear the word of God. So he looked round and saw a couple of boats nearby – the fishermen had left them to go and wash their nets. One of them was Simon's, so Jesus got in and asked him to push out a few yards in order to get some clear water between him and the crowd. Then he sat down and taught the crowds from there. After he'd finished, he said, 'Hey, Simon – shove out into the deeper water, and drop your nets – you may as well catch some fish.'

'Master,' Simon said, 'we've been doing nothing else all night, and a fat lot of good it's done us – there's nothing there. Still, if you say so, I'll do it.'

Now, doing what Jesus said proved to be a wise decision. The net became so full of fish that the men in the other boat had to come and help get it in – and then both boats were nearly sinking! Simon Peter knew something pretty special was happening – scary too. 'Get away from me!' he shouted, as he grovelled in the bottom of the boat. 'I'm not good enough to be around the likes of you!' Well, he was amazed – like everybody else – at the catch they'd pulled in. So were James and John, the sons of Zebedee, who were his partners.

'Don't get frightened,' Jesus said. 'It's people you're going to be fishing for, from now on.' When they got the boats to the shore, they left them – and everything that went with them – and followed Jesus.

---

1. Two points here. Firstly, as has been observed earlier, Jesus may well not have wanted this kind of language to be used about him until his ministry reached an appropriate point – at this stage, it was likely to be counterproductive. Secondly, using someone's name is a way of controlling or exerting authority over them – and Jesus was having none of that from any evil spirit!

Healing a man with leprosy

> According to the laws of the time, people suffering from leprosy
> were strictly quarantined. The illness was regarded as incurable –
> the person was in effect dead already, so a cure would be tanta-
> mount to being raised to new life!

¹²⁻¹⁶ While Jesus was in the cities of that area, a man who was riddled
with leprosy saw him and threw himself on the ground in front of him
begging for help. 'Lord, if you really want to, you can make me well
again – not to mention socially acceptable.'

'I do want to,' Jesus said. 'So be healed.' He reached out and touched
him – not something recommended in polite society.[1] Immediately the
man's skin healed up. Jesus gave him strict instructions not to go telling
everybody about this, saying, 'Just go and see the priest and get all the
legal stuff done – thank offerings, that sort of thing – then you can go
home again.' But, of course, the news just spread all the more quickly,
and crowds gathered to listen to him and to be healed. Jesus retreated
to the desert to pray.

Jesus and the law

Jesus has the authority to forgive[2]

¹⁷⁻²⁶ During that time, while he was teaching, some Pharisees and scribes
were hanging around nearby. Well, they'd actually come in not just
from every village in Galilee and Judea, but even from Jerusalem itself.[3]
And Jesus had God's power to heal.

Then four men arrived, carrying a paralysed friend on a stretcher,
hoping to get him to Jesus, but they couldn't manage it because of the
crowd. So they just took the outside staircase up onto the flat roof, and
calmly started removing it – the roof, that is, not the staircase – until
they'd made a big enough hole to let the stretcher down with the man

---

1. Not only that: Jesus risked being 'quarantined' himself for doing it. How's that for
solidarity!
2. This story is more usually titled something like 'Jesus heals a paralysed man', but if we
take the passage in context we know that the story is really about authority, in keeping
with the others in this section. In this case, the real issue is not the healing but the
forgiving.
3. Evidently, Jesus had them worried.

on it. Jesus was well impressed by their faith and said, 'Friend, your sins are forgiven.'[1]

The scribes and Pharisees responded predictably, of course: 'Who does this guy think he is, to talk like this? Blasphemy – that's what it is! Who other than God has the right to forgive sins?'

Jesus knew exactly what they were saying, and answered, 'Why do you always have to pick holes like that? All right, I suppose anyone could say, "Your sins are forgiven", but to say, "Get up and walk", well, that's another matter, isn't it![2] So, if you want to see some real authority, that's OK by me.' He turned to the man on the stretcher and said, 'I'm telling you to stand up, get hold of that stretcher, and go home.' And immediately he did – glorifying God as he went. And when the crowds saw it, they were completely awestruck and started praising God too. 'Well!' they said, 'we've really seen something today!'

Eating with the undesirables

[27-32] After that, Jesus went out again, and came across a man called Levi, a tax collector, sitting at the custom desk taxing the traders. 'Follow me,' he said, and the man just got up, left everything and followed him. Next thing everybody knew, Levi had prepared a celebration meal in his home, and most of the tax collectors and general undesirables in the area seemed to be sharing in it. 'Hey, what's the idea?' the Pharisees and scribes demanded of Jesus' disciples. 'Why do you fellows share food with characters like this?'

Jesus heard them – he could hardly fail to, the commotion they were causing – and said, 'Well, the people who are fit and healthy hardly need a doctor, do they? Doctors go to those who need them, and so do I. I didn't come to invite the righteous – I came to invite those you call sinners to change!'

Empty rituals

[33-39] 'Look,' they said, 'John's disciples are always fasting and praying, but yours just eat and drink.'

'Oh, right,' Jesus answered, 'I suppose you'd ask wedding guests to fast while the bridegroom's with them, would you? When the bride-groom's been taken away, there'll be plenty of time for that!' Then he

---

1. This doesn't mean Jesus thought the man's illness was a punishment – but it was what people in those days believed, so the man would certainly be *feeling* in need of forgiveness.
2. Because any ordinary person would look a bit silly when it didn't happen!

added a parable. 'No one with any sense rips a piece out of a new shirt to patch an old one; you just end up with a torn new shirt, and it doesn't match. And you don't put new wine into old wineskins either – not if you know your wine. It's just inviting disaster. The new wine will burst out of the skins and they'll both be lost. New wine has to go into fresh wineskins. And, anyway, once people have drunk old wine they don't want the new – they prefer the old.'

The Sabbath

6¹⁻⁵ Then there was the time when Jesus was walking through the cornfields one Sabbath day with his disciples, who were picking some of the heads off the corn as they went, rubbing them in their hands and eating them. Harmless enough, you'd think, but not if you're a Pharisee with an axe to grind. 'Hey, Jesus,' they called, 'what do you think you're doing, breaking the law on the Sabbath?'[1]

'Oh, get real, please!' Jesus answered. 'Try reading your Bibles – don't you remember what King David did when he and his companions were hungry? I mean, he only went into the holy of holies and grabbed the bread intended for worship, which the law says only the priests can eat – *and* gave some to the people with him, too – that's all! The Son of Man has authority even over the Sabbath.'[2]

[6-11] Then, on another Sabbath, when Jesus went to the synagogue to teach, there was a man in the congregation whose right hand was paralysed[3] – so, of course, the scribes and Pharisees were all watching to see whether Jesus would heal on the Sabbath and give them a chance for another go at him. Jesus was well aware of their motives, and said to the man, 'Come and stand here.' The man rose and stood there. Then Jesus turned and said, 'OK, I'm asking you what the law says we should do on the Sabbath: good or harm – save life or kill?'

Jesus looked round at them, and then said to the man, 'Stretch out your hand,' which was suddenly as sound as a bell – well, as sound as a good hand, anyway. The scribes and Pharisees, though, were unimpressed, in fact they were hopping mad, and lost no time getting into an unholy huddle to plot his downfall.

---

1. Now, you might think they meant stealing, but it was even pettier than that. Working on the Sabbath was illegal, and, as far as they were concerned, if you're going to pick an ear of wheat you might as well take a combine harvester to the whole field.
2. Matthew 12:1-8 includes a fuller argument by Jesus.
3. Mark and Matthew simply say it's his hand. Luke tells us it was his *right* hand – which for most people is the one they need most.

Jesus calls the Twelve to be Apostles

¹²⁻¹⁶ It was during these times that Jesus went up a mountain to pray. He stayed there all night, praying to God, and when day came he gave twelve of the disciples the title of 'apostles'.[1] Want to know who they were? I'll tell you. First came Simon (whom Jesus surnamed Peter), and his brother, Andrew; James and John, Philip, Bartholomew and Matthew. Then there were Thomas, another James – the son of Alphaeus – and another Simon – this time Simon who was known as the Zealot;[2] then there was Judas, son of James, and finally Judas Iscariot, the man who was eventually going to betray him.

> Luke is about to introduce us formally to Jesus the teacher. Before he does so, he reminds us of the authority behind the teaching, demonstrated in the banishing of illness and supernatural forces.

Authority to heal . . .

¹⁷⁻¹⁹ Jesus came down with the apostles, to level ground, surrounded by a crowd of disciples and others from all over the place: Judea, including Jerusalem itself, and the seacoast of Tyre and Sidon – a great crowd of people who came to listen to him and be healed of diseases. Some of them were plagued by evil spirits, and he cured them. The whole crowd seemed to be pressing in to touch him, because the power that went out from him completely healed all of them.

. . . and to teach: the sermon on the plain

> The next passage has clear echoes of the Sermon on the Mount (Matthew 5 onwards), but this time it is the Sermon on the Plain. There are other differences too, as we'll see. Some people believe that these are different sayings of Jesus, and Luke has chosen for good reason to record these rather than the ones Matthew used; other people think that it's really the same material, but the Holy Spirit inspired Matthew and Luke to record the detail differently in order that the same basic sayings could address different needs. Whichever explanation you favour, it's still inspired!

---

1. Basically, it meant someone who was commissioned or sent on a mission.
2. The term 'Zealot' identifies him as a member of a fanatical group of freedom fighters.

The Beatitudes

20-26 Jesus looked around at his disciples, and said:
Congratulations[1] to you who are poor
because the kingdom of God is truly yours!
Congratulations to you who are hungry now,
because, let me tell you, you're going to be satisfied!
Congratulations to all of you that are in tears now,
because you are going to laugh for joy!
Congratulations to you when people hate you, and shut you out, and ridicule you, and reject your very names as evil, all because of your loyalty to me.

Be glad about it – jump for joy – because it shows your real faith, and it'll all be made up to you in the end with interest – after all, their ancestors did the same thing to all the prophets, so it's really no surprise, is it!

The Curses

> After the congratulations, the curses. The inclusion of these within the sermon provides a direct counterpart to the previous verses – Jesus knew that if the 'have nots' were going to gain, then the 'haves' would have to give something up. This idea of social reversal is an important theme in the gospels.

But a curse on you[2] who are rich,
because you've already had the comfort you need.
A curse on you who are stuffed full of food now,
because you're going to know real hunger.
A curse on you who're laughing now,
because you're going to shed terrible tears.
A curse on you when all people say what great guys you are,
because their ancestors said exactly the same about the phoney prophets!

---

1. The original word has no direct translation in English. Most people use 'Blessed' and if you want to substitute that I won't mind. Some translations say 'Happy' but that's really not good enough as most people think of happiness as a 'feel good' thing. We could use 'How fortunate'. The point is that Jesus is saying these people are in a good position to be close to God and in tune with his ways.
2. The usual English wording is 'Woe to you', which in the original language was much more than a prediction – it was a condemnation. I think this gets pretty close to the original sense.

Loving enemies

[27-36] But I'm telling you who are listening: love your enemies; do good to people who hate you; bless the ones that curse you, and pray for people who have a go at you. If someone slaps you on the cheek, well, offer the other one too. Someone want to sue you for your coat? Be generous! Give them your shirt as well! Beggars? Don't be selfish – give to them. And if someone takes what belongs to you, don't go steaming off, trying to get your own back! In every situation, treat other people the way you'd like them to treat you.

I mean, what's so special about loving people who love you? – anyone can do that. Even the criminals are canny enough to stick together! And if you only help people who help you, what credit is that to you? Even criminals do the same. There's nothing particularly generous about lending to people who you know are going to pay you back. Even criminals lend to other criminals to get as much back from them. But love your enemies; do good and lend things even when you expect no return at all – you'll find there's a real reward in that. Then you'll truly be children of the Most High, because he's kind to the ungrateful, generous to the selfish. In other words, your example of true kindness should be God, your Father – model yourselves on him!

Judging others

[37-38] Don't get judgemental with others, and they'll have no reason to act that way towards you, will they? Likewise, don't condemn, and you won't be condemned; forgive, and you'll be forgiven; give, and you'll be given to – as if a really generous measure of grain, pressed down, shaken together and running over had been poured into your lap.[1] You get back what you give.[2]

---

1. What a wonderfully vivid image to people at the time – typical of Jesus! Imagine a woman in the market place, buying grain to grind into flour for bread. She's gone to a generous trader who fills up his measure, presses down on it to make space and adds more. Then, for good measure, he shakes the container so that any air-pockets are released and the grain settles, and tops it up again before she gladly holds out her apron for him to pour the generous measure into her 'lap'! That's how God is! Wonderful!

2. Actually, we get back a lot more, according to that passage! We need to be careful not to make God's love conditional – that's not what it's about. The same image is helpful here. If that woman in the market place (see the footnote above) didn't hold out her apron, she wouldn't be able to receive the generous portion no matter how much the trader wanted to offer it. So, Jesus says, when we're good to others, we're holding out our apron to God!

Blind guides

[39-42] He told them a parable too.

Can one blind person guide another? Won't they both end up in the ditch? Are disciples better than their teachers? Of course not – but one who's been well and fully taught will become like the teacher. How is it you can see a speck of sawdust in you neighbour's[1] eye, but you can't see a whacking great roof rafter in your own? How have you got the nerve to say, 'Neighbour, let me take that speck out of your eye', when you yourself can't see the rafter that's still sitting there in yours? Hypocrite! Try dealing with the rafter in your eye first – you might then be able to see more clearly to help your neighbour with that little speck of dust!

Good and bad fruit

[43-45] Look: good trees don't produce bad fruit, do they? There again, bad trees don't produce good fruit either. Every tree is judged by its own fruit. After all, you don't get figs from thorn bushes, now do you – or grapes from brambles? Good people can produce good things because they've got this inner store of goodness – but evil people produce evil from what they've hoarded up inside themselves.

Good and bad foundations

[46-49] Why do you come to me bowing and scraping and saying, 'Lord, Lord,' and not do the things I tell you to? Come to me, hear what I'm saying and live by it, and you'll be like a really wise man, building a house, who dug the foundations deep into the rock. Floods? You've never seen anything like it – but that house stood firm because its foundations were solid. Of course, if you only hear and don't act on it, then you'll be like the other guy who built his house on the surface of the ground – just sort of plonked it there, with no foundations. Seemed easier, see – none of that sweaty labour – until the flood came, and when that house fell, wow, did it fall! What a ruin!

The centurion and his servant

7[1-10] After he'd finished saying all these things to the people, Jesus went into Capernaum. Now, there was a centurion living there who

---

1. Here the word used refers to another member of the faith community – but the word 'Christian' hadn't been thought of yet!

was really worried about his servant. The servant was sick and about to die unless someone pretty special came along. Anyway, he heard of Jesus being in the area, and got some of the Jewish elders to go and ask Jesus to come and cure his servant. When they got to Jesus, they really pleaded with him. 'He's a good guy,' they said. 'He's really sympathetic to Jewish concerns – he built our synagogue, you know.'

Jesus set off with them, but when he got near the house the centurion sent some friends with a message for him: 'Lord, don't bother coming to my house – I'm not fit for it according to your law. That's why I didn't come to you myself. Look, just say the word – that's all it will take, and my servant will be well again. Oh, I know all about authority – I'm under it, and I've got soldiers under me. When I tell someone, "Go", he goes. And if I tell him, "Come here", he comes. I've only got to say the word and my servant will do exactly what I say. Oh, yes, I know authority.'

Jesus was amazed! Turning to the crowd round him, he said, 'I'm telling you, not even in Israel have I found faith like this!' And when the centurion's friends went back to the house, the servant was fit and well.

The widow and her son at Nain

Jesus shows his authority even over death itself, and the faith of the surrounding people is awakened. The point is not that they see a kind of conjuring trick and applaud the conjuror, but that they recognise God in action and praise *him*. They describe Jesus as a 'great prophet' who has been 'raised up' among them – very traditional faith language. And they speak of God 'looking kindly on his people'. This, of course, echoes the words also used by Zechariah in celebrating the birth of his son John.

This story of the raising of a dead man has important secondary resonances. The dead man is met at the city gate on the way out. There are a number of passages where Jesus meets people at the gate, symbolising their marginalised position in society, and enables them to return fully to the heart of community life. To be excluded from the community was to be cut off from the source of life – a living death. Literally dead bodies, of course, were unclean, and would be taken well clear of the city. All associated with the procedure would then need ritual purification. Jesus here reverses exclusion in its most permanent form and enables a return to fullness of life. This story is deeply symbolic of the power of Jesus' ministry and, ultimately, his death and resurrection.

[11-17] Soon after that, Jesus arrived at a city called Nain – with his disciples and the usual crowd following him, of course. Just as he got to the town gate, a dead man was being carried out. A sad case, it was – he'd been his mother's only son, and she was already a widow. There was a sizeable crowd of townspeople following. As soon as Jesus saw her he keenly felt the grief that she was suffering.[1] 'Don't cry,' he said. Then he moved to the bier on which the body lay and touched it, whereupon the bearers stopped and stood still. 'Young man,' Jesus said, 'I'm telling you: rise up!' Well, it was amazing; the dead man just sat up and started talking, as if nothing had happened to him! Jesus presented him to his mother, but the people around were gasping in amazement.

Then they started praising God. 'A prophet!' they said. 'A great prophet has risen up among us!'

'God's truly visited his people now!' said others – and the story spread like wildfire through the whole of Judea and the regions round about.

Jesus, John and great expectations

Even the one who first heralded Jesus is beginning to have his doubts. Jesus doesn't quite fit his expectations somehow. We have a God of surprises, who doesn't always work in the way even his most faithful servants expect.

[18-28] John the Baptiser's disciples went and told him all about it, so he sent them back with a question for Jesus. 'Hey, Jesus, what's the story? I mean, are you really the one we've been waiting for, or should we be looking for someone more like what we expected?'

Now, even as they spoke, Jesus was curing a lot of people of diseases, and chronic conditions – even of demonic possession – and folk who'd been blind were taking their first look at the world. So Jesus answered, 'Why don't you just go back to John and tell him what you've seen and heard: blind people seeing, lame people walking, people cured of leprosy, deaf people hearing, dead people raised back to life, and the good news being targeted on the most needy. And congratulations, I say, to everyone who isn't put off just because I don't fit with their preconceived ideas!'

After they'd gone, Jesus started speaking to the crowds about John. 'Remember how you all went chasing out into the desert? Well, what

---

1. The standard text says he 'had compassion' – which is often badly translated as 'pity', but there's a world of difference. Jesus didn't just feel sorry *for* her, but felt *with* her – actually experienced her pain. Remember, that's what Jesus came for – to share our suffering.

were you expecting to see? Someone weak, like a reed shaken in the wind? Not likely! Or was it someone in beautiful clothes? Look, if you'd wanted that sort of thing you'd have gone to a palace or somewhere. So, what *were* you looking for? A prophet, maybe? Oh, yes – but you got a lot more than that, didn't you! This is the one that scripture foretold: "Look, I'm sending my messenger ahead of you – the one who's going to prepare the way before you."[1] I'm telling you, in the old order of things, there's no mother's son greater than John – but of those who are already in the kingdom of God, even the lowest is greater than he is!'

[29-30] (Everybody who heard this, even including the tax collectors, recognised God's truth – after all, they'd received John's baptism. Not the Pharisees and scribes, mind you – oh, no. They'd rejected John's baptism and, with it, any involvement in God's purpose.)

[31-35] Jesus continued, 'You know what this generation's like? They're like silly children, sitting in a market place playing funerals, and jeering at one another: "We played the flute but you wouldn't dance – we wailed but you wouldn't cry." You really want it both ways, don't you! I mean, along comes John, abstaining from food and strong drink, and you say, "He's possessed by a demon, you know", but when you see the Son of Man enjoying his food and his drink, you say, "Ooh, look – he's greedy, he's drunk and he's got terrible friends, all those tax collectors and sinners!" Well, the things I've done are all the vindication I need.'

A woman and her perfume

> It's hard for us even to begin to appreciate just how offensive the woman's anointing of Jesus' feet must have seemed at the time. It was real toe-curling stuff, and the striking thing about Jesus' response is his calmness. He knows that she desperately needs to do this – and her needs are more important than either cultural etiquette or his own dignity and feelings. Here, in a very special way, Jesus is truly being 'the man for others'.

[36-40] Jesus got an invitation to dinner – from a Pharisee of all people! So, he went to the Pharisee's house and took his place at the table. The word got round, of course, and a particular woman, one with a rather sordid reputation, went to find him, carrying an alabaster jar full of

---

1. Malachi 3:1 and Exodus 23:20.

ointment. She was pretty obviously in a terrible state: for a time, she just stood there, behind Jesus, near his feet,[1] crying; then she began to spread her tears over his feet, as if washing him, and dried them with her hair.[2] Next thing everyone knew, she was kissing his feet[3] and smearing the ointment all over them. It was quite bizarre, yet Jesus didn't seem the least bit embarrassed by it.

The Pharisee who'd invited Jesus noticed – well, he could hardly fail to, could he! 'If Jesus were the prophet he's cracked up to be,' he thought, 'he'd know what a low-life this woman is who's mauling him.'[4]

'Simon,' Jesus said, 'I've got something to ask you.'

'Go ahead, Teacher,' Simon answered.

41-50 'It's like this. There was this man who'd lent money to a couple of other men. One of them owed him about fifty pounds and the other about five hundred. Well, neither of them had the slightest chance of paying, so he cancelled both their debts. Now, which of them's going to be the more grateful?'[5]

'Pretty straightforward really,' Simon answered. 'The one who'd had the bigger debt cancelled, I suppose.'

'Got it in one!' Jesus answered. Then he turned towards the woman. 'See this woman? Well, when I came to your house you didn't even offer me water to wash my feet,[6] but she's used her own tears to do it, and dried them with her own hair! Come to that, you didn't even welcome me – a kiss would have been traditional – but she's been kissing my feet continually. And did you anoint my head with oil? Not likely, you didn't – but she's anointed my feet with perfume. So, I'm telling you, all her sins – and there are plenty of them – are forgiven. That's why she shows so much love. But, then, someone who's so good they've never really needed much forgiveness – mentioning no names, of course – well, someone like that just wouldn't understand that kind of love, now would they?' Then he said to the woman, 'Your sins are truly forgiven!'

---

1. The custom there was not to sit but to recline at the meal table – so Jesus didn't have to be a contortionist for this to happen.
2. Culturally, for a woman to let her hair flow loose in public was an affront to decency.
3. Such intimacy from a stranger would embarrass most of us now. Then, it was simply unthinkable.
4. The text isn't clear what her 'sin' was, but she was almost certainly ritually unclean, so for Jesus to allow her to touch him was scandalous – and at the dinner table too!
5. The exact figures aren't important, but I'm told that the second debt amounted in those days to a pretty daunting sum – the sort of debt we might incur in buying a new car or extending a house.
6. An elementary courtesy in that culture, where roads were dusty.

The people around the table were horrified. 'Who does he think he is, to forgive sins!'

Jesus just said to the woman, 'Your faith has saved you – now go on your way in peace.'

Women following Jesus

8 [1-3] Soon after that, Jesus went on his way through the towns and villages preaching the good news of the kingdom of God. With him were the Twelve, as well as a group of women whom he'd cured of illnesses or in some cases demonic possession. Among them were Mary, known as the Magdalene, from whom seven demons had been exorcised, and Joanna – quite a notable figure, she was, the wife of Chuza who was on King Herod's personal staff. Then there was Susanna, and a lot of others who used their own personal wealth to support Jesus and his companions.

The parable of the sower

[4-8] When a crowd gathered round him, and people from one town after another came looking for him, he told them a parable:

There was this sower who went out sowing seed – as sowers do – and some of his seed landed on the pathway where it got trampled – and what wasn't trampled was snaffled by the birds who thought all their dinner times had come at once. Then some of it fell among rocks, so the wheat died as fast as it grew. No roots, you see – no way of getting water when the sun got up – you know how it is. Anyway, some other seeds fell in the briar patch and the wheat that grew there just got choked to death by all the weeds – so that was pretty fruitless. So far, not so good – but some of the seed fell on good soil, and, wow, did it grow – producing a hundred times its own weight. OK? End of story. If you've got ears, fine – use them.

The nature and purpose of parables

[9-15] When his disciples asked what this riddle meant, Jesus answered:

Well, whether it's a riddle depends on your state of mind.[1] Your minds have been opened to the secrets of the kingdom of God, so

---

1. The word for 'parable' can also be translated 'riddle'. Which it is depends on whether you understand it or not! Here, the openness of mind needed to turn a parable into a riddle is portrayed by Jesus as a gift from God: 'Your minds have been opened', or, as the standard text says, 'To you it has been given to understand . . .'

you understand them – other people's haven't so it's riddles to them: they see but don't really perceive it; they hear but they can't understand.[1] Now, here's what the parable's about: The ones along the path are the ones who've heard the word, but the devil swoops down and grabs it away so they can't believe it and be saved. Then the ones on rocky ground: well, they're the people who hear and get all enthusiastic, but it doesn't last. It's shallow faith, and at the first hint of trouble they're off back to their old ways. Now what? Oh, yes – the seed in the briar patch. Well, some people hear, and they really do have good intentions, you know, but then they get swamped by all the cares and pleasures of the world, and before long it's as if they'd never heard. But the good soil – well, that's something else. People hear the word, they really take it on board, and you start to see the results – it's that good fruit thing again. OK, now?

[16-18] Look, you don't go to the trouble of lighting a lamp only to hide it under a measuring jug, or shove it under the bed, do you? – you put it on a lampstand so that everyone who comes in can see the light. Well, nothing's hidden now that won't all be revealed, and whatever people keep secret now will be brought to light. So really listen, because those who have get more, and those who don't have lose even the little they think they do have.

[19-21] Then Jesus' family turned up and stood outside, but they couldn't get near him in the crush. 'Hey, Jesus!' someone said. 'Your mother and your brothers are standing outside – they say they want a word.'

'My family,' Jesus answered, 'are those who hear the word of God and act upon it.'

Stilling the storm

[22-25] One day Jesus got into a boat with his disciples, and said, 'Let's go across the lake to the other side.' So they pushed off the boat, and Jesus fell asleep. Next thing anybody remembers, there was a storm like a whirlwind, lashing water into the boat, and things were getting distinctly dangerous. So they went to wake Jesus up. 'Master! Master!' they yelled. 'We're dying here!' Jesus had a stern word with the elements, which promptly stopped raging, and everything was quiet.

---

1. An allusion to Isaiah 6:9-10, used in a way to suggest that it was a commonly used saying. It corresponds better to the Aramaic translation (the everyday language of Jesus and his hearers) than it does to the Hebrew or Greek versions.

Jesus wasn't impressed with the disciples, though. 'Where's your faith?' he said.

They were all completely amazed. 'Now, just who is this guy?' they were asking. 'He even gives orders to the wind and the sea – and they do as he tells them!'

Exorcising demons

26-30 Then it was on to the Gerasene region – the far shore from Galilee – where they were confronted by a man who was in the clutches of evil spirits. He was completely naked. He hadn't worn clothes for ages – or lived in a house for that matter, but lived among the graves.[1] When he saw Jesus, he shrieked out and fell on the ground in front of him. 'What business do you have with me, Jesus – Son of the Most High God? Look, I'm begging you, OK? Just don't you start punishing me ahead of time!'

Well, it was understandable, since Jesus had just given the demon its marching orders. It had often gripped the man in the past, and he was under constant guard – even to the extent of heavy chains and shackles, but he just used to rip them apart and the demons would send him charging off into the desert.

Then Jesus asked, 'What's your name?'

'My name?' came the reply. 'My name is Legion.' That was appropriate, because there was a whole colony of demons in the man.

31-39 Then the demons started crawling – begging not to be sent into the place of the dead.[2] And as it happened there was a large herd of pigs, grazing unsuspectingly on the hillside, and the demons begged to be allowed to go into them.[3]

So Jesus agreed to that, and the demons moved into the pigs – and in no time at all those peacefully feeding pigs were charging madly down the steep bank into the sea, where they drowned. The pigmen didn't hang around to ask questions – just took off into the town and

---

1. Living among the tombs would make him ritually unclean anyway, so it was a vicious circle.

2. ('Into the abyss' is one standard translation.) It's interesting: the man they possessed was living in a place for the dead on earth, but the demons were in dreadful fear of the eternal equivalent.

3. Pigs, of course, like demons, demoniacs and graveyards, were ritually 'unclean' under Jewish law, so it does seem grimly appropriate – although I'm not at all sure the pigs would agree.

the countryside round about and told the whole story. So, of course, the entire town got up and came out to see for themselves and found the man who'd been exorcised sitting quietly there, completely sane and fully dressed. They were awestruck – no, they were terrified.[1] The people who had seen the exorcism told them what Jesus had done.

Suddenly, everybody from the surrounding area was pleading with Jesus to go somewhere else because they were terrified. So, he got into the boat and went back.

The man who'd been possessed came scurrying over, begging to be allowed to go with him, but Jesus had a better idea. 'No, don't do that,' he said. 'Go home, instead – back to your family and your friends, and let them see how much God's done for you.' Which the man did – and how! He proclaimed it all over the city.

Jesus gives life to the dead

[40-48] When Jesus got back, the usual crowd were all waiting to welcome him. Then one of the local religious leaders, a man called Jairus, came up and prostrated himself in front of him, begging Jesus to go to his house where his only daughter – just twelve years old – was right on the edge of death. Jesus didn't hang around – he went with him, and the people were pressing in all around him as he walked.

Among them was a woman who'd suffered from a haemorrhage for twelve years. She'd spent all her money on doctors, but no one could cure her. She crept up behind him, touched the fringe of his coat, and immediately the haemorrhage stopped.

'Who touched my coat?' Jesus asked. Everyone denied it, and Peter, of course, thought it was hilarious! 'Oh, get real, Master!' he said. 'You can see how the crowd's jostling around you!'

'Someone touched me,' Jesus insisted. 'I know that some power went out from me.'

The woman knew it was no use hiding, and struggled forward, shaking with fear and apprehension.[2] She fell on the ground at Jesus' feet and poured out the whole story in front of everybody, about why she'd touched him and how she'd been immediately healed.

---

1. Understandably really – they were afraid of Legion, but at least he stayed in the tombs. Jesus was obviously more powerful – and he wasn't going to be confined by one of those!
2. Probably because she knew that her touch would technically have made Jesus ritually unclean – she expected him to be not particularly happy!

'Daughter,' said Jesus, 'your faith has made you better! Go in complete peace.'[1]

[49-56] Even as he spoke, someone from the synagogue leader's house arrived. 'No point in bothering the teacher any more,' he told Jairus. 'I'm sorry, but she's dead.'

Jesus overheard. 'Don't worry,' he said to Jairus. 'Just trust me, and she'll be fine.'

This wasn't a time for public demonstrations, so when he got to the house Jesus told everybody else to stay outside except Peter, James, John, and the child's parents, of course. What a scene! People were weeping and wailing enough to wake the dead – except that they hadn't. 'What's all the fuss about?' Jesus demanded. 'This is one death that's not going to last.'

They all had a good laugh at him over that, because they knew she was definitely dead, but Jesus took her by the hand,[2] and said, 'Child, arise.' The life returned to her and she got up at once. Jesus instructed that she should be given something to eat. Her parents, of course, were totally awestruck by it all, but Jesus warned them in no uncertain terms to keep quiet about it.

The mission widens

9 [1-6] Jesus called a meeting of the Twelve and delegated to them his authority over evil spirits and for healing diseases. Then he sent them out, to preach the kingdom of God, and to do healing. 'Don't get weighed down with provisions,' he told them. 'No fund-raising or getting kitted out with spare gear. Just go in what you stand up in. When someone gives you shelter, stay with them until you finish in that town.[3] If people reject you, then don't let's have any pretence about it. Shake the dust off your shoes as you leave, as a testimony that you've not been welcome.'

So that's what they did – went through the villages preaching the gospel, and healing everywhere.

---

1. This illness would have made the woman 'unclean'. For a full healing, she needed a proper encounter with Christ.
2. Touching a corpse – yet another challenge to the purity laws, since he would then be ritually unclean.
3. Wasting time in hunting around for somewhere nicer to stay wasn't part of the brief.

Now we're introduced to Herod Antipas – not to be confused with Herod the Great whom we met earlier. This is his son – and not one to be particularly proud of – but he knows Jesus is someone special.

[7-9] The local ruler, Herod, got wind of all this, and was really bewildered about it. Some people said that John had been raised from the dead,[1] others that Elijah had been raised,[2] and others believed one of the old prophets had returned. Herod just couldn't get the question out of his mind. 'I beheaded John,' he said, 'but who's this guy I'm hearing all this about?' And he tried to find a way of meeting Jesus.

The missionaries return

[10-11] When they came back, the apostles were brimming over with news about the things they'd done. So Jesus took them on a private retreat to a city called Bethsaida[3] but when the crowds heard, they followed. Jesus welcomed them, talked to them about the kingdom of God and cured any that needed healing.

The feeding of the five thousand

[12-17] Well, the day wore on and the Twelve said to Jesus, 'Send the crowd away and let them go and get some food to eat[4] – this is a pretty isolated place.'

'*You* give them something to eat,' Jesus responded.

'But, we've got no more than five loaves and a couple of fish – unless you're expecting us to go and spend our own money on food for these people.' To be fair, there were about five thousand men there.[5]

---

1. John the Baptiser, that is. Luke doesn't tell us the story of John's execution, but you'll find it in Matthew 14:3-12 (the shorter version) or in more detail in Mark 6:17-29.
2. The return of the prophet Elijah was widely expected by Jews as heralding the Messiah.
3. Mark makes the purpose explicit (6:30-31): Jesus wants to give time and attention to hearing their reports. Matthew links it more to John's execution, Jesus clearly deciding that this is not the right time for his death. Luke is the only one who tells us that Herod specifically wants to see Jesus, although apparently more out of curiosity than anything. Of course, there may have been a number of reasons in reality, but each gospel-writer emphasises the one that brings out his particular emphasis.
4. Exodus 16 and Numbers 11 both recount how Moses fed the masses in the desert – and here's Jesus, the new but greater Moses, in a remote place doing the same.
5. It's interesting that all three of the synoptic gospels (Matthew, Mark and Luke) refer to 'men' specifically, and Matthew makes it clear that the word isn't just a sexist way of saying 'people' by adding 'not counting women and children'.

'Make them sit down,' Jesus told his disciples. 'Get them organised into groups –about fifty in each.' When they'd done that, Jesus took the loaves and fishes, said a prayer of thanksgiving, broke them into pieces and handed them to his disciples who went and served the crowd. The amazing thing is that everyone had as much as they needed. More than that – when they cleared up at the end they collected twelve baskets full of broken pieces!

So, who is Jesus?

Now, the question Luke has been holding in front of us all the way through becomes explicit. Everyone, from the crowds to Herod himself, has been asking, 'Just who is this guy?' Do even the disciples yet know the answer to that? And if they do, do they understand the real meaning of it? Jesus moves quickly to correct any false expectations they may have concerning the nature of true power.

18-21 When Jesus was praying alone, his disciples were with him, and he asked them, 'What is it that the crowd are saying, about who I am?'

'All sorts of things,' they told him. 'Some say you're John the Baptiser come back, others say you're Elijah. Some are even saying one of the other prophets has risen.'

'OK,' Jesus said. 'Now, who do *you* say that I am?'

Simon Peter was right there with the answer. 'You're God's Messiah,' he said. Jesus gave them a solemn warning not to go telling everybody this.[1]

Jesus foretells his death and resurrection

22-27 Jesus continued, 'The Son of Man has to suffer all kinds of things: be rejected by the elders, chief priests and scribes, killed, and finally raised to life on the third day. Then Jesus said, 'If anyone's really determined to be a follower of mine, they've got to be prepared not to call their life their own – ready to take up the cross day after day[2] and follow in my footsteps. Those who are obsessed with safeguarding what they have in this life will lose it. On the other hand, those who are prepared to lose what they have now for my sake will discover real life through letting

1. Again, the time wasn't yet ripe. People still thought the Messiah would be a warlord – so bandying words like that around in such a climate would have been distinctly counter-productive!

2. Only Luke includes 'day after day' here. Following Christ will demand such commitment that we'll be called upon constantly to re-decide for him, re-commit to him.

go. What good does it do to gain the whole world if in doing so you lose your true self? With what do you propose to buy it back again? Put it this way: if anyone finds me or my words an embarrassment, well, don't expect to have it both ways when the Son of Man comes in the glory of his Father, with all the angels with him – that's all. I'm telling you straight, there are people standing here, right now, who won't taste death before they see the kingdom of God.'[1]

Transfiguration: a glimpse of Christ glorified

[28-36] About eight days later Jesus called together Peter, James and John, and went up a mountain with them to pray. And as he prayed, his face was completely changed and his robes were brilliant white. Then Moses and Elijah appeared. They were gloriously presented too, and they talked with Jesus about the great 'exodus' he was to accomplish in Jerusalem.[2] Now, you've got to understand, Peter and his friends were really shattered and had dozed off. So they woke up to see Jesus in glory and the two men with him. It's enough to make anyone speak without thinking! So, just as the two men were leaving, Peter called out, 'Hey, Master, this is terrific! I mean, this is *so* the place to be! Why don't I build three shelters – one for you, one for Moses and one for Elijah?' The poor man just didn't know what he was saying.

Even as he spoke, a cloud came right over all of them, and a voice said, 'This is my special Son – my chosen one – listen to him!'

And that was it! After the voice stopped, Jesus was alone. They didn't tell anybody about it at the time – just kept it to themselves.

Faithless disciples

[37-43a] Next day, after they'd all come down from the mountain, a big crowd met him again. 'Teacher,' one of the crowd said, 'please help my son – my only son. This evil spirit grabs him, so that he screams, and then it convulses him and makes him foam at the mouth, and it injures

---

1. People have argued over what this means for twenty centuries! The kingdom was in an important sense inaugurated with the death and resurrection of Jesus. This verse doesn't necessarily refer to the second coming. (Also, see 'Coming of the Son of Man' in the Glossary of Key Words and Phrases.)
2. The gospels are full of allusions to Moses (see especially the introduction to Matthew 2:13) and this is a great example of the parallel. As Moses led people to freedom via the desert, so Christ will finally lead his people to true, eternal freedom through the 'desert' of death and despair.

him – it hardly leaves him alone at all. I pleaded with your disciples to do an exorcism, but a fat lot of good they were!'

'Oh, great!' Jesus rounded on his disciples. 'You're no better than the rest of this faithless generation, are you! I sometimes wonder how much more of this I'm expected to put up with! Bring the lad over to me.'

As they were bringing him, the evil spirit threw the boy into a massive seizure. Jesus spoke sternly to the spirit, healed the boy and returned him to his father. And everyone was astonished at the sheer, majestic power of God at work.

Jesus foretells his death a second time

[43b-45] While everybody was raving about all the things he did, Jesus said to his disciples, 'Now, listen and listen well: the Son of Man is going to be given up to the worldly authorities.' His disciples just couldn't get it, though – the meaning was hidden from them – and they didn't have the nerve to ask him what it meant!

Real greatness

[46-48] The disciples were bickering amongst themselves about which of them was the greatest! When Jesus realised what they were about, he asked a little child to stand at his side. 'Anyone who welcomes this child in my name also welcomes me,' he told them. 'And anyone who welcomes me welcomes the one who sent me – because whoever's prepared to be least important among you is really the greatest'[1]

[49-50] 'Hey, Master,' John said to him, 'we found this man doing exorcisms in your name, but don't worry, we soon put a stop to that – he wasn't following with us, you see.'

Jesus wasn't impressed. 'So what!' he answered. 'What do you think you're doing, stopping someone who's doing good? You're going to have to learn that anyone who isn't actually opposing you is effectively on your side.[2]

---

1. I've worked with all kinds of people – some, like Jesus' disciples, seemed to be very concerned with their own status, but others were completely unaware of how truly important they were. One person in particular held a very senior position and had absolutely no interest in power or prestige, but just loved the people in the church. Such people are truly great.

2. It's interesting to compare this with Matthew 12:30 and Luke 11:23 where Jesus apparently says exactly the opposite. It just goes to show: we have to read things in context, because Jesus always spoke into particular situations.

Luke's special section

The journey to Jerusalem

'Journeys' are an important part of Christian tradition – the image goes right back to the beginning of Judaism. God calls us on a pilgrimage of faith. The call is his, but the choice to follow is ours – and sometimes it's a choice that has to be sustained and repeatedly re-made over a long time. In this journey we see heightening tension between the religious authorities and Jesus which, like the physical journey, all seem to be pointing towards one thing: the cross. We also here find Jesus placing great emphasis on teaching, as if he's really aware of the increasing urgency of getting his message through. This is a special section in Luke: it's not so much that the material is all unique to Luke (although some of it is); more the way he arranges and uses it.

[51-56] The climax of Jesus' ministry was getting near, and so he set out determinedly for Jerusalem,[1] sending people ahead to prepare his way. They went into a Samaritan village, but the people there knew he was determined to go to Jerusalem and didn't want him around. James and John thought retribution was in order. 'Look, Lord,' they said, 'why not just call down fire from heaven to burn them all up – that'd teach them.' Jesus gave them a real talking to over that – and then they moved on to the next village.

About discipleship

The next section illustrates an important distinction. While Jesus was there for everybody, unconditionally, when it came to people actually becoming *disciples*, he was careful to make sure they knew what it involved – especially now that he'd embarked on this fateful journey. This was not the time for half-hearted experimentation!

[57-62] As they were going along the road, a man came up to him. 'Hey,' he said, 'wherever it is that you're off to, I think I'll tag along.'

---

1. The standard text says that he 'set his face to go to Jerusalem' – we can almost see the determination in his eyes as he prepares to face the final ordeal.

'Oh, you will, will you?' Jesus answered. 'Well, it's not quite as easy as that – foxes have holes to sleep in, birds have their nests, but for the Son of Man there's nowhere that comfortable to get his head down.'

Jesus turned to someone else, and said, 'Follow me!'

'Lord,' he said, 'I'll be very happy to – just as soon as I've buried my father.'[1]

Jesus answered. 'Let the people who are spiritually dead themselves worry about things like that! As far as you're concerned, there's the matter of proclaiming the kingdom of God.'

'I'll follow you,' another one said, 'but you don't mind if I go and say goodbye to my family first, do you?'

'Matter of fact, I do,' Jesus answered. 'People who start off ploughing and are constantly looking backwards aren't a lot of use in the kingdom of God.'[2]

And then there were seventy

Mission is not something for leaders alone! Having previously sent out just the Twelve, Jesus now commissions a large number of people to go and spread the good news.

10[1-12] After that, the Lord chose another seventy people to go ahead of him in pairs to every town he was planning to visit. He told them:

There's a great harvest here, but far too few labourers to bring it all in. So get praying to the Chief Harvester to send in more workers. Off you go, then – I'm sending you into the world to live like lambs among wolves.[3] Don't get weighed down with provisions: no fund-raising or getting kitted out with spare gear – and don't get into idle chatter with passers-by; there's no time. Whenever you enter a house, say, 'Peace to this house!' If the owner is a person of peace, then that blessing will be effective – if not, well, you can't force it on them, can

---

1. Most probably his father wasn't dead. The man was postponing following Jesus for as long as his father remained alive – which could have been years! This would explain Jesus' response.
2. Remember the context: Jesus is resolute about going to Jerusalem. At this stage, anyone following him must be equally so. Any farmer knew that a ploughman who kept looking back ploughed a very crooked furrow, and Jesus wanted people to be completely focused on his mission at this crucial stage.
3. Witnessing for Christ can be a risky business!

you![1] Stay in the same house, and accept the food they offer you – after all, workers deserve their keep. And don't go hunting from house to house looking for better accommodation. When you get to a town and you're welcomed, eat whatever they offer you. Heal the sick, and tell them, 'The kingdom of God has come close to you now.' But if people reject your message, then don't let's have any pretence about it. Find a nice public place to shake the dust off your shoes as you leave, and say, 'Look – we're shaking off even the dust of your streets as a mark of your faithlessness – but just remember this: the kingdom of God has come close to you!'[2] I'm telling you that when the great day comes, Sodom will fare better than that town!

[13-16] Jesus went on:

A curse upon you, Chorazin – and a curse on you too, Bethsaida! Are you in trouble! Even Tyre and Sidon would have turned from their rotten ways and made sackcloth and ashes[3] fashionable if they'd seen the works of power I did for you – but on the day of judgement, they'll come out better than you will![4] And what about you, Capernaum? Reckon you've got a first-class ticket to heaven, do you? Think again – hell's more suitable for you.

Jesus addressed his disciples again, and said, 'When people listen to you, they're listening to me, and if they reject you, then they're rejecting me too – and in that case they've rejected the one who sent me.'

[17-20] The seventy missionaries came back, bubbling over with joy at what had been happening. 'Lord,' they said, 'even evil spirits submit to us when we speak in your name.'

'I know,' Jesus answered. 'It was like seeing Satan fall like a bolt of lightning from heaven. Look, I've given you the authority, haven't I? You can tread on snakes and scorpions; you can defy the power of the

---

1. In the Jewish tradition, blessings aren't just imposed on people; they need to be accepted. It's a bit like giving someone a cheque – if they can't be bothered to cash it, then they're not going to get the benefit and you'll still have the money!
2. Interesting how this term is repeated in opposite ways. To those who in faith accepted the healings, the kingdom of God was good news, but to those who rejected it, that same kingdom would be very bad news indeed!
3. Wearing sackcloth and ashes was a traditional expression of being sorry for sin.
4. Tyre and Sidon, destroyed by God for impenitence (see, for example, Isaiah 23), became a byword for insolence towards God – but the towns Jesus had visited had even less excuse! Sound harsh? The point is that forgiveness can't be forced – it's a two-way process: it simply can't happen unless the guilty party accepts it.

enemy – nothing's going to harm you now.[1] All the same, though, don't let it go to your heads. What matters isn't that you can boss the spirits about, but that your names are recorded in heaven.'[2]

[21-22] So, inspired by the Holy Spirit, Jesus gave thanks to God: 'Father, I really thank you. I mean, you're the God of all things, and you've chosen to make blindingly obvious to simple, uneducated people these matters that the so-called wise and learned just can't get a handle on! Oh, yes, Father – that's truly your will in action!'

He continued, 'My Father's given me authority in all things, you know. We're so close you wouldn't believe. No one's as close to the Son as the Father, and no one understands the Father the way the Son does – unless, of course, the Son chooses to make him known.'

[23-24] Then, in private, Jesus turned to his disciples and said, 'What an honour it is for any mortal eyes to see what yours have – because I'm telling you: there've been prophets and kings who've wanted to see the things you're seeing now – really strained to hear what you're hearing – but weren't able to.'

Love for neighbour, Christ and God

> Christian living is about how we relate to each other, but that in turn is actually an expression of how we relate to Christ – which in turn is linked with a life of prayer. That's the point Luke's making here, when he first tells us two stories that are special to him, and then follows them with the Lord's Prayer. Luke put it in this position in order to make a particular point: Christian ethics don't stand alone but are part of our relationship with Christ, of which our prayer life is an integral part.

[25-28] Just then, a lawyer tried to catch Jesus out. 'Teacher,' he asked, 'what have I got to do to get eternal life?'

'Well, you're a lawyer,' Jesus answered, 'so what does the law say?'

'Love God with all your heart, soul, strength and mind,' the man answered, 'and love your neighbour the way you love yourself.'

'That's right,' Jesus replied. 'Do that and you'll have real life.'

---

1. Amazing, unexpected things will happen when people really believe and live by their beliefs. Such vivid language was quite usual, and evidence of it can be found in the gospels.
2. Ah, now that's the point. It's the kingdom of God that we're supposed to be enthusiastic about.

Good neighbours

[29-37] 'That's all very well,' the man answered, pushing the point, 'but who counts as my neighbour?'[1]

Jesus answered, 'There was a man travelling from Jerusalem down to Jericho, and he was mugged. The muggers took the lot – including the clothes on his back – gave him a hiding and left him for dead. Now, he should've been in luck, because there was a priest who happened to be going that way as well, but he took one look, crossed the road and gave the man a wide berth before scurrying on his way. And in just the same way, a Levite arrived at the spot, but as soon as he saw the man lying there, he also crossed the road and made a bee-line for as far away as possible. Then there was a Samaritan – just happened to be passing that way – and he felt the pain the man was in.[2] He went over to him, bandaged up his wounds using oil and wine to clean them with, and then put the patient on his own donkey to take him to the nearest inn, where he had him properly nursed. "You take good care of him," he told the innkeeper, as he handed over some cash.[3] "Money's no object – I'll square things up with you next time I'm this way." Now, you tell me: which one of these was a neighbour to the man who got mugged?'

'Well, it's obvious,' the lawyer replied. 'It was the one who showed kindness to him.'

'Fine,' said Jesus. 'Now, go and do the same.'

Disciples of Jesus

[38-42] As they went on their way, they came to a village where a woman called Martha lived – and she welcomed Jesus into her own home. Now, she had a sister called Mary – and Mary just sat listening at Jesus' feet, taking in every word he was saying. That didn't please Martha at all, because she was chasing around like a mad thing getting the meal ready. Eventually, she could stand it no longer and went to have a go at

---

1. Is he in for a shock! He's trying to get Jesus to narrow the law down so that he only has to be nice to certain people. Jesus, though, is about to blow things wide open by defining as his neighbour the very last person the lawyer would think of. In other words *everybody*'s his neighbour!
2. The word 'compassion' is used here in standard texts. As observed elsewhere, this is not the same as pity; it means 'co-suffering', and suggests really feeling the pain someone else is in. It's an important point, because Jesus himself came to show our suffering, not just to feel sorry for us.
3. The amount given in the standard text sounds very little to us now, but is actually about as much as an unskilled labourer would earn in two days.

Jesus. 'Lord,' she complained, 'don't you care about the fact that she's left me doing all this work? Oh, you do? Well, tell her to get off her perch and help me, then.'

But the Lord said, 'Martha! Martha! Chill out! I know you're busy, but there's no need to let it get to you. At the end of the day there's one thing that matters above all, and Mary's chosen the better[1] option – no one's going to deny her that.'

People of prayer

11 [1-4] Jesus was at prayer one day and, when he had finished, one of the disciples said, 'Lord, you know how John's taught his disciples their own community prayer?[2] Well, will you teach us one of our own?'

Jesus answered:

> When you pray, say:
> Father,
> may you be truly honoured,
> your reign fully established;
> give us day by day the food we need,
> and forgive us our wrongdoing,
> as we forgive people who wrong us.
> And don't let our faithfulness be tested unreasonably.

Answers to prayer

This is a difficult passage, which seems at first to be saying that God needs to be hassled to give us what we need; and that if we badger him enough we'll get whatever we want. It's more helpful to think of it not as a comparison but as a contrast. Jesus is saying that, while we may have to pester other human beings, God is just longing to give us what's right for us.

---

1. 'Better', not 'good' – which implies that Martha's choice isn't actually bad. Very often we have to choose not between good and bad (which would be relatively simple) but between bad and worse, or – as in this case – good and better. Being a good hostess isn't to be sniffed at – but if it's a choice between that and being a good *disciple* . . .
2. It was usual for a religious community to have its own 'Community prayer'. The disciples were thus asking much more than to be taught to pray: they were asking for a form of prayer that would embody and express their emerging distinctive identity as Jesus' followers.

⁵⁻¹³ Then Jesus said to them:

Look: supposing you've got this friend, and you go knocking on his door at some unearthly hour – say midnight – saying, 'Hi, pal! Any chance you could lend me three loaves of bread? It's just that I've got this friend who's stopped off on the way somewhere, and I've nothing to give him to eat.'

But your friend's not playing ball, is he! 'Push off!' comes the reply. 'Stop pestering me – the door's locked, the whole family's in bed, and I'm not getting up simply to get food for you.' I'm telling you, he may not do it out of friendship, but you keep knocking on that door and he'll crack eventually!

And I'm telling you: ask for something, and you'll be given it; go searching – really searching – and you'll find; keep on knocking, and the door will be opened. Because everyone who keeps asking gets something; everyone who really searches finds, and for everyone who keeps pounding on that door, it *will* be opened.

I mean, look at your own families. So, your child wants some fish – are you going to say, 'Have a snake, instead; they've both got scales'?

Or maybe one of your children says, 'Hey, I'd really like an egg!'

So are you going to say, 'Try a nice scorpion?'

I think not somehow. So if you – poor sinful mortals that you are – know how to be decent parents, how much more will your heavenly Father give the Holy Spirit to you?

¹⁴⁻²³ On another occasion, Jesus was healing a man possessed by a demon that made him unable to speak. When the demon had gone, the man spoke, and the people were awestruck. Not everyone, though. 'Look,' some of them said, 'this guy can cast out demons because he's in league with the devil himself!' Others tried to test him by asking for a supernatural sign.

Jesus knew exactly how their minds were working. 'Use a bit of sense!' he said to them. 'Everyone knows that any kingdom that's divided against itself ends up being destroyed. That's true at every level – a divided city, or even a feuding family – none of them can survive. So if you're saying that Satan is divided against Satan, then clearly the underworld can't stand – look, you're the ones who are saying that I send demons packing by the devil's power! Anyway, put it another way: if it's from the devil that I get my power of exorcism, where do your own exorcists get theirs? I think you've just defeated your own arguments, which rather makes my point! On the other hand, if my powers of exorcism come from God, then it means that the kingdom of God has come and camped on your doorstep – with all that implies. Can you just imagine a strong man, armed to the teeth, guarding his property? I think his stuff's going to be pretty safe, don't you? That is until someone stronger comes, ties him up, disarms him, and makes off with his treasures.[1] Look, you're either with me or against me – there's no neutrality here. You decide whether you're going to be with me – bringing things together – or out there, creating division.'

Evil spirits and vacant possession

24-26 Jesus continued:

You know what happens when an evil spirit leaves a person? It goes walkabout looking for another home. And if it doesn't find one, what does it do? It thinks, 'I know, I'll go back where I was before – nice place, that.' And just suppose that when it gets there it finds it all nice and clean and tidy. 'Hey, this is a bit of all right,' it thinks, 'I'll get a few friends round.' So it goes and finds seven other spirits even more evil than it is itself, and they all move in with it. What a rave that's going to be! And the person ends up worse off than before the original exorcism happened.[2]

27-28 As Jesus said this, a woman in the crowd shouted, 'Congratulations to the womb that gave you birth, and the breasts that gave you food!'

'What you should be saying,' Jesus corrected her, 'is congratulations to those people who hear the word of God and respond to it creatively.'

The demand for proof

29-32 As the crowds around him were growing, Jesus said:

What a completely faithless generation this is – always asking for signs. Well, it's not getting any sign except the sign of Jonah. Remember the kind of sign Jonah was to the people of Nineveh? Well, the Son of Man will be that kind of sign to this present generation. The Queen of Sheba will stand in judgement on this generation,[3]

---

1. 'Binding Satan' was a traditional Jewish image. Jesus is clearly saying the only reason he can do the things he's doing is that he's effectively rendered Satan helpless.
2. So just getting rid of evil isn't enough – there needs to be a positive presence of good to fill the spiritual vacuum.
3. To come under judgement from a pagan foreigner – the Pharisees weren't going to like this!

because she travelled from the other side of the world to listen and learn from the wisdom of Solomon, and you've got something infinitely greater than Solomon right on your doorstep and can't recognise it! And the people of Nineveh too: they're going to rise up at the judgement and condemn all of this generation,[1] because when Jonah preached they repented – whereas you've got something a sight greater than Jonah standing right in front of you and you're rejecting it![2]

Light

[33-36] 'Now, you don't go to the trouble of lighting a lamp only to hide it in the cellar, do you? You put it on a lampstand so that everyone who comes to the house can see the light. Well, think of the eye as a lamp for the body: if it's healthy, you'll be all light, so you'll see things properly. But a bad eye's going to keep you completely in the dark. Take care, then, that what you think is the light in you doesn't turn out to be darkness. Got it? Look, if your whole body's full of light – no murky, dark corners anywhere – then it'll be completely bright, like a shining lamp.

Petty legalism

Here, Jesus lays into the Pharisees who're so hung up on the law that they've lost sight of its true purpose and meaning. They obey every single letter of it, but completely miss the spirit.

[37-41] While he was speaking, a Pharisee invited him to dinner. Well, it would have been churlish to refuse – and Jesus was never that – so he went in and sat down. And the Pharisee was astonished that Jesus didn't wash before the meal.[3] Jesus gave him short shrift:

That's the problem with you Pharisees. You wash the outside of a cup or a dish – but it's the inside that's filthy with greed and ill-gotten

---

1. The people of Nineveh, of course, were also foreigners – Jesus really is laying it on thick!
2. For both Nineveh and the Queen of Sheba, the word was enough in itself and needed no spectacular supernatural sign to verify it.
3. Now, no one's saying it's not a good idea to wash before meals. The point here is that it wasn't the hygiene the Pharisee was interested in, but *ritual purity* – legalism. He didn't care about why the law was there – just that people obeyed it.

gains.[1] You fools! Didn't the one who made the outside make the inside too?[2] So, be generous to the needy and that'll keep you pure inside – then everything else will take care of itself.

[42-44] A curse upon you, Pharisees! Oh, you're so careful about tithing,[3] aren't you? – when it's minute quantities of herbs that are at stake – but the really big legal obligations like justice and the love of God you conveniently forget about! Those are the things you should be focused upon – without neglecting the others, of course.

A curse upon you, Pharisees! Don't you just love the best seats at the synagogues, and to be bowed and scraped to in public!

A curse upon you! You're like graves that are hidden, and people walk over them without knowing it.[4]

[45-48] He'd gone too far for at least one of the scribes present. 'Teacher,' he said, 'now you're insulting us too, by implication.'
Jesus really let fly at that!

A curse upon you, scribes! You load up other people with all kinds of legal baggage, but do you lift a finger to help? Not likely! A curse upon you, because you build monuments to the prophets whom your ancestors killed, which makes you accessories after the fact – they killed them and you build their tombs!

[49-51] And now, the Wisdom of God[5] is sending you prophets and apostles, and you're going to do the same to them, aren't you? – kill and persecute them – and you'll bring on this generation the retribution still pending for every martyrdom since creation began, from Abel to

---

1. Jesus has cleverly pivoted the dirty cup to become a dirty Pharisee – now as far as a Pharisee was concerned, you could insult his wife, kick his dog, steal his best silver, but you just didn't call him unclean!
2. That's God, of course – so just maintaining outward respectability isn't enough. What's inside must be honouring to the Creator as well.
3. The legal requirement to give one-tenth of everything to God (in token recognition that the other nine-tenths are rightfully his also).
4. Jesus has now completely turned the tables. To think, this started out with *them* calling *him* unclean! Graves were about as ritually unclean as it was possible to get, and no Jew would knowingly walk over one. So Jesus is accusing the Pharisees of spreading contamination among unsuspecting, faithful people. This makes them particularly dangerous and abhorrent.
5. In the Hebrew scriptures, the Wisdom of God was thought of as a person – and after Jesus that person became identified by Christians as him.

Zechariah![1] I'm telling you straight, this generation will answer for all these things!

[52] A curse upon you, scribes. First you lock away the knowledge of God, and then you go and lose the key! You didn't enter the kingdom yourselves, and you hindered those that might have.

[53-54] As Jesus left, the scribes and Pharisees were heckling him frantically about all kinds of things, just trying to get him to speak so that they could catch him out.

12 [1-12] Meanwhile, when the crowd had got so big that the people were falling over one another, Jesus said to his disciples:

Beware of the 'yeast' that pervades and corrupts all the Pharisees' teachings – we're talking hypocrisy here. Don't worry, it'll all come out in the end – whatever nasty little secrets they try to hide now will all be made known. On the other hand, we don't have a secret life, do we? – so whatever you say in personal conversations can be shouted from the rooftops.[2] No problem! And I'm telling you, my friends, it's not the civil authorities you need to reckon with. They can take away your earthly life, but that's it. No, I'll tell you whom you should really respect: the one who has life-or-death power over your entire being. Oh, yes, I'm telling you – give him some serious respect! And he's the one you can trust. Look, sparrows are five for a penny, aren't they? But God doesn't forget one of them! As for you, he even counts every hair of your head! So don't go worrying yourselves, because you're worth a sight more than any number of sparrows. And I'm telling you, if you're prepared to speak for me, just to ordinary people, I'll do the same for you in front of the angels of God! But if you disown me to others, well, don't expect to have it both ways. OK? Now, you can say what you like about the Son of Man, but if you start committing blasphemy against the Holy Spirit,

---

1. According to the scriptures of Jesus' time, these were the first and last martyrs – so the persecution of Jesus' disciples is the culmination of the persecution of all God's messengers.
2. In standard translations, you'll find my 'in personal conversations' expressed as 'in the dark', but Jesus is contrasting himself with those who use darkness as cover. When he seeks privacy with his disciples, it's not because he's got something to hide – they can repeat it confidently in public – in 'the light'.

then you put yourself out of reach of forgiveness.[1] So when you find yourself being handed over to civil and religious authorities, don't start fretting about what words you're going to use – just trust God's Spirit to give you the words at the time you most need them.

The parable of the rich fool

[13-21] One of the crowd came up to Jesus. 'Teacher,' he said, 'will you tell my brother he's got to give me my fair share of our inheritance?'

'Now just who do you think has given me the job of arbitrating your family disputes?' Jesus answered.[2] Then he turned to the crowd and said, 'Just watch out you don't fall into the trap of getting greedy[3] – because the value of someone's life isn't about what they've got.' Then he told them a parable:

> Notice in this parable how the central character thinks entirely in the first person. No one else is considered at all. It's all 'Me, me, me'! *My* crop, *my* future, *my* land, *my* property, *my* barns, *my* life. Except that it isn't. The bottom line is that 'his' life is God's to take away. When that happens, the ownership of everything else is a bit academic really – and the life whose entire meaning was vested in ownership of all that stuff has no ultimate meaning at all.

There was a rich man, and his land produced a really terrific harvest.[4] 'Now, there's a poser,' he thought. 'Just where am I going to store my crops?[5] I know – I'll tear down my barns and build bigger ones. Then I'll put all my crops and everything I've got of value into those stores. I'll have no more worries – no need to earn a living – and I'll sit back and enjoy my retirement. Eat, drink and be merry – that's the life for me.'

---

1. It's important to read this in context. The Pharisees and scribes have completely lost sight of what really matters, and convinced themselves that bad is good. In that, they've shut themselves off from the *Spirit of Truth* who, Jesus said elsewhere, leads us into all truth. So it's not that God's withholding forgiveness from them, but that they've got themselves into a position where they can't accept it *because they can't recognise their need of it!*

2. Of course, the man's not really looking for an arbiter – he wants an ally!

3. The man's request may sound fair to our ears, but we don't know the circumstances. Under the system of that time, he could have been talking about his share in a family-owned business from which he wanted to withdraw in order to set up on his own in competition! That would have made Jesus' interpretation of it as greed quite reasonable.

4. Note, 'his land produced', not 'he produced'.

5. So it's suddenly all his, is it? Jesus clearly thinks otherwise – the land produced it, not him!

But God said to him, 'You're quite a fool, aren't you! I'm taking "your" life back, tonight – and whose are all those things going to be then?' That's the way it is, you see, with people who hoard up all the earthly possessions they can, but aren't rich in the things that God values.

[22-30] Jesus turned to his disciples, and said:

That's why I'm telling you: don't get obsessed with things like food and drink, or clothes. Isn't there more to life than that stuff? Take a look at the ravens. When did you last see one digging its garden? But God provides for them, doesn't he, and how much more are you worth to him than they are? And is getting yourself into a stew about things going to give you a single hour's extra life?

So, if you can't do a simple thing like that, why worry about all the rest? Take a look at the wild flowers – when did you see one of them working for its living – or going to dressmaking classes? And yet, I'm telling you that even Solomon in his best ceremonial gear never looked as good as one of those. But, look, if God dresses up the weeds that are going to finish up as fuel for burning, how much more care do you think he's going to take of you? Talk about little faith!

So don't go getting all hung up and anxious about what you're going to eat or drink – those are the kinds of things that people without faith keep harping on about, and your Father knows that you need them.

[31-34] Instead, why not set your sights on God's ways, and trust him to provide all that other stuff as well? Don't be afraid, little flock[1] – God delights in giving you the kingdom. So, just sell your stuff off – you can give the proceeds to the needy – and then you'll have the kind of wallets that don't wear out because your treasure will be safely tucked away in heaven where it doesn't depreciate, and moths and thieves can't get at it. It's simple enough: the things you count as 'treasure' will decide where your true loyalties are.

[35-40] So, be dressed and ready,[2] with lamps burning, like servants waiting for the boss to return from a wedding reception – ready and

---

1. Jesus isn't being patronising – he's recognising how vulnerable the disciples, who have so little, feel, and reassuring them at the same time that God knows their need. And if they're the sheep, then God must be the Shepherd.
2. The well-known biblical injunction to 'gird your loins' is used here. If we imagine trying to move quickly in the flowing robes of the period, we can imagine the need to fasten the robes up at waist height to allow easier movement.

waiting to open the door when he knocks. Congratulations to the ones whom he finds ready to meet him. I'm telling you straight, he'll fasten up his own clothes[1], sit them down at a table and come and wait on them himself![2] And if he comes even later, in the early hours of the morning, and finds them awake and ready, then congratulations to them!

Get this, though: if someone knew what time their house was going to be burgled,[3] they'd stay awake and defend it, wouldn't they? So you'd better do likewise, because the Son of Man will come when you least expect it.

[41-46] 'Lord,' Peter interrupted, 'are you telling this parable just for our benefit, or is it for everybody?'

The Lord answered:

Suppose a servant's given responsibility for caring for the family while his boss is away: if he wants to be in the good books when the boss returns, he's going to care for that family very well, now isn't he? I'm telling you straight, he'll give that servant some serious promotion. But a *bad* servant – well, that's another matter. He might take advantage: drink the boss's best wine, stuff himself with his food, ill-treat the rest of the household. Man, is he in for a shock when the boss arrives home unexpectedly! A fate definitely worse than death, you can safely assume!

[47-48] And what about the servant that knew perfectly well what his boss wanted, but didn't prepare, or do what he should have done? Well, he'll be severely dealt with – but the one who acted in ignorance will be more leniently treated. You see, a lot's expected of people who've got a lot of resources – if people are paying top prices, they expect top service!

The tension rises

Jesus' conflict with the religious establishment is gradually coming to a head. It will not be long before he has crossed the point of no return – where the authorities' rejection of him is complete. Jesus is clearly aware of this, and is preparing his disciples for it.

---

1. Same image again – 'gird himself'.
2. You may like to compare this passage with 17:7-10, and the footnote there.
3. An abrupt change of image here – just go with the flow! It's all about being prepared.

Turning up the heat

49-53 Jesus went on:

I came to set the world alight – and I wish it were already happening. I've got to go through a kind of baptism, and everything I do is hampered until that's been accomplished. I mean, do you think that my coming here is going to make everything hunky-dory, just like that? Real peace isn't that easy! My coming means trouble – big trouble. It'll tear families apart – three against two in a household of five, for example; son against father, daughter against mother, oh yes, and daughter-in-law against mother-in-law.

Signs of the times

54-56 Then he turned to the crowd:

You're priceless! You can look at the sky when cloud rises in the west and say, 'Looks like rain!' And when the wind's in the south, you say, 'It'll be a scorcher today!' And you're right. What a load of hypocrites! You can interpret the weather, but you can't even get close to understanding the other, really important, signs of the times.

Take the opportunity while it's there

57-59 And why can't you think for yourselves about what's right? Someone suing you for something? Settle out of court before it all runs away with you and you find yourself locked up for it – because there'll be no half measures then, and you'll end up paying the full penalty.

There's no 'us and them'

Next, Jesus is faced with the perennial question about why evil things happen. It's a good question, and Jesus avoids simplistic answers. It seems Pilate had killed some Jews and allowed their blood to be used to contaminate the sacrifices in the Temple. A second incident – referred to by Jesus himself – seems to have been a straightforward accident. Both pose different slants on the same basic question, and Jesus uses it to remind people that none of us has any scope for complacency. All of us are sinners; all of us die; but if we want whatever life we have to hold meaning, then we have to respond to God's call to repentance.

13 [1-5] At that exact time there were people there who reported to Jesus that Pilate had mixed the blood of some executed Galileans with the blood of the Temple sacrifices. Jesus countered:

Well? You're surely not suggesting that those unfortunate people were especially bad sinners being punished by God? I'm telling you that's not the explanation – but unless you change your ways, you're all going to die. And, then, what about those eighteen people who were crushed under the collapsing tower at Siloam – you going to try and tell me that they were in some way more guilt-ridden than the people in, oh, Jerusalem, for example? Again, I'm telling you they weren't – but unless you change, you're doomed as well.

The parable of the fruitless fig tree

Scripture is stuffed with images of fig trees, healthy and otherwise, symbolising blessing and judgement. In this parable, the gardener is interceding with the owner for just one more attempt to save the fruitless tree. To people listening, who would know the image well, this was a solemn warning indeed.

[6-9] Then he told them a parable:

There was a man who planted a fig tree in his vineyard. And did he get lots of lovely ripe figs? Not likely – completely unproductive, it was. So he went looking for his gardener. 'Now, see here,' he said, 'this is the third year this tree's been here and given me nothing. Well, that's it – it's a total waste of space. Cut it down and save the soil's goodness for something more worthwhile.'

'Well, sir,' the gardener answered, 'how about giving it one more chance? Let me dig in some nice, smelly manure around it – and if even that doesn't make it fruitful, then you can cut it down next year.'

An oppressed woman in the Synagogue

A healing miracle and so much more besides! Wholeness involves more than the healing of physical ailments (no matter how serious they in themselves may be). When Jesus enables the woman to stand up straight – hold her head up, we might say – in the synagogue, he tells her not that she is 'healed' but that she is 'freed from her oppression'. He also calls her a 'daughter of Abraham' – a remarkable dignifying of womanhood for that time.

[10-13] One Sabbath day Jesus was teaching in the synagogue when a woman came in who'd been oppressed by an evil spirit for eighteen years: she couldn't stand up straight. Jesus noticed her straightaway, of course, and called her over to him. 'Lady,' he said, 'you're free from all that oppression, as of right now.' He reached out and touched her. Her back straightened, her head came up and she looked everybody in the eye. Well, she started praising God as she'd never praised him before!

[14] The man in charge of the synagogue wasn't so happy. According to him, Jesus shouldn't have done the healing because it was the Sabbath when no one's allowed to work. So he announced to all the crowd, 'Look, there are six perfectly good days in every week when it's legal to work. So, if you want healing, you come on one of those days – not on the Sabbath. Got it?'

[15-17] Jesus had an answer for him. 'Oh, you absolute hypocrite!' he said. 'Don't you take care of your animals on the Sabbath – untie them, lead them to water? So, why shouldn't this woman – a descendant of Abraham, and don't you forget it – who's been oppressed by evil for all these years – why shouldn't she be set free from the oppression on the Sabbath day?' Well, that put his opponents in their place! They were hugely embarrassed, of course – but the whole crowd was ecstatic, because of the terrific things he was doing.

Parables of the kingdom of God

Mustard seed

[18-19] So Jesus said, 'What can I use to illustrate the kingdom of God? Well, it's like a mustard seed that someone sowed in a field and it grew into a tree, and the birds came and nested in its branches.'

Yeast

[20-21] And then, again, he said, 'What can I use to illustrate the kingdom of God? Well, it's like a little bit of yeast that a woman mixed with a lot of flour until *all* the flour was affected by it.'

The narrow way

> Does God artificially limit access to his kingdom? Jesus' answer seems to be that God doesn't impose limitations, but many people fail to make it. The problem isn't a rationing of God's love, but our limited willingness to accept it with all its implications. He is also saying that it's a decision we can't put off for ever.

[22-30] Jesus carried on with his journey towards Jerusalem, teaching in the towns and villages, and someone said, 'Lord, is there a limit on the number of people who'll be saved?'

Jesus answered:

Well, you'd better make every effort to get in by the narrow gate, because I'm telling you, there'll be plenty who try and don't make it. Once the door's shut, you can stand outside and knock all you like, shouting, 'Lord, open the door for us!'

'Have we met?' he'll say. 'I don't think I know where you're from.'

Well, of course, you'll begin to protest: 'Come off it, Lord, you must remember! Didn't we share meals with you? Didn't you teach in our streets, right where we lived?'

'Look,' he'll say, 'I don't know where you're from. Just get away from me, you rotten lot!'

Well, you'll wail, you'll gnash your teeth – especially when you see who's there: Abraham, with Isaac and Jacob, and all the prophets, in the kingdom of God, and you left out! And people are going to come from everywhere – from the farthest east and west, north and south – to share in the great feast of the kingdom of God. But an awful lot who are ahead of the game now will come in last, and vice versa.

Time to move on

[31-35] Just at that time, some Pharisees came up to Jesus. 'You'll leave here, if you know what's good for you,' they warned him. 'Herod's out to kill you.'

'Well, take a message from me to that old jackal,'[1] Jesus said. 'I'm going to finish what I came to do; so for a little while longer[2] I'll be exorcising demons, healing people, and then I'll be on my way. If he thinks I'm going to get bumped off in a back street in Galilee, he's got another think coming – the only place for a prophet to die is Jerusalem. Oh, Jerusalem! Jerusalem! The city that kills the prophets and stones God's messengers to death! If you only knew how much I've longed to gather your people together just like a mother hen gathering

---

1. This word occurs several times in scripture as a metaphor for a dangerous and disreputable person.

2. The original text suggests a three-day period. 'Three days' was a Jewish idiom for 'a little while' – rather the way we might say, 'I'll be with you in a second', meaning, 'I'll attend to you very soon'. The point was that Jesus' death was the climax of his work, and he wasn't about to allow Herod to decide when or where it would be.

her brood under her wings for protection – but you wouldn't have any of it![1] Well, you've got the Temple you always wanted, and it's utterly devoid of any spirituality. I'm telling you that you won't be seeing me again, unless and until you're prepared to take me seriously.'

Jesus heals a man with dropsy

14 [1-6] It was a Sabbath day again, when Jesus was having dinner at the home of one of the Pharisees. There was a man there with a particularly unpleasant disease – dropsy.[2] The Pharisees weren't missing anything – watching Jesus secretively, the way a cat watches a bird. Now, Jesus, of course, knew full well that they were watching. So he asked them, up front, 'Is healing somebody lawful on the Sabbath, or isn't it?' Not a word! So Jesus healed the man, and let him go on his way. Then he turned to the Pharisees and said, 'OK, so you tell me: supposing your son – or even an ox, if it comes to that – has fallen into a well on a Sabbath day. Which one of you wouldn't immediately go and rescue him?' Of course, they couldn't answer him.

Humility

[7-14] They weren't the only ones who'd been watching, though. Jesus had noticed how they all tried to grab the best seats – so he told them a parable:

> Look, suppose you're invited to a wedding reception. Don't go and make a bee-line for the top table and sit there, because it's obvious what's going to happen. Someone more important than you's going to turn up and you're going to be asked by the host to move to a lower table. Now, is that embarrassing, or is that absolutely cringe-making? Use a bit of savvy and sit at a nice, obscure, humble table, so that when the host arrives, he can say, 'Hey, what's this – what's a good friend of mine doing there? Please come over here.' Now, that's what I call being publicly honoured! It's obvious, isn't it? – people who go around flaunting their own importance are going to end up being humiliated, but those who show a bit of humility will get some serious respect.

---

1. A vitally important verse, this. The vehemence of Jesus' words is the product of an anger born of love for the nation and its religion – not hatred of it! None of this diatribe has given Jesus any kind of pleasure at all.
2. His limbs would have been swollen up with excess fluid – just the kind of condition that was labelled as ritually unclean in that society.

He hadn't finished yet, though. He turned to the man who'd invited him:

> Next time you throw a party, don't go inviting all the 'right' people – you know, your friends, family, the rich and famous, that sort of thing. If you do, they'll only invite you back and then you get into all that social tit-for-tat stuff and what reward is there in that? Why not do something radical: invite the poor people, powerless people – the ones who can't easily repay you. You can invite them just for the sheer joy of it, not for what you get back. Then you'll be repaid at the end, when the great resurrection happens – there'll be no class distinctions there, make no mistake.

> In the next parable, the metaphor is clear and challenging. Those who consider themselves friends of the host are complacent; they've already committed themselves to going, but then other attractions get in the way. Then we see the invitation going out in stages to a wider franchise: first to the excluded people within the city, and then to the complete outsiders who have no knowledge of the host at all.

The parable of the great dinner

15-24 One of the dinner guests, when he heard Jesus say this, said, 'Well, congratulations to anyone who gets to eat bread in the kingdom of God!'

Jesus answered:

> Think of a man who puts on a big dinner, and invites lots of people. Then when the time comes he sends his messengers out to all the people who've been invited,[1] to say, 'Come on over – dinner's ready.' So, what do they do? They all start making excuses.
>
> 'Well, you see, I've just bought this field,' one of them says, 'and I've got to go and have a look at it. Give my apologies, could you?'
>
> 'Dinner?' says the second, 'When I've just bought myself five pairs of first-rate oxen for my farm? Sorry, but I've got to go and check them out. You'll tell him how really sorry I am, won't you?'
>
> Then the servant went to the third, and guess what? 'Sorry, old lad,' says the guest, 'but I've just got married – you know how it is. Give my apologies – maybe next time.'

---

1. For a formal banquet, two invitations would have been usual – one to let everyone know it was happening, and give them a chance to respond, and then another to tell them the meal was actually ready.

The boss is beside himself with rage when he hears. 'Right!' he tells the servant. 'Now get out there quickly – go into the lanes and the back alleys of the town, and bring in all the down-and-outs you can find. Go!'

'Been there, done that,' the servant reports back later, 'but there's still a lot of space around the table.'

'Then you'd better go further afield, hadn't you?' the boss replies. 'Get out into the countryside, drag the tramps out of the hedgerows, twist their arms if you have to – I'm determined to have my house full. And I'm telling you this – none of those who were first invited are going to get a sniff of my dinner!'

Discipleship and commitment

Jesus is now going to lay on the line the potential cost of being a disciple – but he addresses his remarks not just to the closer group but to the 'large crowds'. The message is clear: the invitation to discipleship is open to all, but relatively few will take it up. We need to remember that our love for Christ finds expression in love for people.

25-33 As usual, there were large crowds travelling with Jesus, and he turned to them to say:

Anyone who comes to me and isn't prepared to lose their parents, their family – yes, even their own life – if it should come to it, can't be my disciple. People who aren't prepared to carry the cross can't be disciples. Look, you've got to be realistic. Would any of you start building a tower without first working out the cost to see whether you'll be able to finish it? I mean, you can just hear the neighbours, can't you, when you've got the foundations done and had to stop for lack of funds? 'Fancy starting something you can't finish!' Or, take another example: imagine a king going to war against the neighbouring one. Won't he sit down first and seriously ask whether his ten thousand soldiers will be a match for his enemy's twenty thousand? And if the answer's no, then if he's got any sense he'll send a peace envoy long before his enemy gets anywhere near. Well, the cost of being a disciple is to give up any sense that anything you have is your own.

Salt

34-35 I could compare you with salt. Salt's good, but if it loses its distinctive flavour, what use is it? You can't use it for fertiliser, or for compost-making[1] – so people just throw it away. Got ears, have you? So, use them.

15 [1-2] Now, every tax collector and general undesirable in the area seemed to be gathering around Jesus, and the Pharisees and scribes muttered, 'This guy doesn't just accept characters like this – he even shares food with them.'[2] So Jesus told them a parable:

The parable of the searching shepherd

[3-7] Think about it: suppose one of you has a hundred sheep and one of them's wandered off. What are you going to do – won't you leave the ninety-nine in the open country[3] and go searching for that one? And when you've found it, you put it on your shoulder and celebrate a little, don't you? Then, when you get back, you call your friends and neighbours: 'Come and celebrate with me – I've found my lost sheep!' Well, in the same way, I'm telling you there's more partying in heaven over one bad person who changes than over ninety-nine who are so good they don't have to!

The parable of the searching housewife

[8-10] Or, think of a woman who's got ten silver coins, and loses one. Doesn't she go and light a lamp and clean the house from top to bottom until she's found it? And when she's found it, she calls her friends and neighbours: 'Come and celebrate with me – I've found my lost coin!' Well, in the same way, I'm telling you you've never seen parties like the angels throw every time a bad person changes.

The parable of the waiting father

This parable brings the set to a dramatic climax. The thoroughly undeserving son is showered with love and forgiveness, while the faithful, eminently deserving one is left feeling unappreciated, bitter and resentful – unable to comprehend this kind of love and

---

1. Just two of the many uses for salt in that culture.
2. As I've observed elsewhere, sharing food with people indicated particular acceptance and commitment. That's why so many Jewish worship rituals include food (we could learn a lot from that!).
3. You may wonder what's good about a shepherd leaving ninety-nine sheep in danger to go and search for one that's lost. It's not unusual to find details that don't quite add up in a parable, since Jesus is pursuing one central point, not trying to cover all the angles. However, in this instance, Jesus and his hearers would probably assume the sheep were under the watchful eye of a friend or colleague.

unwilling to be associated with it. With things like sheep and coins, it's a question of searching, finding, and putting them back where they belong. With people, though, God wants to respect their freedom – which makes it just a touch less straightforward.

The parable is usually known as 'the prodigal son', or 'the lost son', but, of course, that puts the emphasis in the wrong place. The point of the parable is not just the son's lostness – that's the dark background that makes the light of the *father's love* all the more visible!

[11-13] There was this man, and he had two sons. And the younger one came to him and said, 'Hey, Dad, you know all the money I'm going to get when you die? Well, why not give it to me now, so that I can enjoy it?'

Now, it may seem strange, but the father did it – divided his property between his two sons, as if it was a perfectly normal thing to do! Of course, we can all guess what happened, can't we? In about as long as it takes to load up a camel train, the younger son had packed everything he had and hot-footed it to a faraway country where he blew the lot by living it up.

[14-19] Before long, he'd completely run out of money and, to top it all off, a monumental famine hit that part of the world. Things very quickly got a bit tight. So he went looking for a job, and one of the local people took him on to look after the pigs.[1] He was so desperate he'd even have been willing to eat the pigswill – no one ever gave him anything at all.

It didn't take him long to work it out: 'This is barmy!' he thought. 'Even Dad's employees have got more food than they can eat – and here am I, his son, starving to death. Well, there's nothing else for it – I'll have to go home. Now, what'll I say? "Hey, Dad, I'm sorry, right? I mean I've been a fool – OK, I know that now. I've done wrong to God, as well as to you, and I just don't deserve to be called your son – so can I work for you, please?" Yes, that sounds about right – should do the trick.'

[20-24] So off he went, all the way back home, but his father saw him coming from miles away and, being the kind of man he was,

---

1. Pigs! According to the Jewish religion they were ritually unclean. Anybody handling them would be seen as untouchable in the society that this man came from – so his degradation was now absolutely complete – he couldn't sink any lower!

instantly felt sorry for him. He went running out to meet him, threw his arms round him, kissed him and generally fussed over him. The son started to say his piece: 'Hey, I'm really sorry. I know I've done wrong, right? I've well and truly given God some grief – not to mention you – I'm not fit to be your son, am I!'

His father turned to one of his slaves. 'Well, don't just stand there gawping – go and get some clothes – the best ones you can find in the house – put them on him – and get a ring for his finger, and some decent footwear. Then when you've done that, you can go and kill the fatted calf and get a party organised. Are we going to celebrate or what! Look, it's my son who was as good as dead, and he's alive – he was lost, and now he's found again!' So began the biggest party the farm had seen for years.

25-32 Now, the elder son was out working on the farm – where a good, dutiful son should be – and as he came back, he heard the sounds of music, dancing and general partying. So he called one of the servants and asked what it was all about. 'Your brother's only come home, hasn't he!' the servant answered. 'So we've got your dad on a high and the fatted calf on a spit, because he's home, safe and sound!' Now, the elder son wasn't exactly pleased to hear that – in fact, he was so angry you could almost feel the heat! And there was no way he was going inside to celebrate – so his Dad came out to him, but he wouldn't listen.

'All these years!' he ranted. 'All these years of "Yes, Dad", "No, Dad", "Three bags full, Dad"! I've worked my shirt off for you – I've never refused you anything – and for what? I mean, I wouldn't have asked for much – just a goat would have been enough – a baby one, even – to roast so that I could throw a party for my friends. Was I ever offered it? Not rotten likely, I wasn't! But this son of yours comes back – this waster who's spent all your money on fooling around with prostitutes and the like – and he doesn't just get a young goat – he gets the fatted calf!'

His father protested, 'You're my son – you're always here – everything of mine belongs to you already. But can you blame us for celebrating when this brother of yours[1] who seemed dead has come back to new life? I mean, he was lost – and now he's found!'

---

1. Spot the parallel? The elder son dismissively says, 'This son of yours', but the father corrects him, 'This *brother* of yours'. Likewise, God refuses to let us dump responsibility on to him that should rightly be ours!

The parable of the wasteful manager

There are some difficult questions about this parable. One of several possible explanations is that the money the manager is giving away is not his boss's profit but his own commission (Jesus probably wouldn't need to explain this to his audience who would be familiar with the commercial system). He's sacrificing some of his own proceeds now, in the hope of a greater gain later. This isn't the only possible interpretation, but it's one suggestion. The steward might receive different rates of commission for oil and wheat, which would explain the differences below. If this is correct, he is doing nothing dishonest, but has shown wisdom in taking a longer-term view of how to use his own resources. The application to the temporary sacrifices made by disciples is now much easier to see.

16 $^{1-9}$ Jesus said to his disciples:

There was a rich man, who had a manager looking after his business. Well, he got word that his manager wasn't really managing – not being too careful with the funds, to put it simply. So he decided to get things straight. 'I've been hearing things about you,' he said to him, 'and I don't like them. I want an account of everything you've done, spent or even thought. Got it?'

Of course, the manager knew the game was up. 'What am I going to do?' he thought. 'I mean, I'm hardly built for manual labour, and I'm certainly not going to be seen begging around here – oh, the indignity! I know – friends are what I'm going to need, and I'm going to make sure I've got a few. Then, when I lose my job as manager, at least I won't be on the street – nasty, unpleasant places, streets.'

So, he called in a few people who had accounts to settle. 'What do you owe?' he asked the first.

'I still owe for a hundred jugs of your olive oil.'

'Well, I think we can make that easier for you – shall we just say fifty?'

The manager turned to the next customer. 'What does your account stand at?'

'A hundred containers of wheat,' the man answered.

'Mmm. Let's call it eighty, shall we?'

Now the boss was impressed with the intelligent way the manager had acted. You see, the people of this world are, in their way, a lot shrewder than the people who've seen the light.[1] So, I'm telling you: in similar ways, use your own resources wisely, with an eye on the eternal reception committee that will be waiting for you![2]

[10-13] What you need to recognise is that people who can be honest in little things can be trusted to be the same where the big issues are concerned – so, of course, anyone who can't be trusted in small matters shouldn't be given too much leeway in the big ones, either. If you've not been faithful in handling ordinary worldly wealth, who's going to trust you with the kind of riches that really matter? And if you've been dishonest with someone else's stuff, then who's going to trust you where your own affairs are concerned? You see, a servant can't have two bosses. They'll either hate the one and love the other, or be committed to the one and cheat the other. You can't serve God and selfish gain!

The rule of law and the rule of God

[14-16] The Pharisees scoffed at him – well, they would, since they were all very loyal servants where money was concerned! So, Jesus said:

Well, you're the ones who're obsessed with your own reputations, but God knows what's really in you. The trouble is that the things that make you popular with people are offensive to God. The law and the prophets that you're so keen on were all you had up to the time of John, but since him you've got the Good News of the kingdom of God – and I've been passionately urging – almost bullying – you all to join it.[3]

[17-18] Don't get me wrong, though – it'd be easier for heaven and earth to fade into nothing than for a single letter of the law to become

---

1. Think, for example, of the 'loss leaders' used in commerce. They hope that if they give something away now, they'll make more profit from you in the future!
2. In other words, to take it in context, we should use our money and possessions in ways that get us respect and affection for our generosity – and we'll benefit by it in the longer term.
3. The Greek is very difficult, here. Often, it's translated in such a way that it sounds as though people are fighting to get into the kingdom – which pretty obviously was not the case. My research suggests that this is a pretty accurate reflection of what Jesus was saying – that his own preaching had been so passionate that it was almost as if he were bullying people. And, even then, the Pharisees were resisting!

redundant![1] For example, anyone who divorces his wife and marries someone else is committing adultery. And if someone else does it, don't go thinking you can move in on her afterwards, because you'll effectively be committing adultery too.

The parable of the rich man and Lazarus

[19-24] You know, there was once a rich man – and, do I mean rich! Beautiful purple robes, fine linen underwear – no kidding! – and food – well, you've never seen anything like it. And that was just the everyday style! Outside at his gate it was quite a different matter for Lazarus, a man so poor that he could hardly be said to be alive[2] – his body was covered in open sores. He used to lie there longing to get the scraps from the table, while the dogs licked his running sores.[3] As you'd expect, he died, but the good news is he was taken by angels to be with Abraham – a fate better than death if ever I knew one! The rich man died, as well,[4] but he didn't come out of it as well as Lazarus. So there he was, in hell, looking across to see Lazarus with Abraham in heaven in the far distance. Well, he thought it was worth asking: 'Hey, father Abraham,' he called, 'do me a kindness, and just ask Lazarus to pop over here and wet his finger so that I can cool my tongue.[5] I'm in agony here!'

[25-31] 'My son,' Abraham answered, 'You might just remember the luxury you enjoyed in life and Lazarus at the same time put up with that horrible existence? Well, that's how it goes – now he's in luxury and you're in agony. There's a massive canyon between us, and no one can cross it either way, so I'm sorry but it's no go.'

'Well, if he can't come over here, could he take a message to my family, do you think? I've got five brothers, you know – at least I could save them from coming to this hell-hole.'

---

1. Jesus adds this because he wants to be clear – it's the Pharisees' idolising of the law that he's getting at, not the law itself.
2. He depended on others for food, and he had open sores on his body. According to custom, either of those would have meant that he counted as effectively dead.
3. If Lazarus hadn't been ritually unclean already, the dogs would have made him so.
4. Surely, Jesus must be making a point about shared mortality here? For all the fancy monuments we erect to the famous, the final experience of death is still, in the end, a great social leveller!
5. Interesting: he could ignore Lazarus in life, but in death Lazarus was expected to wait upon him.

Abraham looked puzzled. 'Now, how would that help?' he answered. 'They've got the whole of scripture to warn them – Moses, all the prophets – I mean, why can't they listen to them?'

'Oh, no, father Abraham,' the man answered, 'I mean, someone coming back from the dead – well, that's really spectacular stuff, isn't it! I mean, they'd be bound to listen then, wouldn't they? – *then* they'd all instantly change their ways and be really nice, you know!'

'Oh, get real!' Abraham answered. 'If they won't listen to Moses and the prophets – thousands of years of history – they're not going to take notice of someone who rises from the dead!'[1]

Various teachings of Jesus on discipleship

17 [1-4] Jesus said to his disciples:

The world's always going to have stumbling blocks[2] in it, but a curse upon those people who deliberately put them in place! What's coming to anyone who does that will make them think that being drowned would have been preferable to tripping up one of these humble people.[3] Take care of yourselves. If you think another disciple's going off the rails, have a quiet word when you're alone, and if that works, then leave it at that. And even if the same person offends you seven times in the same day, but genuinely regrets it and tries to change, then you just keep right on forgiving.

[5-10] 'You'd better give us a bit more faith!' the apostles said.

Jesus answered:

If you only had faith as tiny as a mustard seed, you could say to this mulberry tree, 'Uproot yourself from here, and go and plant yourself in the sea', and it would obey you.[4] Look, if you'd got a servant,

---

1. There *must* be a resurrection reference here – what a wonderful bit of irony! The people whom Jesus accused of ignoring (and worse) the prophets were to be completely unimpressed by the resurrection.
2. A familiar image used by Jesus. This is what he accused Peter of being in Matthew 16!
3. Often called 'little ones' or 'the least'. In other gospels, Jesus uses this teaching subtly to merge the child image with people who choose service over self-aggrandisement.
4. A couple of important points here. Firstly, Jesus' emphasis in talking about faith was always on the power of God working through even the tiniest faith – not upon the power of the human will. Secondly, since a world where this was happening all the time would be unthinkable, Jesus was clearly using a picture to say that God would do impossible things if only there were an atom of faith for him to work with.

ploughing your land, say, or keeping your sheep, and you saw him coming in after a day's work, would you say, 'Hey, you look whacked – come and sit here and eat dinner'? Wouldn't you be more likely to say, 'Go and cook dinner, then get properly dressed and serve it to me – and then when you've done that you can get yourself something'? Well, the same goes for you. When you've done all you can, you'll have done no more than your duty.[1]

Jesus heals ten people

[11-19] On his way to Jerusalem, Jesus went through the border country between Samaria and Galilee, and as he approached a village ten people with leprosy started shouting to him, while keeping their distance. 'Hey, Jesus! Master! Do us a kindness!'

As soon as Jesus saw them he said, 'Just go and show yourselves to the priests.' So off they went, and on the way they were suddenly healed of their leprosy.[2] One of them turned back as soon as he saw it, shouting and singing his praise to God, and threw himself down at Jesus' feet to thank him. And the really interesting thing is that this man was a Samaritan.

'You know, it's a funny thing,' Jesus said. 'I was sure I healed ten of them – and wasn't there one who could come back and praise God for it, other than this outsider?' Then he turned to the man who'd been healed. 'Get up,' he said, 'and get on your way. Your faith has made you well.'

The coming of the kingdom – part 1

In Matthew and Mark, these sayings of Jesus about the coming kingdom are kept together as part of his conversation with his disciples on the Mount of Olives. In Luke, however, they are in two parts (the other begins at 21:5). Here the Pharisees prompt the first of these discourses by asking about the Kingdom.

---

1. This passage is intended to stop us thinking all the time about how much we deserve! It's interesting to see the contrast with 12:35-40 in which Jesus says apparently the exact opposite! God longs to provide for his people – the whole of the incarnation was an expression of God's 'service' to us. The point is, though, that this is because of God's goodness and not because we've done anything to deserve it. When we respond appropriately to God, as in that other passage, we make that kind of relationship possible, but we haven't 'deserved' it!

2. So, there was an act of faith here – they set off before they were healed, apparently trusting that Jesus would heal them.

[20-21] When the Pharisees asked Jesus when the kingdom of God was going to come, he rounded on them and said:

Well, it's not going to come with some obvious, predetermined signs of the kind that you can observe. And you're not going to have people saying, 'Look, here it is,' or 'I've found it – it's over there!' because the kingdom of God is right here among you already.[1]

[22-33] Then Jesus turned to his disciples:

You know, the days are coming when you'll long for the great day of the Son of Man but won't see it. And people will say, 'Look here!' or 'Over there!' but don't go chasing after them. You know how lightning lights up the entire sky – you can hardly be in any doubt about it, can you? Well, that's how the Son of Man will be when the great day comes. But before that he has to suffer all sorts of things and be completely rejected by this generation. And it will be like the story of Noah. Remember that? There they all were, eating and drinking, marrying and planning their futures together, right up until the last moment when Noah went into the ark – and the flood hit them and destroyed them all. Then you may remember the story of Lot – people eating and drinking, buying and selling, planting crops, building houses,[2] right up until the moment Lot left Sodom, and then the fire and sulphur poured out of the heavens and killed the whole gaggle of them – well, it'll be that sudden, when the Son of Man is finally fully made known. Now, when that happens, if someone's up on the rooftop and their stuff's down in the house, it'll be no good just popping inside to get something – and people who are in the fields had better not try to get back to fetch their belongings – remember what turning back did for Lot's wife![3] Life's a funny thing – the more you grasp at it, the more it eludes you, but those who put their lives and lifestyles on the line for me will find what real living is about!

---

1. This is part of what has been called the 'now and not yet' of the kingdom. Although it's a future hope, it's also a present reality – rather as we might say that the day has begun when the first rays of dawn appear in the east. That light is a sign that the day will come – in all its brightness – but it also means that it is already here. The sign of the future is part of the present reality. Jesus now turns to the 'not yet'.
2. Both of these last two are, of course, statements of confidence in the future.
3. She was turned into a pillar of salt. The moral's easy enough: there are times when forward is the only way to be looking!

[34-37] I'm telling you, in that night there'll be two people in the same bed and one will be taken and the other left behind.[1] Or it could be two women grinding corn together – one taken, one left.

'So, where's this going to be, Lord?' they asked him.

'Don't worry,' Jesus told them, grimly. 'You'll know – just look for where the vultures are gathering, and that's where the bodies will be.'

Prayer: what's the point?

It might be helpful to refer back to the introduction to Luke 11:5, here: it's another contrast parable intended to address an important question. Not only is God all-seeing and all-knowing, but he's also just longing to do good things for his people and relieve their suffering. So, what's the point of telling him what he already knows or asking him for what he already wants to give?

But, of course, prayer isn't just about asking and getting, is it? We talk to each other – tell each other the obvious very often – just because it's part of our relationship. We put our children into other people's care with words such as 'Take care of her', not because we think they need telling but as a way of showing our care and our trust.

So our prayers to God are nothing like our dealings with, say, a judge, to whom we might have to plead our case very powerfully. God knows our needs and longs to meet them. We talk to God because we love him – not because we want something from him.

That's the contrast Luke now tries to bring out in the next parable, which is unique to his treatment of the gospel.

The unjust judge

18[1-8] Jesus told them a parable to show how they shouldn't get disheartened about prayer.

In the city, there was a judge who really didn't care – not about God or about people. And there was a widow in the same city who

---

1. Now, if we ask, 'Taken where?' the text isn't very helpful – but then it doesn't need to be. Whether it's one person taken to heaven and the other left out, or one taken to judgement and the other spared, the principle's the same: commitment to Christ, not family ties or friendship, is what's going to matter, and it will often divide people from those closest to them.

needed a bit of backup against someone who was harassing her.[1] 'Tell this guy that I'm in the right,' she kept pleading.

Well, the judge didn't bother much at first – just told her to sling her hook – but then he thought, 'This is silly – I may not care about God or about people, but I certainly care about me! I'm going to judge in this woman's favour, and then maybe I'll get a bit of peace before she wears me out with her nagging.'

So take notice of what this lazy judge says – and won't God be even more eager to judge in favour of his people, who're always calling on him, day and night? What – do you think he's going to keep them hanging around like that? I'm telling you, he'll give them good judgement, and quickly. But the question still remains, though: when the Son of Man comes, is he going to find faith here on earth?

[9-14] He told another parable – this one was aimed at those who trusted their own piety and looked down on others as inferior.

OK, so two men go up to the Temple to pray – one of them's a Pharisee, and the other's a tax gatherer.[2] So the Pharisee stands there and prays to himself.[3] 'Oh, God,' he says, 'I really thank you – you know? Because I'm not like other people, am I? I mean, other people run extortion rackets, pervert justice, commit adultery, all that kind of stuff.[4] And I really thank you – no, God, *really, really* thank you – that I'm certainly nothing like that tax gatherer over there. Well, there's no comparison, is there? I do ritual fasting, twice every week; I give tithes[5] of everything I get. I mean, I'm really a pretty all-round OK sort of a guy! Thank you, God.'

Well, the tax gatherer's in a real state – he can't even raise his eyes towards heaven, but keeps his head down and beats his chest in anguish. 'God be merciful to me,' he says, 'for being such a bad lot!' I'm telling you, that man went home in a better relationship with

---

1. Widows are one of the representative groups that stand for powerless people. And you don't get much more powerless, in a society with no social security and where women have no rights – thought of as someone's property, and if the 'owner' died, their fate was in the hands of others.
2. Collecting taxes for the Roman occupiers made these people top of the 'Hate and Despise' list, even if they weren't cooking the books and defrauding the poor.
3. Get it? 'Prays *to himself'* – not to God!
4. Clever, isn't it! First, he narrowly defines 'sin' as all the really dreadful things, and then he can say that because he doesn't do those he must be a good man!
5. The law required that a tenth of all crops, earnings, etc., should be offered as token recognition that *everything* we have is really God's.

God than the other one did. You see, people who put themselves on pedestals are likely to come crashing down, but those who humble themselves are going to be lifted up.[1]

---

1. Luke has recorded Jesus saying something like this before (14:11) and it also echoes the words of the *Magnificat* in 1:51-53. This is a significant theme in Luke – again, not entirely absent elsewhere, but highlighted by Luke in particular.

Jesus in Judea

Luke doesn't specifically say, 'Jesus entered Judea' at this point, but both Matthew and Mark provide that information. Although Luke arranges his material rather differently, he has recently told us that Jesus has left Galilee towards Samaria, and soon we will find him in Jericho. It's very clear that he's on his great self-offering journey to Jerusalem. So this main section heading has been placed here to enable the relationship between the three Synoptic gospels to be seen more clearly.

¹⁵⁻¹⁷ Some people were bringing children – even babies – to Jesus, so that he could lay hands on them. When the disciples saw it, they told them to get lost, but Jesus wasn't having that. 'Get out of the way and let the little children come to me,' he said, 'because it's to people like these that the kingdom of God truly belongs. I'm telling you straight, you've got to change your whole outlook on things – forget the rat-race and learn to live without all that status-obsession, the way children have to – before you even get a foot in the door!'

The rich man's ambition

This man wanted to know what he could *do* to secure eternal life. The idea that it can be either earned or bought isn't exactly uncommon today, is it! We find it so hard to accept a gift, don't we? – so hard, in fact, that we sometimes end up missing out on the best things in life.

¹⁸⁻²² One of the local dignitaries[1] came up to Jesus and said, 'Good teacher, can you advise me – I'd like to do something that'll guarantee I get eternal life.'

'Save the flattery for God,' Jesus answered. 'He's the only one you should be calling good – and he's what this is all about, isn't he! Look, it's God's laws, not human achievements, that count – and you know his commandments: don't commit adultery, don't murder, don't steal, or lie about people; *do* honour your parents . . .'

---

1. The man would be a lay person – not a priest – from a wealthy aristocratic class that exercised influence and leadership.

The man persisted, 'I've done all that since I was just so high – but it doesn't seem enough.'

When Jesus heard that, he said, 'There's just one thing missing. Go and sell all your stuff, and give the money to the poor. Then you'll have real treasure in heaven – the kind that lasts for eternity. And when you've done that, come and follow me.'

23-27 Well, talk about a let-down! The poor fellow's face was a picture of gloom! That wasn't what he'd wanted to hear at all – because he was remarkably rich – and he was a very unhappy man.

Jesus looked at him. 'It's tough,' he said. 'If there's one thing the rich can't afford it's a ticket to the kingdom of God. You'd see a camel go through the eye of a needle before you saw a rich person earn their way in.'

The people listening were aghast. 'Well, in that case, what hope is there for anyone at all?' they asked.

'Ah, now there's the heart of it,' said Jesus 'What's impossible with mortals is quite possible with God!'

28-30 'Fine,' Peter said. 'Well, we've given up our homes to follow you.'

Jesus said to them, 'I'm telling you straight, there's no one who's given up their homes or families for the sake of the kingdom of God, who won't get it back countless times over.[1] I'm talking about now, in this life – and afterwards, in eternal life, as well.'

Jesus again foretells his death and resurrection

In Luke, this is Jesus' sixth reference to his future suffering – although not always specifically to death or resurrection. Sometimes he has referred just to his betrayal (9:44) or to his suffering and rejection. However, he's twice specifically said that he's going to be killed, and made another clear reference to it in his message to Herod (13:32-33), which only Luke records. Very clearly, Luke wants to highlight just how great the misunderstanding of Messiahship was even among those who knew Jesus best. After all these attempts he still hadn't got it through to them! How interesting that this final prediction is immediately followed by a miracle of opening blind eyes!

---

1. Think about it: if everyone's sharing everything, and 'holding all things in common ownership' (Acts 2:44) then everyone 'owns' countless houses, etc! It's really saying that everyone will be abundantly provided for because of the community principles.

[31-34] Jesus took the Twelve to one side again and said, 'Look, we're going to Jerusalem – so it's showdown time. Everything that's been prophesied in scripture about the Son of Man is going to be fulfilled. He'll be handed over to the Gentile authorities where he'll be humiliated, abused and spat on. Then they'll have him flogged and killed, and on the third day he'll rise to life.' But they didn't have a clue what he was talking about – the meaning was hidden from them, and they just couldn't get their heads round it.

Sight for the blind

[35-43] As Jesus approached Jericho, a blind man was sitting by the side of the road, begging. When he heard the crowd going by, he asked what was happening, and they said, 'Jesus – from Nazareth – he's on his way past, right now!'

That was all he needed. 'Jesus!' he shouted. 'Son of David – will you do a kindness for me?' The people in front tried to shut him up, but he wasn't having any of it and just kept shouting more loudly, 'Son of David – will you do a kindness for me?'

Jesus stopped, and ordered that the man should be brought over to him.

When he got near, Jesus asked, 'What is it you want me to do for you?'[1]

'Lord, I just want to be able to see!'

'Accept your sight,' Jesus said. 'Your faith's healed you.'

Immediately the man got his sight back and followed Jesus, glorifying God – as did all the other people who saw it, too.

Jesus and Zacchaeus

19 [1-10] So Jesus reached Jericho, and was passing through. In Jericho there was a man called Zacchaeus – a superintendent tax inspector, and a rich man by any standards. Now, he was trying to get a good look at Jesus, but the crowd was so dense he couldn't see through – he was a touch on the short side, you see. You don't get to be a superintendent tax collector – and survive – without being resourceful, though, so he ran ahead and shinned up a sycamore tree to get a better view. He knew Jesus would have to pass right by where he was. Reaching the spot,

---

1. This is the humble servant talking – not the expert of people's expectations. You or I would probably have just assumed that blind people wanted to see, but Jesus knew better than to make assumptions.

Jesus looked up, and saw Zacchaeus. 'Hey, Zacchaeus,' he called, 'what's the good of being up there? Come on, hurry up and get down – I'm coming to your place today!'

Well, that was the first Zacchaeus had heard of it, but he wasn't about to argue. He came down at full speed and gave Jesus a warm welcome to his house. Everyone else who'd witnessed the encounter was less happy about it and started whinging among themselves. 'See what he's done?' they complained. 'He's only gone in to share food as the guest of a low-life like that!'

Zacchaeus stood up, and said, 'Look, Lord, I'm going to give half of everything I've got to the poor. And that's just for starters. If I've conned anyone, I'll repay them four times over.'

'Well,' Jesus said, 'salvation's certainly come to this house today, and no mistake – because whether you lot like it or not, this guy's a descendant of Abraham too. You see, it was the ones who'd wandered away and got lost that the Son of Man specifically came to save.'

The parable of the king's return

> This parable is very like the parable of the talents – headed 'A parable of trust and responsibility' in Matthew 25:14-30 – but Luke's detail is slightly different. Did Jesus tell both as separate stories, or did God inspire Matthew and Luke to tell the same story in different ways to give it a complementary slant?
>
> Luke's different detail keeps the point of the parable but sharpens the focus on the second coming of Jesus. The point is crystal clear: we should expect Christ's return, but be prepared to give account for how we've used the time before it.

[11-14] As the people listened to Jesus saying these things, he went on to tell them a parable – he knew that he was close to Jerusalem and he also knew that they thought what *they* called the 'kingdom of God' was going to appear instantly.[1] So he said:

I want you to think about a nobleman who went on a long journey to a really distant country where he was going to be crowned king – then he was planning to return.[2] So he called ten of his staff to a

---

1. So Jesus wants to point them to the fullness of the kingdom in the more distant future.
2. So, far from inaugurating the kingdom as a quick fix, he's going away, to return as king later – and in the meantime he's going to entrust everything to his followers.

meeting, and gave each of them a pound,[1] saying, 'Trade with this money until I come back.'

Some of his people hated him, and sent envoys after him, saying, 'We don't want this man as our king, thank you very much!'

[15-19] Anyway, he came back after his coronation, and issued orders for his servants to be called in front of him so that he could check their accounts. The first one arrived and said, 'Sir, the pound you gave me has made ten more.'

'Great!' exclaimed the king. 'Well done! You're a good servant, and you've done a good job with the little bit I gave you, so now I'm going to make you governor of ten cities!'

Then the second servant came up. 'Sir, the pound you gave me has made another five.'

'Terrific!' the king said. 'You'll be governor of five cities!'

[20-27] Another servant came forward. 'Well, um, sir – er, I've got your pound here – kept it safe – folded up in a napkin. It's like this, you see. I, um, well . . . look, you're a good businessman, right – tough and ruthless? I mean, you make profits out of nothing! I knew I couldn't measure up to your standards.'

'You're condemned out of your own mouth!' his master said angrily. 'Oh, so you knew I was tough, did you? You knew I was ruthless? Then why didn't you at least put the money in a bank where it would get interest?' Then he turned to the people around them and said, 'Take his pound away from him and give it to the guy who ended up with the ten pounds.'

The people said, 'Sir, he's got ten pounds already!'

'That's the way it is,' the king answered. 'Those who have, get more, and those who don't have, lose even the little they have already. Now, what about those enemies who said they didn't want me as their king? Have them brought here and executed right in front of me!'

---

1. Luke has levelled the playing field: in Matthew people were given different amounts according to their ability; in Luke, we all have equal responsibility as stewards of the things of God's kingdom. A mina, which modern translations call a pound, was actually about three months' earnings for an unskilled man.

Jesus in Jerusalem

Here begins the ultimate journey, on which Jesus calls us to follow him. But it is the hardest journey of all, as it calls us finally to relinquish all our ideas of status, power, victory, and so forth, and recognise the greatest victory in defeat, the highest success in failure, the way to the best possible life in a preparedness to die.

28-34 After saying this, Jesus went striding ahead towards Jerusalem. As he approached Bethphage and Bethany at the Mount of Olives, he said to two of his disciples, 'I'd like you to go into the village, and when you get there you'll find a colt tied up – one that's never been ridden. Just untie it and bring it to me, here. Oh, and if anyone says, "Why are you untying it?" just say, "The Lord needs it."'

The disciples went off on their errand and found everything just as he'd said. As they untied the colt, its owners said, 'Hey! Why are you untying that colt?'

The disciples said, 'The Lord needs it.'

Jesus enters the city

35-38 They brought it to Jesus, threw their own coats over its back, and sat Jesus on the colt to ride into town. Then people spread their own coats on the road in front of him – talk about putting out the red carpet! As they got nearer, descending the Mount of Olives, all the disciples started celebrating and praising God at the tops of their voices, for all the great works they'd witnessed. 'Congratulations to the one who's coming in God's name!' they shouted. 'Peace in heaven! Glory in the highest!'

The next passage contains a terrible judgement, but we must remember that it's spoken through floods of tears. Jesus is not so much angry as grief-stricken. The principle is that God has offered his love to his people – but you can't force good relationships on anybody. God is being rejected, and is respecting the people's choice. He won't be on the outside, though, saying, 'I told you so', but right at the heart of the pain, suffering it with them. The siege outlined below happened in AD 70 when the rejection of God's way of love led to violent revolution that was brutally put down by the Romans.

[39-44] Some of the Pharisees in the crowd said to Jesus, 'Hey, teacher – could you shut your disciples up, do you think?'

'What?' Jesus answered, 'Stop them celebrating? I'm telling you that if they weren't doing it, the very stones themselves would shout for joy!' But when he got closer to the city, he was in tears for it. 'If only you knew,' he wept, 'even at this late time, the things that would really be for your true peace and wellbeing![1] But now all of that's hidden from you, because the days are going to come when your enemies will besiege you, build big banks around you, hem you in from every side, before they flatten you to the ground, complete with all the babies still waiting to be born; there won't be a single stone left standing on another – and all because you couldn't recognise the time of God's visitation of you!'

A confrontation in the Temple

[45-48] Jesus went to the Temple and laid into the traders. 'You know what scripture says,' he roared at them. '"My house is to be a place for prayer"[2] – you've turned it into a thieves' kitchen!'

From then on, Jesus was in the Temple, teaching, every day. As far as the chief priests and the scribes were concerned, he'd finally pushed things too far – he definitely had to go. But, plot as they might, they couldn't see what they could do, since the people all hung on his every word.

Who does he think he is!

20 [1-8] One day, he was teaching in the Temple, preaching the gospel, when the chief priests and scribes, with the elders, came to have a go at him. 'Tell us what authority you think you have for the things you're doing,' they challenged him, 'and just who you think gave it to you!'

'I'll ask you a question too,' Jesus countered.[3] 'Was the baptism that John introduced done on heavenly authority or was it just a human invention?'

That did it – suddenly they were arguing amongst themselves. 'Look, we can't say it was from heaven,' they muttered, 'or he'll ask why we

---

1. Modern usage too often reduces the word 'peace' to little more than the absence of conflict. For Jews of Jesus' time, though, 'peace' meant real wellbeing, based on good values and deep relationships. In such a world, war wouldn't merely be prevented – it wouldn't even be in the vocabulary.
2. Isaiah 56:7.
3. Countering a question with another question was a standard technique in theological debate in those days – a good way of getting to the heart of the matter.

rejected it. And we can't say it was just a human invention, because the people will stone us – they all think John was a prophet!' So they had to say that they didn't know.

'In that case,' Jesus retorted, 'you won't mind if I don't tell you where *my* authority comes from – will you!'

The parable of the vineyard

> The religious authorities would be familiar with images of Israel as God's vineyard. Jesus highlights the point that God's prophets have traditionally been abused and murdered, and his Son doesn't expect to be treated any better.

9-19 Then Jesus started telling them this parable:

There's a landowner, and he plants a vineyard. He lets it out to tenants and goes abroad for a long time. When the time comes, he sends a servant to bring him some of the profits from his vineyard. What do the tenants do? They beat the servant and send him back empty handed. So the landowner sends another – and that one gets his dignity shredded and likewise goes back with nothing. So he sends another, and this one is wounded and thrown out. Then the owner of the vineyard says, 'Well, what am I to do now? I know – I'll send my son – my own beloved son – it's possible they'll respect him.' So do they? Not a bit of it.

'It's the son,' they say, 'the one who's down to inherit it all. If we get rid of him, perhaps we can take over!' So they drag him outside the vineyard and kill him. Now, what's the owner going to do? He'll come down on those tenants like a ton of grapes, destroy them completely and re-let the vineyard to others.

'God forbid that anything like that should happen!' said the people who were listening.

Jesus looked at them, and said, 'So what do you think this Bible passage is about? "The stone that the expert builders rejected has turned out to be the cornerstone."[1] Anyone who trips over that stone's going to be broken in pieces – but if it falls on them, they'll be completely crushed.'[2]

---

1. Psalm 118:22.
2. Jesus used this kind of word-play very effectively. The stone that supports and strengthens can also be a 'stumbling block' that trips people up – or, as here, a stone that falls on them and destroys them. Whether God's word is about grace or judgement depends upon how we respond to it. Compare Jesus' words to Peter in Matthew 16:23, and the footnote to that passage.

The scribes and the chief priests would have arrested him on the spot, but they were too afraid of the people. The penny had finally dropped that the parable was against them!

More catch questions

The stakes are really rising now: the conflict between Jesus with his Good News of grace and the legalistic old guard with their bad news of rules and regulations.

Should we pay taxes?

[20-26] Then they sent spies to pretend to be sympathisers and try to trap Jesus so that they could hand him over to the real authority in the area – the Governor. 'Excuse us, Teacher,' the spies oiled, 'but we know you're a man of integrity and all that stuff – not afraid of anyone, always ready to speak the truth. So we were wondering whether you think it's right for Jews to pay taxes to the Roman Emperor or not. Should we pay, or refuse?'[1]

Jesus knew a cunning plot when he saw one. 'Show me a coin, somebody,' he said. 'Now, tell me, whose head is this on the coin? Whose inscription?'

'Caesar's,' they answered.

'Exactly!' Jesus responded. 'So give to Caesar whatever he's got a right to, and to God what belongs to God. That plain enough for you, is it?'

That told them – they just didn't seem to be able to catch him out in public. He'd left them completely dumbstruck.

Marriage in heaven

[27-33] Next to try their luck were the Sadducees, who didn't believe in life after death. They had a question for Jesus. 'Teacher,' they said, 'you know that according to the law of Moses if a man dies leaving his widow childless, then his brother has to marry his widow so that she can have children? Well, we've got an interesting case for you. There were these seven brothers, see, and the first one got married but then died without having become a father. So the second and then the third married his widow, but they didn't have any children either. Well,

---

1. They must really have thought they'd got him now. If he said, 'Yes', he'd lose his street cred among devout Jews, and if he said, 'No', then he could be tried by the Romans for sedition.

would you believe it – all seven of them in turn married her and died childless – and then she died, herself. So, we were wondering – in the afterlife,[1] whose wife will she be? I mean, she's legally married to all seven, isn't she?'[2]

[34-40] Jesus answered, 'People marry in this life – but, for those who attain it, resurrection life is a totally different order from this one – marriage and remarriage don't enter into it! People don't die any more, you see – like the angels.[3] "Children of the resurrection" means "children of God". And as for resurrection itself, haven't you read in the book of Moses – you know, the bit about the burning bush – the title God gives himself, "I am the God of Abraham, Isaac and Jacob" – which, since he's the God of the living, not of the dead, would be pretty difficult without a resurrection, wouldn't it? Sorry, lads – wrong again!'

Well, what could they say, except, 'Well said, Teacher – there's no answer to that!' They just didn't dare to go on asking catch questions.

Who is the Messiah?

[41-44] Then Jesus said, 'It's a funny thing, the way they call the Messiah "Son of David". I mean, David himself – in the Book of Psalms – says, "God said to my Lord, 'Take your place on my right, while I make your enemies a rest for your feet.'"[4] I mean, if David calls him Lord, how can he be David's son?'[5]

[45-47] With everybody listening, Jesus said to his disciples, 'Now, be careful not to be taken in by the scribes, parading their fancy outfits and revelling in the public glory. Oh, and don't they just love the best seats in the Synagogues and the top table at official functions! At the same time as they're depriving widows of their homes,[6] they'll make long pretentious prayers in public. Oh, yes, they'll find they get the worse judgement!'

---

1. In which, you may remember, the people asking the question didn't believe!
2. This was supposed to show that belief in resurrection was unrealistic – as if God would be defeated by a simple problem like that!
3. Jesus isn't endorsing the popular sentimental idea that people become angels after death – he's simply saying that, like them, we'll be immortal, so that the kind of arrangements that were right for this mortal life won't be appropriate.
4. Psalm 110:1.
5. Jesus isn't denying that he's a descendant of David. He's saying he's not *only* that, but actually much, much more.
6. Remember, a widow would have no legal rights, and no rights to property. So the religious establishment's strict legalism was directly contrary to the compassionate demands of Jesus.

The widow's generosity

21 $^{1\text{-}4}$ Jesus looked up and saw wealthy people putting money into the offertory box. The rich put in sizeable amounts, but then he saw a really poor widow drop in two copper coins. 'I'm telling you straight,' he said, 'this really hard-up widow's given more than all those others put together. They only gave what they wouldn't miss, didn't they? – but she, for all her poverty and need, has given everything she had to live on.'[1]

The coming of the kingdom – part 2

The destruction of the Temple

> This is the second of Luke's two discourses on the coming of the kingdom. The introduction to Mark 13 also fits here, but Luke includes an additional point in his narrative: the glory of the Temple included 'gifts'. Evidently, generous donors were recognised in some way or other in the fabric of the Temple.

$^{5\text{-}7}$ People were waxing lyrical about the Temple – about how it was decorated with impressive stones and gifts from wealthy people. 'You think so?' Jesus replied. 'Well, take a good look while you can, because the day will come when there won't be a single stone left standing on top of another – the whole thing's going to be razed to the ground.'

'When, Teacher?' they asked him. 'When's this disaster going to happen? What sort of clues should we be looking for?'

> This next passage needs to be interpreted with care. People have often used it to predict the end of the world, but if we read closely we find Jesus is warning us against trying to do precisely that. You might like to flip back to the introduction to Matthew 24, to see how Jesus is drawing a parallel between the short-term temporal showdown that can already be foreseen, and the longer term, cosmic one that is not for us to predict.

The apocalypse

$^{8\text{-}11}$ Jesus answered:

Oh, don't get hung up on that! Don't be fooled – all kinds of frauds and posers will come along in my name, saying, 'Hey, guys, I'm the

---

1. Now, you need *real* faith to do that!

one – the time's come!' Don't go chasing after them. Oh, and the same goes for wars and conflicts – I mean, you're always going to have those things going on, but that doesn't mean the end's just round the corner. Of course nations will make war on one another, there'll be all the usual earthquakes and famines and things – fearful times, and great signs in the sky.

Persecutions

¹²⁻¹⁹ But even before that, there'll be the persecutions: they'll put you on trial on trumped-up charges; they'll have you thrown in prison – and that's just the religious people. You'll be tried by the highest human authorities, just because you're committed to me – but that'll be your opportunity to testify – tell my story! So get it into your heads that you're not to fret in advance about what words you're going to use – because I'll give you words and wisdom that none of your opponents will be able to answer. Oh, it's going to get nasty: you'll find families split apart, all turning on one another – and people will hate you with a passion, just because of me. But not one hair of your head will be lost, and anyone who keeps the faith through it all will be saved.

The destruction of Jerusalem

²⁰⁻²⁴ When you see Jerusalem besieged by armies, then you'll know that the time of its destruction is near. That is *not* the time to hang around! Take to the hills, pronto: if you're in the city, get out – and if you're not, then *stay* out – because these are the days of retribution, when the prophecies of doom will be fulfilled. It'll be particularly ghastly for pregnant women and nursing mothers. At that time there'll be dreadful misery on earth, great judgement on the nation – people either killed or taken into exile as captives – and Jerusalem totally overrun by the surrounding nations.

The coming of the Son of Man

²⁵⁻²⁸ You'll see ominous signs in the sun, moon and stars, and on earth the entire order of things will be shaken up – seas threatening to engulf the world,[1] people fainting with fear and foreboding at

---

1. We've noted elsewhere how water was a traditional metaphor for overwhelming chaos, and hence it was natural for Jesus to refer to it in that way. He probably means more than just flooding, here – a huge, overwhelming return of the primeval chaos that God brought under control (as distinct from destroyed) in the creation story.

what's happening – then they'll recognise 'the Son of Man coming in clouds',[1] with all the glory and power of God. Now, when all this begins, stand up tall, hold your heads high, because your redemption is very, very close.

Remember the fig tree

[29-33] Jesus went on to tell them a parable:

Take the fig tree as an example – any tree at all, come to that – when the leaves start to sprout, you see for yourselves that summer's coming. Well, in the same way, when you see these things happening, you'll know that the kingdom of God is near. I'm telling you straight, this generation won't have disappeared until it's all happened.[2] Trust me on this – I'm giving you my word on it, and that's more solid and reliable even than the universe itself!

[34-36] But you watch yourselves – don't go getting dragged down into debauchery and drunkenness, and so submerged in the problems of this life that these times are sprung upon you like a trap – because no one's going to escape it. So you'd better keep watching and praying that you'll be able to get through all of this and finally present yourselves before the Son of Man.

[37-38] Jesus was teaching in the Temple daily, going back to his lodgings on the Mount of Olives at night. And early every morning people would be in the Temple waiting to hear him.

The Passion Narrative

22 [1-2] It was just before the Passover – the feast of unleavened bread – and the chief priests and scribes were in an unholy huddle, plotting to put Jesus to death, but they were afraid of the reactions of the people.

---

1. Daniel 7:13-14. In that passage, the 'Son of Man' doesn't come to earth, but comes *to* God to receive glory and power. So while, of course, this *may* be about the second coming, there again it may very well not.
2. There's the key to the issue. If Jesus had been accurately predicting the literal end of the world in the previous verses, then you wouldn't be here to read this. However, if he was predicting the worldly events of that same century, then we don't have a problem with this verse. The point is that he's using the imminent historical apocalypse as an image *foreshadowing* the big one – not predicting it exactly.

Betrayal!

³⁻⁶ Then Satan finally got to Judas Iscariot, one of the Twelve, who went and plotted with the chief priests and Temple officers about how he would let them know when it would be safe to grab Jesus. They thought all their birthdays had come at once, and promised to make it worth his while – money-wise. So Judas was on the lookout for a chance to betray him when the crowd wasn't around.

The Last Supper

⁷⁻¹³ On the day of the Festival period, when the Passover lamb was due to be sacrificed, Jesus went to Peter and John, and said, 'Go and get everything ready so that we can have our Passover meal.'

'Fine,' they answered. 'But – like, where?'

Jesus told them, 'When you get to the town, you'll be met by a man carrying a water jar.¹ Follow him. And when he goes indoors, say to the householder, "The Teacher asks you, 'Where's the guest room you've provided so that I can celebrate Passover with my friends?'" He'll show you a big upstairs room, all furnished – set the table there.' The disciples went and found everything the way Jesus had said. So the Passover meal was prepared.

The Lord's Supper

> The Church has debated this next passage for centuries. What we can say is that it's a graphic acted parable of what's about to happen: Jesus' body torn and broken, his blood poured out, and in some infinitely mysterious way that sacrificial self-giving is going to strengthen and sustain his people like food. We, as it were, 'feed on the life and death of Christ'.

¹⁴⁻²³ That evening they sat down together – Jesus and the Twelve. 'I've really longed to share this Passover with you before I face the pain ahead,' he told them, 'because I'm telling you, I won't eat it again this side of the kingdom of God.' Then he took a cup, gave thanks and said, 'Take this and share it among yourselves. I'm telling you, I shan't be

---

1. There wouldn't be many of those – carrying water was seen as women's work and beneath a man's dignity. What a sign of the kingdom! If we want to serve Jesus, then we need to be prepared to 'follow', in more senses than one, the Man who carries water!

drinking the "fruit of the vine"[1] again until the kingdom of God comes!'

Then he took a piece of bread, gave thanks, broke it and gave it to them. 'This is my body,' he said, 'which is given for you. Do this in remembrance of me.'[2]

Then, after supper, he did the same with a cup. 'This cup, poured out for you, is a new covenant – a whole new relationship with God – sealed in my blood. But, look, the one who's going to betray me is right here at this table – actually sharing food with me![3] Well, the Son of Man is fulfilling the scriptures, but a curse on the one who betrays him!' The disciples started wondering among themselves which one of them it could be.

More jockeying for position – they still haven't learnt!

Here's another interesting example of the gospel writers' different perspectives. The argument about status, prompting Jesus to teach about the true nature of greatness, occurs in a different place in Matthew and Mark. This conversation may well have taken place several times – the gulf of understanding between Jesus and his disciples is a constant theme – but, if so, why does Luke record this particular instance? Perhaps because it provides a stark contrast with the image of Jesus portrayed at the supper. Here he literally serves his disciples, and speaks of much humbler, more costly service in the giving of his own life. He will, for them, become the very least. And it is precisely at that time that the disciples are squabbling over which of *them* is to be great! Luke could not more graphically show just how little the disciples have yet understood just who Jesus is and what he means.

---

1. Jesus is quoting the traditional Jewish blessing that he has just used – it's not specifically recorded but its omission from a Passover celebration would have been unthinkable, so the gospel writers can safely leave their readers to assume that it would have been used.
2. These words are difficult to translate, and we need to think of 'remembering' in the Jewish way, as 're-membering'. When we remember the past, we do more than reminisce – in some way, the past becomes real again in the present. However, all agree that Christ is always present among us.
3. For Jews, to share table fellowship included an obligation to be at peace – at the very least while the food remained in the body. Judas was contemplating an even more unspeakable act than we would immediately appreciate.

24-30 And what were the disciples doing in these solemn moments? Would you believe, squabbling over which of them was the greatest? 'Look,' Jesus said, 'you know how it is in the old order of things: kings on thrones giving orders to everyone else, bullies having all the clout – and for some bizarre reason people seem actually grateful for it! Well, you'd better get it into your heads that it's not going to be like that among you. One of you wants to be thought of as great? Fine, then take on the attitude of the most junior member. And if you want to be a leader, then get down to being a good servant. Think about it – who's greater, the people who sit at table and eat the food that's served to them, or the one who does the serving? And yet here am *I* serving as your waiter! You're the ones that have been with me, and stood by me through all the tough times, and I'm conferring on you what my Father has conferred on me: a kingdom. Yes, you're going to share in the great banquet that is my kingdom, and you'll be seated on twelve thrones, ruling over the twelve tribes of Israel.[1]

Jesus foretells Simon's denial

31-34 'Simon, Simon!' Jesus continued. 'You know, Satan's already tried to stake a claim for all of you[2] – wants to break you into little pieces.[3] But I've prayed for you – prayed that your own faith won't fail completely, and once you've turned back to me you'll be a source of strength for the whole group.'

'Lord,' Peter answered, 'whatever it takes, I'm ready to follow you – prison, death – no question about it.'

'I'm telling you, Peter,' Jesus responded, 'before the morning cock-crow, you'll say three times that you don't even know me.'

Be prepared

35-38 Jesus continued, 'Remember when I sent you all out on that mission – with no money, no provisions, no spare clothes – did you find that you were lacking anything?'

'Nothing at all,' they answered.

---

1. Historically, these have been among the most horribly misused words of Jesus; they are not a licence for un-Christian arrogance and anti-Semitism.
2. Although the words are apparently addressed to Simon, the Greek word translated 'you' is plural. So Jesus is using Simon as a focus for all the disciples.
3. The local image that Jesus used was 'sift you like wheat', but this was much more about destruction than sorting – as Amos 9:9 shows.

'Well,' he said, 'now you'd better get prepared. If you've got money, keep it with you – same goes for spare clothes and shoes. And if anyone hasn't got a weapon, maybe they'd better sell their coat and get one[1] – because I'm telling you that the prophecy's got to be fulfilled in me that says, "He was counted among the transgressors".[2] In fact, all that's been written about me is right on the brink of fulfilment.'

'Look, Lord,' the disciples said eagerly, 'we've got two swords, so we're ready!'

'Oh, enough of all this!' Jesus answered.

Jesus' agonising prayer

> Luke's account of this is briefer than Matthew's or Mark's, but it has a particular intensity of its own. Only Luke recalls the famous 'blood-like sweat' and the angel appearing during the prayer.

[39-46] Jesus went out and walked, as he often did, to the Mount of Olives, with the disciples following him. When they got there he said, 'Now, pray – pray that you'll have the strength to resist temptation.' Then he went a little way away from them – just a stone's throw – and knelt down to pray. 'Father,' he pleaded, 'if you're willing to, then please take this bitter cup[3] away from me! But in the end, the only thing that matters is your will, not mine.' Then an angel appeared from heaven, strengthening and encouraging him. Even so, he was dreadfully frightened, and he prayed all the harder[4] – he was sweating what seemed to be enormous drops of blood that landed and stained the ground around him. Then he went back to his disciples and found them asleep – they just couldn't stay awake and face the horror of it all. 'Why are you sleeping?' he asked. 'You should be awake and praying – praying that you don't get tested more than you can take.'

---

1. The passage is unique to Luke, and it's hard to believe Jesus meant it literally, especially in view of the conversation that follows (where he seems already to be discouraging any fighting talk) and also in terms of his response to the use of swords at his arrest. Generally, it's thought that Jesus is telling his disciples to prepare for *spiritual* warfare (as in Ephesians 6:10-18).
2. Isaiah 53:12.
3. The 'cup of suffering' was a familiar Jewish image. Jesus used it when challenging James and John in, for example, Mark 10:38.
4. The angelic presence must have been a two-edged experience: strengthening, yes, but by implication confirming that there was to be no release from this – Jesus was going to go through it. So his terror, and with it his prayer, intensifies dramatically. In Jesus, God is sparing himself nothing of the human experience!

The arrest

⁴⁷⁻⁵³ Even as he spoke, a crowd arrived, led by Judas – who, you'll remember, was one of the Twelve. He began to approach Jesus, to give him a kiss of greeting, but Jesus said, 'Oh, really, Judas! Are you seriously going to betray the Son of Man with a mark of friendship?'

The people around him saw what was happening. 'Lord,' they said, 'shall we use our swords – strike quickly now?' Without waiting for an answer, one of them lashed out and caught the High Priest's servant a glancing blow that cut off his right ear.

'Enough of this!' Jesus said. 'Don't let's add to the evil!'[1] And he reached out, touched the man's right ear and healed it. Then he turned to the chief priests, Temple police and elders who had come for him. 'Just look at you!' he said. 'You come after me, armed to the teeth as if I were some sort of dangerous desperado – but I've been teaching openly in the Temple every day, so why didn't you just take me then? Still, you've got your moment now: the hour of the powers of darkness.'

⁵⁴⁻⁵⁵ They seized Jesus and led him away to the High Priest's house. Now, Peter had followed at a safe distance and when the guards had made a fire in the middle of the courtyard and sat around it, Peter went and slipped in among them.

> Luke has brought us here with breathtaking pace as though he cannot wait to show us the fulfilment of Jesus' ministry and God's purpose. Now he will slow the pace again: the cosmic confrontation between good and evil will be presented graphically to us, scene by scene.

Peter denies Jesus

⁵⁶⁻⁶² It wasn't long before Peter found himself being mercilessly hounded by a solitary slip of a servant girl! She took a good look at him in the light from the fire, and said, 'Hey, this guy's one of his friends!'

---

1. This intervention by Jesus sums up one important aspect of the cross. Faced with evil, we have a choice whether to respond in ways that add to it or that limit it – and the latter may have to be very costly for us. We might prefer not to imagine what sort of bloodbath could have ensued if Jesus' followers, with their two swords, had been pitched in battle against a determined, well-prepared opposition. Jesus knew it was he whom they wanted, and his intervention contained the situation at the cost of sacrificing himself. As Paul would say, 'Do not be overcome by evil, but overcome evil with good' (Romans 12:21). To put it another way, had Jesus responded violently, then evil would have won.

Peter quailed. 'What are you on about, woman? I don't know the man!'

Then, soon afterwards, someone else recognised him. 'You're one of them,' he asserted.

Peter said, 'Not me, man! I'm nothing to do with him.'

There was no hiding place, though – about an hour later one of the others went for him. 'I know this man must be one of them,' he said. 'It's obvious he's a Galilean!'

Peter got really flustered then. 'Man,' he said, 'I just haven't got a clue what you're on about!'

Immediately, even as he spoke, the cock crowed, the Lord turned and looked straight at Peter. Peter remembered what he'd said: 'Before the cock crows today, you'll deny three times that you know me,' and he went out and dissolved into terrible tears of remorse.

Jesus is mocked and beaten

63-65 The men who were holding Jesus really laid into him, taunting and beating him. Then they blindfolded him and said, 'OK, then – prophesy. If you're so all-fired special, tell us who hit you!' And they went on hurling insults and abuse at him.

Jesus is brought before the Council

66-71 Come daybreak, the elders' assembly, including chief priests and scribes, gathered together, and led Jesus away to the Council, where they said, 'If you're the Messiah, then tell us plainly.'

'Look,' Jesus said, 'let's be realistic here – whatever I tell you, you don't believe, and whatever questions I ask you, you don't answer – but from now on, the Son of Man will be seated at the right-hand side of God's throne.'

'What?' they responded. 'Are you expecting us to believe that *you* are the Son of God?'[1]

'You've said it!' Jesus answered.

'That's it!' they concluded. 'What more testimony do we need? He's convicted himself!'

---

1. The very idea would appear ludicrous, with Jesus standing in front of them, bound and humiliated!

Jesus is brought before Pilate

23 [1-5] The whole assembly rose as one and took Jesus to Pilate.[1] There they started slinging accusations at him. 'We found this person,' they said, 'spreading sedition around the nation. He told us – oh, you'll love this one – he told us that we shouldn't pay taxes to Caesar.[2] And he said he's the Messiah – our king.'

Pilate asked, 'Are *you* the King of the Jews?'[3]

'Those are your words,' Jesus answered.

Pilate turned to the chief priests and to the crowds. 'Oh, come on,' he said, 'he's harmless enough – I don't see anything dangerous about him.'

Then they really started laying it on. 'Well, you should just hear him,' they said. 'He's always stirring up trouble among the masses – he's been teaching his dangerous nonsense all through Judea, Galilee[4] – even in this holy city itself.'

Jesus is brought before Herod

[6-12] Pilate pricked up his ears. So, this man was a Galilean, was he? That meant he came under Herod's jurisdiction, so the buck could be passed to him[5] – especially as he happened to be conveniently in Jerusalem at the time.

Herod was glad of the chance to meet Jesus. He'd heard all about him and thought this would be a good chance to see him perform some spectacular stunt. But although Herod spent a long time questioning him, Jesus wasn't going to give any answers. Through it all, the chief priests and the scribes were standing on the touchlines throwing accusations at him. Herod eventually had to satisfy himself with letting his soldiers abuse and taunt him. Then he had him dressed in a glorious, royal robe and sent him back like that to Pilate. Pilate clearly appreciated the joke,

---

1. Pontius Pilate, that is – the Roman Governor of Judea and the only person who could legally sentence anyone to death.
2. See 20:20-26 for what Jesus really said. They tried to trap him, but he skilfully avoided the trap, so they just went ahead anyway! Well, why let a little detail like truth get in the way of what they want!
3. Pilate could well have been relishing the irony of the situation. He hated the Jews and would enjoy humiliating them by referring to this unlikely figure as their 'king'!
4. Galilee – that mention was calculated to worry Pilate, since Galilee had a reputation as a breeding ground for political hotheads.
5. Pilate would then always be able to say that it was the Jews who condemned him, not the Romans. Since Jesus was a religious figure and Rome was always very sensitive about local religious matters, it might make Pilate's somewhat fragile position a little safer.

because from then on he and Herod settled their differences and became friends.

Jesus is sentenced to death

[13-25] Pilate called together the chief priests and leaders of the people. 'Look,' he said, 'you brought this character to me, claiming that he was some sort of dangerous revolutionary – but, look at him! I've listened to you nicely, asked him all the right questions, and I didn't find him guilty of any of the things you were accusing him of. Now, Herod's had a go and he doesn't find him a problem either, or he wouldn't have sent him back the way he did. Look, he's obviously not done anything to deserve the death penalty, so I'm going to give him a good thrashing and release him.'[1]

'No, no!' everybody shouted. 'Take him away – give us Barabbas instead!' That was a man who was in prison for starting a rebellion in the city, not to mention murder!

Pilate tried again to appeal to them, but they just shrieked all the more loudly, 'Crucify him! Crucify him!'

'Now, why should I want to do a thing like that?' Pilate asked. 'What harm's he done? I didn't find him guilty of anything that justified the death penalty – so I'm going to thrash him and release him.'

The crowd went mad at that – screaming out for Jesus to be crucified. And, as so often happens in these situations, the mob won. Pilate gave his sentence, to grant their wish. This meant that he released the man who'd already been found guilty of rebellion and murder – just because they wanted it – but Jesus he handed over to meet their demands.

The crucifixion

[26-31] As they led Jesus away, they grabbed a man called Simon, from Cyrene, who was coming in from the country, and they forced him to carry the cross behind Jesus. They were followed by many people – including a lot of women who were crying out in grief for Jesus, but he turned to them and said, 'Listen, you daughters of Jerusalem: it's not me you should be crying for – it's your own children and grandchildren – because the days are most assuredly coming when people will say, "How fortunate are those who never had children – never carried them,

---

1. So, if Pilate thinks he's innocent, why's he going to thrash him? Obviously, he feels that he's got to keep the mob happy.

gave birth to them, never nursed them at the breast!" Then they'll cry out in desperation to the mountains, "Fall on us!" and to the hills, "Bury us!" Because if this can happen to a young, green sapling, just imagine what destruction can be visited on a dried-up, withered old tree!'[1]

[32-43] There were two others as well – a couple of revolutionaries – who were led away to be executed with him, and when they got to the place called 'the place of the skull', they nailed Jesus to the cross with the rebels on either side of him. It was then that Jesus said the most amazing prayer. 'Father,' he said, 'please forgive them. They just don't have a clue what it is that they're doing.'

Meanwhile, some of the people around were gambling for the condemned men's clothes, while others just stood by and watched. The leaders, though – they jeered at him. 'Oh, he was very good at saving other people, wasn't he!' they said. 'Now let's see whether he can save himself, shall we! That is, of course, if he's really the Messiah – the one specially chosen by God.'

The soldiers got in on the act too. They came and offered him sour wine. 'Oh, so you're the King of the Jews, are you?' they scoffed. 'Well, show a bit of kingly power and save yourself!' And just by way of really rubbing things in, they put a placard over his head. 'This,' it said, 'is the King of the Jews!'[2]

Even one of the criminals crucified with him thought Jesus was fair game too. 'Oh, come on,' he taunted him, 'you're the Messiah, aren't you? So act like one and save yourself – and us along with you!'

The other criminal turned on him, though. 'Don't you have any respect for God at all?' he blazed. 'You're condemned, the same as he is, aren't you? Except, of course, that we thoroughly deserve what we're getting, but this guy's totally innocent!' Then he turned to Jesus, and said, 'Jesus, remember me, won't you, when your enthronement is complete.'

Jesus said, 'I'm telling you straight, this very day you're going to be in Paradise with me.'

---

1. Remember how, in 13:6-9, he compared the religious cult to a fruitless fig tree (see also Mark 11:12-19)? Well, now they're destroying the 'tree' that could have been so fruitful for them – Jesus – and if that can happen to a good tree, then the fate of the fruitless, dried-up tree that is the nation hardly bears contemplation.

2. There's a real irony here, isn't there? While the religious leaders were mocking Jesus for being helpless, the Romans were taking the chance to mock *them* by saying, in effect, 'Is this the best you lot can do for a king?' The great, final climax of Jesus' ministry has arrived, and both the 'insiders' and the 'outsiders' alike are completely missing the point.

The death of Christ

[44-49] It was now about midday, and there was an eerie darkness everywhere. It lasted until three o'clock in the afternoon, when the sunlight fled completely, and the curtain that hid the holy of holies in the Temple was ripped in two. And at three, Jesus gave a great cry. 'Father,' he said, 'I commit my spirit into your hands!' And, saying that, he breathed his last. When the supervising centurion saw how he died, he praised God and said, 'Surely it must be true that this is an innocent man!'

The crowds who had originally gathered to watch the spectacle went home full of regret and remorse,[1] while his friends, including the women who'd followed him from Galilee, stood at a distance, watching everything that happened.

The burial

[50-56] Joseph, from Arimathea, knew he had to move quickly. (Joseph was a respected council member who was also searching for the kingdom of God and had dissented from the council's purposes and from their actions.) So, in the evening, he plucked up his courage and went to see Pilate to ask to be allowed to take Jesus' body.[2] Then he took it down from the cross, wrapped it lovingly in a clean piece of linen, and placed it in a brand-new, completely empty[3] tomb, hewn out of the rock. This was the Day of Preparation – the Sabbath would begin at dusk.[4]

The women who had followed Jesus from Galilee were still following, even now; they noted the tomb, and the way the body was laid in it,

---

1. Poor crowds! Remember whom this word represents. These are those who followed Jesus but never really heard him, because they thought and hoped that he would be the Messiah of traditional expectation. When it was finally made clear that he wasn't going to meet those shallow hopes, their disappointment turned to anger and the crowd condemned him. Now, when it's too late, the crowd appear to realise their mistake and bitterly regret it. No one, of course, is saying that this is necessarily exactly the same crowd all the way through – they'd have to be committed for that to be the case, and then they wouldn't be called the crowd! The word is used symbolically to represent the general superficial response to Jesus in contrast to that of the closer disciples who, for all their blindness, nonetheless followed in a different, deeper sense.

2. Joseph's a somewhat mysterious character of whom we know very little. Are we, like Joseph, going to stay safely in the shadows, until the stage where there's really nothing more we can do for the oppressed but give them a decent burial?

3. In those days it was not uncommon for numerous bodies to be buried in the various chambers within a tomb of this kind.

4. No time, then, for the proper burial rites that would normally be required (although, interestingly, most crucified criminals wouldn't get a burial at all, but be left on the cross to rot as a warning to others or, if the same cross were needed again, burned on the rubbish tip).

and then went away to prepare spices and ointments. On the next day, the Sabbath, they rested as the law required.

The Resurrection

The gospel will end as it began: women, considered of no value in these matters, will be the first to hear and proclaim the good news. What a God we have, who will entrust the proclamation of the most important moments in his good news to those whom the world values least!

24[1-12] When the Sabbath was over, though, they wasted no time. As the first day of the week dawned, they went to the tomb just after daybreak, carrying the spices they'd got ready. When they arrived, they found that the stone was already rolled back, but when they went inside the tomb – no body! While they were standing there, completely baffled, there were suddenly two men with them, in dazzling white robes. The women were completely terrified, and kept their heads down, but the men asked, 'Why are you looking for the living among the dead? He's not here – he's risen! Don't you remember how he said to you, back in the Galilee days, that the Son of Man would have to be handed over to evil people, be crucified, and then on the third day rise to life?'

Of course! They remembered Jesus' words, turned away from the tomb and went back to tell everything to the eleven and the rest of the disciples. Among the group of women were Mary Magdalene, Joanna, and Mary the mother of James. Were they believed? Not on your life, they weren't. 'Idle chatter' was one of the more polite reactions. Peter couldn't help himself, though – he got up and ran for all he was worth to the tomb. When he got there, he stooped and peered into the burial chamber where he saw only the grave clothes, lying neatly in a place of their own. He went home full of amazement at what had happened.

The walk to Emmaus

This story only occurs in Luke, and we're enormously in his debt for giving it to us. Picture, if you will, the scene: the two disciples are walking away from the scene of the most devastating failure, disappointment and bereavement they have ever known. We all recognise the need to get away when places take on such horrible significance. Now, you know, and I know, that Jerusalem was very much the place to be. God, as always, was bringing hope right from

the very heart of despair – so, if we'd been there, knowing what we know, we'd probably have been standing in the way, shouting at them to turn back. Jesus doesn't. He knows they need to make this journey, and he joins them, discreetly, inconspicuously, and walks with them – but they were prevented from recognising him.[1]
'What are you discussing together, on your journey?'[2] he asked.

[13-18] Later that day two of them were walking to Emmaus, a village about seven miles from Jerusalem, and discussing the recent events on the way. As they were deep in conversation, Jesus himself joined them and walked with them – but they were prevented from recognising him.[1] 'What are you discussing together, on your journey?'[2] he asked.

Cleopas, one of the two, looked at him in amazement. 'Are you the only visitor to Jerusalem who doesn't know?' he asked incredulously. 'Haven't you heard the things that have happened these past days?'

[19-24] 'What things?'

The two disciples thought this man needed his eyes opened! 'The things about Jesus from Nazareth,' they explained. 'A prophet, he was – definitely a prophet – powerful in words and in actions, honoured by God and the people. And our chief priests and leaders handed him over to the authorities, got him sentenced to death and demanded he be crucified. And the real let-down is that we'd really thought he was the promised one who was going to redeem the nation of Israel. Oh, yes, and to cap it all, some women in our group really got us going. Apparently, they were at the tomb early this morning and couldn't find the body – so they came tearing back to us with some tale about a vision of angels who'd said that he was alive. Well, a few of us went to have a look – the tomb was open and empty all right, but we didn't see anything else.'

[25-29] 'Oh, dear, oh, dear!' Jesus answered. 'Are you still missing the point? Don't you recognise all the prophecies being fulfilled in front of you? Don't you see that all this was part of that fulfilment – that the Messiah was to suffer all of this before being glorified?' Then he began

---

1. People speculate endlessly about why they couldn't recognise him: that misses the point. Luke says they were actively *prevented* from recognising him. It was Christ's purpose to be discreet. He wanted to help them understand, not just leap in with a 'Wow, folks, it's me, and everything's OK now!' kind of quick fix!
2. Let's never lose sight of the symbolic importance of journeys in religious thought – it's as we 'walk' through life that we learn.

with Moses, and went through the prophets, interpreting the things in scripture about himself.

When they got near to the village, he went ahead as if he were going to continue his journey. 'Don't go,' they urged him. 'It's late, and the day's as good as over.' So he went in to stay with them.

[30-35] During supper, around the table, he took some bread and gave thanks to God for it. Then he broke it and gave it to them,[1] and they were able to recognise him. And as they did so, he disappeared![2] They turned to each other. 'Didn't he make our very hearts burn as he talked with us on the road!' they said. 'Remember how he opened and explained the scriptures to us!'

So, right then, they jumped up and went back to Jerusalem.[3] The eleven and all the others were gathered together there, and greeted them with the words, 'It's true! It's true! The Lord really is risen – he's appeared to Simon!' Then they told their story about what had happened on the road, and how Jesus had been made known to them in the breaking of bread.[4]

Jesus appears to his disciples

[36-43] Even as the room was buzzing with all this, Jesus himself was suddenly visible among them. 'My peace to you all!' he said. Well, 'peace' was hardly their initial reaction to this – they were absolutely terrified, convinced they must be seeing a ghost![5] 'What are you frightened

---

1. Note the four actions: taking, giving thanks, breaking and sharing bread. Echoes of the feeding of the five thousand and of the Last Supper are very clear. And it's in this action – not in the earlier words, however important they were – that Jesus is recognised. For those interested in the structure of worship, here's an example of 'Word and Sacrament' being kept together. The word is expounded verbally on the road, but the living Word is made visible in the breaking and sharing of bread.

2. Very powerful symbolism here. Christ reveals himself when and in the ways he chooses. And as soon as we think we've got him sussed, we lose sight of him! We can never think we've got Jesus pinned down – he's beyond any category or description we can find, and there's always more to search for, to wonder at and to give thanks for.

3. So, as Jesus has gone with them to their refuge and revealed himself there, they're able to return to the place where the pain was – because they know that it's from that very pain that hope is springing!

4. Firstly, he'd been 'made known' – this was God's revelation, not their recognition. Secondly, it was in the sharing of food. Could it be we need to recover the tradition of informal table fellowship as part of church life? Should we be surprised to find the risen Christ revealing himself afresh in that context?

5. Hearing about it is one thing – really believing is another. Clearly, they haven't fully taken it on board, just through words. Only an encounter with the living Christ can actually enable them fully to accept it. So we should never think that Christian mission is about winning arguments with words – people need to *meet* Jesus!

275

of?' Jesus remonstrated. 'Why are you so difficult to convince? OK, then – take a look at my hands and feet – see for yourselves that it's really me. Touch me, if you like – after all, this is real flesh and blood, and no ghost ever had that!' So saying, he showed them his hands and feet. While they were still lost in a mixture of elation, doubt and fear, he said, 'Look, have you got anything to eat here?' They found some broiled fish, and he took it and ate it right there in front of them.

[44-49] 'Let me recall for you,' he said, 'the words I spoke before, when I was with you – that everything the scriptures say about me had to be fulfilled.' Then he opened up their minds, helped them understand the scriptures, and said to them, 'You see, it's written that the Messiah is to suffer, and to rise from the dead on the third day. Then the gospel of repentance and forgiveness is to be proclaimed in the name of that same Messiah to the whole world – starting right here in Jerusalem. Now, you're my witnesses of all this. And, look, I'm going to send you the special gift that the Father promised. So don't go rushing at things like a bull at a gate – wait here in the city until you've been clothed with the power from above.'[1]

The Ascension

[50-53] Then Jesus led his disciples out to the village of Bethany, where he lifted his hands up to bless them, and, even as he was doing it, the last, mysterious journey began. First, he moved a short distance from them, and then he was completely removed and taken to heaven while they worshipped on the mountainside. The disciples went back to Jerusalem, absolutely buzzing about it, and spent all their time in the Temple praising God.

---

1. This image, related to the Hebrew scriptures, foretells the gift of God's Holy Spirit to empower his disciples for mission, which Luke will describe early in his second volume, The Acts of the Apostles. The disciples are not to rush out impetuously before they're properly equipped. Once again, it's all about relying on God's power, not our own.

John

The Gospel according to John

This gospel stands out as distinctive from the other three in various ways – one or two of which have been touched on in the General Introduction to the Gospels at the front of this book.

Like the other writers, John wants to proclaim his faith that Jesus is the Son of God – but he wants to give it particular emphases. He wants to say that Jesus *is* God, and has been from eternity – no beginning and no ending. Jesus was not created by God as a kind of lesser deity, but *is* God. That is John's overriding preoccupation. However, he is most emphatic that in Jesus God became truly human. He shows Jesus experiencing intensely human emotional upheavals, because he wants to emphasise that this was no pretence, no play-acting by God. The wonder of God becoming fully human and yet remaining God may be a mystery too high for our minds to reach, but John doesn't let us off the hook by allowing us to forget either his divinity or his complete humanity. In Christ, all things are complete (a theme of John's) and that applies both to his humanity and his divinity.

To help us understand the death of Jesus and its significance, John presents it as a sacrifice – or rather, *the* Sacrifice. He uses the familiar tradition of the Passover and shows Jesus as the ultimate Passover Lamb whose blood signifies ultimate life and freedom for his people. For this reason, Passover will be a recurrent theme.

In this gospel, the reader has the greatest opportunity to dig for buried treasure as the process reveals layer upon layer of subtext, each with special significance to add to an already luminous text. Some of the heavily symbolic phrases used in the gospel can be difficult for modern Western minds, but I have generally chosen to retain them and offer some help with interpretation rather than simplify, which would certainly be even less helpful.

John has given us a great piece of writing. I certainly won't have done justice to it, so you're going to need to turn back to the standard text eventually – with the help of a commentary. Meanwhile, I hope this version may serve as an introduction to some of the treasures God has inspired John to give to us.

Enjoy it.

Many times.

John Route Planner

You might find this helpful to give you a quick overview of the journey ahead.

The Prologue

It's well worth reading Genesis 1 before this – the parallels are striking and deliberate. In Genesis 1, God, by his word, created the world, overcoming darkness with light and inviting life in all its abundance to blossom. Reading further through scripture, we can see that the word of God came to be thought of in personal terms, from expressions like 'The word of God came to me, saying . . .' John now brings this whole idea to its height. He will spend the next twenty-one chapters telling us that the Word of God is indeed a Person, seen in the flesh in Jesus. The Word through whom creation came to be, through whom light was first called to drive out the darkness, has come into this world to be its light, to overcome the darkness in which we can lose ourselves, and to bring to completeness the work of creation. He deliberately echoes the Genesis opening, 'In the beginning', and goes on to tell us that the Word of God was there at the beginning, was with God, and in fact *was* God.[1] John is telling us that when we speak of the word of God, we don't merely mean a letter or message from God; in hearing the word of God we are hearing no less than the Person of God speaking.

I want to emphasise that a mystery as deep and wide as this can't be simplified without losing its power. I've tried to make it accessible (not the same thing as understandable) without losing too much, but I really would urge you to read this passage in a standard Bible – hoping that this introductory version may help prepare for it – and simply revel in the wonder of God who is so far beyond our understanding that even the little we know is too much for our language to express!

1 [1-5] In the beginning was the Word. And the Word was right there with God – in fact, the Word *was* God, no less. He was right there, before all things, with God, and all creation was made through him. Without him, not one single created thing came into existence. In him was real life – true living – and that life was the light of all people. So the light shines in the darkness – and the darkness hasn't a hope of overcoming it!

---

1. You might find it very helpful here to look up the word Trinity in the Glossary.

[6-8] There was a man sent from God – John, his name was – who came as a witness, to testify to the light, so that through him everybody might believe.[1] Now, get this straight: he wasn't the light himself – he came to testify to the light.

[9-13] The true light – the one that gives light to everybody – was coming into the world.[2] So: he was in the world; the world was made through him; so the world was bound to recognise him – right? Wrong! The world simply didn't know him. He came to the world he owned[3] – and his own people didn't accept him! But to all those who *did* – all those who believed *in* him[4] – well, that was another matter: they were enabled to become children of God, no less! And that's a kind of 'birth' you can't get by the joining of blood-lines, or by the desires of the flesh, or because a human husband wishes it – it's something that comes from God.

[14-18] And the Word became flesh and made his home[5] among us, and we all saw his glory for ourselves – the glory of a father's unique son,[6] full of amazing grace and truth. (John,[7] of course, testified about him when he shouted out, 'This is the one I meant when I said, "There's one coming after me who ranks ahead of me, because he *was* before I was."') And from his fullness[8] we've received grace on top of grace! The law

---

1. You'll find a lot about 'testifying' in John – often linked with the idea of believing. It's a law metaphor, frequently used in connection with legal concepts of the time. God has sent witnesses, who have given their testimony – so, now, what's our verdict? We, incidentally, are both jury and defendant (God, of course, is the judge), since whether we believe or not will affect the judgement we receive!
2. This same phrase will be repeated by Martha in 11:27 and by Jesus (including the reference to light) in 12:46.
3. The Greek here means 'his own property'.
4. John makes a real distinction between believing Jesus – a matter of intellectual assent to his teachings – and believing *in* him, which means a life-commitment.
5. The Greek says that he 'pitched his tent'. We could take that nomadic image as meaning that God in Christ 'shared our journey', but that metaphor is much more appropriate to the Synoptic gospels than to John. It could also mean that he shared the impermanence and uncertainty of our life – again, that would fit more in the Synoptics, especially Luke, than in John. What really rings bells in terms of this gospel is the idea of 'tabernacle' – the tent that travelled with the Hebrew people during their time in the desert and was in effect their first Temple. Now all you need to do is look up 'Temple' in the Glossary and the whole thing should become a lot clearer!
6. This is good educational practice. John first introduces a familiar idea – 'like father, like son' – to prepare the ground for an unfamiliar one: *the* Father's only Son.
7. The Baptiser, not the writer.
8. Remember, John just said Jesus was '*full* of grace and truth'.

was given through Moses – saving grace and truth came through Jesus Christ. No one's ever truly seen God,[1] until God the unique Son – who's really close to the Father's heart – has finally made him fully known.

---

1. According to the Hebrew Scriptures, some people had seen God. However, the overwhelming conviction was that a close encounter with God himself would be fatal, and that these references were to people who met *manifestations* of God, rather than God in all his unveiled majesty. John is saying that Jesus has made even that possible in himself – although, as the gospel itself reveals, the very humanity that revealed him also paradoxically concealed him: many people found it a barrier.

The Evidence

> John has stated the belief that underpins the whole gospel. Now he will call his witnesses to testify to his case: that Jesus is the Son of God. There's a lot in this gospel about 'testimony'. You might like to look the word up in the Glossary.
>
> The witnesses are many and varied. As well as John the Baptiser (not to be confused with John the writer) they will include not only Jesus and his friends, but also his enemies who sometimes quite unwittingly testify in his favour and strengthen his case in the very act of trying to disprove it!
>
> The written/verbal statements will be supported by six pieces of solid evidence: the six 'signs' that Jesus performed. John is the only evangelist to call Jesus' miracles 'signs', and we need to be clear that these are not *proofs* to convince the unbelieving, but signs which confirm and strengthen faith for those who have eyes to see. God always gives us the option, because he wants us to respond *in faith*, not because we've got no alternative.

The testimony of John the Baptiser

[19-28] This is the testimony given by John when the religious authorities sent priests and Levites[1] from Jerusalem to ask him, 'Look, just who are you?'

John was honest with them, right from the beginning. He made no pretence about it, but said, straight out, 'Well, first off, I'm not the Messiah – you can get that clear for a start.'

'Who, then?' they insisted. 'Are you Elijah?'

'Nope!'

'Well, the promised prophet, then?'

'No, again.'

'Oh, come on, play fair – who are you? Give us something we can take back to the ones who sent us. How do *you* describe yourself?'

---

1. Levites were part of the spiritual leadership. They're only mentioned twice in the whole of the New Testament, but frequently in Hebrew scriptures where they often feature alongside priests. If you'd like to know more, then Numbers 18 gives an account of who they were and what they did.

'Oh, well, if you're asking *that,* he said, 'I'm "a voice, calling out in the desert, 'Make the way straight for God!'" as the prophet Isaiah said.'[1]

The Pharisees had sent these people – so they really had to go back with an answer. 'OK, then,' they persisted, 'so if you're not the Messiah, and you're not Elijah, and you're not the prophet – why are you going around baptising people?'

'What I'm doing,' John answered, 'is baptising with water. Now, there's someone right here among you, whom you don't know – the one whose way I'm preparing – and I'm not even good enough to help him undo his shoes.'

This happened in Bethany-over-Jordan,[2] where John was baptising.

Jesus is the Lamb of God

Remember how the Synoptic gospels, Matthew in particular, used Moses to give the readers a set of images they could use to help understand Jesus (see the introduction to Matthew 2:13)? Well, here's John doing the same thing with the Lamb. The sacrificing of lambs as part of the atonement rituals was an honoured tradition with which every Jew was very familiar. For people who had grown up understanding these concepts and a whole lot more besides, John's image would immediately 'ring bells'. For those of us who haven't grown up with it, it's more difficult. You may find it helpful to look up 'sacrifice' in the Glossary.

[29-34] Next day, John saw Jesus walking in his direction. 'Here he is,' he declared, 'the Lamb of God – the one who takes away all the sin of the world. Remember I told you, "There's someone coming after me who actually ranks before me"? Well, here he is – I didn't know him myself, but he was the reason for my coming – so that he, and all that he's about, could be made known to Israel.'

John continued his testimony: 'I saw the Holy Spirit of God coming down out of heaven in the visual form of a dove, and it settled on him. I didn't know him myself, but the one who sent me to baptise with water said to me, "Look for the person on whom my Spirit comes down and settles – he's the one who'll baptise people with the Holy

---

1. Isaiah 40:3
2. No one seems to know where this was! We assume that John gives it this title to distinguish it from the other Bethany mentioned in the gospels – just outside Jerusalem.

Spirit."[1] And now I've seen for myself, and I've given my testimony that this is no less than the Son of God.'

Jesus calls his first disciples

> Here, in an apparently minor anecdote, we have a cameo of Christian discipleship. First, the prophets, represented by John the Baptiser, point to Jesus, and then those who hear his words and follow Jesus are invited to the 'place where Christ lives' – the Christian community – where they stay, and invite others to join them.

[35-42] Next day, John was again standing with two of his disciples and saw Jesus walking past. 'Look!' he pointed to Jesus. 'There's the Lamb of God!' As soon as they heard that, they went and followed Jesus.

Jesus turned and saw the two of them following him. 'What are you looking for?' he asked them.

'Rabbi,'[2] they answered (that's a word meaning 'teacher'), 'where are you staying?'

'Why don't you come and see for yourselves?' Jesus answered.

So they went with Jesus to the place where he was staying, and remained with him for the day – it was now about four o'clock in the afternoon. Now, one of the two was a man called Andrew, who was the brother of Simon Peter. He went shooting off to find his brother, and told him, 'We've found the Messiah!' – in other words, God's 'anointed'.

Andrew brought Simon to where Jesus was. Jesus sized him up very quickly. 'You're Simon,' he said, 'the son of John. Well, you're going to be known as Cephas.' (Cephas is a name meaning 'Peter'.)

[43-51] Next day, Jesus decided he'd go to Galilee, where he found Philip. 'Follow me,' he said. Now, Philip came from the same place as Andrew and Peter – Bethsaida – and he went off to find Nathanael. 'Hey!' he

---

1. To put it very simply, John's baptism was important but it was about good human intentions – a sign of the people themselves 'turning away' (the true meaning of repentance) from their old ways. John (the writer) will be emphasising all the way through the gospel that humans just don't have the power to do that on our own. We need God's Spirit within us to enable that to happen, and only Jesus, not John, could give us that. (You might like to compare Jesus' parable, *Evil spirits and vacant possession* in Matthew 12:43/Luke 11:24.)

2. The title shows they recognise Jesus as special, but they're a long way from fully recognising him. It will be some time before they call him 'Lord'.

told him, 'you know the one that Moses wrote about and all the prophets foretold? Well, we've found him. It's Jesus – you know, the son of Joseph, from Nazareth.'

'Nazareth!' Nathanael exclaimed. 'Are you telling me that something good's come out of Nazareth?'[1]

'Well, you'd better come and see for yourself, hadn't you!' Philip insisted.

As soon as Jesus saw Nathanael coming, he said, 'Now here's a good, honest, "what-you-see-is-what-you-get" Israelite!'

'That's incredible!' Nathanael exclaimed. 'Just how do you know anything about me?'

'Oh, I've seen you before,' Jesus answered. 'I got a good look at you while you were under the fig tree, before Philip called you.'

'Rabbi,' Nathanael answered, 'it's true – "something special" doesn't begin to describe you! Son of God, more like it – you're the King of Israel!'

Jesus answered, 'Now, do you believe that, just because I told you that I'd sussed you out when you were under the fig tree? Well, you've got greater things than that to see. I'm really telling you straight, you'll see heaven itself wide open, and the angels of God ascending and descending on the Son of Man.'[2]

The first sign: the wedding at Cana in Galilee

John's ordering of the narrative moves us straight on to the first of these 'greater things': the first 'sign' in Jesus' ministry. It's appropriate that this should take place at a wedding. Not only was the banquet or wedding feast a familiar metaphor for heaven but a wedding is above all a celebration of relationship. We need to remember also that in those days they hadn't privatised it the way we have – it was a community event, where the love of husband and wife was inextricably linked to the bond within the wider community. All

---

1. We don't know that Nazareth was a specially bad or dull place. It's more likely that Nathanael, like most of us, has a kind of prejudice that important people can't be local but always have to come from somewhere else! We can see this at work also in Luke 4:16-30.
2. Nathanael would have understood this image instantly from Jacob's dream in Genesis 28:10-17 where he saw a ladder set up from heaven to earth and angels ascending and descending on it. We could say that wherever Christ is, Jacob's words are truly fulfilled: 'What an awesome place! It must be the very gateway to heaven!' This also relates to Jesus' use of the 'Temple' image, in referring to his own body. The Temple was, if you like, Jacob's ladder – the place where humanity encountered God, where God's presence among people was focused.

these things make it a perfect setting for this sign of the new order. But it gets better . . .

The water in the jars was a sign of the old order – the law that dominated people's lives, which had originally been intended as a blessing and had become a burden. That was all to change in the new order, the kingdom of God, where it would be the undeserved grace of God, freely given without being earned, that would matter – not points earned by keeping every detail of the law. So the old, distasteful, washing water of law is transformed by Jesus into the new, full-bodied wine of grace! It's a wonderful, vivid sign of the kingdom of God that was becoming a reality in Jesus.

2 [1-5] On the third day[1] there was a wedding in Cana, in Galilee, and the mother of Jesus[2] was one of the guests – as were Jesus and his disciples. Part-way through the celebrations, things got seriously embarrassing when the drink ran dry.

'They've run out of wine,' the mother of Jesus said to him.

'Oh, really, Mother,'[3] Jesus answered, 'this isn't the time, you know.'[4]

'Don't worry, he'll help – just do whatever he tells you to do,' his mother said to the servant.

[6-11] There were some water jars standing near the door, used for foot-washing to comply with the Jewish purity laws, and each of them would hold about twenty or thirty gallons. 'OK,' Jesus said, 'you'd better fill those jars with water.[5] Done that, have you? Good – now draw out some water, and take it to the head waiter.'

---

1. 'The third day' probably indicates a day's break between events which may well have been the Sabbath. In that case, this 'sign' – with all its associations with renewal – took place on the same day of the week as the resurrection.

2. John never refers to Jesus' mother by her first name, but always by her title. This is certainly a point of honour for her position as mother of the Saviour, but may also serve a secondary purpose in distinguishing her from the other women named Mary who appear in the text.

3. Here, and also at 19:26, Jesus addresses his mother as 'Woman'. He wouldn't, though, be using the term as we often do, but in an affectionate way. 'Mother' gives a better sense of it in our understanding.

4. Traditional texts say, 'My time is not yet come'. Christ's glorification was to happen at Golgotha – a different kind of glory from the public acclaim that conjuring up wine at a wedding would be likely to bring! Jesus is reluctant to risk the latter kind of response.

5. They would most probably have been almost empty after guests had washed on arrival and before eating.

The head waiter took one taste and said, 'Terrific!' Now, remember, only the servants knew what had happened – *he* had no reason to expect the wine to be special. Then he called the bridegroom. 'This is really something,' he said. 'You could have given out the best wine first, and dished up any old rubbish once the guests had drunk too much to notice – but you've saved the best until the end. Great stuff!'

This first sign by Jesus was performed in Cana in Galilee – and it really showed his glory[1] and confirmed his disciples' faith.[2]

[12] After this Jesus went away with his mother, his brothers and his disciples, to spend a few days at Capernaum.

The cleansing of the Temple

This event follows after the wedding 'sign'. Having turned the water of the old order into the wine of the new, Jesus then proceeds straight to the ultimate symbol of the old order, the Temple, and confronts it with the new Temple – himself. The glory of God has been shown in the 'new Temple' in his turning of water into wine. Now he will drive the point home with this daring challenge to restore the glory also to the 'old'.

Jesus isn't throwing out and replacing the old, though – he's transforming and renewing it. His respect for the law and for the Temple is never in doubt in any of the gospels. What he wants is for them to fulfil their proper purpose.

[13-17] It was getting on for the time of the Jewish Passover – so Jesus went up to Jerusalem. When he got there, he found all kinds of trade going on – people selling cattle, sheep and doves for the sacrifices, and

---

1. This seems to contradict what I said in the introduction, but not so. Firstly, Jesus' reluctance to 'show off' indicates that his *own* glorification was definitely not the *motive* behind his actions. Secondly, the story indicates that it was done as discreetly as possible – the head waiter didn't know what had happened. No doubt the story got out, but that's a different matter. There was no flamboyant 'Look at me, I'm the Son of God' stuff here. However, John's making a deeper theological point. Christ's body is the new Temple, in which the glory of God is revealed – but the full revelation will of course be a very different kind of glory – on Golgotha.
2. Again, care is needed! That the disciples already had faith, without needing signs of this sort, is obvious because they were already following him. This sign confirmed their faith – it wasn't a precondition of faith, which is the kind of sign other people were always after.

money-changers sitting at their tables.[1] Jesus went ballistic! He got some rope and made it into a whip, and then drove all the animals – and the traders with them – right out of the Temple. Then he sent the money-changers' money rolling all over the floor. 'Get all this stuff out of here!' he roared at the dove-sellers. 'I won't have my Father's house turned into a street market!'[2]

This reminded his disciples of the Bible text that says, 'My enthusiasm for your Temple will completely consume me.'[3]

[18-22] In no time at all, the religious authorities were at him about it. 'Hey, like, who do you think you are?' they demanded. 'Give us a sign of your authority to do this kind of thing.'

'Give yourselves a sign!' Jesus retorted. 'Wreck this Temple, and then watch me raise it up in three days. How about that, then?'

'You're mad!' the religious authorities said. 'Forty-six years we've spent building this Temple – and you reckon you can do it over a week-end!' But Jesus, of course, was talking about the Temple of his own body – and later, after he'd been raised from the dead, his disciples understood that. Then, of course, they grasped what scripture was saying as well as what Jesus himself had said.

[23-25] During his time in Jerusalem, during the Passover, a lot of people saw the signs and their faith in him grew stronger. But Jesus knew better than to rely on their support. He knew what made people tick, and he didn't need to listen to anybody else's testimony to know what they were really like.

---

1. In itself, this would seem reasonable. The livestock was guaranteed suitable for Temple rituals, and the money was free of idolatrous images – so this wasn't like renting out the church foyer to a supermarket chain!

2. Jesus doesn't mention the dishonesty, although it's clearly implied in the synoptic equivalents: it seems to be the trading *as such* that is the problem. Perhaps also he saw just turning up at the Temple and buying something to use as an offering as a bit of a cop-out. The original idea was to give sacrificially; so, having painstakingly raised your livestock, stayed up all night for the lambing, lost sleep worrying over the lack of good grazing, etc., you then took the very best that all your own sweat and tears had produced and offered it to God. The traders made it possible to shortcut all that – just turn up, buy something and sacrifice it (and if you'd got something even better at home, well, you could just hang on to it for yourself). If I'm right, then this completely fits in with Jesus' passion for the *spirit* of the law as distinct from the letter.

3. Psalm 69:9, but put into the future tense so that it points forward to the crucifixion.

Nicodemus: a closet Christian?

Having just referred to people who believed, but whom Jesus knew better than to trust, John immediately introduces us to Nicodemus – who comes to Jesus *by night*. Nicodemus was a Pharisee; could it be that he was trying to be a half-hearted follower of Jesus, but keep all the social privileges and status that his position carried? It seems likely that by the time John was writing there were many like him who wanted to 'have their cake and eat it too' as the gap widened between the traditional religion and Christianity, which certainly underlies John's stark 'make a choice' message. We know that Jesus' words were addressed not to an individual but to all the people he represented, because when he says, 'You must be born from above', the Greek word for 'You' is plural, not singular: 'You all'. It's not surprising that this story, which only appears in one gospel, should be John's choice at this point in his story. Jesus wants committed disciples – prepared to stand up and be counted – and he challenges Nicodemus to open himself up to the new birth of conversion which will lead to full-blooded commitment.

Nicodemus then fades out of the story and Jesus continues to lay stress on the need for us all to make the choice Nicodemus is putting off. We need to keep the dual perspective here. 'Born from above' means that only God can do this – it's not something we can achieve by hard work, or by saying or thinking the right things. It's a gift. But it's a gift that God won't force on us, and we have to be open to receiving – which is where our own decision comes in.

3 [1-8] Nicodemus was one of the Pharisees – which might explain why he only felt able to approach Jesus at night. 'Rabbi,' he said, 'look, we all know you're a teacher sent by God – I mean, you couldn't do the things you are doing, otherwise, could you?'

'I'm really telling you straight,' said Jesus, 'if you want to have any idea what the kingdom of God's about, you need to be born from above.'

'Oh, right!' Nicodemus answered. 'Like, someone who's old can actually go back into the womb and be born again – that'd be quite something, that would.'[1]

---

1. Nicodemus is thinking of natural birth – just being born again. Jesus is talking about a supernatural 'birth' – a conversion experience that begins a completely new life. Nicodemus thinks that being born into a faith community is enough in itself. Jesus challenges him to open himself up to the Spirit of God and receive new life. It's that 'old' and 'new' thing again.

'I'm really telling you straight,' Jesus repeated, 'you can't enter the kingdom of God without being born of water and Spirit.[1] Look, it's simple enough: flesh can only give birth to more flesh; Spirit is what gives birth to spirit. So don't stand gaping in amazement because I said you've got to be born from above. Look, the wind[2] blows where it decides to blow, doesn't it? Mystery – that's what it is – you can hear it, but you don't know where it comes from or where it's going.[3] Well, that's what life's like for those who are born of the Spirit: mysterious, but effective.'

9-15 'I just can't get my head round this!' Nicodemus gasped.

'How come?' Jesus answered. 'A teacher of Israel like yourself can't understand what I'm saying? I'm really telling you straight, we talk about the things we know – we testify to things we've seen, but you Pharisees don't believe our testimony. I've talked about things to do with this world, and you can't get your head round it – so how are you going to manage if I talk about the things of heaven? I mean, no one's ever been up to heaven – except the one who came down from there, the Son of Man. And you remember how Moses lifted up the snake in the desert – well, in the same way the Son of Man's going to be lifted up too, so that everybody who believes in him may have eternal life.[4]

16-21 'What you need to get your head round is just how much God loves this world – so much that he gave his unique Son so that everyone who really accepts him needn't die but may have eternal life.[5]

---

1. It's the 'Spirit' that's crucial here. 'Water' might well refer to the waters of baptism, but it's probably not insignificant that water is involved in our natural birth too. Jesus isn't dismissing – still less, condemning – natural processes – just saying they aren't enough on their own.

2. 'Wind' and 'spirit' are very close in biblical thought – the same word is used for each in both Greek and Hebrew, and the Holy Spirit was also known as the 'Breath of God'.

3. OK, so you can tell the general direction, but that's not the same thing as knowing the point of origin or the precise destination, is it?

4. Numbers 21:8, onwards. The serpent standard, when raised up, offered healing to people bitten by poisonous snakes. Jesus is clearly looking ahead to his own crucifixion and its life-saving effect.

5. Deservedly one of the most famous verses in the Bible, this is particularly important in John, since it's the only time he talks about God loving *the world*. In his enthusiasm to present a choice to his readers, to show Christ's way as the only way, he runs the risk of suggesting that love is only for the Christian community. Unlike the other gospel writers, he doesn't, for example, show Jesus telling us to love our enemies, but only one another. He is also in danger at times of making 'the world' appear in a negative light. This verse is the vital corrective to both of those. The world is God's creation, and he loves it.

'God didn't send the Son into the world as a judgement – he sent him to save it, and everyone who puts faith in him has nothing to fear. Of course, if people are determined to reject him, then in effect they've already judged themselves – they've rejected the unique Son of God, and all that goes with him.

'And do you know what the judgement actually is? Light's come into the world, and people have chosen to remain in the dark and keep their nasty little ways under cover. You see, people who're up to no good really hate the light – stay well away from it, so that no one'll see what they're doing. But people of integrity – people who "do the truth" – well, they'll always choose the light so that everyone can see they've nothing to hide.'

Jesus and John the Baptiser

22-30 After this, Jesus took his disciples off into the countryside of Judea and spent some time with them, baptising people. John was baptising too – at Aenon, near Salim, where there was plenty of water, and people just kept on coming to him for baptism (this, of course, was before John was thrown into prison). So, one member of the religious authorities started an argument with John about the purification laws. 'Hey, Rabbi,' they said, 'you know that guy who was with you when you were the other side of the river – the one you kept pointing us to[1] – well, he's baptising now, and everyone's going to him.'

'Well, whatever success he's having must have been sent from heaven, mustn't it!' John retorted. 'All of you can witness that I said right from the start, "I'm not the Messiah – just the one who's been sent to announce him." Look, if you go to a wedding, it's the guy with the bride who's the bridegroom, isn't it? His best mate will be there beside him, but he's just sharing the bridegroom's happiness.[2] Right, so I'm happy for him – OK? Now he's got to become greater, and I've got to become less important. That's the way it is.

The one from heaven and the one from earth

31-36 'It's obvious, isn't it? – someone who comes from above will always be "above" the one who's just from the earth. Someone from earth can

---

1. Or, more accurately, 'giving testimony to'.
2. In a Jewish wedding, the bridegroom would go to the bride's house, to claim her and take her to his own place. His best friend would go with him and, as they approached, would call out, 'Behold, the bridegroom comes!' So that was John the Baptiser's role – an important one, but Jesus was the main man.

only speak about earthly matters, but the one from heaven, well, he's above all, isn't he! He comes and testifies about the things that only he's seen and heard first-hand, and do they believe his testimony? Not a bit of it. Anyone who *does* accept his testimony, though – well, that person shows the truth, that God sent him. The one that God sends speaks God's words – right? Because that guy can give you God's Holy Spirit like no one else can.[1] The point is that the Father loves the Son so much that he's put everything into his hands. Believe him, and you find true life. Reject him, and – well, you reject the life that comes with him. That's the judgement.'[2]

The Samaritan woman at the well

> Jesus now finds it necessary to move away from Judea – the place where he should have found acceptance – and it's in what would be expected to be hostile territory that he finds recognition and real faith. The Samaritan woman gives her testimony: that in Jesus she has met the Messiah.

4 [1-6] Jesus got wind of the fact that he'd been noticed – word had got to the Pharisees that 'he's doing more baptisms than John' (although to be strictly accurate it was Jesus' disciples who were baptising, not Jesus himself). So he left Judea and went back to Galilee[3] – which meant he had to pass through Samaria on the way.

So it was that he arrived at Sychar (not far from the plot that the Patriarch Jacob had given to his son Joseph all those centuries ago) in need of a rest. He sat down by Jacob's well – the noonday sun was high in the sky.

[7-15] When a Samaritan woman came to get water, Jesus saw his chance.[4] 'Do you think you could give me a drink?' he asked. His disciples had gone off to buy food, by the way, so he was all alone.

---

1. As sometimes happens, the different ancient manuscripts don't entirely agree here and the meaning isn't clear. What I've put is one possible interpretation, but if you care to go digging in the commentaries you'll find some real treasure.
2. The old text says 'wrath of God' here – the only use of that word in this gospel (it's used quite a lot in Revelation). Research suggests that the word 'judgement' is appropriate, but you can always mentally change it back if you prefer.
3. He was probably avoiding a premature confrontation with the authorities. Although the exact word isn't used here, you might like to check 'Retreat' in the Glossary.
4. Jesus, the much greater 'Jacob' – patriarch of the New Israel – meets a woman at the well. You might like to play a game of 'spot the connections and contrasts' by looking up Genesis 24:15 where Jacob's servant meets Rebekah.

'Now, hang on a moment, there,' the woman answered. 'You're a Jew, right? And you're asking me – a Samaritan woman – to give you a drink?[1] Now, there's a turn-up!' It's important to understand here that traditionally Jews wouldn't touch anything handled by a Samaritan.[2]

'If you only knew,' Jesus replied, 'what God can give to people who're open to him – and if you knew who was asking you for this – it would be you asking me. And it would be for *living* water . . . you'd get that!'

'Sir,' the woman said, 'you've got no bucket – have you any idea how deep this well is?[3] So just how are you going to get hold of this living water?[4] I suppose you think you're greater than Jacob himself, do you? You know: our ancestor, who gave us this well, and who drank from it himself, along with his family and his livestock? Are you greater than him?'[5]

'Oh, this well's fine,' Jesus said, 'but people who drink from it are going to be thirsty again, aren't they? Now, the water that I can give, on the other hand – that'll satisfy people for ever. No more thirst! They'll have their own internal spring,[6] bubbling over with eternal life.'

'Oh, I'll have a bit of that – yes, sir, I will!' the woman said. 'Just think – no more getting thirsty, no more coming to this well every day to get water. Oh, yes – that'll do nicely.'

16-26 'OK,' Jesus said. 'Go and get your husband, why don't you? Bring him back here.'

'Husband? I've no husband.'

'No, but you have had, haven't you? – five of them, in fact. And, of course, the guy you're with right now, well, you're right, he's not your husband, is he?'

'OK, OK, I can see you're a prophet, sir,' she said. 'I'll give you that. Look, our ancestors worshipped on this mountain – right? – and that

---

1. Race- and sex-discrimination in one sentence! Apart from Jews not engaging with Samaritans, no respectable Rabbi would speak to a strange woman in a public place. Jesus is shattering the taboos here.
2. It's that old ritual purity thing again – Samaritans followed a kind of hybrid religion, and were therefore 'unclean'.
3. The word used here for 'well' indicates that it would be one built over an underground spring, and over 100 feet deep.
4. In the local idiom, she would understand 'living water' as being from a spring or river, as opposed to stagnant water from a tank. So at this point she thinks the living water is in the well!
5 Wonderful irony! So often, those who ridicule Jesus are saying more truth than they know! Another example is the mocking at the trial and crucifixion.
6. Not one that's 100 feet underground . . .

was good enough for God. But your lot say everyone's got to go up to Jerusalem, and what we do here doesn't count.'

'Look, lady, I'm not getting into all that,' Jesus said. 'Believe me, the time's coming when places won't be important. You people worship a God you don't really know, whereas we worship one we know – because salvation comes from within the Jewish tradition.[1] But the time's coming – and, in fact, it's now – when genuine worshippers will worship the Father in spirit and in truth, because that's the kind of worship the Father wants. God is life-giving spirit – so worship's an offering of our lives to him – lives lived in spirit and truth.'

'Oh, well – I know the Messiah's coming,' the woman answered (another word for Messiah is Christ), 'and I guess we'll understand all this stuff, then, won't we!'

'I am the one you mean,'[2] Jesus told her. 'And I'm speaking to you right here and now!'[3]

[27-30] At that point the disciples came back and were absolutely amazed to find Jesus talking to a woman he didn't know.[4] Mind you, they didn't quite have the nerve to say, 'Do you want something, lady?' or, 'Hey, Jesus, what do you think you're doing, talking to her?'

The woman dashed off – didn't even stop to pick up her water-jug – and went back home to tell her friends. 'You've just got to come and meet this guy,' she told them. 'He knew all about me, even though we'd never met! I mean, he surely can't be the Messiah, can he?' And in no time, they were all high-tailing it out of the city to see him.

[31-38] Meanwhile the disciples were really nagging at Jesus – with the best of intentions, of course. 'Come on, Rabbi,' they were urging him, 'you've got to eat something, you know.'

'Oh, don't worry about me,' Jesus told them. 'I've got food to eat that you know nothing about.'

'What? But no one's brought you anything, have they?'

---

1. Jesus might have accused his contemporaries of having lost the plot, but he believed the plot was still there if they cared to see it. The Samaritan religion was a bit like the 'pick 'n' mix' spirituality we sometimes come across, the people, having picked bits out of various philosophies, losing sight of the really important things at their heart.

2. Now, that's odd – in the synoptic gospels, Jesus seems to be always telling people not to say who he is. Perhaps in Samaria he feels it's a bit safer to risk the misunderstanding that the term 'Messiah' would certainly have caused in Judea.

3. In other words, 'Don't keep putting it off – the time is now!'

4. Again, a complete breach of social taboos – a sign of Jesus' freedom from the prejudice that surrounded him.

This next passage is a timely warning against complacency. While the disciples are behaving as if the only thing that matters is food, the Samaritan woman has gone rushing off to get her friends. The complacency of the 'chosen' ones' is vividly contrasted with the sense of urgency of the 'heretic' Samaritan who can recognise that the spiritual harvest is ready, even though they can't! The idea that salvation was offered to Samaritans would have been offensive. The point is, though, that the harvest is God's gift, not anyone's right.

'As far as I'm concerned,' Jesus told them, 'doing the will of the one who sent me's the only food I need – completing his work.[1] Look, how often have you sat around, saying, "We've got a good four months before harvest"?[2] Well, look around yourselves – the corn's ripe and the harvesters are already at work gathering fruit for eternal life so that the sower and the reaper can both share in the celebrations. You know, that old saying's got a lot of truth in it: "One person sows, but someone else reaps the harvest"! Well, you're going to gather what you haven't worked for – others did the work, but you've got a place at their harvest festival.'

[39-42] Many of the Samaritans in that city turned to faith in Jesus because of what the woman had testified – 'He knew all about me even though we'd never met'. They asked Jesus to stay with them – which he did for two days – and even more of them believed once they'd heard him for themselves. 'It's not just because of what you said,' they told the woman. 'We've heard for ourselves now – and we believe this truly is the Saviour of the world.'[3]

The second sign: healing an official's son

Here comes the second 'sign' of John's first group of three. Remember what was said about Jesus in 1:4? 'In him was life' – which means much more than the fact that he was breathing! 'In him was the fullness of life'.

---

1. We'll see a vivid example of this 'completing' idea in John 9.
2. Not a very accurate picture of modern farming, but in those days you wouldn't disturb the soil by working on it while the seed was growing. It may be that Jesus was quoting a familiar lazy person's saying – 'What's all the rush for – there's loads of time!'
3. This is the grand climax of the passage – and the words come not from one of Jesus' own followers, but from members of the 'untouchable' nation, the Samaritans.

[43-49] After the two days were over, Jesus returned to Galilee (remember, he himself had testified that prophets don't exactly get the honour they deserve in their home areas).[1] In Galilee he was given a real welcome – people from that region had been up to Jerusalem for the festival and had seen what he'd done there. So he went on to Cana in Galilee – the place where he changed water into wine at the wedding, remember? – and found a local official there whose son was ill in Capernaum. As soon as the man heard that Jesus was back in Galilee from Judea, he hot-footed it over to him to ask him to heal his son – otherwise the lad would die.

'You people[2] are always looking for signs and wonders before you'll believe, aren't you!' Jesus sighed.

'Look, sir,' the official persisted, 'the point is my little boy's dying – are you going to come and heal him?'

[50-54] 'Go home,' Jesus told him. 'Your lad's going to live.'

That was all the man needed – Jesus' word was enough – so he started back home, and on the way his slaves came running to meet him shouting that his son was OK. And when the official asked what time the recovery began, guess what? 'Yesterday, about one-ish,' they answered. 'That's when the fever died down.'[3]

The father knew that was exactly the time Jesus had said, 'Your lad's going to live', and then he *really* believed – no lingering doubts at all – and his entire household came to faith as well. Now, this was the second sign Jesus did after coming from Judaea into Galilee.

The third sign: healing a sick man

We move straight on to the third of this first group of three signs. As Lord of life, Jesus now turns his attention to someone whose social isolation means he cannot enjoy life in all its fullness.

---

1. This comment by John sits less easily here than the equivalent saying in the Synoptics – it doesn't seem to fit with the success Jesus seems to be having in his own region. One possible explanation is that John's really saying that Jesus has no 'home country' here on earth.
2. The 'you' in Greek is plural – so Jesus isn't having a go at the official in particular but the people in general.
3. Now, why the official took overnight to travel twenty miles (presumably on horse-back) we're not told. Perhaps it's an indication of his complete confidence in Jesus that he didn't need to hurry home and check. We just don't know.

> Without friends to help him, he cannot get the healing he needs. This sign is pure, unconditional grace – Jesus sees his need and meets it, without any prior indication of faith by the sick man.

5 [1-9] After this there was one of the Jewish festivals, and Jesus went to Jerusalem again. Now, there's a place in Jerusalem called the Sheep Gate, where there's a pool with the Hebrew name 'Bethzatha' – grand sort of place – five porticoes – and in them were all kinds of ill and disabled people: blind, paralysed, you name it. One of them had been ill for thirty-eight years – can you believe that? Jesus knew he'd been there for yonks, so he said, 'Do you want to get well?'

'Look, sir,' the man answered, 'I've got no one to help me into the pool when the waters get stirred up,[1] and some other guy always barges in ahead of me.'

'Well, just stand up, pick up your mattress and walk,' Jesus told him.

No problem: the man was cured instantly, rolled up his mattress and started walking away. Now, this took place on the Sabbath.

[10-18] The religious authorities weren't happy about it at all. 'Hey, just you hang on a minute!' they called to the man. 'It's the Sabbath day – you can't go doing hard work like carrying a mattress!'[2]

'Look,' he said, 'the guy who healed me said, "Pick up your mattress, and walk". I've picked it up. I'm walking. If you're not happy, take it up with him.'

'Oh, we will!' they answered. 'So who was it who told you to carry a mattress on the Sabbath?'

That was a problem – Jesus hadn't waited around to be recognised but had melted into the crowd. He found the man in the Temple later, and said, 'There – you've been made well. Now, mind you don't sin, because there are worse things than being ill, you know.'[3]

---

1. A regular disturbance of the water was believed to be the moment when people could be healed by getting into the pool. The disturbance didn't last long, though. There were two kinds of people there – the quick and the disappointed.
2. I mean, come on – the guy's just been healed after 38 years, and they're quibbling about a legal technicality! God's loving provision for his people, which is what the Sabbath originally was, can all too easily be turned into a burden.
3. Jesus warns the man not to sin, so that nothing worse will happen. This shouldn't be read simplistically as saying that particular sins caused his illness. All creation is less than it should be, and sin and illness alike manifest that – but that's not the same as saying that committing sin x leads to illness y.

The man went off and told the religious authorities that it had been Jesus who'd healed him, and, of course, they got stuck in to Jesus straightaway, because he was doing terrible things like making sick people well on the Sabbath!

'Look, it's simple enough, even for you,' Jesus answered. 'My Father's been working non-stop right up until now, so I'm working too.' That made the religious authorities all the more determined to get him – not only breaking the Sabbath,[1] but now calling God his Father too – in other words, making himself equal with God!

[19-24] Jesus said to them:

I'm really telling you straight, the Son doesn't do anything independently – only what he's already seen the Father doing. What the Father does, the Son does too. You see, the Father really loves the Son, and lets him see everything he does. And he's going to show things that'll have you completely dumbfounded – which'll make a nice change in itself – because just as the Father can give new life to the dead, so the Son brings the whole fullness of life to people wherever he chooses. And it's not the Father who brings about judgement – he's given that prerogative to the Son as well,[2] so that people can honour the Son as they honour the Father. Now, if you dishonour the Son, that's your choice – but in doing so you dishonour the Father who sent him, too. I'm really telling you straight, people who're open to my word and believe the one who sent me – those people have eternal life already. No judgement for them – they've passed over[3] from death to life.

[25-29] I'm really telling you straight, the time's coming – and, in fact, it's now – when those who are spiritually dead – and physically too, come to that – will hear the Son of God's voice, and those who attend to it will really live![4] You see, as the Father has life in himself,

---

1. Worse, actually – he'd completely contradicted the scriptural basis for the Sabbath (Genesis 2:2-3), thus apparently cancelling all Sabbaths from then on! Of course, it's not that simple. Jesus was really saying that God had never stopped caring – and if caring is work, then he was guilty!

2. Doesn't this contradict 3:17? Well, no, it doesn't. Judgement wasn't the *purpose* of Christ's coming, but if we flatly reject him, then it's a *consequence* we invoke (see 'Judgement' in the Glossary).

3. An unmistakable allusion to the Passover festival, celebrating the nation's liberation from slavery. See 'Passover' in the Glossary for an indication of the breadth of meaning in this.

4. Jesus is the Lord of *all* life – physical and spiritual. Later we'll see him raising the dead as an acted parable of his calling the *spiritually* dead to find life in all its fullness in him.

he's granted the same to the Son – to have real life in himself, along with the authority of judgement because he's the Son of Man. And you can stop all the 'stand back in amazement' stuff, because the time's coming[1] when all the people now in their graves will hear his voice and come out – for those who've done good it'll be a resurrection to life, and for those who've done harm, a resurrection to judgement.

30-38 I don't just go around acting on my own whims, you know. I judge by the evidence I hear, and that's a just judgement because I'm not looking to my own interests, but the will of the one who sent me.

OK, so my own testimony to myself isn't acceptable evidence; but there's someone else who testifies on my behalf too – and I know that his testimony's reliable. I mean, it was you who sent people to question John in the first place – and he gave his testimony to the truth. Not that the testimony of a human witness is particularly important to me anyway, but I'm putting myself through this for *your* sake – so that *you* can be saved! You know, that man was a fiery, shining lamp, and you were happy enough to bask in his light for a while, weren't you? But I've got a testimony that can knock John's into a cocked hat – the evidence is in the tasks that the Father assigned to me to complete. The things I do speak for themselves – *they're* my testimony that the Father has sent me. And it's the Father who really testifies for me. OK, I know you've never heard his voice – or seen him – but how can you expect to have his word within yourselves when you don't believe the one that he's sent?

39-47 You're priceless, you are, do you know that? You hunt high and low in the scriptures, because you think that eternal life's contained in them – and it's those same scriptures that testify to me! But will you come to me? Not likely, you won't! Oh, I'm not interested in the kind of glory people can give me – that's not what bothers me – what matters is that you haven't got the love of God in you! I've come to you in the name of my Father, and you won't accept me. If someone else comes along, in his own name – oh, that'll be different, won't it? You'll accept that person. How can you ever really believe when you're only interested in the vain flattery you get from

---

1. This time Jesus doesn't add, 'and, in fact, it's now' – indicating that he's looking ahead to the future, and the final general resurrection of the physically dead.

each other, and not in the true glory that God can give? Oh, don't worry – I'm not going to be making accusations about you to God – I don't need to – Moses is already doing that! Remember Moses – the one you always claim to be so keen on? Well, if you really believed him, you'd believe me, because he pointed to me in everything he wrote. But if you won't believe what he wrote, I suppose it's far too much to ask you to believe what I say.

The fourth sign: the feeding of the five thousand

John now introduces his second set of three signs, beginning again with a nature miracle. The opening sentence of the chapter indicates that there were other signs too – but John is focusing on the ones that emphasise what he particularly wants to say about Jesus. He will tell us himself later that he's only covered a tiny bit of Jesus' story.

As we read this narrative, we need to be aware that John has linked it to some very explicit teaching by Jesus that relates, with hindsight at least, to the Communion service. He feeds us with bread, but later he says that he can give us a better kind of food that sustains an infinitely more desirable kind of life. That idea is coming up shortly, but it's helpful to be aware of it as we read this.

This chapter gets a bit heavy going later on, but it's worth persevering with because John gives us a lot of clues about how to understand Jesus. Two tips might be helpful.

1. Read the introductions and footnotes – I hope they'll make things rather less obscure.
2. Don't expect to grasp it all straightaway. Read it, get the gist, and move on. You can come back again later to dig a little deeper.

6 ¹⁻¹⁰ After this, Jesus was off across the Sea of Galilee – also known as the Sea of Tiberias – with a huge crowd following him because of the signs he was doing in healing sick people. Jesus went up the mountain, where he sat down with his disciples – this was near the time of the Jewish Passover festival.

Looking up, Jesus saw the crowd making straight for them, so he said to Philip, 'Where are we going to buy bread, so that these people can eat?' He was just testing really – he knew exactly what he was going to do.

'What!' Philip answered, 'You couldn't earn the money in six months to buy enough to give everyone even a crumb!'

Andrew, the brother of Simon Peter, interrupted. 'Well, there's a boy here with five barley loaves[1] and a couple of small fish – but just how far do you expect that to go among all these people?'

'Get the people to sit down,' Jesus ordered. There was plenty of open grassland, so they all sat down – about five thousand altogether.

[11-15] Then Jesus took the loaves, and after he'd given thanks he gave them out to the people sitting around him. He did the same with the fish too, and everyone had as much as they needed. Then he turned to his disciples. 'You'd better collect all the fragments,' he said. 'We don't want any to be lost,[2] do we?' So they did – and filled no less than twelve baskets with the leftovers from those five barley loaves.

When the people saw this sign, they went crazy. 'It's him!' they said. 'It's the prophet that was promised to come into the world!' Jesus knew they'd got it all wrong again, and that they were going to try to drag him off to a worldly throne that he had no interest in, so he beat a retreat to the mountain on his own.

Jesus walks on the water

We need to remember that water had enormous symbolic meaning for Jews. The waters brought under control at creation symbolised the primeval chaos and disorder that had existed before – a state of 'non-being'. Those waters had been allowed to break out again in the flood, and, in fact, were seen as always threatening. Psalmists, for example, who wanted to say how desperate they were feeling, would sing about being overwhelmed by powerful waters. So, here are the disciples, without Jesus – who is the Lord of life – threatened by overwhelming waters until that same Lord of life shows his complete mastery of the waters of chaos by simply walking on top of them!

---

1. Barley loaves were the cheapest kind of bread – eaten by poor people. This makes the miracle all the more amazing in that the people were completely satisfied with this.

2. The specific Greek word John uses for 'lost' here (remember, Jesus would almost certainly have been speaking Aramaic, so even the Greek is a translation) is the same word he uses for 'lost' people who are saved.

[16-21] Come evening time, the disciples decided they couldn't wait any longer, got into a boat and pushed off for Capernaum. It was dark[1] by now – and Jesus wasn't there. Soon the wind had whipped up the waves into a frenzy and a half. They'd managed to row about three or four miles when they saw something that made their hair stand on end: Jesus, walking towards them *on the surface of the water* – and he was getting closer every second! Terrified? That's one way of putting it.

'Oh, come on, get a grip!' Jesus told them. 'It's only me – no need to get your loincloths in a twist.'

Then, of course, they changed their tune completely and wanted to get him straight into the boat – which immediately reached the shore they'd been aiming for.

> We now come to a key passage for understanding John's portrayal of Jesus. Jesus, he says, is the source of our spiritual life. By attending to him we 'feed on him' – draw spiritual nourishment from him. However important the material things may be, they won't give us the kind of life that Jesus can. Even the famous manna that came from heaven didn't give people that kind of life. So Jesus offers himself to us as our spiritual food – and the image reaches its height when we see how sacrificial that self-offering ultimately was.

Bread from heaven

[22-27] Next day, the penny dropped for the crowd – who were still waiting on the other side of the sea. Like – there's only one boat there, and there should be two. They realised that Jesus hadn't got into the boat with his disciples but had let them go on without him. Then some other boats, from Tiberias, came near and, seeing that both Jesus and his disciples had clearly moved on, the crowd got into the boats and went to Capernaum to look for Jesus – and they caught up with him on the other side of the sea. 'So, since when have you been here, Rabbi?' they demanded.

'I'm really telling you straight,' Jesus answered, 'you didn't come tearing after me because you understood the signs – it's the bread that filled your stomachs you care about. What you've got to learn is not to break your backs trying to build up stocks of perishable food – go after the

---

1. It's a particular theme of John that we're all in darkness without Jesus, who is the Light.

food that lasts for eternal life – the food that the Son of Man can give you, because it's on him that the Father's set his seal of approval.'

[28-34] 'OK, then, so what do we have to do to be fulfilling God's expectations?'[1] they asked.

'This is what God expects,' Jesus told them, 'that you believe in the one he's sent.'[2]

'Fine,' they said, 'so give us a sign[3] – a great work that we can see and believe you.[4] Well – what are you going to do, then? In the old days, our ancestors had manna to eat in the desert. You know the bit in the Bible: "He gave them bread from heaven, to eat."'[5]

'I'm really telling you straight,' Jesus retorted, 'Moses didn't give you the bread from heaven – only my Father can do that. Look it's so simple it's almost embarrassing – the bread that God gives comes down from heaven and gives life to the world.'

'Now you're talking, sir!' they responded. 'You can give us that bread for ever, thank you very much!'

[35-40] Jesus answered, '*I am* the bread of life. Anyone who comes to me won't ever be hungry – anyone who believes in me will never be thirsty. But then I've already pointed out that you've seen and still don't believe, so what's surprising about all this! It's about giving and receiving: I'm open to what the Father wants to give, so of course I can receive it. And anyone else who responds in faith and turns to me – well, I'm not going to turn them away, am I?[6] After all, I haven't come down from

---

1. They've correctly understood that the 'food' Jesus refers to consists in doing the will of God.
2. So it's not good works, but faith in Christ. And that means more than merely believing the right things – it means allowing him to change us so radically that it's like a new birth.
3. Why? Wasn't the feeding of the five thousand a sign? Yes, it was – and that was enough for them to hail him as 'the prophet' and want to make him king. Now, they realised that Jesus was staking a much higher claim – and for that he'd need to do something bigger and better.
4. Interesting things, prepositions – especially when there aren't any! 'Believe you' is a very different matter from 'believe *in* you'. They just haven't caught on, at all.
5. Now, that would do it. The common expectation was that when the Messiah came, the people would be given more of the 'manna' that they'd had in the desert under Moses' leadership. I mean, making an ordinary bread roll go round a thousand people is all very well, but calling down bread from heaven itself – well!
6. God offers – we can respond or not as we choose. Jesus' point is that we can't earn salvation by human means – it's God's gift. But it's a gift he won't force on us, so it's also about our willingness to *receive*.

heaven just to do my own thing – I'm here to do what the one who sent me expects of me. And what he who sent me expects is that I shouldn't lose any of what he's given to me, but raise it all up on the last day. What my Father expects is that all people who really pay attention to the Son – really believe *in* him – they'll have eternal life and you can be sure I *will* raise them up on the last day.'

[41-51] Then the religious authorities started moaning about Jesus' saying that he was the bread from heaven. 'Oh, come on, get real!' they said. 'This is Jesus – Joseph's son – we know his parents. "Come down from heaven", my eye!'

'Now, don't go whinging among yourselves,' Jesus told them. 'The only people who can come to me are the ones that respond to the Father's call[1] – and, yes, I'll raise them up on the last day. You know what it says in the writings of the prophets: "They'll all be taught by God".[2] So everyone who listens and learns from the Father[3] comes to me in faith. Not that anyone's seen the Father, of course, except the one who's actually from God – *he's* seen the Father. I'm really telling you straight, everyone who believes already has eternal life – I am the bread of life. Look: your ancestors ate the manna in the desert, and what happened to them? They died, that's what. But now you're looking at the bread that comes down from heaven for people to eat and then never die. I am the living bread, sent down from heaven. Everybody who eats this bread will have real life – the kind that lasts for ever[4] – and the bread that I give so that the whole world can really have life – well, ultimately, that's going to be my own body.'

> So far, Jesus' words could be seen simply as a metaphor: 'feeding' on him could be understood in terms of learning and growing through our contact with him. However, he's now going to raise the stakes by speaking in terms that immediately call to mind the Last Supper and our celebration of that in Holy Communion. Quite what these words would have meant to Jesus' contemporaries is

1. It's that 'offer and response' thing again.
2. Isaiah 54:13. Again, it's not something we can do for ourselves – it's God who teaches . . .
3. . . . but it *is* up to us to respond.
4. So, we're being told, Jesus is essential to real life – and if people thought that the manna in the desert showed God's love and care for his people – well, they've got something infinitely better now being offered to them. Here's life that Moses never dreamt of!

difficult to imagine (the reaction of the people around Jesus indicates that they completely misunderstood him) and there are various theories about that. What really matters for us, though, is what they can say to us now – why did John choose to record these sayings? And that question seems to point us directly to the Communion.

⁵²⁻⁵⁹ Well, he'd really pushed it too far now! The religious authorities all started bickering among themselves again. 'Unbelievable!' they said. 'How can this guy give us his own flesh to eat?'

Jesus said to them, 'I'm really telling you straight, unless you do eat the Son of Man's flesh – and drink his blood too – you'll have no life in you that means anything. Those who eat my flesh and drink my blood – they'll have eternal life, here and now, and I'll raise them up on the last day. You see, my flesh is the food that truly counts – my blood is the drink that really matters. And when people eat my flesh and drink my blood – well, they really invest their lives in me, and I put my life in them. It follows, if you think about it. The Father, who really is life, sent me, and my life flows from him. So, in the same way, whoever feeds on me will have the life that flows through me. Got it? Now, this really is the bread that came down from heaven – not like the stuff our ancestors ate in the desert, and then later died – you eat this bread, and you'll live for ever.' Jesus said all these things during his teaching in the Capernaum synagogue.

Faithful and unfaithful disciples

⁶⁰⁻⁷¹ This was more than a lot of the disciples could handle. 'Tough teaching, this,' they said. 'No one can cope with ideas like these!'

Jesus knew that even his own disciples had now started whinging, and said, 'Oh, so this offends you, does it? So, how are you going to cope if you should see the Son of Man ascending back to the place he came from? It's the spirit that generates life – without it, the flesh is no use at all. And the words I've been speaking are, in fact, spirit and life.[1] Yet there are unbelievers, even among you.' Jesus knew, right from the

---

1. In Jesus, spirit and flesh (flesh in its true, unfallen state, as God meant it to be) are perfectly united: flesh alone is nothing without the life in it, but it's the flesh that provides, if you like, a vehicle for the life. We need physical food, and we need spiritual food which is conveyed in the words of Jesus – who himself took human flesh in order to do it. So, at the Communion we read the scriptures so that the Word and the sacrament – spirit and flesh – are kept together, and symbolically we feed on both.

start, who the fickle ones were in his group, and which one of them was eventually going to betray him. 'That's the reason,' he told them, 'why I've been drumming into you that no one comes to me other than by accepting the gift of faith from the Father.'

After that, it's hardly surprising that a lot of his disciples recoiled from this and went their own way. So Jesus turned to the Twelve. 'Well?' he challenged them. 'Are you going to leave me, too?'

'Lord,' Simon Peter answered, 'who else is there we can go to? You're the one who's got the words of eternal life. I mean, we've come to believe in you now – and we're completely convinced that you're God's holy one.'[1]

'Didn't I personally hand-pick all of you?' Jesus said. 'And yet there's one of you who's a devil.'[2] By this, of course, he meant Judas, the son of Simon Iscariot – because although he was one of the close circle of the Twelve, he was going to betray Jesus.

The Festival of Tents: the controversy gets hotter

7[1-5] After this, Jesus went walkabout in Galilee – he knew better than to do that in Judea because the religious authorities were just waiting for a chance to kill him. Now, this was about the time of the Jewish Festival of Tents,[3] and his brothers said, 'You know, you should go to Jerusalem – take your disciples along so they can see the terrific things you do. I mean, if you want people to take notice of you it's no good skulking around in secret, now is it?' So, you can see, even his brothers hadn't a clue what he was about.

---

1. This is a Messianic title – so why didn't Peter just say, 'Messiah'? I don't know – but it could well be that the term 'God's holy one' is meant to show Jesus as the Messiah *and much more* – since the general expectation of the Messiah was simply a military saviour and worldly ruler.

2. A strong word, specifically chosen by Jesus. To some, this verse means that Jesus chose Judas because someone *had* to betray him. This view raises serious questions about God and his relationship with people – did God 'use' Judas as a helpless pawn in his plan? Clearly that presents great difficulties. We could say that knowing what is going to happen isn't the same as planning or encouraging it. Judas, like the other eleven, was called – but how he responded was his own free choice. Remember, Jesus has just made it plain that *all* the Twelve had the freedom to turn away. Jesus wants true friends – people who freely choose him – not robots.

3. In autumn, when the grapes were harvested, the workers would live in tents for eight days as a reminder that the Jews had begun as a nomadic people. There's a reminder here that nothing's for ever. God is constantly calling us to journey and to change as we follow him in faith.

[6-13] 'My time hasn't come yet,' Jesus answered, 'but that's not an issue for you, is it? Of course the world hates me – I keep telling it where it's going wrong! Look, you just go to the festival yourselves – I'm not going because the time's not right.'[1] So, he stayed in Galilee – that is, until his brothers had got well clear, and then he went to Jerusalem in secret. The religious authorities[2] were hunting for him, and there was a lot of argument about him in the crowds. Some people said, 'Hey, lighten up – he's a good guy.' But others said, 'He's pulling the wool over the crowds' eyes.' All this was in hushed tones, mind you – no one spoke openly about him because they were terrified of the religious authorities.

[14-24] The festival was about half-way through when Jesus went up to the Temple and started teaching – and the religious authorities were absolutely amazed. 'Where does this guy get it all from?' they asked. 'He's never been trained for this, after all.'

'It's not *my* wisdom you're hearing,' Jesus told them. 'It comes from him who sent me – and anyone who was seriously interested in the will of God would know whether this is from him or merely my own invention. People who just spout their own thoughts are only interested in self-glorification, but someone who's focused on what the one who sent him expects – what *he* says is true, nothing false about it. Look, it was Moses who gave you the law, wasn't it – but do you keep it? Not likely, you don't, or why are you waiting for the chance to kill me?'

'You're mad!' the crowd answered. 'Whoever do you think's trying to kill you?'

'Look,' Jesus said, 'we all know what this is about: I do one piece of work on the Sabbath and you get all open-mouthed and wide-eyed about it. Now, you take your lead from Moses, don't you – and you say that he gave you the circumcision laws? (Actually, the tradition goes back to the patriarchs, not Moses, but we'll let that pass.) Well, you're

---

1. Jerusalem would be heaving with pilgrims – just the place for Jesus to be if he wanted to be famous, and didn't mind risking coming to a sticky and untimely end. But Jesus wanted to do the work of the one who sent him – and that didn't include fifteen minutes of fame and then getting mugged in some back alley somewhere.
2. John seems in this passage to be referring to three different groups: the 'Jews', as he terms them, meaning the theologically educated religious authorities; the 'crowd' of pilgrims, up for the festival, who are more easily deceived; and in between them the people of Jerusalem who are a bit more politically and theologically aware than the crowds.

perfectly happy to 'work' at circumcising a man on the Sabbath.[1] So if a man can be circumcised on the Sabbath, to avoid violating the law of Moses, why complain when I heal the whole body?'[2] Stop making these superficial judgements and use a bit of sense!'

[25-31] By now the people of Jerusalem were really buzzing about him. 'Isn't this the guy they've been trying to kill? So, what's he doing talking openly like this and getting away with it? Do you think the movers and shakers have decided that he really is the Messiah? Oh, come on, though – we know where the guy comes from, don't we? And everyone knows that when the Messiah comes no one's going to know where he's from.'

So Jesus shouted out, as he was teaching in the Temple, 'Of course you know me – and you know where I'm from, but only in earthly terms. I'm not here on my own account – the one who sent me is the one you can really rely on – and you don't know him at all. I do, though – I know him – because I'm from him, and he sent me.'

Then they decided they'd really got to arrest him, but no one actually laid a finger on him because the time wasn't right.[3] But there were a lot of people in the crowd who did believe in him. 'Well, come on,' they argued, 'are they saying that the Messiah's going to do even more signs than this man's done, when he comes?'

[32-36] The Pharisees heard the crowd arguing like this about him, and colluded with the priests to send some Temple guards to bring him in. 'Oh, I'll be around for a bit yet,' Jesus told them, 'and then I'm going back to the one who sent me – but you won't find me, and you can hardly come chasing after me, where I'm going.[4]

Then the religious authorities started discussing among themselves, 'Where's he going, then, that we won't be able to find him? Probably to the Jewish people in the Greek regions – or maybe he's going to preach

---

1. Abraham was first commanded to carry out circumcision on the eighth day (Genesis 17:12) and where that fell on the Sabbath the 'work' was allowed.

2. Simple argument: if Moses said that it was right to care for a small part of the man on the Sabbath, isn't it even more so if the entire person is in need of healing? And since it's the law of Moses that Jesus is accused of breaking . . .

3. John is emphasising his point that the people who thought they were in power weren't actually controlling anything. No one took Jesus' life away. He laid it down, at a time and in a manner of God's choosing.

4. So, Jesus will never really fall into their hands – rather, they'll be the unwitting agents who bring about his purpose *at the time God chooses.*

to the Greeks themselves? What does he mean by all this stuff about "You can look but you won't find", and "You can't come where I'm going"?'

> John now emphasises that we have got to the final day of the festival – a day of high ceremonial when people would pour out large offerings of water as part of their worship. At this point Jesus makes two dramatic contrasts. He, the new Temple, stands within the old, effectively offering himself as the way we can truly encounter God. And, as he does so, he adopts the style of a market-trader and offers people the water of life. We remember his meeting with the Samaritan woman, beside Jacob's well, where he offered living water. Now he does it in the place where good, pious worshippers believe they find it.

37-44 When the festival reached its grand climax on the last day, Jesus stood there and shouted out, 'If anyone's thirsty, come to me – if you really believe, then drink the water I offer. Remember what scripture says? "Living water will flow in torrents out of the heart of the true believer!"[1] He was talking, of course, about the Spirit that would be given to people who believed in him, but the Spirit wasn't yet fully given to anyone – that would come after Jesus' glorification.[2]

This set some of the crowd off again. 'We're right!' they crowed. 'This really is the great prophet.'

'Well, in fact, he's the Messiah!' others corrected.

'No,' yet others said, 'the Messiah won't come from Galilee, will he? Scripture says the Messiah's to be descended from David and come from Bethlehem – the city where David lived.'

So the crowd were completely divided about the issue. Some of them thought he should be arrested, but in the climate at the time no one was actually going to do it.

45-53 The chief priests and the Pharisees weren't exactly delighted when the Temple guards reported back. 'So, where is he? Why didn't you arrest him, as you were ordered to?'

'Well, er, it's not that easy,' the guards answered. 'I mean, we've never heard any ordinary man speak like that.'

---

1. I don't think there's an exact match for this, actually – it's likely that Jesus was paraphrasing Isaiah 58:11.
2. For the gospel writers, but especially for John, Jesus was supremely glorified at his death.

The Pharisees scoffed. 'Oh, great – so he's fooled you too, has he! Tell us this, then – has anyone with any real clout believed in him? Well? Only the crowd – ignorant peasants who're already damned because they can't be bothered to study the law for themselves!'

Nicodemus, the one who'd gone to Jesus before but was still one of their party, said, 'I think we should be careful, you know – condemning someone without a hearing, and all that – not strictly legal, is it? – er, hope you don't mind my saying so.'[1]

They rounded on him viciously. 'Really! We never knew you were from Galilee – something you're not telling us? Go, check the scriptures – be as thorough as you like – and you'll see that there's nothing about a prophet arising in Galilee.' Then they all went home.

Self-righteousness, trickery and adultery

> The next passage stands out as very distinctive in a number of ways, and we could have a very interesting time investigating all the arguments scholars have had about this text. I mention this just in case you wonder why, in some Bibles, this story is put in brackets; but, we can simply thank God that the story was preserved for us. It may help us keep our own judgementalism in check.

8[1-11] Jesus went to the Mount of Olives, and then early next morning he went back to the Temple where people flocked to him again, and he sat down and started teaching them, but he hadn't got far before the scribes and Pharisees came in, dragging a woman they'd caught in the very act of adultery – and they made her stand in front of everybody before they turned to Jesus. 'Teacher,' they asked, 'we need your advice – you see, we caught this woman with someone else's husband, and – well, the law of Moses says she's to be stoned to death. OK, what do you say?' Not that they were the least bit interested in justice – they just wanted to catch him out.[2]

---

1. That was Nicodemus's big chance, and he bottled out! He could have pulled the rug from under the Pharisees by giving an unexpected answer to their rhetorical question: one of the people in authority *did* believe in Jesus! But instead he appealed to a general legal principle and kept his head down – and safe. Let's not be judgemental, though – I'm not at all confident that I'd have been any braver than he was. The important thing is for us to learn from him.

2. They must have thought they'd got him. It was, of course, a catch question, to which he could legally give no safe answer. If he said, 'No', then they could tell everybody that he had no standards and didn't care about Moses' law, whereas if he said, 'Yes', he could be presented to the Romans as a danger to public order.

Jesus didn't answer straightaway – just bent down and wrote in the dust on the floor with his finger-tip.[1] They got impatient and kept on at him, and eventually he stood up straight again. 'OK, then, I'll tell you,' Jesus said. 'The person to start off the stoning will be the one who can claim never to have committed *any* kind of sin. Now, who can say that?'[2] Then he bent down again to write on the ground.

That did it! One by one, they turned and went away – the elders first – until there was just Jesus there with the woman in front of him. Jesus straightened up. 'Where's everybody gone?' Jesus asked her. 'Isn't anybody pressing the charge against you?'

'No, sir – nobody is.'

'Then neither will I,' Jesus told her. 'Go and make a new start – no more sin from now on.'[3]

[12-20] Jesus spoke to the people again. 'I am the light of the world,'[4] he said. 'People who follow me won't be living in darkness – they'll have the very light of life itself.'

'That's what you say,' the Pharisees said, 'but a person's testimony about themselves isn't acceptable as evidence – is it!'

'Look,' Jesus told them, 'even if I do testify about myself, it's still valid because I can do it with a bit of authority: I know where I'm from – and where I'm going, for that matter – but you don't know either of

---

1. Why? Was he playing for time, perhaps? There's no reason why he should be shown as doing so, and it would suggest that Jesus had been caught on the hop – which the gospel writers are all careful to show that he never was. Some people think that he was silently refusing to play the judge, but there's another interesting possibility. Judges had a tradition that they always wrote the sentence down before pronouncing it. Jesus could be saying, 'You're asking me to do the job of a judge – well let's do it properly', and thus highlighting (by contrast) the fact that the accusers are not really interested in the law at all, just in using it for their own ends.

2. Under Jewish law, the main prosecution witnesses were obliged to take a lead in carrying out sentence. So these words are addressed, by implication, directly to the people who are accusing her.

3. It's interesting that Jesus has twice referred to 'sin' but never to adultery. We're very good at producing our own league-tables of sins, with the ones we frequently commit always at the bottom! Jesus says that sin is sin; we can't just say that we're less sinful than others and that this entitles us to judge them – only the sinless one can do that, and he's just turned down the opportunity!

4. At the Feast of Tabernacles, the whole Temple would be illuminated – a spectacular symbol of God's glory. And here is Jesus, the new Temple – the new meeting place between God and humanity – claiming that the real light is himself. He doesn't need any artificial lighting.

those.[1] You lot judge everything and everybody by outward appearances,[2] don't you. Me – I don't judge anyone – well, OK, I do judge, in effect, but the judgement's a valid one because it's not just me alone, but my Father who sent me, who judges with me.[3] Look, it's your own law that says that the testimony of two witnesses counts. OK, so you've got two witnesses. I testify about myself – and my Father who sent me testifies about me too.'[4]

'OK,' they challenged him, 'so where is this Father of yours who can speak for you?'

'You don't really know me at all,' Jesus replied, 'and you don't know my Father either. If you knew me, then you'd also know my Father well enough not to ask daft questions like that.' He said all this while he was teaching in the treasury in the Temple[5] – so they could easily have arrested him, but no one did because it still wasn't the right time.[6]

Jesus foretells his death

> There's a sense of urgency developing – the people who are rejecting Jesus are now at the Last Chance Saloon. This is not the time for neat theological point-scoring – it's the time for repentance and a change of life!

[21-30] 'Well,' Jesus said, 'I'm going away, so you'll soon have had your chance. Oh, then you'll all be searching for me, of course – but you'll all die in your sin, because you can't come looking for me in the place where I'm going.'

---

1. The fact that they don't know where he's from, as we've seen earlier, is relevant to the claim that he's the Messiah. And since he himself *does* know, his is the only testimony that can possibly count.
2. Or 'according to the flesh'.
3. This judgement, as observed elsewhere, is not the purpose but the inevitable *consequence* of Christ's coming. So he can say that judgement isn't what he's really about, even if it happens as a consequence of people's rejection of him.
4. The things Jesus does are not his own work, but his Father working though him and thereby testifying to him.
5. No one's really sure why John mentions this specifically, but here's one possible significance: the treasury was probably located in the Court of Women, which was not a particularly sacred part of the Temple – so there was no legal or religious reason why they shouldn't have arrested him there and then.
6. Again, John emphasises who is really in charge of events here. Jesus will offer himself – not be taken – at a time of his own (or, rather, his Father's) choosing.

'What's this?' the religious authorities started speculating. 'Is he going to top himself or something? Where else could he be going where we can't get to him?'

'The problem is,' Jesus said, 'you belong below and I belong above. You're completely tied to the things of this world; I don't belong to this world[1] – and I told you you'll die in your sins, because that's exactly what you will do if you don't believe that I am the one.'[2]

'But what "one"?' they insisted. 'Just who are you?'

'Oh, why do I even bother to try to get things across to you!' This was almost too much even for Jesus' patience. 'But I've got to try, because I've got so much to say – so much evil to expose! But the one who sent me is concerned about truth, and it's *his* message of salvation that I'm going to speak to the world even if I have to shout you down to do it.'

They just couldn't grasp that he was speaking to them about the Father! So Jesus went on, 'You know, when you've raised the Son of Man up,[3] *then* you'll get it – that I am the one – that I don't act on my own behalf but speak for the Father. And the one who sent me is always with me – he and I are never separated, because I always fulfil his expectations, not just my own.' And as Jesus drove this message home, a lot of people believed in him.

True discipleship

[31-38] Jesus turned to those of the religious authorities who believed him.[4] 'If you really hang on to my word,' he said, 'then you'll be truly my disciples – and you'll know real truth – truth that will set you free.'

'Free?' they objected. 'Why "free"? We're descendants of Abraham, we are – we're slaves to nobody, let us tell you. "Free", indeed!'

'I'm really telling you straight,' Jesus told them, 'everyone sins, so everyone's enslaved by sin. And you know that slaves don't count as full members of the family, whereas the householder's sons do – they'll always be part of it. So, if the Son makes you free, then you'll be free in the best possible sense of the word. Yes, I know you're descendants of Abraham – but that doesn't stop you looking for a chance to kill me,

---

1. This shouldn't be taken as devaluing God's creation – Jesus simply isn't locked into it, physically or spiritually, as he accuses his hearers of being.
2. The one who saves.
3. Raised on the cross, that is – only God who is life could finally 'raise him up'.
4. Note, 'believed him' – not 'believed *in* him', which meant faith rather than mere intellectual assent.

does it, because you're just not open to my word. I tell what I've seen at my Father's side – you, then, should live by what you're hearing as from the Father.'

[39-47] '*Abraham's* our father!' they told him.

'Oh, right,' Jesus answered, 'and if you really regarded Abraham as your father, then you'd be following in his ways, wouldn't you? And what are you doing? Trying to kill me – that's what – someone who's done nothing worse than tell you the truth I received directly from God himself. Now, that is *so* not what Abraham did! But you *are* doing what the person you really treat as your "father" does. Oh, yes.'

'What're you calling us?' they said. 'Illegitimate or something? Look we've got one Father – and that's God.'[1]

'"God"!' Jesus retorted. 'You call God your Father? If you really called God your Father, you'd treat me as a brother! I came from God, after all, and now I'm right here in front of you. And I didn't just come on some whim of mine – he sent me. So why do you struggle to understand what I'm saying? It's because you're just not open to my word – and *that's* because the person you really treat as your father is the devil, and you're very good children to him – really fulfil his expectations! He was a murderer[2] from the start, and has nothing to do with truth because there's no truth in him in the first place. And the lies he tells show his true nature – a liar and the father of all lies. Go on, then – which of you can make any charge stick against me? Well? You can't – so if I'm telling the truth, why don't you believe me? People who are God's children in the real sense will pay attention to God's words – you don't, because you're not.'

[48-59] 'Oh, come on,' they said, 'you know we're right when we say that you're a heretic in the grip of a demon.'

'It's not me that's possessed,' Jesus answered. 'I'm the one that honours my Father – you're the ones that won't honour me. I'm not into self-glorification – there's just one whose judgement matters in these things. I'm really telling you straight, anyone who seriously keeps my words won't see death.'

---

1. Every good male Jew could call himself a 'son of God', so there's no blasphemy here. They mean this differently from the way the term is used about Jesus.
2. The Greek word used here only comes twice in the whole New Testament. The other time is also by John, in 1 John 3:15, where he's making a connection with Cain. It's also a contrast between God who is the source of life and the devil who is all about death.

'There!' the religious authorities were angry and overjoyed at the same time! 'That just proves you're possessed! Abraham's dead, isn't he? – and so are the prophets – and here are you saying that people who keep *your* word won't die. So are you greater than Abraham – our father – who died? And the prophets who all died, too? Just who are you claiming to be?'

'Oh, I'm not glorifying myself,' Jesus said. 'A poor sort of glory that would be! It's my Father who glorifies me – the one you claim is your God, even though you clearly don't know him. *I* know him, though – and I'm not going to say I don't and make myself a liar like you. I *do* know him – and I keep his word. Want to talk about Abraham? OK, let's talk about Abraham – your ancestor. He celebrated the fact that he was to see my day – overjoyed, he was.'

'What!' the religious authorities answered. 'You're not yet fifty years old,[1] and you're telling us you've seen Abraham?'

'I'm really telling you straight,' Jesus said, 'before Abraham was, I *am*.[2]

That did it! They picked up stones to hurl at him. But Jesus concealed himself and left the Temple.[3]

There's none so blind . . .

It is said that Helen Keller was asked whether she could think of anything worse than blindness, and she answered, 'Yes: to be able to see, but to have no vision.' In this passage, Jesus has no difficulty helping a blind man to see, but those sighted people who *refuse* to see are a more difficult proposition by far. This gospel in particular is full of vivid imagery, both in the words Jesus uses and in the things he does. There's so much to see for those who have the vision to get behind the literal meaning of the words!

1. The choice of words might have been highly symbolic. Although no one's suggesting this was actually Jesus' age, 'not yet fifty' could imply forty-nine, which is the square of seven – the number that symbolised completeness. Tradition puts Jesus' age at his death at about thirty-three. John would not necessarily be implying that he was literally forty-nine, but there is a very strong hint here that John is using this figure symbolically to show Jesus' life, death and resurrection as the ultimate 'completeness'. We might say that in him completeness is itself complete! This ties in with the last word on the cross.
2. The divine name of God used again, with devastating effectiveness. The apparently bad grammar highlights the point. Abraham had a beginning and an ending: he 'was'. God has no beginning or end, and so is always 'present'.
3. Again not cowardice but mastery of the situation. Being stoned by the mob was not the means by which his mission would be fulfilled – and neither was this the time.

I'll pick out just two of the significant themes in the subtext: *light/darkness*, and *creation* (themselves, of course, linked in the Genesis 1 and John 1 passages). When Jesus, the Light of the world, meets and heals the blind man, light meets and overcomes darkness (see 1:5). However, the darkness in the minds of his opponents is a more difficult proposition. John has already reminded us that light overcame darkness in the Genesis creation, and he goes on to make this creation connection explicit: we're told the man has been blind *from birth* – so we have the Word through whom all things were created (1:3) completing an incomplete 'work' of creation by giving the man his sight. The symbolism is huge! Christ, the eternal Word through whom God first lit up and then created the universe, comes as the Light of the world to overcome darkness (personal, political or spiritual) and complete God's 'work' of creation.

So, we have the fifth sign – light overcomes darkness and creation is complete.

The fifth sign: Jesus heals a man blind from birth

9 [1-2] As Jesus walked along, he saw a man who'd been blind right from the day he was born, and his disciples were curious. 'Teacher – why's he blind? Is it punishment for his own sins, or for something his parents did?'

[3-5] 'Sin's got nothing to do with it,' Jesus answered. 'Bad things can happen to good people, you know – but since he's blind, it's an opportunity for the glory of God's love to be seen. That's who sent me, and we've got to do his work while the light is here because before long it's going to be as dark as night – and no one's going to want to do any work at all. But as long as I'm in this world, I'm the light that lets people see how terrific God is – so let's go to it!'

[6-12] Then Jesus made some mud using dust[1] from the ground and his own saliva, and he spread it on the eyes of the blind man. 'Now, off you go,' he told him, 'and wash in the pool of Siloam.' Well, that was

---

1. Remember dust? According to Genesis 2:7 it's the raw material from which God made us. So Jesus takes some of God's raw material to 'complete his work'.

appropriate because the name 'Siloam' meant 'Sent'.[1] Of course, the blind man didn't need telling twice, so he went to the pool to wash the stickiness away, and came back with his eyes in full working order.

People noticed – understandably. 'Hey,' they said, 'isn't this the man who used to sit begging for money?'

'No,' some others said, 'it's like him – that's true enough – but no way can it be the same guy.'

'Oh, it's me, all right – honestly it is,' the man kept telling them.

Of course, then they wouldn't leave him alone: 'So, how did you come to be able to see all of a sudden?'

'All I know,' he said, 'is that a chap called Jesus came along, plastered some sort of gunge over my eyes, and said, "Go to Siloam and wash". Well, I didn't need telling twice, and now here I am, able to see!'

'So where's Jesus now?'

'How should I know?'

The blindness of the Pharisees

[13-17] The next thing he knew, the man who used to be blind was taken off to the Pharisees[2] – which was a little unfortunate, because the day when Jesus made the mud and opened blind eyes was the Sabbath, and we all know how the Pharisees felt about that! Of course, they wanted to know how he'd been given his sight.

'Look,' said the man, 'he put the mud on my eyes. I washed. Now I can see. Got it, now?'

Some of the Pharisees really got going then. 'Well, it's obvious he's a bad guy,' they said. 'He breaks the law by healing on the Sabbath – so he can hardly be from God, now can he!'

'But, if he's not from God,' others of them said, 'how come he can perform signs like this?' So party unity went out of the window, and they started arguing among themselves. Eventually they turned back to the man who'd been healed, and said, 'Well, what do you think – after all, it was your eyes he opened?'

'No problem,' said the man. 'He's a prophet.'

---

1. Jesus, that is, had been 'sent' on this work-completing mission, to bring 'wholeness' (the true meaning of 'salvation') to the world, and now he was in turn sending this man to seek the wholeness – completeness – salvation – God wanted for him. The baptism symbolism is unmistakable as Christ, with water, brings about salvation, or 'wholeness'.
2. . . . who still were blind! This is a powerful symbolic confrontation between the once-blind and the still-blind.

[18-23] That wasn't the answer they wanted at all – they preferred to believe that the man had never been blind in the first place – so they called in the man's parents, and asked them, 'Is this your son – the one you've always said was born blind – because if he is, how do you explain the fact that he's suddenly able to see?'

'All we can say,' his parents replied, 'is that this is our son, and that he was born blind. As for how he comes to be able to see, well, we haven't a clue – and we don't know who did it for him either. Anyway, he's a big boy now – he can speak for himself – so why not ask him?' You see, the trouble was that they were afraid of the authorities. They knew perfectly well that anyone who said they believed in Jesus was likely to be banned from the synagogue – that's why they passed the buck back to their son!

[24-34] So, for the second time that day, the authorities sent for the man who used to be blind. 'Stop dishonouring God by taking his part,' they said. 'We know he's a sinner.'

'Oh, well, as to that,' the man answered, 'who am I to judge him? There's just one thing I know: once I was blind, now I can see – end of story!'

'Yes, but what did he *do* to you – *how* did he give you your sight?'

'Look, you lot,' said the man, 'I've told you once already, and you obviously weren't listening. Or maybe it's that you want to hear the story again because you want to join his disciples as well?' he added mischievously.

'How dare you!' they ranted. 'You're the one who's a disciple of his. We're disciples of Moses, we are! We know that Moses came from God, and God spoke through him – we don't know anything about where this guy comes from.'

'Well, that's a funny thing!' the man mused. 'You don't know where he comes from – and yet he helped me to see. Use your brains: we know God doesn't work through people who're against him – but he does listen to those who are faithful to him and fulfil his purpose. I mean, there's never been a case in the whole history of creation where someone who was born blind had their sight given to them by a human being – if this man were not from God, he wouldn't be able to do things like that!'

'Oh, you!' they shouted. 'You're a bad 'un, and you've always been a bad 'un – who are you to try and teach us!' And they threw him out.[1]

---

1. Recognise the technique – if you can't win the argument, blame the other guy for not understanding you! It's a case of 'argument weak – shout louder'!

³⁵⁻⁴¹ Jesus heard what had happened, and went to find the man who had been blind. 'Tell me,' he said, 'do you believe in the Son of Man?'

'Well, now,' the man replied, 'I'm not really sure. Who is this "Son of Man" anyway, sir? You tell me who he is, and then I might be able to say I believe in him.'

'Oh, you know him,' Jesus answered, 'and you're talking to him, right now.'

'Well, now, that's a horse of a different colour,' said the man. 'Yes, Lord¹ – of course I believe in you.' And he worshipped him.

'It's a sad thing,' Jesus said, 'but my coming into this world was always going to end up in judgement. People who used to be blind find that they can see – but then people whose eyesight is perfect turn out to have no vision at all!'

'Hey,' said some nearby Pharisees, 'are you calling us blind? We're not the blind ones!'

'Oh,' said Jesus, 'for once you've got it right. Now, if you *were* blind, you'd have some excuse for having no vision – but you've just said you're not, so you've got only yourselves to blame, haven't you?'

Jesus, the Good Shepherd

> The shepherd image is familiar enough. Shepherds in those days would initially call the sheep out of the fold into the yard, from where they would go ahead, leading them. This meant that a solid relationship of trust was important – the sheep would only follow the person they recognised. The false shepherd in this image could be intended to refer to the religious authorities of the time or to the false messiahs mentioned in the Synoptic gospels. 'Shepherds' was a term often used in scripture for the leaders of the nation, who are often denounced as incompetent or even corrupt. We've just seen the blind man, his eyes open, choosing Jesus in preference to the established authorities whom he clearly regards as blind impostors.

10 ¹⁻⁵ Jesus said:

I'm really telling you straight: anyone who chooses not to go into the sheep-pen by the door, but clambers in by some other route – well,

---

1. 'Lord' and 'Sir' (which the man used earlier to address Jesus) are actually translated from the same Greek word, 'Kyrios'. Some English translators make the change because it seems the man himself might by now understand the word differently. In verse 36 he was merely being polite, but now he's acknowledging who Jesus is.

it's pretty obvious that that person's a rustler, or a robber. The one who goes in by the gate's the sheep's own shepherd. The gatekeeper willingly opens the door for him, and the sheep recognise his voice too. Because he knows them, he can call the sheep by their own names, and then he leads them out. And once he's got them all out into the yard, he can lead from in front – the sheep follow because they recognise his voice. Now, they're not going to follow a stranger, are they? – they'll run well clear of anyone whose voice they don't recognise.

[6-10] Jesus offered this analogy, but it was completely lost on them. So he went on:

I'm really telling you straight – I am the door for the sheep.[1] The ones who came before me were rustlers and robbers,[2] and the sheep knew better than to listen to them. I am the door. Anybody who comes in by me will be saved – go freely in and out,[3] and find good food. The rustler only has one interest in the sheep – to kill them. I've come to give them life – life in all its abundance.[4]

[11-18] I am the *good* shepherd[5] – and the good shepherd will lay down his own life to save the sheep. Now, there's the difference: the hired hand's not really the shepherd and the sheep aren't really his – so he sees a wolf coming and takes to his toes, abandoning the sheep. The wolf grabs them and they're scattered.[6] Now, the hired help runs

---

1. This is similar to 'I am the way' – Jesus is saying that it's through him that we come to God and to salvation.
2. Whom Jesus means by this is a little uncertain, but we can be assured he wasn't referring to the great prophets of the Hebrew scriptures. As is often the case in occupied countries, the place was teeming with people who were making all kinds of claims for themselves and calling people to follow them.
3. The ability to 'go in and out' was the privilege that denoted a trusted servant. Here it represents the true freedom Christ offers – which needs to be kept in mind, to balance the negative connotations of 'sheep'. We're not following blindly, but freely.
4. The Greek word means 'more than necessary' – so Jesus doesn't want life to be simply about 'getting by' (which is not the same as saying he's going to make us all millionaires!)
5. The contrast is changing, and the accusing finger is turning to point not at 'rustlers and robbers' but at bad shepherds. The leadership of Israel were said to be its 'shepherds' and to have failed the 'sheep' (see Ezekiel 34 and, by implication, Matthew 9:36 and Mark 6:34).
6. Jesus' main emphasis here is supernatural (the wolf = the devil) – but he's also foreshadowing a political parallel in the destruction of the Temple, when the Roman 'wolf' mauls and scatters the nation which is then dispersed into the surrounding regions. This is a vivid traditional image of judgement upon a nation whose spiritual leadership is bankrupt.

because he's got no real interest in the sheep – just the wages. I am the *good* shepherd – I know my own, and my own know me – just as the Father knows me, and I know the Father. And I lay down my own life to save the sheep.[1] I've got other sheep too, though – they aren't all in this sheepfold. I've got to bring them in as well – they'll listen to my voice, and there'll ultimately be just the one flock and the one shepherd. This is why the Father loves and trusts me so much – because I lay down my own life, ready to take it up again. Now get this: no one's taking it from me; I'm laying it down of my own free will. That's my decision – it's within my power to lay it down, and it's within my power to take it up again. This is the command I've received from my Father.

[19-21] Once again the religious authorities were in disagreement over the words Jesus had spoken. 'He's possessed,' some of them said, 'barking mad – why listen to him?'

Others thought differently. 'How can he be possessed?' they said. 'Can demons open the eyes of blind people?'

Jesus is rejected by his own people, and withdraws from Jerusalem

[22-30] It was the festival of the dedication in Jerusalem – winter time – and Jesus was walking though the Temple, in Solomon's portico, when the religious authorities gathered round him. 'Look, are you going to give us a straight answer?' they demanded. 'Are you the Messiah, or aren't you?'[2]

'You don't believe what I tell you anyway,' Jesus retorted. 'The works I do in my Father's name – they're my testimony. You don't believe, of course, because you don't belong with my sheep. My sheep hear and recognise my voice – I know them, and they follow me. I give them eternal life, and they're never going to die. No one is ever going to grab them from my hand. They're my Father's gift to me – more precious than absolutely everything else put together – and no one can grab anything out of the Father's hand. And the Father and I are one.'[3]

---

1. Again, note the emphasis: Jesus' death will be no ordinary murder or execution, brought about by others. His life isn't taken; he *offers* it – at a time and in a manner of his choosing. It's a *sacrifice*.
2. This is a dilemma for Jesus. He can't deny the truth, but, in fact, he's not the kind of Messiah they're looking for, and to say 'Yes' would be misleading and might precipitate a crisis before time.
3. So Christ's hand is as safe as his Father's.

[31-39] The religious authorities picked up stones, to stone him to death.[1] 'Oh, right,' Jesus said, 'so, out of all the good works I've shown you, from my Father, which is it that you're going to stone me for doing?'

'You know perfectly well!' they answered. 'It's nothing to do with good works – you've just committed blasphemy: you – a human being – making yourself out to be God!'

'Well, it's your own law,'[2] Jesus replied, 'that says, "I said, you are gods".[3] And the scriptures can't be just declared null and void when it suits you, so what are you going to do with *that* text? If the people to whom the word of God came could be called 'gods', then how can you say that the one the Father has sanctified and sent into the world is blaspheming by saying, "I am God's Son"?[4] Look, it's simple enough: if I'm not doing my Father's works, then don't believe me – but if I am, then even if you don't believe me you should believe the works themselves, and then you'd know that I am in the Father, and the Father is in me.' At this, they tried to arrest him again, but he slipped away from them.

[40-42] Jesus went back across the Jordan,[5] to the place where John had earlier been baptising, where he stayed for a time, and many people came to him there, and said, 'Well, John didn't do any signs, but everything he said about this guy was completely true.' And many people believed in him in that place.[6]

The sixth sign: the death and raising of Lazarus

The raising of Lazarus is a vital sign pointing us to the greater resurrection – but *in itself* it isn't resurrection in the full sense and we

---

1. The penalty for blasphemy under the law of Moses, but since there had been no trial this would have been much closer to lynch-mob activity.
2. The very same one that they're appealing to in accusing Jesus.
3. Psalm 82:6.
4. It is not for any human being to *claim* Sonship, but for God, through his word, to confer it. If it can be conferred by the spoken word, then it is clearly an appropriate title for the living Word himself.
5. Jesus appears now to have come full circle – back to the place where his ministry began in 1:28, and where people now recognise the truth of John the Baptiser's words. Completeness is one of John's themes, and this return to his starting point could represent the closing of the circle – the completion of this stage of his ministry. From here on, the final journey begins that will take him to Jerusalem, the cross and the true 'completion' of his work there.
6. It may well be that the writer is contrasting the faith found across the Jordan, 'in that place', with the lack of faith in Jerusalem which should have been the epicentre of faith.

mustn't confuse the two. Lazarus came *back* to *this* life and, presumably, died later. Resurrection, in the full Christian sense, is about going *on* to *new* life, which will have no death.

This distinction implies no suggestion whatever that Lazarus was not truly dead – the text is very clear that he had been in the tomb for four days and certainly smelt dead! It is not the death that's at issue here, but the importance of distinguishing between his coming back *from* death and Jesus' going on *through* it to new life.

Here we are presented with Jesus not only as Lord of life, but as life itself.

11 ¹⁻⁶ Now, there was a man who was ill – Lazarus, of Bethany, the village where Mary lived with her sister Martha. Mary was the woman who anointed the Lord with her perfume and wiped his feet with her hair – we'll come to that later.[1] Well, anyway, her brother Lazarus was ill – so the sisters sent Jesus a message. 'Lord, the friend you love so much – he's ill.'

Jesus didn't go rushing over, though. 'This illness isn't going to be final,' he said, 'but it's a way that the Son of God can be glorified.' So, although he loved Martha – and her sister, and Lazarus – deeply, he stayed where he was for another two days.

⁷⁻¹⁶ And indeed it was only after that[2] that he said to his disciples, 'Let's go to Judea again.

'What!' the disciples were aghast. 'Rabbi,' they said, 'it hardly seems five minutes since the religious authorities were trying to stone you – and you want to go back there?'

'Oh, come on!' Jesus answered. 'There are twelve hours of daylight, aren't there? In daylight, honest people can move about without fear, because the light of this world's there for them. But those who choose to skulk in the night come to grief because they're completely without the light.'[3] When the disciples didn't answer, he followed up with, 'Our friend Lazarus has fallen asleep – I'm going there to wake him up.'

---

1. John 12:1-8. John uses the past tense because it is in the past in relation to the time of writing, rather than in terms of this point in his story.
2. John's choice of Greek words here puts heavy emphasis on the delay – once again he's careful to show Jesus doing things at his own pace, supremely in command of the situation.
3. For Jesus, to 'walk in the light' was to obey God's calling. He wasn't afraid as long as he was doing that, because he had confidence that God would work out his purpose.

'But, Lord, if he's just fallen asleep, he'll get better!'[1] Jesus, of course, had been referring to death, but they thought he was literally talking about sleep.

So Jesus had to tell them straight out: 'Lazarus is dead. Now, do you understand? Actually, I'm glad I wasn't there to save him – for your sakes, that is – because this is a chance to strengthen your faith. But let's go to him.'

Thomas – the one who was also known as 'the Twin' – said to the others, 'Well, let's all go too – if he's going to die, we can die with him.'[2]

[17-27] On his arrival, Jesus found that Lazarus had been dead and buried for four days already. Now, Bethany was only about two miles from Jerusalem, and a good number of people had arrived from there to mourn with Martha and Mary.[3] When Martha heard that Jesus was near, she hurried off to meet him, leaving Mary sitting at home.[4]

'Lord,' Martha said to Jesus, 'if only you'd come when we asked, my brother wouldn't have died, would he! Still, I know that even now God would give you anything – if you were to ask him . . .'

'Your brother,' Jesus assured her, 'is going to rise again.'

'Well, yes, I know – at the resurrection on the last day.'

Jesus said to her, 'I am the resurrection – and life itself. People who have faith in me – even if they experience death, they'll live again. And those who live in faith won't finally die.[5] Now, do you trust me on this one?'

'Yes, Lord,' Mary answered. 'I trust you – you're the Messiah, the Son of God, the one whose coming into the world has been promised.'

---

1. The Greek word here actually can also mean 'be saved'. As so often happens in the gospels, the disciples are stumbling on to truth by accident. Caiaphas does something similar in the trial of Jesus, and later the soldiers' mockery, putting Jesus into royal garb, actually foreshadows his 'enthronement' at Golgotha.

2. Thomas's name has become a byword for lack of faith. Here, though, he's the one who shows *real* faith – ready to die with Jesus if need be. It reminds us that faith's about commitment – not just intellectual assent to an idea or a dogma.

3. The very strong sense of community meant that both joy and sorrow were shared. At a wedding, everybody celebrated; at a death, everybody mourned. What happened to one affected everybody.

4. This shows the familiar characters we know from Luke: Martha getting up and doing, Mary sitting (as etiquette required mourners to do) to receive visitors.

5. I've added 'finally' to indicate one possible meaning of this text – which is very difficult to understand on a literal level. There are various ways people seek to explain it, but the important thing about the whole verse is that faith in Jesus gives us confidence in eternal life.

[28-37] After she'd said this, Martha went to fetch her sister, Mary. She whispered to her, 'The Teacher's here – he's calling for you.'[1] Mary got up straightaway and went to meet him. Jesus hadn't come into the village yet – he was still where Martha had met him. The people from Jerusalem who were comforting her followed, assuming that she was going to mourn at the graveside. Mary went and knelt at Jesus' feet. 'Lord,' she said, 'if only you'd come when we asked, my brother wouldn't have died, would he!' When Jesus saw her tears, and the visitors from Jerusalem crying with her, he felt an almost overwhelming sense of horror and grief.[2] 'Where've you buried him?' he managed to ask.

'Come and see, Lord,' they answered, and Jesus burst into tears.[3]

'See how much he loved his friend?' some of the visitors said.

'Well, in that case,' some others argued, 'since he can give blind people their sight, why couldn't he have saved the guy from dying?'

[38-44] Jesus was still churned up as he approached the tomb – a cave with a stone across the front. 'Take the stone away,' Jesus ordered.

Martha, the dead man's sister, protested, 'Lord, he's been dead four days – there's a revolting stench in there.'

'Didn't I tell you,' Jesus answered, 'that if you had real faith you'd see God glorified?'

They took away the stone.

Jesus raised his eyes towards heaven, and said, 'Father, thank you for having already heard me. Yes, well, I know you always do hear me, but I've got to say that for this crowd to hear, haven't I! Then they can really believe that you sent me.'[4] Then Jesus raised his voice to a loud shout and called, 'Lazarus! Come out!'

---

1. This may be a vivid bit of characterisation: John doesn't tell us that Jesus asked for Mary; it looks as if Martha's organising again!
2. The particular word John chooses to use here indicates an enormous emotional upheaval. The same terrible word is used four more times – two of which occur as Jesus contemplates his own death, and two as he prepares his disciples for it. Is this coincidence? Since Jesus knows he is about to raise Lazarus, he's not likely to be experiencing the same grief as the others around him. More likely, here in the shadow of Jerusalem, his coming encounter with and triumph over death in Lazarus is foreshadowing for him the dreadful confrontation with death, on a cosmic scale, that is coming.
3. We need to remember here that it's a relatively modern and particularly Western (maybe even just British) hang-up for men to see crying as a sign of weakness. Again, Jesus knows he's going to raise Lazarus, so the tears are most probably a natural expression of the emotional earthquake referred to in my previous note.
4. Merely working the miracle would just confirm what they clearly already thought – that Jesus was a pretty impressive wonder-worker. Jesus' audible, public prayer pointed them away from him to the Father who had sent him.

The dead man shuffled awkwardly out to the entrance of the tomb, with the burial bindings still on his feet and hands, and the cloth still wrapped round his face. 'Unbind him!' Jesus ordered. 'Set him free!'[1]

The plot to kill Jesus

[45-54] So it was that a lot of the visitors from Jerusalem who'd followed Mary and seen what Jesus did came to faith in him – not all, though. Some went running off to tell the Pharisees about it. They, with the chief priests, called a council meeting to discuss the crisis. 'What are we doing, letting this go on?' they said. 'All these signs[2] and wonders he's doing – if we let this go on we all know where it'll end: the people will believe in him, and then the Romans will have to crack down and that's it – goodbye, holy Temple – goodbye, entire nation!'

Caiaphas – the High Priest during these momentous times – said, 'You just don't get it, do you! It's in the public interest for him to die. One man dies to save the people – and so that the entire nation doesn't end up non-existent.' Now, Caiaphas might have thought this was all his bright idea, but he was actually speaking prophetically – as the High Priest – in saying that Jesus would die for the nation. Not just for the nation, though – his death would gather into one all the people of God scattered throughout the world. So, that very day, they formalised their decision to kill Jesus.

From then on Jesus decided to keep a low profile in the Jewish areas, and retreated to a remote place called Ephraim where he spent some time with his disciples.[3]

---

1. Huge symbolism here! Jesus is seen not just raising the man to life but commanding that the bonds that 'bind' him in death be broken and that he be set free. The new life that Jesus offers, here in this world, which is itself a taster for the infinitely greater life to come, is characterised by being set free from the restrictions that our preoccupation with and fear of death involve.
2. They, of course, were using the word differently from the way Jesus would – and the way John would about Jesus. 'Signs and wonders' fits their understanding better.
3. John's used this expression just once before – in 3:22, where Jesus was preparing at the start of his public ministry. It seems he's now indicating another time of preparation when his mission is about to move into its final phase.

The Sacrifice

The tension is mounting: this Passover will mark the climax of Jesus' life on earth: his sacrificial death, and his resurrection. John is highlighting the Passover parallels. He will also show us this not as a terrible tragedy but rather as Jesus' 'coronation'. The cross on Golgotha is the true throne of God, where his victory over sin and death is 'complete'.

John has specifically shown us six signs – one short of the symbolic perfect number representing completeness. The seventh and ultimate sign, which will 'complete' everything, will be displayed publicly and dramatically on the hill of Golgotha.

55-57 Now, the Jewish Passover was coming up, and people were flocking to Jerusalem from the surrounding regions – they wanted to get there in good time to make sure they were ritually pure.[1] They were looking out for Jesus in the Temple, and wondering whether he'd show or not. 'Well, get real!' some of them said. 'He's not seriously going to show his face here, now is he!' The chief priests and the Pharisees had given orders that anyone who knew Jesus' whereabouts should inform on him so that they could pick him up.

Jesus is anointed

12 1-8 It was now just six days before the Passover, and Jesus went to Bethany, where Lazarus lived – the one he'd raised from the dead. He was eating a meal, served by Martha, and Lazarus was there at table with him. Then a most extraordinary thing happened. Mary suddenly took a jar of perfume – real nard of pistachio, none of your cheap substitute rubbish – and anointed Jesus' feet with it. Then she wiped them with her own hair. Now, this was powerful stuff, and the scent of it wafted through the house until there wasn't a nook or cranny that didn't smell of it.

Not everyone appreciated the gesture; Judas Iscariot, one of the disciples (the one who was shortly going to betray Jesus, in fact) said, 'Well, how about that for waste! You know, that perfume would have fetched about ten months' wages[2] – think what difference that could make to

---

1. If they weren't, they'd have to wait another month before they could celebrate it.
2. An unskilled worker earned about one denarius a day, and Judas reckoned this would fetch about 300 denarii.

the poor.' (Now, let's get this straight: Judas didn't care about the poor any more than he cared about his friends – and if I tell you that he was the group's treasurer and was filching money out of the common purse they shared, well, enough said.)[1]

Jesus rounded on Judas. 'Now, you leave her alone! Do you hear? She bought that specifically to keep for the day of my burial. I mean, you'll always have ways of showing you care for the poor, but you won't always have the chance to do this kind of thing for me.'

Now they're out to get Lazarus too

[9-11] When the crowds of Jewish pilgrims heard that Jesus was in the area, they came flocking over – not just to see him, but to gawp at Lazarus whom he'd raised from the dead. So now the chief priests were plotting to kill Lazarus as well – because it was on account of him that so many people were turning to faith in Jesus.

Jesus enters Jerusalem

[12-19] Next day, the crowd of pilgrims at the festival heard that Jesus was on his way to Jerusalem – so they grabbed palm branches and hot-footed it to the outskirts to meet him.

'Saviour!'[2] they shouted. 'Congratulations to the one who's coming in God's name – the king of Israel!'[3]

Jesus got hold of a young donkey and sat on it – which fulfilled the old prophecy:

> Don't be afraid, daughter of Zion.
> Look – here comes your king,
>   sitting on the colt of a donkey![4]

---

1. Putting everybody's money into a common purse was a mark of a special community in which both the property and the needs of each were owned by everybody. See Acts 2:44-45 to see this principle still applied in the early Church. The sharing also showed the complete trust among the members and it was that trust that Judas was betraying. John is making a point of telling us this to prepare us for the ultimate betrayal of trust to come later.
2. The word 'Hosanna' literally means 'Save us', but had come to be used as a shout of praise more than as a prayer in itself. Here the crowd are praising Jesus as Saviour.
3. Clearly the crowd are looking to Jesus to do what was traditionally expected of the Messiah – to get rid of the occupying Romans and restore the throne of David.
4. Zechariah 9:9. Actually, 'Don't be afraid' isn't part of it, but it was a common reassurance offered in scripture when people came face to face with God, and would have been a natural enough phrase to use in conjunction with the prophecy. It also reinforces John's message about the status of Jesus.

Now, at the time the disciples really didn't understand this at all – but after Jesus had been glorified it all fell into place for them and they remembered what had been prophesied about him, and how it had all been done.

So the crowd who'd seen him raise Lazarus continued to give their testimony[1] about Jesus – it was because of that particular sign that they'd gone out to meet him – and the Pharisees were just about tearing out their beards by this time. 'You can't do *anything* about him, can you!' they accused each other. 'The guy's unstoppable – just look at the way the whole world's running after him!'[2]

Gentiles as well as Jews

[20-26] Now, there were some Greek pilgrims at the Festival too. They went up to Philip – probably because he was from Bethsaida in Galilee[3] – and said, 'Sir, we'd really like to meet this Jesus guy – can you arrange it?'[4]

Philip went to Andrew, and they approached Jesus together.

'What – now?' Jesus answered. 'This is the crucial moment – the pivotal point of history – I mean, the Son of Man's going to be seriously glorified. I'm really telling you straight: a grain of wheat's no use to anybody until it falls into the ground and dies. Now, if it does *that*, well, it's another story – in dying it releases the power to produce incredible amounts of fruit. So, if people are so in love with their lives that they won't let go, well, just look what they're losing by the very act of clinging on! On the other hand, people who reject that kind of "life" in this world will end up with eternal life.[5] For any disciple of mine, "serving"

---

1. Ironically, it's the right testimony but with the wrong meaning: they've recognised Jesus as the Messiah, but they've got completely the wrong idea about what that actually means!
2. Another delightful bit of irony: the Pharisees just mean that everybody's going after Jesus, but in saying 'the world' they're unconsciously prophesying on his behalf.
3. A town with a sizeable Gentile population.
4. We're getting a real sense here of Jesus as the great Misunderstood Messiah. The way John tells us the story suggests that they were looking to shake hands with a local personality – a wonder worker, maybe – rather than wanting seriously to follow him. John is painting a vivid picture for us of Jesus standing alone. Everybody wants him, but none for the right reasons.
5. The actual words are much stronger. Jesus highlights the paradox by talking about 'loving' and 'hating' life in this world. My version weakens the paradox, unfortunately, but helps make the meaning clearer. The verse has been over-literally interpreted at times, leading to people thinking that life in this world was meant to be detested in itself, which is a million miles from Jesus' intention. Our life here is God's gift, to be appreciated but not to be made the be-all and end-all of our existence. A similar thing could be said for the contrast between 'this world' and 'eternal life'. John told us in 3:16 that God loves 'the world' – and the events that are coming up will show us just how much!

means "following" – being right there with me, wherever I am and whatever's happening to me. And my Father will seriously honour anyone who "serves" me in that sense.'

Jesus foretells his death

[27-36a] Jesus went on, 'Now I really am going through mortal terror![1] And what am I supposed to say – "Father, save me from this dreadful hour"? A fat lot of sense that would make, since it's for this very thing that I came into the world! No, there's only one prayer for a time like this, and I'm going to say it: "Father – show your glory!"'

A voice came from heaven. 'Oh, I have – no question about that. And I'm going to show that glory again – with a capital G!'[2]

The crowd standing around heard the voice, but thought it was thunder. Some others said, 'No – it was an angel talking to him.'

'That voice was for your benefit,' Jesus told them, 'not mine. Now's the time of judgement for this world – the devil who thinks he's the boss of this world's going to be kicked out. I, on the other hand, am going to be lifted up – exalted – and when I am, I'm going to draw all people to me.'[3]

This saying was meant to give people some insight into the death he was to die, but – well, judge for yourself. The crowd just answered, 'We know from what's written in scripture that the Messiah's going to stay here, like, for ever. What's all this stuff about the Son of Man being taken away?[4] And who is this Son of Man guy anyway?'

'Oh, dear – do wake up!' Jesus replied. 'Look, you've not got the light here for much longer. You'd better do your best to get on, while you have – before the darkness completely overwhelms you. Because if you

---

1. Here's the wonder of the Incarnation in a simple sentence: Jesus, the eternal Son of God, takes our human nature so completely that he experiences the depths of fear that we should feel in those circumstances. In becoming flesh in Jesus, God spared himself nothing!

2. This is not God showing off! We must remember that the glory of God is his love: the love that led him to give his unique Son to the world. And the glory of that love – which God reveals for us – has been revealed and will be further revealed in Jesus.

3. It will look as though the darkness has won – the apparent triumph of evil will, in fact, be its downfall when the cross, which is intended as the instrument of Jesus' defeat, becomes the means of his glorification as the love of God shines out as a glorious light from the darkness of Golgotha – and the deepest darkness the world could ever know fails to overcome that light (as promised in 1:5).

4. They've misunderstood the words 'lifted up', completely – just as they've misunderstood the whole Messiah thing.

try to move after it's dark you'll not have a clue where you're going! *This is the time to make a commitment – while you've got a bit of light around you – so that you can be people of the light.'*

They still don't get it!

[36b-43] After saying this, Jesus withdrew from public ministry. They'd seen so many signs – right in front of their eyes – and yet they still didn't believe in him. This fulfilled the word spoken long ago by the prophet Isaiah:

Well, God, so who's believed us – eh?
I mean, has the revelation of your power actually made an impression on anybody?[1]

But, then, that was only to be expected: they just weren't open to it, as Isaiah had also said:

He's blinded them completely,
hardened their hearts,
so they wouldn't use their eyes to see,
or their minds to understand, and change,
and then I'd heal them.'[2]

Isaiah had originally said this because he foresaw his[3] glory and spoke of him all that time ago. Even so, though, there were a good number of dignitaries who did believe in Jesus. But be reasonable: they were hardly going to admit that in front of the Pharisees, now were they? – not at the risk of being kicked out of the synagogues. You see, they were so hooked on other people's respect that they wouldn't give that up even in exchange for God's!

Jesus sums up the challenge of his ministry

[44-50] Then Jesus shouted out, 'Look, it's not just about me: if you believe in me you believe in the one who sent me – that's the point. Recognise me, and you're recognising the one who sent me! I've come into the world as its light – I'm your ticket out of the darkness! And I'm not

---

1. Isaiah 53:1
2. Isaiah 6:10. John is citing the prophecy to show the unbelief as being part of God's purpose. The time for Jesus' glory to be made public would be at his enthronement at Golgotha – then, those with eyes to see would recognise him.
3. (Christ's)

going to stand in judgement on people who hear my words but then ignore them, because I didn't come to judge the world – I came to save it. If you reject me – and my word – then you'll be judged all right, on that final day, but not by me. It'll be that very word itself – the word I've spoken and you've ignored – that'll be your judge. Because I didn't speak on my own account; the Father who sent me told me what I was to say – and I know that his command carries eternal life. So, what I say is what the Father told me to say.'

The Last Supper

13[1-2] As the Passover festival approached, Jesus knew that the time had come – soon he was to leave this world and go to the Father. He'd always loved the ones who'd been his friends in the world – and he loved them to the end. Judas, son of Simon Iscariot, was already harbouring sinister intentions – the devil was really getting at him to betray Jesus.

Jesus washes his disciples' feet

> Some people think it rather mysterious that Jesus waited until the meal had started before washing his disciples' feet. It should strictly speaking have been done on their arrival, and certainly before the food was served. The meal itself was a community event – it was also a symbol of the kingdom of God. Naturally, Jesus wanted to make as close a link as possible between the community meal and the principle of service: 'This is the kind of community we must be: sharing the whole of life together (symbolised by food and drink) and humbly serving each other (shown in the foot-washing).'

[3-11] During the supper Jesus knew what a significant moment this was – the Father had entrusted him with everything; he'd come from God, and now he was going back to God. He got up from the table, stripped off his tunic and wrapped a towel round his waist. Then he poured some water into a bowl and proceeded to go round washing his disciples' feet[1] and carefully wiping them dry on the towel.

---

1. This was the traditional courtesy (actually required by law) extended to guests on their arrival at someone's house. Just as we might offer a visitor the use of the cloakroom to freshen up, so in those days of dusty roads and open sandals a slave would be detailed to wash the guests' feet. The difference, of course, is that Jesus does it himself – he becomes the slave.

As he approached Simon Peter, Simon protested, 'What's this – *you're* surely not planning on washing *my* feet, are you?'

'I know it looks odd now, but one day you'll understand,' Jesus assured him.

'Oh, no!' Peter was adamant. 'I'm not having that! Never! Absolutely out of the question!'

'OK,' said Jesus, 'so you don't want me to wash you – that means that you don't have anything to do with me or what I'm about. If that's what you want . . .'

'Oh! Right, well, that puts a totally different complexion on it, doesn't it! Look, why not do my hands and my head as well, while you're at it?'

'You're missing the point, Peter,' Jesus told him. 'You've already had a bath – right? So you just need your feet washed after the walk. That's because you're basically clean. And you all *are* clean, aren't you?[1] – well, actually, not *all* of you are.' He knew, of course, which of them it was that was about to betray him – and that's why he said, 'Not *all* of you are clean'.

[12-20] After he'd washed their feet, got dressed again and gone back to his place at the table, he said:

Have you any idea what I've *really* done for you just now? I mean, you call me things like 'Teacher' and 'Lord', right? And that's fine, because that's exactly what I am. OK, then – so if I – Lord, Teacher and all that stuff – have just knelt on the floor washing your feet, then you might perhaps get the point that I'm expecting you to do the same for each other – because I've given you an example to follow – a pattern: do as I've done. I'm really telling you straight: slaves aren't greater than their masters, are they? Neither are people who carry messages superior to the ones who send them out. If you know that – well, congratulations are in order if you also apply it.

Now, sad to say, that won't be for all of you. I mean, I know the ones I chose, but – well, this fulfils what scripture foretold: 'Even my trusted friend, who shares my bread, aims his foot at me.'[2] I'm warning you about this – now, before it happens – so that when it does happen

---

1. I've added the 'all' here to show that the 'you' is plural. Jesus is talking about the group of disciples, not just Peter. But, of course, there was one who wasn't 'clean' in the ritual sense in which Jesus meant it. Once again, we must remember that this is very symbolic stuff: Jesus wants his disciples to think about something deeper than just having dust-free feet!
2. Psalm 41:9.

you can believe that I am the One. I'm really telling you straight: anyone who welcomes those I send is really welcoming me – and welcoming me is really the same as welcoming him who sent me.'

Jesus highlights the betrayal

Like me, you may be struggling with the role of Judas: did he have any choice in what he did, or was he predetermined to do it? I'm convinced that God doesn't 'use' people like pawns, and wouldn't ask a human being to damn themselves. It might be helpful to reflect that God's knowing something is going to happen – and planning to use that to achieve his purpose – isn't the same thing as his specifically ordering the event itself. This is consistent with this story: Jesus didn't exclude Judas from the foot washing, but Judas excluded *himself* from being part of what it meant.

There are indications that Jesus was giving Judas every chance to change his mind – emphatically not for Jesus' sake but for Judas'. By now the die was cast; the authorities were determined to arrest Jesus and put him to death, even if Judas didn't help them. Whether Judas allowed himself to be used in that was up to him, and Jesus seems here to be trying his best to save him from himself.

21-30 Jesus was in a terrible state of inner turmoil now. 'I'm really telling you straight,' he declared solemnly, 'one of you's going to betray me.'

Well, the disciples looked at each other in bewilderment. Whom could he possibly mean? One of the disciples – Jesus' closest friend[1] – was reclining next to him, and Simon Peter signalled to him to ask Jesus about it. So he leaned closer to Jesus and whispered, 'Lord, which one is it?'

Jesus answered, 'It's the one I'm going to give this bread to, after I've dipped it in the dish.'[2] Then he dipped the bread in the dish and passed it to Judas Iscariot. And as he took the bread, Judas' decision was sealed. Satan finally got really into him, and his mind was made up. Jesus

---

1. Friendship, of course, is two-way. No one can be forced to be someone's friend. So while Jesus offered love equally to all, there would be different levels of friendship according to people's different responses.
2. This was a highly symbolic action. Jesus was reminding Judas of the depth of his treachery. To share food with someone and then do that person harm was an unspeakably vile act.

spoke to him once more. 'This thing you're going to do,' he whispered, 'why don't you just get it over and done with?'

The rest of the people at the table had no idea why Jesus had said that to him.[1] There was some speculation that Judas – who was the group's treasurer – had gone to do a bit of last-minute festal shopping for Jesus, or maybe to give a donation for poverty relief.

Judas knew the score, though – and as soon as he'd taken the bread from Jesus he went out. And it was a dark night.[2]

A new commandment

[31-35] After he'd left, Jesus said:

Just now you saw the Son of Man glorified,[3] and that means you saw God glorified in him. And if God's glorified in him, then God will also glorify him in his own right. Right? And he'll do it now![4] Oh, my dear friends! I'm only going to be with you for a little while longer. You're going to be looking for me, but it won't help – remember what I said to the people who were attacking me, that they couldn't come where I'm going? Well, now I'm saying it to you too. So I'm giving you a new commandment: love[5] one another.[6] The

---

1. This seems odd, but it could be that only Jesus' closest friend had heard his answer – or that they couldn't or wouldn't believe that the events Jesus had foretold would really happen.

2. John's bluntly laying it on the line. The closeness of the acts of fellowship and betrayal couldn't be more plainly stated – and remember what Jesus has said about people who choose to do their work under cover of *darkness*.

3. The Greek indicates that Jesus is talking about a recent but past event. He seems to be referring to the foot-washing in which his true glory was shown in humble, loving service – and which pointed forward to his ultimate glorification when love and humility would shine out from the cross.

4. Putting it simply – the glory of God is the glory of the Son of Man, and vice versa.

5. Now, we all know people are never going to 'love' one another just because they're told to – but that's to do with our understanding of the word 'love' which is primarily an emotional thing. Nothing wrong with that, but what do you do when the emotions aren't there – or the wrong ones are? People often feel guilty because they can't *feel* love for some kinds of people. The love that Jesus refers to is a different form of love – an act of the will. I may not be able to have wonderful warm feelings about a mugger or a thief, or someone who just gets on my nerves, but I can and should decide that I'm going to treat this person as a human being who is loved by God. This may not sound much like 'love', but it's no small thing to achieve.

6. Not new in the literal sense – see Leviticus 19:18. It's new for three reasons: firstly, it now becomes *the* command – the defining quality of their community – whereas in Leviticus it was just one of a whole mass of legislation; secondly, the quality of the love is of a whole new order, as demonstrated in Jesus; and thirdly, Christians would come to understand this mutual love in a very special way – as an earthly expression of the love that exists within the Trinity.

way I've always loved you is how you should love one another. That's how people are going to know that you're my disciples – by the quality of the love you share between you.[1]

Jesus foretells Peter's denial

[36-38] 'But, Lord – where is it you're going?' Simon Peter asked anxiously.

'I've already told you, you can't follow me there,' Jesus said. 'But don't worry – you will follow me later.'

'Later? Later? So, why can't I follow you now?' Peter protested. 'Lord, you know I'd lay down my very life for you.'

'Would you lay down your life for me?' Jesus asked him. 'I'm really telling you straight, before the morning cock-crow, you'll have denied no less than three times that you even know me.'

This way to the Father

14 [1-7] Jesus went on, 'Now, stop getting yourselves all horror-struck[2] about this. You believe in God, don't you? Then believe in me too. There's no end of room in my Father's house – otherwise, why would I have told you that I'm going to get your place ready for you? And when I've gone – and got your place sorted out – well, then I'll be able to come back and take you to myself, won't I? – so that wherever I am, you can be too. And, anyway, you know perfectly well where it is that I'm going.'

'First I've heard of it, Lord,' Thomas replied. 'We haven't a clue where you're going – so how do you expect us to know the way?'

'I am the way!' Jesus told him. 'And the truth too – and the life.[3] Everyone who comes to the Father comes through me. And if you know me, then by definition you must know my Father as well – and from now on you know him, and you've seen him face to face.'

---

1. This isn't a completely inward love – we aren't told to love *only* one another, but to do that first. The quality of Christian community will then be the best witness we can bear to Christ, and the most powerful form of evangelism, leading others to know his love as well.

2. The Greek word used here was used first to describe Jesus' emotions at 11:33.It portrays really tumultuous feelings – so Jesus isn't saying that his disciples are wrong to be *sad* – he's talking about something much more dangerous than that: the kind of grief that ultimately paralyses people.

3. So, now they've found the right *way* to go; they've been given their travel directions ('Truth') and the energy to do it ('Life').

[8-14] 'Lord,' Philip said, 'just show us the Father – that's all we're asking!'
Jesus answered:

How long have I been around you, Philip? All this time, and you still don't know me better than that! Anyone who's seen me *has* seen the Father. So why do you say, 'Show us the Father'? Don't you believe that the Father and I are completely united? All those words I've spoken to you – they didn't just come from me, you know – the Father who's right here within me is the one who's really at work. So, you'd better believe it – the Father and I are undivided. And if you can't believe that, then just take a look at the works he does through me. I'm really telling you straight, people who believe in me are going to do all the works that I do, and then some. That's what my going to the Father will mean, practically speaking.[1] I'll do anything you ask that's really in my name, so that the Father can be glorified in the Son. Ask me for anything, if it's in keeping with my purpose, and I'll do it.[2]

Jesus promises the Holy Spirit

[15-21] Loving me really means you're going to do as I say, doesn't it? And then I'll ask the Father and he'll give you your very own Advocate who'll be with you for ever. This is none other than the Spirit of Truth – the one the world can't accept because it refuses to see or recognise him. You, on the other hand, *do* know him because he's right here with you and he's going to be within you.[3]

I'm not going to leave you permanently bereaved – I'm coming to you. Just a little while from now and I won't be visible to the world any more – but you'll be able to see me; and because I'm alive, you'll really live! On that day you'll know that I'm united with my Father, and you with me, and I with you – all part of the same divine life!

---

1. During his earthly life, Jesus' power was exercised through his mortal body – which was limited by the constraints of time and space. Going to the Father would mean that he would be freed from those constraints, and his power could be available throughout the world.
2. Two things. Firstly, 'in the name of Jesus' isn't a kind of magic spell that makes God do what we want! This is about us being genuinely involved in Jesus' work so that our will and his are completely aligned. Secondly, he doesn't say he'll do it instantly! Of course, faith tells us that if we're asking for things that are part of God's purpose, then the prayers are going to be answered. But they will be answered in a time and a manner of *his* choosing.
3. Like breath within a body, giving it life and enabling speech.

The ones who hold on to my commands and live by them – well, they'll be really close to my Father and to me, and we'll come and live among them.

²² Judas (not Judas Iscariot, the other one) said, 'Lord, how come you're just going to make sure we can see you, and not the whole world?'

²³⁻²⁴ Jesus answered:

The ones who hold on to what I say and live by it – well, they'll be truly close to my Father and to me, and I'll make myself known to them. People who don't love me won't keep my words – and it's not just *my* word we're talking about, but it's from the Father who sent me.

²⁵⁻³¹ I've said all these things to you while I've been physically present with you. But the Advocate – the Holy Spirit, whom the Father's going to send in my name – now, he's going to make sure all that's understood and remembered. Peace is what I'm leaving with you – peace is my gift to you. And I don't give peace the way the world does.[1] So don't be terror-struck and cowardly. You heard what I said: I'm going away, and I'm coming back – OK? I mean, if you really loved me you'd be glad for me because I'm going to the Father, the one I respect and obey. And I've told you this in advance so that when it all happens you'll know I can be trusted.

Well, the time for words is nearly over – the one who rules this world is on his way. Not that he's got an atom of power over me, you understand – he's going to find that out – but my acceptance of this is going to show my love and obedience toward the Father. Now, let's get up and go!

Jesus is the true Vine

In this passage Jesus comes very close to using a parable – but without the direct 'story-telling' element that the Synoptic writers tell us about. The branches depend for their life on the Vine of which they're a part. And the life that the Vine supplies is

---

1. The world makes peace by coercion and deterrence – the kind of peace that is no more than the absence of war. Peace is actually made by force and by fear! Christ gives peace by offering himself sacrificially and paying the cost of healing broken relationships. 'Peace' in his terms is not just a tense stand-off but a state of wholeness, trust and mutual love that makes war just plain unthinkable!

intended to bear fruit for the world – which is the will and purpose of the Gardener. So Vine and branches unite in one another to serve the Gardener's will. We might think of Christ's word as the sap that carries nutrients to the branches. As long as the branches are 'in' the vine – and vice versa – the branches can be kept healthy and produce good fruit. And we stay 'in the Vine' by accepting the word of Christ and living by it.

15 [1-6] Jesus continued:

Here's another way to think of me: I am the true Vine – OK? And my Father – well, think of him as the gardener. Now if there are branches in me that don't bear any fruit, then, he'll remove them, won't he! And the ones that do bear fruit – those are the ones he prunes and tends, to make them even more fruitful than they are. Now you're healthy branches, because of the word I've spoken to you. So, live in me – just as I live in you. I mean, did you ever see a branch that was chopped off, carrying on bearing fruit? No – exactly! Neither can you. So: me, Vine; you, branches – OK? People who invest their lives in me – and I in them, because it goes both ways – people like that will always live fruitful lives, because they're depending on me. But those that don't – well, what do you do with a withered branch? Bundle it up with the rest and throw it into the fire, of course.

[7-11] So, if your life's really rooted in me, and my words are like life itself to you, then anything you care to ask for will be done for you.[1] This is what glorifying my Father is about – that you become the kind of disciples whose lives bear fruit. Because just as the Father has always loved me,[2] in that same way I've always loved you – so ground your lives in my love. Keep my commandments, and you'll stay in my love – just the same as I keep my Father's commandments and stay in *his* love. I've said all this to you for one purpose: so that you can have my joy right inside yourselves – and you can't get any better joy than that!

---

1. This expands a little on what Jesus said in 14:14 – if our lives are completely at one with his life, then we're not going to be asking for things that he's not willing to give – although, again, he still doesn't commit himself to do it in the way or at the time that we expect.
2. In the Greek, the 'aorist' tense is used, indicating that this love is eternal – from before things began.

[12-17] And what *is* my commandment? Just this. Love one another, the way I've always loved you. There just isn't any greater form of love than to lay down life itself for one's friends. And you certainly are friends of mine if you obey my commands. I'm not going to call you servants any more – because servants don't need to understand their master's business. But I've always called you friends, because I've taken you into my confidence right from the start – told you everything I've heard from my Father. You didn't choose me as your teacher, remember – I chose you as my disciples.[1] And it was my decision to appoint you to go producing all that fruit I've just been talking about – fruit that will really last – so that the Father will give you whatever you ask for in my name. Get it now? The whole point of all these commands I give you is for you to love one another.

Expect to be rejected

[18-25] If you find that the world hates you, don't be surprised – just remember it hated me first. Now, if you were on the world's side in this, it would love you, wouldn't it? – but you're not, so it doesn't. Just remember the earlier word I had with you – slaves shouldn't expect better treatment than their masters. If they've hounded me, then they'll hound you too. On the other hand, if they accepted my word, they'd accept yours – but no, they'll do all this to you on account of me, because they can't recognise the one who sent me. Now, if I hadn't come and spoken to them face to face, they'd have an excuse, of course – but I have, so they haven't! Make no mistake, anyone who hates me hates my Father as well. If I'd never done all those works, right in front of them – works that no one else ever did – they couldn't be counted guilty. But as it is, they've seen all that, and continued hating both me and my Father – and they've gone and fulfilled the scriptures, because it says there, 'They hated me for no reason'.[2]

[26-27] Now, when the Advocate comes – the one I'm going to send you from the Father – the Spirit of Truth who comes from the Father – when he comes, he'll testify for me. And you're to testify as well, as eye-witnesses – because, after all, you've been with me right from the start.

---

1. This reversed the usual process – and speaks of God's grace very powerfully. Imagine getting a letter from a university, completely out of the blue, saying, 'We'd really like you to come and study with us.' I mean – an honour, or what?
2. Psalms 35:19; 69:4.

16 ^{1-4a} Jesus went on:

I've said all these things to you so that you don't get tripped up. Be prepared: they're going to kick you out of the synagogues – in fact, the time's going to come when anyone who kills you will think they're doing God a favour. And why? Because they've never recognised the Father or me. But I've said all this so that when their moment of so-called victory comes, you can remember what I said.

The Holy Spirit as Advocate

^{4b-11} I didn't say these things to you from the start – didn't need to, because I was right here with you – but now I'm going to the one who sent me. Yet none of you seems to be asking, 'Where are you going?' You're really churned up about what I've said, aren't you! All the same, I'm telling you straight, it's for your benefit that I have to go away. If I don't go, then the Advocate won't come – but if I return, I can send him.[1] And when he comes, he'll show just how wrong the world is about sin, and about matters of acquittal and judgement. It's sinful in that it doesn't believe in me; it's missed out on acquittal because I'm now going to the Father; and it's all set for judgement because the ruler of this world is already under sentence.[2]

¹²⁻¹⁵ I've got so much to say to you! But you wouldn't be able to cope with it all now. When the Spirit of Truth comes, though, he'll guide you to a deeper understanding of me, because he won't just speak on his own account, but he'll speak as he himself has heard, and he'll tell of the things that are to come. And he'll glorify me by taking everything that's mine and telling it to you. Everything that belongs to the Father is mine too – that's why I said he'll take what's *mine* and tell it to you.[3]

Through sadness to joy

¹⁶⁻²⁴ 'In a little while you won't be seeing me,' Jesus went on, 'but give me a little while more, and you will!'

---

1. See my note on 14:12. Jesus now clarifies that it's through the Holy Spirit that this is to happen. And having his Spirit within them will be an even greater gift than his physical presence.
2. It's worth repeating that God is not rejecting the world. God loves the world and wants it to be free – which means he must respect its freedom to reject *him*.
3. So the Holy Spirit will lead us into deeper understanding of Christ, and what we learn about Christ we can also say of God.

'Eh?' the disciples were bemused. 'What's all this "a little while" stuff? Now we see him, now we don't – and all because he's "going to the Father", whatever that means. What *is* all this "a little while" stuff? We haven't a clue what he's harping on about!'

Jesus knew what they were bursting to ask him, so he said:

Are you wittering on among yourselves about what I meant when I said, 'In a little while, you won't be seeing me, but give me a little while more, and you will'? I'm really telling you straight, you'll be completely grief-stricken, but the world will be celebrating. You'll go through mental torture, but the pain will all turn into joy. Look, think of a woman in childbirth. She feels pain during the labour, but as soon as the child's born she puts all the terrible memories behind her because all that matters is that she's brought another human being into the world! OK, so right now you're hurting, but I'm going to see you again and you'll have a kind of happiness that no one can ever take away from you. When that day comes, you won't be questioning me about anything. I'm really telling you straight, if you ask the Father for anything, genuinely in my name, he'll give it to you.[1] You haven't done that up to now, so go ahead – ask – and you'll receive, and you'll know the best joy!

[25-33] I've said all these things to you in figures of speech – but the time's coming when I won't use figures of speech any more: I'll tell you straight, about the Father. And then you really will ask 'in my name'. Now, note that I don't say I'm going to ask the Father on your behalf; the Father actually loves *you* – because you've loved me and believed in me, that I've come from God. I came from the Father, into the world, and now I'm leaving the world to go to the Father.

'Ah,' the disciples said, 'now you're talking our language, not riddles – we can get our heads round this! Now we understand: you know everything, and there's nothing more we need to ask. "We believe you came from God" – job done – end of story.'[2]

'Oh, so you understand already, do you?' Jesus challenged them. 'Well, the time's coming – and, in fact, it's now – when you'll all scatter, scurrying off to your own homes and leaving me all alone. But I'm never alone, of course – the Father's always with me. I've told you this,

---

1. See my notes on 14:14 and 15:7.
2. The disciples may have been the first to think they'd got Jesus neatly summed up and needed no further explanation, but they weren't the last!

so that you can go on trusting me. I know you're in for a rough time from the present world, but be assured: I've already conquered the world.'[1]

Jesus' great prayer for all his disciples

The narrative from here to the time of Jesus' arrest illustrates what I said in the General Introduction to the Gospels. The writers choose which details to include in order to emphasise the particular aspects of Jesus that they want to highlight. John tells us none of the detail from the Last Supper that has become part of the Communion Service (although he's told us things about it in Chapter 6 that the Synoptists didn't include), but he does show us this great prayer in which Jesus sums up what his life and death are about and offers a real insight into the relationship of the Father and the Son. This will bring Jesus' earthly ministry to its high point in preparation for his 'enthronement' on the cross at Golgotha.

This is a prayer of great dignity and serenity, prayed by one who knows he's about to die in unimaginable pain.

17[1-5] After he'd finished saying these things, Jesus looked up towards heaven and spoke to God directly:

The time has come, Father – time to glorify your Son so that your Son can fully glorify you. After all, you've given him full authority – authority over all flesh – to offer the gift of eternal life, right here and now. And what is eternal life, but to know you, the only true God, and Jesus Christ whom you've sent?[2] I glorified you on earth, by bringing your work to completion just as you asked me to. So now, Father, I ask you to return me to the glory I shared with you before the world was even begun.

---

1. Christ has already dealt with the 'ruler of this world' (see 12:31, 16:11) so whatever the outward appearances may be, his disciples are to trust that *he* is the true ruler of the world. The difference is that his rule of love will be much less easy to see than the kind of 'rule' to which we're more accustomed.
2. Knowing God, in traditional Hebrew thought, was something for the future. God is unknowable – way beyond our understanding – while we're in this world. Jesus, in summing up his life, makes the extraordinary claim that in him God has broken through the barriers and revealed himself to us in a 'knowable' way. The Hebrew thinking was, of course, right: we can't aspire to know God who is beyond our thoughts – that knowledge is a gift that only God himself can give, and he has.

[6-10] I made known your name to the ones you entrusted to me out of the world.[1] They were your gift to me, and they've been faithful to your word. They understand now that my whole life and ministry is truly from you; because the very words I received from you, they've in turn received from me – so they truly know that I came from you, and they've really believed that you sent me. It's on their behalf that I'm praying now – not on behalf of the world, but of those you entrusted to me, because they're your own.[2] It's a mutuality thing, isn't it? – everything that's mine is yours, and yours is mine, and what glory that gives me!

[11-19] And now I'm not in the hostile world any more, but they still are – and I'm coming back to you. Holy Father, keep them safe, really close to you. Let them live completely in your name – the name you gave to me – so that they can be united the way you and I are united. While I was with them, I took really good care of them, and didn't lose a single one – except the treacherous one, but even he's fulfilling the scriptures. But now I'm coming to you. And I'm saying these things here in the world so that they can have my joy – the best joy – within themselves. I've given them your word, and the world has rejected them, because they're not on the world's side in this any more than I am. I'm not asking you to take them *out* of the world, but I do ask that you strengthen them against temptation. They're not on the world's side any more than I am. Let your truth make them holy – the truth that is your word. Just as you sent me into the world, now I'm sending them. For their sake, I'm offering myself fully to you,[3] so that they can be completely committed to you in truth.[4]

---

1. The suggestion that God took people 'out of the world' does not mean that Christians are meant to be 'so heavenly minded we're no earthly use'! It denotes a change of loyalties and priorities, not a rejection of the world God created. Jesus' friends will make their choices by a different set of criteria from those that applied before they met him.
2. Again, this isn't that Jesus doesn't care about the world, but rather that the world has rejected him and the gift he has offered. If someone won't let you give them something, you can't force it on them. This idea doesn't conflict with God's sovereignty – God has chosen to leave *us* free to choose.
3. Jesus is looking ahead to the cross, where he will offer himself sacrificially, 'for their sake'.
4. It's through Christ's sacrificial death that his followers will be able to be fully committed and offer themselves to God. Our self-offering is only possible because Christ's has opened the way to a full relationship with God.

20-24 I'm asking not only on behalf of these, but of all the ones who are going to believe in me because of their word: I'm asking that they might be fully united, Father. Just as you and I are completely caught up in one another,[1] so may they be in us – so that the world will be able to believe that you sent me. I've given to them the same glory you have given me, so they can be united just as we are united – I in them and you in me – so that the world will be able to know that you have sent me, and that you've always loved them just as you've always loved me.[2] And, Father, I earnestly want these, that you've given to me, to be right where I am and truly to see my glory – the glory you've given me because you loved me before the world was even begun.[3]

25-26 Holy Father, the world doesn't recognise you – but I recognise you, and all these know that you sent me. I made you visible to them, and I'll make you even clearer, so that the love that you've always given to me can be known in them, too – and, in fact, I myself can be in them.

The self-offering of Jesus

Jesus' long discourse over, we return to narrative and to the final climactic events leading to the crucifixion. All the gospels tell us about this – but John highlights particularly that Jesus is in control of events. He gives himself up for arrest at a time of his choosing, and his self-sacrifice means that his disciples are saved. So the drama in a particular time and place – the garden – is a little

---

1. The relationship of perfect love and trust between the Father and the Son is what Jesus wants for all his disciples. But I don't think he's after uniformity with us all being exactly the same as one another. He is talking about that *relationship*. The doctrine of Trinity tells us that in God the Three are perfectly One while remaining fully Three; the model for disciples of Jesus, then, is to be perfectly united in love and trust while yet treasuring the brilliant, God-given diversity that makes each of us special and enriches the whole.
2. Jesus wants his disciples to know that the Father's love for them is timeless, just like his love for the Son. God loved them before they were even thought of in human terms – before anyone was, in fact.
3. This works on all kinds of levels. Jesus wants the *friends* the Father has given to share the glory the Father has given. That glory is already manifest in Jesus because the Father has sent him – the very act of sending was a glorious act by God; it will reach its greatest earthly manifestation in the crucifixion, after which Christ will 'enter into his glory' in heaven. So Jesus is really asking that those who have been God's gift to him should witness his glory (also God's gift to him) at every possible level.

> miniature of the cosmic drama that is unfolding, the effects of which will be similar but quite literally 'cosmic', for all creation.

18

[1-6] After he'd said these words, he led his disciples out across the Kidron valley to a garden, which they all entered. Now Judas – the one who was already in the process of betraying him – knew the place well, because Jesus often used to meet his disciples there. So along he came with a troop made up of soldiers and the Temple police sent by the chief priests and Pharisees, carrying torches, lanterns, and a pretty fearsome armoury of weapons. Jesus, of course, knew everything that was going to happen to him, and went to meet them. 'Who are you looking for?' he asked.

'Jesus,' they answered, 'the guy from Nazareth.'

Jesus said, 'That's who I am.' Judas was just standing there among them. When they heard Jesus say, 'That's who I am,' they recoiled[1] and fell to the ground.

[7-11] Jesus asked them again, 'Who are you looking for?'

'Jesus,' they repeated, 'the guy from Nazareth.'

Jesus said, 'I've already told you that that's who I am. So if it's me you're looking for you can let these people go – OK?' Here, Jesus was fulfilling the word he'd said earlier: 'I didn't lose a single one of the ones you gave to me.'

Then Simon Peter, who was armed with a sword, whipped it out and lashed out at the High Priest's servant, catching the man a glancing blow that cut off his right ear. The servant was called Malchus. 'Put that thing away!' Jesus said. 'Are you trying to ensure that I don't drink the cup the Father's given me?'[2]

Jesus in front of the Religious Council

[12-14] So the Roman soldiers, their officer and the Temple police arrested Jesus and tied him up. Then they took him to Annas, who was the

---

1. John's used this word once before, in 6:66 where Jesus' disciples 'recoiled' from his hard teaching and some of them left him. The guards may have thought that Jesus was about to use the divine Name to cast a spell on them as a sorcerer might do in popular imagination.

2. This is the only use of this image in this gospel, but we find some helpful cross-references in the Synoptics. In Matthew 20:20-23 (and Mark 10:35-45), Jesus challenges James and John to share his 'cup', meaning his suffering, and in Matthew 26:36-46 (also Mark 14:32-42 and Luke 22:40-46) he uses the word in the same way in his prayer in the garden. It would have been a familiar image to people of that time.

father-in-law of Caiaphas, the High Priest at that time. Caiaphas, you may remember, had already said that it would be better if one man died to save the people.[1]

Peter denies Jesus the first time

[15-18] Simon Peter, and another disciple, followed where Jesus went. Now that other disciple was a good friend of the High Priest and just went straight into the courtyard, but Peter hung around outside the gate. So his friend came back out and had a word in the ear of the young woman on the door so that Peter was allowed in.

'You aren't another of this guy's disciples, are you?' the woman asked Peter.

'Me?' Peter gasped. 'Not likely, I'm not!'

The slaves and the police had a fire going in the courtyard – it was a cold night – and were standing around it keeping themselves warm. Peter went and stood with them, warming himself too.

The High Priest's interrogation

[19-24] Then the High Priest[2] started firing questions at Jesus about his disciples, and about the things he taught. 'What's your problem?' Jesus answered. 'I've spoken quite openly for anybody and everybody to hear, haven't I? I've taught in the synagogues – even in the Temple where all the people get together. I've not kept any secrets, so why are you asking me all this stuff? Go and ask the people who heard me – they know exactly what I said.'

One of the police angrily slapped Jesus in the face.[3] 'What sort of way's that to answer the High Priest!'

'Look,' Jesus said, 'if I'm wrong in what I say, then testify to that – *show* that I'm wrong. But if I'm right, why hit me – what's that going to prove?'

Then Annas sent him, still tied up, to Caiaphas the High Priest.

---

1. 11:50 is the reference. Caiaphas, of course, didn't know how fully he was speaking the truth without meaning to. Jesus' death was 'to save the people', but on a quite different level. This is another of those delicious ironies in the gospels where people in opposition to Jesus speak profound truths without realising it themselves. Prosecution witnesses inadvertently testifying for the defence!

2. Here John means Annas, who had been High Priest before his son-in-law, Caiaphas. He no longer held the substantive position, but no doubt commanded respect and could well have continued to be thought of as 'the High Priest' by many people.

3. The use of the open hand, or the back of it, was a sign not only of anger but of contempt.

Peter denies Jesus the second and third times

[25-27] Now, Simon Peter, you may remember, was standing warming himself, and the people around started getting nosey. 'You're not one of this man's disciples, are you?' they asked.

'Me? Not likely!'

Then one of the High Priest's slaves – related to the one whose ear Peter had cut off – asked, 'I saw you with him in the garden, didn't I?' Peter denied it again – and at that very moment the cock crowed.

Jesus in front of the Roman Governor

The way John lights this scene, we can see both Pilate and Jesus as victims of the frightened bigots who are actually behind things but are temporarily shut out of sight. Pilate knows that he's being manipulated, and probably would free Jesus if he weren't terrified of a riot breaking out. However, the difference between Pilate and Jesus is profound: Pilate technically has all the power he needs but finds himself powerless, whereas Jesus ostensibly is the powerless one but knows himself to be completely in command of the situation. Here is an image of worldly power when it is most threatened, and therefore most dangerous, contrasted with the authentic power of God's truth.

[28-32] From Caiaphas, Jesus was taken to the official residence of Pilate – by now it was early morning – but they didn't go in themselves, because that would make them ritually unclean[1] and they wouldn't be able to celebrate the Passover.[2] So Pilate went out to them. 'What's the charge against this man?'

'Well, if he weren't guilty of *something*, we wouldn't have brought him here, would we!'

'Oh, take him away,' Pilate said. 'Judge him under your own law.'

'Fine,' said the others, 'but there's just one problem – we can't put him to death, can we!' (This was to fulfil what Jesus had said about the kind of death he was going to die.)

---

1. All gentile houses were classed as 'unclean'.
2. I can't help thinking John makes a point of telling us this to highlight the hypocrisy. They were about to commit perjury and ritual murder against the Son of God, but were punctilious in observing the detail of the law where religious observance was concerned. Jesus had a lot of interesting things to say about this kind of inconsistency – see, for example, Matthew 23:23-28.

[33-38a] So Pilate went back into his headquarters and sent for Jesus. 'Am I supposed to believe that *you* are the King of the Jews?'

'Is that you speaking?' Jesus asked him. 'Or are you just repeating what someone else has said?'

'Oh, get real – I'm not a Jew, am I? Look, your own people – your own chief priests – have dumped you on me, so what did you do for either of us to deserve that?'

Jesus answered, 'My kingship bears no relationship to what this world understands by that term. I mean, if it did, my servants would be fighting for me, wouldn't they, to stop me being handed over to the authorities? But my kingship's about something quite different from that.'[1]

'Oh,' Pilate countered, 'so you clearly *are* a king, then?'

'It's you that say I'm a king,' Jesus replied. 'The real reason I've been born, and come into the world, is to testify to truth. Anyone who's on the side of truth listens to my voice.'

'What *is* truth?' Pilate shrugged.[2]

[38b-40] After saying this, he went back out to where the religious authorities were waiting, and said, 'I find no case against this man at all, but let's compromise. You know that custom you have, that I release a prisoner for you at Passover time – how about I release this "King of the Jews" character?'[3]

There was absolute uproar! 'Not on your life – we don't want this guy at any price! Give us Barabbas!' Now, Barabbas was a rebel.[4]

---

1. The disciples did try, but Jesus stopped them. So the point testifies to the nature of his kingship, not their lack of courage.

2. The question is left hanging – because there is no simple answer that can be given in a court. God's truth is not simply about fact versus fiction but about meaning and integrity. In one sense, the whole gospel has been an attempt to explore that very question.

3. Another of those ironies: Pilate thinks he's being sarcastic, but he's speaking the truth on a level he can't begin to comprehend. It may also be that he's hoping to appeal to the larger crowd who may see Jesus in this way, so that they will outvote the authorities. If so, it's a vain hope.

4. Ironically, Barabbas, who was released, was exactly what Jesus was accused of being and wasn't (or not in the political sense, anyway)! This was incredibly dangerous stuff: Barabbas was quite capable of inciting rebellion and bringing about the very kind of Roman crackdown that Caiaphas feared Jesus would invoke.

Jesus is mocked

19 [1-7] Then Pilate sent Jesus for a merciless flogging.[1] That wasn't enough for the soldiers, though: they literally added insult to injury – wove a crown from thorns and put it on his head, and dressed him in a purple robe. Then they kept coming up to him, saying, 'Hail, O King of the Jews!'[2] and slapping him.

Pilate went outside again. 'Look,' he said, 'I'm bringing him out here and I want you to be in no doubt about it – I don't find anything against the guy.' So Jesus came out, complete with the crown of thorns and purple robe. 'There,' Pilate said. 'Look at the man!'[3]

As soon as the chief priests and Temple police set eyes on him, they started yelling hysterically, 'Crucify him! Crucify him!'

'Oh, take him and crucify him yourselves!' Pilate snapped back. 'I don't see any reason to do it.'[4]

'Look,' they told him, 'we've got a law too, you know – and by that law he's got to die because he set himself up as the Son of God – no, honestly – Son of God!'

[8-12] At this, Pilate became seriously scared. He went back inside his headquarters. 'Just where are you from?' he asked Jesus.

Jesus wasn't going to try to answer *that* in words of one syllable so he kept quiet.

Pilate could hardly believe it. 'Are *you* refusing to speak to *me*?' he demanded. 'I mean, have you any idea of the power I've got? I'm the guy who can decide whether to release you or have you crucified.'[5]

---

1. We cannot begin to imagine the pain this involved: the scourge would rip deep into the flesh at every stroke and the combination of shock and loss of blood would effectively begin the execution process even before crucifixion.
2. Yet more irony: Jesus *is* the King, but in a very different sense, and the mockery will ultimately be turned back upon themselves.
3. The Greek word used here is actually the Greek equivalent of the Aramaic word meaning 'Son of Man'. Pilate is making an unconsciously prophetic statement. In effect, he says, 'Now, you see the coming of the Son of Man'.
4. Pilate knows full well, of course, that they can't do any such thing. Apart from not having the authority to do it, their form of legal execution was stoning. This was not going to happen to Jesus – he was to be 'lifted up' and glorified. And by trying to make it all look legal they were, in fact – another irony – ensuring that the enthronement happened!
5. The poor man's deluded! In worldly terms, he's completely in the power of the religious authorities – and he knows it! If he *really* had the power to do it he'd already have released Jesus.

'You wouldn't have any power in my case at all,' Jesus retorted, 'if it hadn't been given to you from above. That's why the really guilty party here is the one who's handed me over to you.'[1]

Pilate became seriously determined to release Jesus after that, but the religious authorities shouted out, 'You let this guy go and you're no friend of the Emperor's. Anyone who claims to be a king is setting up in opposition to the Emperor.'[2]

[13-16a] When Pilate heard that, he brought Jesus outside and sat on the judgement seat in a place called the Stone Pavement – in Hebrew, it's Gabbatha. This was about midday on the day of Preparation for the Passover.[3] 'Here's your king!' he said to the people.

'Take him away!' came the shout. 'Take him away! Crucify him!'

'What?' Pilate asked. 'You really want me to crucify your king?'

The chief priests shouted back, 'We haven't got any king other than the Emperor!'[4]

Then Pilate handed Jesus over to the soldiers to be crucified.

The crucifixion

Early in his account of the gospel, John reported Jesus as being called 'the Lamb of God', and the gospel has included many, many allusions to the Passover tradition, where John is highlighting for us the connections with Jesus' life and death. Christ is the final sacrifice reconciling us to God, enabling the relationship God has always wanted with us to be a reality. Jesus is God's Passover Lamb. And now John has just been careful to ensure we know the time and date of the crucifixion: after midday on the Day of Preparation for the Passover. The afternoon of that day would be taken up with the ritual slaughter of the Passover lambs in the

---

1. He means Caiaphas. The fact that Judas tried to play with the big boys doesn't mean he was a serious factor.
2. So, suddenly they want to be loyal to the emperor? Where did that come from? Political expediency, that's where.
3. Make a mental note of the time and day – it will be important when we get to the crucifixion itself.
4. When it comes to blasphemy, this is a cracker! The whole theological basis of the Jewish nation state was that they had no king but *God*! Here, the enormity of it is brought into stark relief because the God they are rejecting as king is standing right before them in the flesh.

Temple. The priests who were doing that were unaware of the significance of the ritual simultaneous slaughter of the perfect – and
therefore final – Passover Lamb on the hill of Golgotha. A major
theme of John's gospel reaches its mind-blowing climax.

[16b-24] So they took Jesus and, carrying his cross on his own back, he set
out for what's called 'The place of the skull' – or, in Hebrew, Golgotha –
where they crucified him along with two others, one each side and
Jesus in the middle. Pilate ordered that a big placard be fixed over his
head, saying, 'Jesus of Nazareth: KING OF THE JEWS'. And plenty of
people read it – Pilate made sure of that by having it written not only
in Hebrew but in Latin and Greek as well!

Of course, the religious authorities didn't like that one bit![1] 'You
can't say that!' they objected. 'Say that *he claimed* to be king of the
Jews!'

'What I have written,' Pilate said tersely, 'I have written – live with it.'

Once they'd finished the actual crucifixion of Jesus, the soldiers
divided up his clothes among the four of them – all except his tunic.
The tunic was seamless – woven in one continuous piece.[2] 'It's a shame
to rip it up,' they said, 'so why don't we gamble for it?' This was to fulfil
another scripture: 'They divided my garments among them – gambled
for my clothes.'[3]

[25-30] That's exactly what the soldiers did. Meanwhile, standing near Jesus'
cross were his mother and her sister, Mary – wife of Clopas – as well as
Mary Magdalene. When Jesus saw his mother – and the disciple who
was his closest friend – standing there, he said, 'Mother – there's your
son, now.' Then he turned to the disciple: 'Call her your mother,' he told

---

1. It's not surprising that they didn't like it. Pilate was really enjoying himself. He might
as well have put, 'This is the best they can do for a king'! He was also in effect accusing
them of treason for their declared loyalty to the Emperor (he probably knew enough
about their religion to know the enormity of what they'd said). In all this, too, he
continued as an unwitting witness for Christ, declaring the truth about him without
knowing it.
2. This was how High Priests' robes were made. By specifically giving us this detail John is
making a theological statement: as well as the Lamb who is sacrificed, Jesus is the true
High Priest who *offers* the sacrifice. Again, John reminds us, no one took Jesus' life away –
he offered it. This is a reminder that his High-Priesthood is as far removed from the
earthly office of priest as the Good Shepherd (who offers his life for the sheep) is from
the hired hand.
3. Psalm 22:18.

him.[1] So, from then on the disciple took her into his own home. After this, when Jesus knew that everything was complete, he spoke in fulfilment of the scriptures: 'I'm thirsty!'[2] There was a jar of bitter wine standing there and they dipped a sponge in it, speared it onto a hyssop[3] branch and held it up to his lips. When he'd accepted the drink, Jesus said, 'Everything is accomplished!'[4] Then he bowed his head and gave up his life.[5]

Jesus' side is pierced

[31-37] Now, remember, this was the day of Preparation for the Passover. The religious authorities didn't want bodies on crosses on any Sabbath day – but especially such a significant one as that. So they went to Pilate and asked him to have the convicts' legs broken to get it over with and the bodies removed.[6] The soldiers came and smashed the legs of the other two crucified with Jesus, but when they came to Jesus himself and found he was dead already, they didn't break his legs, but a soldier plunged a spear into his side and a mixture of blood and water came

---

1. It seems strange for Jesus to commend his mother to the care of a friend – why would his brothers not care for her? However, we know from both John and the Synoptic gospels that Jesus not only foresaw family divisions but found his own family confused and probably divided about him. So it may be that he could not rely on his family to care for his mother which, in that culture, would leave her terribly vulnerable. Jesus, right at the point of agonising death, remains not only 'the man for others' but, as John has shown us throughout, supremely in charge of events.

2. Possibly Psalm 22:15, or more probably 69:21: 'When I was thirsty, they offered me vinegar!' Maybe this highlights the bitterness of Jesus' rejection. He offered the world living water for its thirst (4:13-15). The best the world can do for him, in his, is bitter vinegar!

3. In Exodus 12:22 a sprig of hyssop was used to smear the blood of the Lamb on the doorposts so that the Israelites would be saved. It subsequently came to be closely associated with cleansing (see, for example, Psalm 51:7). Once again, John is giving us an apparently trivial bit of detail that actually is bursting with symbolism about the meaning of the death of Jesus.

4. Some standard texts translate this, 'It is finished'; others, 'It is complete'. Not only Jesus' life but his work and indeed the salvation of the world is finished, complete, accomplished. It also relates to Jesus' 'completing' of his Father's work in creation. That's the difficulty with translation sometimes – we really need at least three words to translate one original!

5. Again, John words things extremely carefully. Jesus didn't simply 'die' – he *gave up* (or 'laid down', cf. 10:11-18) his life in obedience to his Father.

6. Without the support from the legs, the weight of the body on the arms would constrict the chest and hasten death.

out.[1] (This comes directly from an eye-witness, who's given his testimony so that you may believe – his testimony is accurate and well vouched for.) These things all happened in fulfilment of scripture, which said, 'Not a single one of his bones will be allowed to be broken'.[2] Then there's that other text from scripture, that says, 'They'll look upon the one they stabbed'.[3]

The burial of Jesus

Joseph of Arimathea and Nicodemus finally put their heads above the parapet. Where had they been until now? Nicodemus was the secretly believing Pharisee who'd come to consult Jesus under cover of darkness in Chapter 3, and then put up a feeble defence in Chapter 7; Joseph hasn't appeared before. You might like to glance back to Luke 23:50 and my footnote on that. Another point brought out from this by John's detail is how Nicodemus and Joseph, unwilling to make a choice earlier, now finally take their stand with Jesus. The death of Jesus precipitates a crisis which demands that we finally make our choice.

[38-42] After all this had happened, Joseph of Arimathea came into the picture. He was a disciple of Jesus, but he kept that close to his chest because he was afraid of the religious authorities. Anyway, he asked Pilate to let him take Jesus' body away. Pilate gave him the go-ahead, and he went and took the body. Nicodemus turned up too – the man who'd come to Jesus by night – and he brought a hundred pounds' weight of myrrh and spices. So they took Jesus' body and wrapped it with the spices in linen – this was the traditional form of burial. Now there was a garden in the same place, with a new tomb in it in which no one had yet been buried. Well, time was short, what with the Preparation and everything, and the tomb was handy, so there they laid Jesus to rest.

---

1. Again, this detail – only spelled out by John – is full of significance. At the death of Christ, his blood is availed to the world (see 6:52-59 and introduction). The significance of water is slightly less clear, but could symbolise the pouring out of the Spirit or the living water Christ offered the Samaritan woman at the well in Chapter 4 – or indeed both. In addition to that, John makes it very clear that Jesus' death was real, which is important for the resurrection.

2. John is probably pointing us to Exodus 12:46 or Numbers 9:12, both of which are instructions about the Passover lamb, which would fit with John's particular emphasis on Passover.

3. Zechariah 12:10. The original language shows this to be forward-looking: the one they've stabbed is going to return and they'll have to face him.

The Resurrection of Jesus

20$^{1\text{-}10}$ Early in the morning of the first day of the week – while it was still dark, in fact – Mary Magdalene arrived at the tomb to find the stone rolled away from the entrance. So she ran off to find Simon Peter and the other disciple – Jesus' closest friend – and said, 'They've gone and taken the Lord out of his tomb and we haven't got a clue where they've put him.'

Peter and the other disciple didn't hang around, but hot-footed it to the tomb. To start with, they were together – but the other disciple soon got ahead of Peter, and arrived first. He bent down and peered in. He could see the linen grave-clothes lying there, but he didn't venture inside. Then Simon Peter arrived and he had no hesitation – straight into the tomb. He, too, saw the linen grave-clothes lying there, and the cloth that had been put over Jesus' head – that wasn't with the grave clothes but was rolled up separately. Then the other disciple – the one who'd got there first – went inside too; and he saw and understood what had happened. You must remember they still didn't understand the scripture that said that he was to rise from the dead. Then the disciples both went home.

The appearances of Jesus

There is a real sense, in John particularly, that something truly awesome is happening. Perhaps we've lost our sense of wonder because the story's too familiar to us – it *should* be awesome, but oh, how lightly we speak of it! Both here and in the Synoptics we find examples of the risen Jesus not being recognised. Obviously, we can accept a psychological explanation for that – resurrection is hardly an everyday occurrence! – but when the gospel writers go out of their way to tell us such obvious things, we know it's pretty safe to bet that they're showing us a bit more than that.

Firstly, the aim is to help readers to grasp that Jesus is with us even when we don't recognise him. Secondly, it is to stress that knowing the risen Christ is something that is in his gift, not our grasp – see the Emmaus story in Luke 24 where Jesus reveals himself in the way he chooses but doesn't let them grab hold of him, and compare this with Mary Magdalene's encounter, below. We don't *find* Christ – he makes himself known to us, in ways that are of his sovereign choosing. If anything should help us remember that we haven't got God in a box, it's this!

Jesus appears to Mary Magdalene

[11-18] Mary stayed, though, crying, outside the tomb, and as she cried she bent down to look inside and saw two angels dressed in white. They were sitting there – one at the head end and the other near the feet of where Jesus' body had been lying. 'Lady, why are you crying?' they asked her.

'They've taken my Lord away,' she told them, 'and I haven't any idea where they've put him.' As soon as she said it, she turned round and saw Jesus himself behind her – except that she didn't recognise him straightaway.

'Lady,' Jesus said, 'why are you crying? Who are you trying to find?'

Mary thought he must be the gardener. 'Oh, sir!' she blurted out. 'If you're the one who's moved him, can you just tell me where you've put him so that I can go and take him away?'

Jesus said just one word: 'Mary.'

At that, she turned right round to face him and said, in Hebrew, 'Rabbouni!' – the word for 'Teacher'.[1]

'No,' Jesus said, 'don't cling to me – I haven't yet ascended to my Father.[2] Go and find my brothers,[3] and tell them I'm starting my journey back to my Father – and that means *your* Father – to my God, who is also your God.'

Mary took off to announce to the disciples, 'Hey, guys, guess what? I've seen the Lord!' And she told them the things that he'd said to her.

Jesus appears to the disciples

> On his appearance to his disciples after resurrection, Jesus does three vital things. He first gives them his peace; then he sends them out on his mission; and finally he empowers them with his Holy Spirit. So the encounter with the risen Christ equips the Church to *be* the Church: resting on the security of his peace, commissioned with his authority and empowered by his Spirit.

---

1. Her name is all it takes: the Good Shepherd calls his sheep by name, and they recognise his voice (10:3 onwards).

2. Mary's use of 'Rabbouni' falls woefully short of Christ's full title. This, combined with her implied attempt to take hold of him, betrays a desire to go back to the way things were. And who can blame her for that? – if any of us, in the depths of grief, found the person we had lost to be alive again, no doubt we should feel exactly the same. But Jesus is not to be confined either to past ideas or to this earth.

3. His followers, that is – not the literal brothers who had not believed in him (see 7:1-5).

[19-23] In the evening of that same day – the first day of the week – the disciples were huddled together behind locked doors, terrified of the religious authorities, when Jesus came, stood right in the middle of them, and said, 'Peace be with you all.' Then he showed them his hands and side, and the disciples were completely overjoyed when they recognised the Lord, risen and among them. Again, Jesus said, 'Peace be with you all. Now, just as the Father has sent me, so I'm sending you.'[1] And after saying this, he breathed on them.[2] 'Receive the Holy Spirit,' he said. 'If you say anyone's forgiven, then they are – and if you say they're not, they're not.'[3]

Honest Thomas

[24-29] There was one disciple, Thomas (known as the Twin), who, although he was one of the Twelve, wasn't there when Jesus appeared. Of course, the other disciples told him, 'We've seen the Lord!' but he didn't believe them.[4]

'Yes, well, I'm not believing a word of it until I've seen and touched the nail-wounds in his hands and actually felt the wound in his side,' he said.

A week later he got his wish. The disciples were in the house again, and this time Thomas was with them. The fact that the doors were shut was no barrier to Jesus, who just came and stood among them. 'Peace be with you all,' he said. Then he turned to Thomas. 'Well, what are you waiting for? Put your finger here – those hands wounded enough, are they? Reach out you hand – go on – put it right into the gap in my side. Now, don't doubt any more. Believe!'

'My Lord!' Thomas said. 'And my God!'

---

1. In other words, with the same authority.
2. Two points here: firstly, we've already noted the association between 'breath' and '*spirit*', for which the same word was used both in Hebrew and Greek. Secondly, the action recalls Genesis 2 where God breathed his spirit into the man to give him life. Put those two together, and we have a whole rainbow of images to do with the new life of the risen Jesus being shared with his people.
3. This saying causes a lot of difficulty. It's doubtful that Jesus really meant that his disciples had power over people's eternal salvation. The Greek verbs used are actually to do with 'opening' and 'closing', and could be to do with granting or refusing people re-admission to the community after exclusion for some serious sin.
4. Neither had the others (with one exception) until they'd seen him, so let's not be unfair to Thomas.

'You believe, do you, now that you've seen me?' Jesus said. 'Well, congratulations to all who haven't seen, and yet have believed.'[1]

[30-31] Now, the disciples saw Jesus do plenty of other signs right in front of them that aren't included in this book. But these are written so that you can come to faith in Jesus as Messiah – Son of God – and that by faith you may have true life in his name.[2]

---

1. At this point, as far as we know, only Jesus' closest friend fitted that category. The rest of the disciples hadn't believed until they'd had the kind of evidence Thomas asked for. However, the combined testimony of the entire community should have been enough – and was going to have to be enough for generations of Christians to come.
2. So John is specifically saying that he's selected carefully from a wealth of material, in order to achieve his purpose. He has been inspired by the Holy Spirit to produce a book that gives a distinctive picture of the complex and many-faceted person that is Jesus.

The Epilogue: Jesus' final appearance to seven disciples

21 [1-8] After these things had happened, Jesus revealed himself to his disciples again – by the Sea of Tiberias – and he did it like this. Simon Peter, Thomas ('the Twin') and Nathanael (from Cana in Galilee) had all met together, along with the two sons of Zebedee and a couple of other disciples. 'I'm going fishing,' Simon Peter said.

'OK,' said the rest, 'we'll come with you,' and they got into a boat. They didn't catch a single thing that night, though.

The miraculous catch

It was just after daybreak when Jesus stood on the beach – unrecognised by his disciples – and called out, 'Hey, friends! You haven't caught any fish – have you!'

'No!' came the disconsolate reply.

'Well, throw the net over to the right side of the boat – you'll find some there.'

They did as he said, and suddenly it was so full of fish they couldn't haul it in. Jesus' closest friend turned to Peter and said, 'It's the Lord!'

As soon as Simon Peter heard it was the Lord, he threw on some clothes – he'd stripped off to be able to work freely – and jumped into the sea, but the others stayed in the boat. They had to drag the net full of fish, still in the water, to the shore, but that was only a matter of about a hundred yards.

[9-14] When they got to the shore, what should they find but a charcoal fire with fish and bread cooking away on it.[1] 'Bring over some of that fish you've just caught,' said Jesus. Simon Peter went back to the boat and dragged the net ashore. It was bursting at the seams with enormous fish – a hundred and fifty-three of them altogether – but the net wasn't torn.[2]

---

1. Is Jesus making a connection with the fourth sign – the feeding of the five thousand – which also involved fish and bread? Could he be saying, 'Feed the world with the food of eternal life'?

2. The significance of 153 is obscure – although the fact that John cares to mention it means it probably had some special meaning. It used to be thought that 153 was the total number of species of fish known in those times, but this is now less certain. Other interpretations are based on combinations of numbers that had symbolic meaning at the time, or the numerical values attached to Hebrew letters. It's all beyond me but the general consensus is that the number somehow foretells the eventual completeness – and the unbroken net the security – of salvation.

'Come and have breakfast,' Jesus said to them. None of them dared ask, 'Who are you?' because deep down they knew it was the Lord.[1] Jesus took the loaves, and gave these out to them. He did the same with the fish too. This was the third time Jesus appeared to his disciples after he was raised from the dead.

Jesus reconciles Peter

> There's a bit of unfinished business between Jesus and Peter. Peter's denials, while utterly understandable, need to be dealt with. It won't help Peter if Jesus just ignores them, or reassures Peter in a way that treats them lightly. They matter – and Peter needs to be helped to come to terms with them. So Jesus gives him three opportunities to state the friendship he has three times denied – now with perhaps a little more realism born of bitter experience. And each affirmation is met with a commission which is both a chance to make amends and an assurance that Peter still has Jesus' trust – and, by implication, that he's going to be more faithful. Peter is brought face to face both with his own failure – so that he can deal with it – and with the love of God.

[15-19] When they'd finished breakfast, Jesus turned to Simon Peter. 'Simon, son of John,' he asked, 'do you love me more than these others?'[2]

'Yes, Lord – you know that I love you!'

'Feed my lambs,' said Jesus.[3]

Then Jesus asked a second time: 'Simon, son of John, do you love me?'

'Yes, Lord,' Peter repeated. 'you know I love you.'

---

1. This may seem odd – why should they even want to ask, if they knew? Again, I see this as part of the awesome mystery that meeting the risen Christ involves. They were enabled to recognise who he was at a superficial level, but the very appearance of the risen Saviour would also beg the question, 'Who are you?' at a much deeper level, although they would be unlikely to feel able to ask it.

2. The language is, perhaps deliberately, ambiguous. The Greek could mean 'more than these other disciples do' or it could equally be interpreted 'more than these other things' or 'more than all else'. The former might seem somehow not in keeping with Jesus – in effect encouraging his disciples to compete – but in Matthew 26:33 and Mark 14:29, we find Peter specifically claiming to be more loyal to Jesus than the rest, so this could be a challenge. It may well be that both meanings are intended, and the ambiguity is deliberate.

3. In typically symbolic language, the Good Shepherd is putting the care of his sheep in Peter's hands. How's that for trust!

'So, take care of my sheep,' Jesus said.

Then he asked a third time, 'Simon, son of John, do you love me?'

Peter was seriously upset about being asked this three times. 'Look, Lord,' he said, 'you know everything, don't you? So you know perfectly well that I love you.'

'Feed my sheep,' Jesus answered. 'I'm really telling you straight, when you were young you were free to do your own thing – get dressed, go out wherever you wanted. Well, that's fine, but when you're old you're going to hold your hands out and someone else is going to dress you[1] and take you where they choose, even if you don't want to go.'[2] (He said this to point to the kind of death by which Peter would glorify God.) And then he said, 'Follow me.'

Jesus and his closest friend

[20-25] Peter turned and saw Jesus' closest friend following them – you remember, the one who'd been reclining next to Jesus at the supper, and had said, 'Lord, which one's going to betray you?'

Seeing him, Peter said to Jesus, 'Hey, Lord, what about this guy?'

'That's not your business,' Jesus said. 'Even if I decided that he was going to stay until I come again, what business would it be of yours? Your job is to follow me.'[3]

That did it! The rumour went round that this disciple wasn't going to die – but that wasn't what Jesus had said, was it! What he'd said was, '*Even if* I decided that he was going to stay until I come again, what business would it be of yours?'

This is the disciple who's written his testimony about all these things – and we know that his testimony is reliable. But you need to know that this isn't all there is – there are countless other things that Jesus did, and if they were all written down, well, I reckon the whole world wouldn't be big enough to hold all the books that would be written!

---

1. The image Jesus uses is, I think, deliberately ambiguous. It could also show Peter being bound as a captive, as Jesus has been.

2. As so often, the text works on at least two levels. The image is of Peter losing his independence in old age, as happens to many people, but it's also clearly an image of captivity and, as John indicates in his note, the manner of his death.

3. So, forgiveness doesn't make us perfect. I feel real empathy for Peter. It seems that whenever he'd got it right with Jesus he went straight out and fell over his feet again, which makes him pretty much like most of us! Immediately after his reconciliation and commissioning, he takes his eye off the ball and starts minding other people's business. The 'closest friend' is already following Jesus without being asked, but Peter has to be reminded.

Glossary

Glossary of key words and phrases

The interpretations below are a guide to *some* of the important terms used in the gospels. One difficulty is that the writers wrote in Greek (sometimes translating source documents from the more generally used language, Aramaic) rather than in modern English! Translation is not always 100 per cent accurate because some words really can't be expressed at all well while others could be translated in different ways. An example of the former is 'congratulations', usually translated 'Blessed' in the Sermon on the Mount, while one of the latter is shown in the use of 'Master' and Lord', which clearly overlap, and which different translators will handle differently.

Above	In John, 'above' is used to signify the things of heaven, as distinct from the things of earth which are 'below'. The people of Jesus' day would, of course, have taken the words quite literally, whereas we would see them in more symbolic terms: God is always 'above' in the sense of being 'superior'.
Advocate	This translates a Greek word that only occurs in John's writings. That word really means someone who stands with you and speaks in support of you. So, when the disciples were being challenged about their faith, the 'Advocate' God would send would speak for (or, to be more precise, through) them. The word 'advocate' is becoming more widely used now in English, not only to refer to a barrister who speaks for a client in court, but also anyone who speaks in support of someone else.
Christ	Originally, simply the Greek version of the Hebrew word 'Messiah', and now often used as another name for Jesus. Apart from a very few instances, the word is generally rendered 'Messiah' in the texts of the gospels, and appears in this book mainly in my notes and headings.
Coming of the Son of Man	There are several references to this, which are generally taken to point back to Daniel 7:13-14 and forward to Christ's second coming. In Daniel, however, the

'Son of Man' doesn't come to earth, but comes to God to receive glory and power. So it's quite possible that when Jesus uses this expression he's referring to his own glorification in crucifixion and resurrection. This would be in keeping with his consistent desire to change people's image of Messianic power. That, of course, doesn't mean that it can't also be pointing forward to the final great event, but we need to be open to a bigger and less simple meaning than immediately comes to mind.

Congratulations This word replaces the traditional 'blessed', used famously in the Beatitudes, and elsewhere too. Some translations say 'Happy' but that's really not adequate as most people think of happiness as a 'feel-good' thing. The word really means that people are in a good position to be close to God and in tune with his ways.

Covenant This word only occurs four times in the gospels – twice in Luke – but it is nonetheless a key concept. Putting it very briefly, it describes God's relationship with creation – and the human race in particular. In early times, people thought of it as a *conditional* covenant. God would do certain things for us if we were faithful to him. Later, thinking moved on to an *unconditional* covenant which put no strings on God's love at all – it's a completely free gift. However, we all know that gifts can be accepted or rejected, and a truly free gift is never imposed. So, while God's love is unconditional, it is still up to us to accept it. And we all know in human relationships that if we want fully to benefit from someone's love, then we need to make some contribution ourselves. So the covenant is a free one – no strings attached – but we won't get a lot out of it unless we actively accept it ourselves.

Crowd The more distant 'crowds' around Jesus are distinguished from the closer followers, the 'disciples'. Sometimes the crowds are friendly, sometimes hostile, but either way it's helpful to distinguish Jesus' words to the disciples from those addressed to the crowds.

Curse   Traditional versions often use 'woe' to represent the opposite of 'Blessed' (see 'Congratulations'). However, it really doesn't convey the strength of the Greek word, which was much more than a prediction – it was a *condemnation*.

Dark   See 'Light'.

Elders   To give them their full title, the 'Elders of the people' have a long history in the Hebrew scriptures. Strictly speaking, they were what would now be called 'laity', members of the civil authorities, but their historical influence meant that they carried a great deal of weight, and shared in the oversight of religious affairs through, for example, representation on the Temple Council, the Sanhedrin. See also 'Unholy alliances/huddles'.

Eternal life   This term is used a few times in the Synoptic gospels, but more often in John. In both cases, it means much more than merely 'everlasting'. As well as looking ahead to the life to come after death, it also anticipates the new life we can have here and now in Christ. 'Eternal' is about quality of life: the life we expect to share in eternity can be entered into now, within this world, and the life can spread from us out into the world.

This clearly overlaps with the Synoptic writers' 'kingdom of God/heaven', and John, in fact, uses it pretty much as his version of that phrase.

Father (for God)   The different writers have subtly different ways of using this term. You could spend a lot of time looking into the nuances of this, but one or two things are worth noting. In Matthew and John, Jesus often calls God '*my* Father' (see below for Matthew's particular use of it). Luke only uses that exact title for God three times, and Mark never at all. 'Our Father' is only used once for God – in Matthew's version of the Lord's Prayer; Jesus refers to God as *'your* Father' frequently in Matthew, rarely in Mark or Luke and only once in John – which, significantly, is after the resurrection. *'The* Father' occurs very rarely in the Synoptics but with remarkable frequency in John, where the term Father is often coupled with 'Son'. This reflects John's much heavier emphasis on Jesus' divine status, and specifically on his *equal* divinity as God incarnate. This in itself could well be related to the later period in which John was writing, by which time the idea of Trinity was beginning to be explored (it would be the fourth century before the doctrine was officially established) and, alongside that, various heresies were gaining ground which represented Jesus as less than fully God. We might see John's account of the gospel as an important contribution to those debates.

Father in heaven   In Matthew, Jesus often refers to God this way. It reflects God's fatherly relationship with those who choose to 'enter his kingdom', but at the same time the expression 'in heaven' acknowledges that he is to be worshipped, not treated in a 'matey' fashion. It is a very Matthean phrase: Mark only uses the precise form of words once, against Matthew's thirteen, while Luke and John never use it.

Flesh   In John particularly, and to a lesser extent in the Synoptic gospels, this word refers not merely to human tissue as such but to human as distinct from divine (spirit) life. There is a common misconception that all flesh is bad and only things of the spirit are good – but we need to remember that human flesh is God's creation too. What Jesus, in the gospel according to John especially, is saying is that whatever our birth circumstances may have given us isn't enough: we need a spiritual (supernatural) life *as well as* a 'fleshly' (natural) one.

Follow

This is a very important word. To 'follow' Jesus was much more than just tagging along behind: it expressed a degree of commitment to him, or at least an active interest in his work and mission. That commitment varies: the crowd followed him, but not so closely as the disciples. Of course, even the disciples were in many ways a million miles behind him, but at least they had a serious commitment even when they completely failed to understand. So the gospel writers are using the word to contrast the different degrees of commitment of the various groups.

(this) Generation

This word appears many times in the Synoptic Gospels (Matthew, Mark and Luke) but not in John. Just as Jesus is the culmination of God's purpose throughout history, so 'this generation' – Jesus' contemporaries – are the culmination of centuries of human blindness to and rejection of that purpose. Jesus is saying that matters are really coming to a head in him. His coming precipitated a crisis then – and he can do the same thing in our lives now.

Glory

John's gospel in particular emphasises the glory of God in Christ. God's glory is revealed to us as the love that moved him to send his Son into the world and that found its supreme revelation at Calvary. This important theme of 'sending' (see 'sent') means that while John wants to show us that Jesus' glory was supremely revealed in the cross, he also wants to emphasise that it was visible throughout his ministry to those who had eyes to see, because the very sending of his only Son was itself a glorious thing for God to do. He particularly emphasises at least two important connections.

Firstly, the glory of God and the glory of Jesus Christ are one. In the unity of their relationship they glorify one another; the Father glorifies the Son by revealing his love through him, and the Son glorifies the Father by the obedience that acts as a lens for the light to shine out.

Secondly, the glory revealed in Jesus' earthly ministry is the same glory as the glory he has in heaven. John wants us to be very clear that this glory is timeless, with no beginning and no end: the glory of God's eternity.

Grace

Not a word you come across often in the gospels (just four times, in John) but massively important to Christians all the same and used here in my introduction and notes. It was Paul, in his letters, who developed the use of the word so that it became a mainstay of Christian thought, and we shouldn't confuse Paul's thinking with John's, but there is an overlap. Paul teaches that we're saved by God's undeserved love (grace), when we respond to it in faith. God won't force his goodness on us, because he wants us to be free, so he offers and then leaves it up to us to respond. Paul also – and this is where he overlaps with John – contrasted grace to law. There was a general popular opinion that people earned their salvation through keeping the law – 'works', as Paul called it. The Christian belief is that this is impossible – we can never be good enough to deserve to be saved, which is why it all depends on God's grace. The nearest we get to 'salvation by works' is by emphasising that God leaves us free to respond or not as we choose.

It's like accepting a gift. Someone can be longing to give, but until we hold out our hand and say, 'Yes, please!' there's no way we can actually receive it. Although John only uses the word 'grace' four times, all in the first chapter, the concept dominates his writing as he shows the whole story to have been God's doing, right down to the precise timing of Christ's death.

In contrasting law and grace, however, we should not be too rigid. The law was also God's gift – in that sense, it was also 'grace' – and has value in helping us order our lives and the world healthily. But the law isn't *saving* grace, because we're simply

374

not capable of living up to it. The only thing that can save us is something that depends on God, rather than on us.

Hear See 'Listen'.

I am This was the name God gave himself in revealing himself to Moses at the burning bush. In John, Jesus introduces a number of self-revealing statements with these words – scholars call them 'the "I am" sayings', and believe that the fact that John chooses to record these sayings is another example of his especially strong emphasis on Jesus' divinity.

I'm telling you These words, traditionally rendered 'I say to you', indicate an authoritative statement by Jesus. They are found more often in Matthew than the other gospels, and are sometimes preceded with 'but', as Jesus is stamping his authority on the tradition: 'You've heard it said . . . but *I* say to you . . .'

I'm really telling you straight See below, 'I'm telling you straight', and then make it even more so! John actually used a double 'Amen' here which is found nowhere else in scripture. Jesus could hardly have added more weight to his words, whatever else he said.

I'm telling you straight See 'I'm telling you'. Sometimes Jesus would add 'truly' – or 'verily' in the Authorised Version – to give extra weight to particularly solemn utterances.

Immediately Mark especially uses this word to keep his narrative moving. Other writers also use it, but it's Mark in particular who makes it a feature of his writing and a device for pacing his narrative.

In my/your name In biblical days, as now, people would invoke the name of Jesus for various purposes, some very good and others more self-serving. Jesus uses this expression in the gospels for people of both sorts, but, as you'd expect, he takes a different attitude according to how his name is being used. Jesus is referring to a specific appeal to his name or to the things he's said, but it can be argued that if people know we are Christians, then *everything* we say or do is, by implication, 'in Christ's name'.

This phrase is also used to express a relationship: to act or live 'in Christ's (or God's) name' is to be really in tune with his mind so that our desires and actions will be fully aligned with his.

See also 'Name'.

Into the (or this) world

This phrase occurs a number of times in John, always in reference to Christ (although one – 16:21 – is metaphorical, the metaphor still points to Christ). In all but that example, it begins with the verb 'to come' or 'to send'. We are being pointed back to John 1:9, where the phrase is first used: Christ is the one who was to come into the world as its light. So when such a title is applied to him it carries a statement, a recognition, of who he is.

Judgement

Now, here's where Christians get into all sorts of debates – and actually get quite judgemental of one another! Many struggle with the idea of a God who loves unconditionally and longs only to save, but who is also portrayed as harsh in judgement – often to the point of apparent vindictiveness. I could write a book on this word alone, but here's a rather over-simplified summary: God truly loves us, wants us to be free, and knows that free people can't be forced to love and accept him. Free people have to be allowed to make decisions, but that's only genuine if those decisions have consequences. So (to put it terribly simply and risk distorting the idea) God allows us to make the free choice, but then allows us to live with the consequences. So if we reject him, and decide to stay outside his 'kingdom', we 'judge' ourselves, and God 'judges' that we must be allowed to do so. But it doesn't end there – the Good News is what this book is all about – that God doesn't leave us to face that alone, but suffers it with us.

You might find the entry under 'Light' illuminating.

Kindness   The more usual word is 'mercy', but in our culture that's too much associated with forgiveness. In the gospels it doesn't necessarily have the same connotation – people ask for 'mercy' who have no obvious, specific guilt. So, where it's appropriate, I've rendered 'have mercy' as 'do a kindness', and 'I prefer mercy' as 'I prefer kindness', etc. This also makes the demand greater: we might think we only need show *mercy* to those who offend us, but *kindness* is something we should show to everybody.

Kingdom of God/heaven   (Generally speaking, Matthew uses 'Kingdom of heaven' while the other evangelists say 'Kingdom of God'.) This is not a place, but a condition of life: the 'kingship' of God might be a better way of expressing it in our language. We should remember that God seeks to rule by relationships of love, rather than by worldly standards of coercion, so it's something that happens here and now where the will of God is accepted and done. We mustn't limit our understanding of it to the afterlife. Jesus often talks about 'entering the kingdom of heaven', meaning 'entering into God's new life', or 'becoming fully committed to God's ways'. It's something we can be part of here and now! Scholars talk about 'the now and not yet of the kingdom' – the belief that the fullness of it is promised, but it's already been inaugurated in Jesus. So it's also present, now.

Kneel   A posture specifically showing deference. Matthew uses it most, and often associates it with use of the word 'Lord' (see below). However, like the name 'Lord' it can also be a mockery, as the soldiers showed at Jesus' trial.

Lamb of God   This phrase only occurs twice in the whole Bible – both times early in John – but it is still a key phrase. So much so, in fact, that it's worth searching a little further, and there are two places in this book that should help. Try looking up 'sacrifice' in this glossary, and then the introduction to John 1:29.

377

Light and
darkness

Light is often used in contrast to darkness. Its connotations are generally good: Jesus is 'the light that enlightens all people'; people who do good things 'live in the light', and so on – in contrast to the darkness where evil things can be covered up and therefore where evil people choose to be. We can also choose to be in the darkness by refusing to see the light; and darkness is also used in reference to isolation from God – for example, Matthew 8:12.

This is an excellent image for modern people to understand how evil can exist in a world created by a good God. We know that as the earth turns away from light it becomes dark. In the same way, if creation turns away from God who is its light, it is turning into darkness. We can choose to be 'in the light' or 'in the darkness'. Finally, as Jesus himself pointed out, the light can be very uncomfortable – it shows up an untidy room something rotten! See John 3:19 for light portrayed as judgement. Christ's coming is good news and bad news – grace and judgement – according to where we ourselves stand and how we respond.

Listen

Listening to Jesus is a significant theme, particularly in Luke. This doesn't mean that the other evangelists don't think it's important, but Luke makes a special point of emphasising it.

Lord

Generally, the Greek word translated 'Lord' might mean nothing more than a polite 'Sir', and indeed it's used that way in the Gospels – for example, by Jesus in some of his parables. However, it was also the title commonly accorded to God – who, of course, is Lord of lords (note the upper- and lower-case 'l's) and again it's used that way in the Gospels, particularly when citing prophecies, and by Jesus in reference to God. Finally, it's used sometimes as a title for Jesus, and in such cases it usually signifies a recognition of Jesus' special authority. However, Jesus was also at pains to point out that simply saying

'Lord' really isn't enough on its own. In this paraphrase, I've used 'Sir', 'God' and 'Lord' respectively for these different nuances, as far as I can be confident of them, but you must remember that the edges are very blurred and I probably haven't always got it right about where 'Sir' ends and 'Lord' begins.

See also 'Lord and Master' below.

Lord and **Master**

These two words do seem extremely close, and people with a lot more scholarship than I have still seem pretty vague. Since Luke uses both terms, we can assume that he's making some sort of distinction, but no one's really clear what it is. I have a feeling that it's to do with the speaker's own humility. Since 'Master' was also used for a slave-owner, it could be that when people say 'Master' they're not just showing respect to God but expressing their own position before him in the humblest possible terms.

What we must remember is that even the disciples, who saw Jesus face to face, took a long time to learn what calling Jesus 'Lord' really meant.

Master

This word is very close to 'Lord' and in some cases, notably in Luke, seems in English translations to overlap considerably. Matthew uses the term a great deal, but always in terms of a slave-owner – either a householder or employer in our terms. John uses it a few times and Mark just once in that way. In Luke, it has much more overlap with 'Lord'.

See also 'Lord and Master' above.

Messiah

The expectation was of a human liberator, descended from King David, to restore the Davidic kingdom to Israel – the term 'messiah' would not have had anything like the breadth or depth of meaning for the early readers that it has for us. The gospel writers had a difficult task, then: to present Jesus as the Messiah, and as the fulfilment of the prophecies, but also to show that that fulfilment would take a very different form from the popular expectation!

Passover   A great annual festival, celebrating liberation. In its
                  narrowest sense, it refers to the angel of death 'pass-
                  ing over' the houses of Israelite slaves in Egypt with-
                  out striking their firstborn, but it also developed
                  rich sub-strata of meaning: the Israelites themselves
                  then 'passed over' from slavery to freedom, from
                  death-like existence to true life – all kinds of ways
                  the term could be applied. Particularly dramatic
                  was the 'passing over' from one side of the Red Sea
                  to another – which for Christians symbolises the
                  fearful journey through death from this life to a
                  much greater one (imagine walking between two
                  high walls of water, and the imagery's pretty vivid!)
                  and where we believe Christ led the way for us in
                  his crucifixion and resurrection. We are invited,
                  with Christ, to 'pass over' from death to life, from
                  slavery to freedom, from brokenness to wholeness,
                  from – well, I'm sure you can think of others, but
                  the list just goes on and on.

                  The Passover feast would feature a lamb, sacrificed
                  as part of the ritual. That's how Jesus became
                  known as the 'Lamb of God' – the final, perfect sacri-
                  fice securing our liberation from evil and enabling
                  us to 'pass over'.

                  It's worth studying Passover further. It is the key
                  to many layers of even deeper meaning in the
                  Christian gospel.

Pharisees   Despite getting pretty savage treatment from Jesus,
                  the Pharisees were actually not that dishonourable
                  (as he himself reminds us in Matthew 23:2). As a
                  party, they attributed Israel's political problems to
                  failure to obey God's law, and to give them their
                  due they kept it assiduously. Their real problem lay
                  in their rigid and unimaginative interpretation of
                  it, and in their determination to defend the *status
                  quo* at all costs. See also 'Unholy alliances/huddles'.

Priests   You couldn't aspire to be a priest – you had to be born
                  to it. This made the priests in effect an aristocratic,

unaccountable closed shop with a lot of personal vested interests to protect. To suggest they were simply corrupt, however, is to over-simplify. Like the Pharisees, they had a misguided zeal to protect their wing of the establishment. They wielded enormous power, as is clear in the gospel, including the power to readmit excluded people to society – hence Jesus' instruction to some of the people he healed to go and see the priest. See also 'Unholy alliances/huddles'.

Private The same Greek term is used several times – especially by Mark – to indicate that Jesus made a point of having 'time out'. This principle could be applied to private prayer, retreats, or walks in the park with the nearest and dearest, but in any event it's obviously God-given.

Rabbi To a certain extent, this overlapped with 'teacher' (see later in this glossary). A rabbi was a particularly well-respected teacher. Unlike our term 'reverend', it was not reserved to those with specialist training (hence it could be applied to Jesus), but the general perception was similar – it was a term of special respect.

Religious authorities I've used this term in a particular way in John, replacing his 'the Jews'. Mostly, when John says 'the Jews' in his narrative he doesn't mean the people as a whole, but the leadership who were opposed to Jesus.

Retreat The gospels repeatedly show Jesus 'retreating' from an area, apparently to avoid trouble. This would be a matter not of cowardice but common sense. There are some things that are worth dying for and others that aren't – and Jesus was saving himself for when it really mattered. The term is also used for times when he sought solitude, as in a spiritual retreat.

Sacrifice

The word itself occurs relatively rarely in the gospels – and not always with the same meaning. However, the concept runs right through the Hebrew and Christian scriptures, and we can't get any understanding of what Christians believe about Jesus' death without having at least a basic grasp of it.

There were numerous sacrifices in the Jewish tradition, but two aspects of them stand out.

Firstly: forgiveness and atonement are really about reconciliation – about putting right our relationship with God. This is an enormously 'costly' process, as anyone who has ever been seriously wronged, and then genuinely forgiven the other, will recognise. That is where God is – the wronged party, but longing for reconciliation. The early Hebrew people recognised that the alienation caused by sin was too big a problem for human beings: only God could achieve reconciliation. However, it was essential that the humans in the relationship found a way of experiencing and expressing for themselves something of the sacrifice that God was making in forgiving us. So people were called to sacrifice a flawless lamb (there were alternatives to lambs, but it's the lamb that applies here) – a high price in the time of Jesus, as a lamb would be the family's 'pension fund' – promising security for the future by the production of more animals. This would be as close as the community could come to feeling a tiny part of the 'cost' of God's forgiveness of us.

Secondly: blood was the sign of life – it was believed that life was, quite literally, contained in the blood. So, after the lamb had been sacrificed, its perfect blood would be ritually scattered over the people. Since sin was seen as leading to death, this was the obvious antidote.

So, the perfect, unblemished lamb, ritually slaughtered for the people, showed costly atonement and by its blood enabled the sinful people to be saved from death. The early Christian communities, steeped in this tradition, immediately recognised Christ as the perfect sacrifice, provided by God, as Abraham had promised (Genesis 22:8).

Sadducees

An extremely aristocratic party, mainly consisting of priests, who dominated the Sanhedrin, the Temple Council in Jerusalem. The impression given is that they were rude and officious, and generally disliked as a result. They did not accept the Pharisees' tortuous extensions of the law as binding, and they did not believe in, for example, resurrection. For these and other reasons, they were at daggers drawn with the Pharisees, and when Matthew reports these two groups as colluding against Jesus it's a sure sign that they were desperate! See also 'Unholy alliances/huddles'.

Scribes

Scribes were lawyers. Their responsibilities included defending the law as well as instructing students and interpreting it. Some scribes sat on the Sanhedrin, the supreme religious council at the Temple in Jerusalem. See also 'Unholy alliances/huddles'.

Sent/sends (where Jesus is the object)

The theme of Jesus being 'sent' of God is, of course, present in all the gospels, but is particularly strong in John, where he repeatedly emphasises that his authority is not his own but is given by God who sent him. The use of this term places Jesus firmly in the divine purpose – God's sending of his Son. Even in John, then, with his heavy emphasis on Jesus' divinity, the signpost always points back from the Son to the Father as the source of his authority. So, in our life and worship, we do not honour Jesus by allowing our recognition of his divinity to eclipse the Father. The Son is 'seated at the right hand of the Father' – not standing in front of him, blocking our view!

Sign

Where this word is used in direct reference to Jesus, it has special significance. In the gospels, Jesus was asked several times to give 'signs' as proof of his authority, and he always refused. The demand for such 'signs', he said, indicated faithlessness. Such signs would, he said, be given by impostors, and should be treated with caution. The 'signs' that Jesus endorsed were the 'signs of the end times' – intended not to show off his own power, or to satisfy faithless people, but to be interpreted by people of faith as indications that God's final intervention was imminent. That's why, in Mark, the disciples are represented as performing 'signs' after the resurrection.

The fourth evangelist, John, is the only one who uses the word for the miracles of Jesus, and that's led to the mistaken – or at least simplistic – idea that the miracles were 'proofs' of Jesus' authority – the very signs Jesus refused to give! John's point is that the 'end times' have begun in Christ, and the miracles are the 'signs' of it. They are indications of the inbreaking of the kingdom of God.

Son (for Jesus) Most of this is covered in the next entries, but see also the entry under 'Father (for God)'

Son of David The people were expecting a Messiah to restore the just reign of King David. That's why Matthew is particularly (although not uniquely) concerned to place Jesus firmly in a line of descent from David. When people use the term as a form of address to Jesus, they're showing that they recognise his special role.

Son of God This is a title that can have many meanings. It's applied in scripture to the king, to the nation of Israel as a whole, and to any faithful Jew – well, any male Jew, anyway. However, it's very clear that the gospel writers intend us to read something much more specific into it, and the divine Sonship of Jesus is a clear underlying theme in the gospels, especially Matthew and John.

Son of Man This is a key phrase in the gospels, used by Jesus to refer to himself. There's no equivalent modern phrase that would carry the meaning any better, so I've left it as it is. In common usage it meant 'a human being', but Jesus gave it more significance. It's possible that the vital word is 'the'. Jesus is not any old 'son of man' but *the* 'Son of Man' – rather as someone might now say of a friend or colleague, 'he's the man', meaning the significant person in that setting. It may also refer to the glorified 'son of man' in Daniel 7:13f., in which case it's significant that Jesus uses the phrase often in predicting his own suffering. The radiant glory of Daniel's 'son of man' will be realised in the suffering of the 'Son of Man'. Whole books have been written on this subject, but that'll do for our purposes.

Spirit

In John, this word is used in more than one way. Sometimes it's contrasted with 'flesh' (see that entry in this glossary) to mean 'supernatural' as distinct from 'natural' – qualities, values, etc., that come from God as distinct from human ones (but heed the cautionary note under 'flesh', above). It is also used to represent the essence of our life – see Genesis 2:7 – the word for 'breath' was also the word for 'Spirit'. We get this sense in John's 'worship in spirit and in truth', where Jesus is saying that the quality of the lives we bring to worship is more important than the place where it happens.

Where the word occurs with a capital 'S', it's referring to the Holy Spirit – traditionally portrayed as the 'Breath of God', which to a Jew would have meant, again, the essence of the life of God.

We also find the word 'spirit' joined with 'evil', to refer to malevolent supernatural beings, but this use of it should, of course, always be kept distinct from the others.

Synoptic

This word doesn't appear *in* the gospels, but you'll often hear it used *about* them, so you may find it helpful to know what it means. It refers to the first three gospel accounts – Matthew, Mark and Luke –

and distinguishes them from John, which is quite a distinctive approach. If you want to know more than this, take a look at the General Introduction to the Gospels.

Teacher

When the word 'teacher' is used by others about Jesus, it generally indicates a rather limited understanding of Jesus, and what it would mean to follow him. Jesus was, of course, a teacher, but he was also much, much more!
See also 'Rabbi'.

Temple

The Temple, in Jewish tradition, was the place of meeting between people and God. Enlightened Jews didn't think it was the *only* place, but it was the special one. Since the reforms of King Josiah, the Temple had been the only place where sacrifices could legally be offered. Christians believe that Jesus himself is the ultimate meeting point with God, and the gospels – most especially John – use the metaphor of the 'new Temple' very powerfully. It also links in with his sacrificial death. Christ is everything to us: he is the Temple where the sacrifice is offered, the Priest who makes the offering (he wasn't merely killed – he *offered* himself) and the Lamb who is sacrificed. And in each and all of those images, he enables us to encounter God, as the Temple did in the old days.

Testify

The language of the law-courts is used in a Christian setting to indicate a solemn witness statement. When made by Jesus and his associates these statements are claimed to be utterly reliable, in contrast to the testimony of his enemies, notably at his trial. John uses this word and its variants almost twice as often as the Synoptic gospels put together, and frequently links the idea to issues of belief and acceptance of Christ.

The time's coming – and, in fact, it's now

This phrase occurs a number of times in John. It's related to the 'now and not yet' idea (see 'Kingdom of God'). Jesus is saying that God's promised time, although fully to be manifest in the future, is actually beginning in him.

Trinity

This word never occurs in the Bible, but it's vital to understanding how Christians interpret the scriptures, and I've been unable to avoid using it in my own comments. I'll try and put it very simply. The Jewish belief in one God was of great importance also to Christians. They certainly couldn't let go of that principle. And yet they felt they'd experienced God fully in Jesus, who had called God 'Father'. Their experience of God in him was just too powerful to be second-hand – they were convinced that in some mysterious way, Jesus *was* God in human form. Then they also had a similarly vivid experience of God in the Holy Spirit – not, like Jesus, visible and tangible, but intensely real for all that. How were they to explain this? Well, can you imagine a relationship with someone else in which, while fully able to be yourselves, you also felt that you were in some way deeply united? Christians believe that God is like that. While we mortals struggle with the tension of valuing individuality while also treasuring our relationships, God manages to combine both perfectly. So we can say that God is three – three perfectly distinctive Persons – while also saying that the three are not 'almost' or 'as if', but absolutely one.

One helpful way of thinking about the relationship is in terms of the traditional images of the Spirit as 'breath' (both in Greek and in Hebrew one word is used for both) and Jesus as the 'Word'. The Father 'breathes' the Word: we can think of the Holy Spirit as the energy who makes the Word known, the breath that is the life in the Word. In all this, though, let's remember that we're using images to express a mystery that's too great for them.

Truth

We have a very limited concept of 'truth' in the modern West. Eastern cultures are much more aware that 'truth' is not precisely the same as 'fact'. Jesus' parables, for example, are certainly full of 'truth'. In the Bible – and especially in John – truth isn't merely a forensic commodity but a quality of life. John calls us to 'do the truth' – to let our whole lives be rooted and grounded in all that is good and holy. So the 'truth' about Jesus is much more than historical facts. It's about the whole quality of his life, the integrity of his being, and it's shown not in the things we say, or believe, but in the way we *live* in response to him. Merely not telling lies isn't enough to allow us to claim to be 'truthful'. We are called to be 'truth-full' – allow Christ's integrity to suffuse our entire lives.

Unholy alliances/ huddles

Definitely my expression, not the gospel writers'! Scribes and Pharisees got on pretty well on the whole, but in the Gospels, generally speaking, the more of these distinctive authority figures there are grouped together in one place at the same time, the more desperate they're probably getting!

(God has) Visited

Luke uses this image a number of times: this is a key time in history – the 'time of God's visitation'. Basically, Luke is trying to emphasise that God is actually present among his people in Jesus. Jesus is not a mere messenger. The word, then, points to a very dramatic moment – an opportunity for great things to happen. However, Luke would not want this word to be misunderstood by being taken too literally. Visitors come and go, but this was no temporary stay on God's part. In 'part two' of his book, The Acts of the Apostles (not included here, but you'll find it in a standard Bible), Luke will show from his first-hand experience that God is very much present and active in the world after Christ's ascension.

Voice
In John, Jesus' voice is the vehicle for his word (see 'Word'). So the voice of Jesus, the voice of the Son of God, is described as having similar power to his word.

Word
John uses this word himself – and shows Jesus using it also – in a very specific way. In the first verse of the gospel, he points us back to the Old Testament idea of the effective Word of God, directing us to the very beginning of Genesis – the Creation story in which God speaks and something happens. He tells us that Jesus is himself that living Word, through whom God's purpose is accomplished. Then he shows us Jesus speaking of *his* word as something people must accept in order to benefit from the salvation he brings. If he is the Word, then his word carries the same effectual power. In John's narrative, Jesus also passes this on to his disciples: their word is really his word, which is the Word of God.

John only says 'word' when this is what he means. I've used it more often, because in English there's often no alternative, but it shouldn't be difficult to distinguish my usage from John's.

There is, of course, a subtle distinction between the Word and the words of God. In John's presentation, though, Jesus' words are special because they're, if you like, 'the words of the Word'.

Work
This word has particular significance in John. He carefully highlights the point that by his work or works Jesus is bringing to completion God's work in creation. The fallen world is redeemed, the original relationship with God made possible again. This supremely happens at the cross, on Calvary, where John emphasises it by specifically telling us that Jesus said, 'It is complete.' Of course, his life and work are complete, but we are invited to see something wider and deeper: because of the cross, we can now have the full, unhindered relationship with God that was intended for us in the beginning – so the 'work' of God in creation is complete.

World

The people reading the gospel according to John would think of 'world' both in terms of space and time. So the term 'the world to come' could also mean 'the age to come', or 'the world order to come'. John would actually see both as being relevant, since the world order that was to come in a future age was the world order in which God lived and from which Christ had come – and from which he would one day return. 'This world' is contrasted with 'the world to come' and can have both emphases, both temporal and spatial. Sometimes in John we find Jesus talking about 'this world' or 'the world' in apparently hostile terms, and we need to remember that it is the world that is hostile to God, not the other way round. God has shown us how much he loves the world precisely in the way he endured that hostility.

Index

Index of key words and phrases

This index might be helpful if you want to track the use of the words and phrases in the Glossary, through the gospels. Just a couple of points to bear in mind:

1. Variations of a word come under the same heading in this index. So, for example, 'Truth' includes 'True' and 'Truly'; 'Glory' covers 'Glorify', 'Glorification', etc. This is to enable you to trace the concept that the word represents, without having to do a separate search for nouns, adjectives, etc.

2. Some of the words don't necessarily carry the same significance every time they're used: 'Word' is a good example of this; I've only indexed the instances where they do have significance (which could of course be on the same page as a more general example, so you'll need to exercise a bit of judgement occasionally in these cases).

Happy digging!

Select bibliography

I am deeply indebted to a large number of scholars, authors, friends and colleagues whose expertise has been invaluable to me in working on this book. It would be impossible to list them all, but the works most frequently consulted have been:

Barton, John and Muddiman, John (eds.). *The Oxford Bible Commentary.* Oxford University Press.

Black, Matthew & Rowley, H. H. (eds.). *Peake's Commentary on the Bible.* London: Thomas Nelson & Sons.

Bock, Darrell L. *Luke.* Illinois: Inter-Varsity Press.

France, R. T. *Matthew.* London: Inter-Varsity Press.

Juel, Donald. *Luke-Acts.* London: SCM.

Kee, Howard Clark (ed.). *Cambridge Annotated Study Bible.* Cambridge University Press.

Laymon, Charles M. (ed.). *The Interpreter's One-Volume Commentary on the Bible.* Nashville: Abingdon Press.

Sanders, J. N. & Mastin, B. A. *A Commentary on the Gospel According to St John.* London: A & C Black.

Schweizer, Eduard. *The Good News According to Mark.* London: SPCK.

Throckmorton, Burton H., Jr. *Gospel Parallels.* New York: Thomas Nelson Publishers.

Electronic searches of scripture have played an important part in the research for this book, and these have been carried out using 'Quickverse 6', from Parsons Technology.